RACIALLY WRITING THE REPUBLIC

RACIALLY

WRITING

THE

REPUBLIC

Racists, Race Rebels, and Transformations of American Identity

EDITED BY Bruce Baum and Duchess Harris

Duke University Press · Durham and London · 2009

© 2009 Duke University Press

All rights reserved

Printed in the United States of America
on acid-free paper ∞

Designed by Heather Hensley

Typeset in Minion Pro by Achorn
International

Library of Congress Cataloging-in-
Publication Data appear on the last
printed page of this book.

For

JESSICA STUART
FRANK HARRIS JR. (1934–2007)
JON V. THOMAS
and MIRIAM M. HARRIS

Contents

Acknowledgments

This book has had a long gestation period, and we have benefited from the assistance and advice of many people. We want to thank the following people in particular for their help: our editor at Duke University Press, Valerie Millholland, for her patience and support; Robin D. G. Kelley, Philip Deloria, J. F. (Frank) de la Teja, and Martha Menchaca for helping us round up some contributors; two of our former students from Macalester College, Adam Waterman and Brett Baldwin, for early research assistance; Katrina Chapelas and Diana Witt for their work on the index; the anonymous reviewers of the book for Duke University Press for their helpful comments; and, most importantly, our great contributors. We are deeply appreciative of George Lipsitz for writing the afterword. We couldn't have asked for a better end to our work on the book.

Bruce Baum would also like to thank his parents, Rosalyn and Charles Baum, and three contributors who offered extra help along the way: Joel Olson, Ben Keppel, and, especially, for her love and friendship, Laura Janara, who may be as happy as he and Duchess are to see this project finished. Bruce dedicates his work on the book to his niece, Jessica Stuart, with love, in the hope that her generation will realize more fully the promise of America in a more just and peaceful world.

Duchess Harris would like to thank the Mellon Mays Undergraduate Fellowship and the Woodrow Wilson Career Enhancement Fellowship for their generous support; the Macalester College American Studies Department; Jane Rhodes, Karin Aguilar-San Juan, Jason Ruiz, and Kathie Scott; and for their careful readings Nikol Alexander-Floyd, Sarita McCoy Gregory, Hilary Jones, and Evelyn M. Simien. She is also grateful for the love of her children: Austin Harris Thomas, Avril Noelle Thomas, and Zachary Harris Thomas. Duchess dedicates her work on the book to the memory of her father Frank

Harris Jr. (1934–2007) and to the two pillars who hold her up: her husband, Jon V. Thomas, and her mother, Miriam M. Harris.

....

Some of the essays in this book have been published previously: Laura Janara's essay was originally published in a longer version under the title "Brothers and Others: Tocqueville and Beaumont, U.S. Genealogy, Democracy, and Racism," in *Political Theory* 32 (December 2004): 773–800; some material in Cari M. Carpenter's essay appeared in her book *Seeing Red: Anger, Sentimentality, and American Indians* (Columbus: Ohio State University Press, 2008) and in "Tiresias Speaks: Sarah Winnemucca's Hybrid Selves and Genres," *Legacy: A Journal of American Women Writers* 19, no. 1 (2002): 71–80; the essay on Samuel Gompers is abridged from Gwendolyn Mink, *Old Labor and New Immigrants in American Political Development: Union, Party, and State, 1875–1920* (Ithaca: Cornell University Press, 1986), chapter 3; Gary Gerstle's essay, "Theodore Roosevelt and the Divided Character of American Nationalism," is a revised version of an essay that originally appeared under the same title in the *Journal of American History* 86 (December 1999): 1280–1307; Joel Olson's essay was published under the same title, "W. E. B. Du Bois and the Race Concept," in SOULS: *A Critical Journal of Black Politics, Culture, and Society* 7, no. 3–4.

Introduction

I am the poor white, fooled and pushed apart,
I am the Negro bearing slavery's scars.
I am the red man driven from the land,
I am the immigrant clutching the hope I seek—
And finding only the same old stupid plan.
Of dog eat dog, of mighty crush the weak . . .
O, let America be America again—
The land that has never been yet—
And yet must be—the land where every man is free.
The land that's mine—the poor man's, Indian's, Negro's

     ME—

Who made America,
Whose sweat and blood, whose faith and pain,
Whose hand at the foundry, whose plow in the rain,
Must bring back our mighty dream again.

—LANGSTON HUGHES, "LET AMERICA BE AMERICA AGAIN"

Langston Hughes's poem "Let America Be America Again" (1938) bridges the gap between the American dreams proclaimed in Thomas Jefferson's *Notes on Virginia* and the *Declaration of Independence* and the American nightmares of James Baldwin's *The Fire Next Time*. Baldwin himself speaks to this gap when he says, in 1960, "This country is yet to be discovered in any real sense." Writing in the midst of the civil rights movement, he is pondering the responsibility of the writer to lay bear the myths that shroud the often oppressive, racialized character of American national identity. Baldwin elaborates as follows: "There is an illusion about America to which we are clinging which has nothing to do with the lives we lead . . . this collision between one's image of oneself and what one actually is is always very painful and there are two things you can do about it, you can meet the collision head-on and try to become what you really are or you can retreat and try to remain what you thought you were, which is a fantasy, in which you will certainly perish."[1] The character of American myths has surely changed since 1960, in no small part because of activists in the civil rights movement and visionary thinkers like Baldwin. These brave souls dared to instruct people about how, when they consider the racial history of the United States, the American dream has too often been, in Baldwin's words, "something much more closely resembling a nightmare, on the private, domestic, and international levels."[2]

In this critical spirit, we propose in this book to revisit the debasing role of "race" and racism in the development of American political thought and national identity and in constructions and transformations of what it has meant to be an American.[3] As we will explain later, we regard the terms *America* and *American* as somewhat dubious since the Americas span the Western Hemisphere, and the nation-state that encompasses our inquiries is the United States of America. Yet *America* and *American* remain symbolically and ideologically potent self-designations for the United States of America and its citizens. Thus, we still see the same need that Baldwin sees to confront two contending Americas: the mythical America of the Founders' rhetoric, which proclaims freedom and justice for all, regardless of race, sex, religion, or national origins, and the historical nation-state, haunted by its legacy as an exclusionary, white, *herrenvolk* republic.[4] In short, for much of U.S. history the country's liberal and democratic ideals, along with full-fledged American identity and citizenship, have been reserved for those who were racially defined as white and also for those who were Anglo-Saxon, Protestant, male, propertied, and sexually "upright." Yet the crux of the matter lies deeper than this formulation suggests: white supremacy and racialized slavery arguably were the ground upon which the American ideals and practices of civic freedom and equality were established.

As Edmund Morgan has shown persuasively, it was no coincidence that American freedom—particularly the rise of revolutionary republicanism and white male democracy in the 1820s and 1830s—emerged in tandem with racialized and racist slavery.[5] Tellingly, the democratic republican ideals of freedom and equality were celebrated more boldly by republican commentators in the United States than by English ones and within the United States by members of the southern planter elite—for instance, Thomas Jefferson and James Madison—more than by northern elites—such as John Adams and Alexander Hamilton. The rather unique (at the time) Virginian (and American) love of freedom and equality caught the attention of Sir Augustus John Foster, the English diplomat who served in Washington during Jefferson's presidency. Foster observed that the Virginians "can profess an unbounded love of liberty and democracy in consequence of the mass of the people, who in other countries might become mobs" but who in the United States "nearly altogether composed their own slaves."[6] Morgan comments, "Aristocrats could more safely preach equality in a slave society than in a free one. Slaves did not become leveling mobs, because their owners would see to it that they had no chance to." The Virginian elites could celebrate republican ideals more boldly than the English and New England republicans "partly because they had solved the problem [that the poor posed to democratic republican ideals]: they had achieved a society in which most of the poor were enslaved."[7] He notes further that in republican thought poverty "was as much a threat to liberty as the ambition of monarchs and of over-rich landlords."[8] Morgan's analysis sheds light on Jefferson's well-known concern about the threat posed to a virtuous democratic republic by urbanization and the kind of concentration of poor working people in cities that he had witnessed in France (see the essay by Harris and Baum).[9]

In short, as the essays in this collection make clear, it is no coincidence that the United States, which was deeply shaped from its beginnings by racism, led the way among the North Atlantic nation-states in asserting democratic ideals.[10] The relatively early development in the United States of a democratic ethos was closely connected to the *herrenvolk*, white supremacist character of the polity.[11] Ever since there has been a profound, ongoing tension in the country's egalitarian commitments: notably, U.S. egalitarianism has been limited across classes *and* across racialized groups (as well as between men and women) by the investments of the white majority in what W. E. B. Du Bois called the "wages of whiteness."[12] Thus, the project to achieve the larger promise of democracy in the United States—and of the American dream—is integrally bound up with the stalled effort to overcome fully the legacy of the country's white racism.

The Racial Politics of American Studies
and American Political Thought

Like Baldwin, we see two options in responding to this gap between American myth and reality: the people of the United States can either meet it head-on and strive to make the reality approach the ideal, or retreat to what they thought they were, which was often a perilous fantasy. To envision new ways to close the gap between American ideals and American actuality, we will pursue another closely related but somewhat different contrast: that between the exalted ideals, entangled with racism as they are, of canonical American thinkers and leaders like Jefferson, Lincoln, and Samuel Gompers and the as-yet-unrealized hopes of American race rebels such as the Paiute activist and memoirist Sarah Winnemucca, the African American activist Ida B. Wells-Barnett, and the Filipino writer Carlos Bulosan for an antiracist, egalitarian republic. While the canonical thinkers are deeply associated with constitutive American ideals—freedom, equality, democracy, a living wage—the race rebels have worked, as Ben Keppel says, to redraw "the boundaries of political possibility" regarding the race-inflected promise of America.[13]

Our approach to this task is rooted in a merging of our respective academic disciplines: political theory and American studies. While American political theory goes back to the seventeenth-century Puritans of New England and to the eighteenth-century founding of the United States (notably, in Jefferson's Declaration of Independence and *The Federalist Papers* of James Madison, Alexander Hamilton, and John Jay), the field of American studies was established between the late 1930s and the 1950s. Its founding scholars sought to clarify, describe, and analyze a way of thinking and acting that was unique to the historical experience of the United States—that is, to comprehend the defining features of "American exceptionalism."[14] They focused on several characteristic images operating in the national culture—chiefly myths and symbols—including the ability of Europeans to start life anew in a new world or virgin land; the relative strength of liberal democratic society in relation to a weak aristocracy; a personality type called the American Adam, characterized by extravagant optimism, individualism, and innocence; and especially the Western frontier, which promised escape from the corruptions of the Old World and the renewal of American values. These themes were assumed to relate more or less uniformly to all citizens but to be expressed with special clarity and profundity by selected elites—for example, novelists like Nathaniel Hawthorne and political leaders like Thomas Jefferson.[15]

In this book we engage the field of American studies primarily through the tradition of American political thought. We reconsider this tradition, which has expounded on American identity from its colonial beginnings, in two ways. First, we reread the legacy of canonical, white, and generally racist American political thinkers—George Washington (1732–99), Thomas Jefferson (1743–1826), Abraham Lincoln (1809–65), Theodore Roosevelt (1858–1919), Samuel Gompers (1850–1924), and Margaret Sanger (1879–1966)—along with Alexis de Tocqueville (1805–59), the great French chronicler of Jacksonian America. Their writings and activities put forward noble republican and democratic visions of America and Americans, but at the same time constructed a racially (and often otherwise) exclusionary republic. Tocqueville stands somewhat apart among this group, not only because he was a French visitor to the United States, but also because he critically scrutinized the racialized contradiction in Jacksonian democracy.

With regard to the tribunes of the white republic, our intent is not to simply dismiss their contributions—such as Jefferson's declaration that "all men are created equal," Gompers's call "to secure a larger share of the [national] income" for workers, Roosevelt's "New Nationalism," or Sanger's advocacy of women's liberation.[16] Rather, we wish to show how their beneficial ideas can be realized only by racially rewriting the republic—that is, by fully dismantling its racially exclusionary character. With this goal in mind, we are committed to exposing the false neutrality of a racially white America that their theories presume and to making visible the various ways in which exclusionary racialized power has been deployed in the construction of American identity, freedom, and citizenship.

Second, we look to a set of race rebels who improvised audaciously on the salutary parts of the American dream while vigorously contesting its oppressive manifestations.[17] Our rebels range from the well-known African American writer-activists W. E. B. Du Bois (1868–1963) and James Baldwin (1924–87) to several important but lesser-known figures: the Mexican Texan Juan Nepomuceno Cortina (1824–92), who led an armed resistance to Anglo racism against Mexican Texans; Sarah Winnemucca (c. 1844–91), a memoirist and daughter of Chief Winnemucca of the Northern Paiutes, a tribe of Nevada and California; Ida B. Wells-Barnett (1862–1931), who crusaded against lynching and for women's rights; the Filipino American poet and migrant worker Carlos Bulosan (1911–56); and the playwright Lorraine Hansberry (1930–65). As race rebels, these thinkers struggled for social justice from perspectives that were explicitly informed by their own subordinated, racialized identities. And yet, their visions of a good society—their not-yet-visible republic—are, in Martin Luther King Jr.'s famous phrase, "deeply rooted in the American dream."

In this task, the essays in this collection build upon the recent flourishing of critical race scholarship to reexamine the racial transformations in American identity from the founding of the republic up to 1965.[18] We have chosen this time period because the 1770s mark a pivotal moment in the racial writing of the American republic and because U.S. racial formations have changed significantly—i.e., have been substantially rewritten—after 1965, the culmination of the civil rights movement, the so-called second reconstruction that followed the epochal events of 1963: the assassination of the civil rights leader Medgar Evers; the March on Washington, featuring Martin Luther King's "I Have a Dream" speech; the publication of Betty Friedan's *The Feminine Mystique*; and the assassination of President John F. Kennedy.[19] The great victories of the civil rights movement, especially the Civil Rights Act of 1964 and the Voting Rights Act of 1965, ushered in a new era; equally important was the Immigration Law of 1965, which produced major demographic changes in the United States, opening the country to new immigrants from Mexico and Latin America, Asia, Africa, and Europe.

The post-1965 period was marked by the rise of the Black Power movement and related radical insurgencies—the Black Panthers, the American Indian movement (AIM), the Chicano movement, the second wave of the women's movement, and the Revolutionary People's Constitutional Convention. Through these movements members of subordinated groups asserted vigorously their claims to dignity, nationhood, freedom, and power. Yet the past forty years have also been deeply shaped by a white backlash to the civil rights initiatives of the sixties.[20] Our contention is not that the country's ethnic and racialized hierarchies have been magically dismantled in this era. Instead, we maintain that these hierarchies are still alive, though in altered form, and that understanding the racial writing of the republic between the 1770s and 1965 is crucial to tackling current racial challenges in the United States.[21]

As scholars of political theory and American studies, we are responding to the traditional ways in which American political thought and American culture have been framed. The essays that follow focus on representative U.S. public intellectuals from different racialized groups—Founding Fathers and other influential figures, racists and race rebels—who helped constitute and transform the racial character of the country at key junctures.[22] Typically, figures like Jefferson, Washington, Roosevelt, Lincoln, and Gompers have been whitewashed in texts and monographs on American political thought.[23] That is, the political thought of, say, Jefferson, Roosevelt, and Gompers commonly is presented in such a way that readers encounter samples of their more seemingly inclusive, republican, and humanistic speeches but find little evidence of the racist and nativist elements of their thinking and activism.[24] Meanwhile, many important writer-activists from subaltern racialized groups—including Cortina, Winnemucca, Wells-Barnett, and Bulosan—have generally been excluded from the canon of American political thought. Moreover, while thinkers like Du Bois and Baldwin are sometimes included in the canon of American political thought (along with Frederick Douglass and King), they are frequently considered in narrow ways: for example, Du Bois is sometimes presented primarily as the more militant counterpoint to Booker T. Washington's accommodationism and Baldwin as the literary voice of the civil rights movement.[25]

Such selectivity in the construction of a canon of American political thought is perhaps defensible insofar as this tradition of thought is construed expressly in terms of systematic theories of government, constitutionalism, democracy, political economy, and abstract citizenship. Yet, when we shift our angle of vision to reconsider American political thought in terms of racial writings and rewritings of the republic, we must rethink the existing canon and reread established, canonical thinkers in new ways. This calls upon readers to confront how canonical thinkers often articulated ennobling ideals within racist frames. In addition, we need to look outside the established canon for race rebels who have perceptively reworked ideals of freedom, equality, dignity, race, republic, and nationality to envision an antiracist America—or, as Hughes says, to "let America be America again—The land that has never been yet—And yet must be."

Of course, we cannot avoid being selective in our choice of representative figures;. and we are aware of the problems involved in putting forward any group of thinkers, no matter how seemingly diverse, as truly representative of the diverse but intertwined racialized struggles for justice in the United States. Therefore, we make no claims about offering a definitive account of racial formations in the United States between the 1770s and 1965. Our aims are more modest. First, we believe there is much to be learned about the racialized and often contradictory character of American political ideals and American nationalism by focusing on the ideas of influential public intellectuals.[26] Second, while any choice of presumed representative public intellectuals is bound to be selective, we are convinced that our selections enable us to tell important stories about the racial writing and rewriting of the republic.

Furthermore, we are well aware that there is much more to say about each of the individuals and each of the eras that this book examines. For instance, some of the rebels whom we discuss have notable limitations of their own that these essays only begin to address. These limitations range from Baldwin's nearly exclusive focus on the black/white divide to the failures of other rebels to incorporate adequately social justice struggles concerning gender, class, and sexuality into their emancipatory visions. In this regard, we recognize that all individuals hold "multiple social locations." That is, all people simultaneously have racialized, gendered, class, national, and sexual identities, each of which informs or shapes the other aspects of their social identities.[27] Hansberry, for example, was a black, middle-class lesbian, straddling positions of subordination and privilege at the same time. Jefferson and Washington, by contrast, were white, male members of the landed gentry and thus were persons of privilege in a quite all-encompassing way.

Several of the essays that follow highlight such intersections of race, class, gender, and sexuality in the construction of American nationality: the essay by John Kuo Wei Tchen, on Washington, addresses the entwinement of race, class, and gender in American orientalism toward China; the essays on Jefferson and Sally Hemings and on Wells-Barnett highlight issues of race, gender, and sexuality; the interplay of race and class is featured in the essays on Tocqueville, Gompers, Du Bois, Baldwin, Sanger, and Bulosan, while those on Sanger and Bulosan also address notions of sexuality; and the essays on Washington, Cortina, Roosevelt, and Bulosan foreground the role of visions of masculinity in American racialized nationalism. The essays on Washington, Roosevelt, and Hansberry also begin to consider the interplay of global racial politics and U.S. domestic racial politics. Inevitably, each essay highlights some aspects of the identities, ideas, and struggles of its subject (or subjects) at the expense of others. Here we invite further critical investigation, dialogue, and debate to complement our work.

Finally, we have made a conscious effort in this book to go beyond the narrow black/white model of reading the racialization of America. The way we have done so will surely not satisfy everyone—not least because scholars disagree about the extent to which the black/white divide has overriding significance for understanding the racialized politics of the United States.[28] We maintain that from the start, given the virtually concurrent English colonial projects of conquering the indigenous peoples of North America and enslaving Africans, the racialized hierarchies in colonial America and the United States have been more complex than a simple binary opposition between one dominant group (whites) and one subordinate group (blacks). Accordingly, we have tried to address not only the changing places of blacks and whites in American racialized hierarchies, but also (at least tentatively) the respective and changing places of Native Americans, Asian Americans, and Latinos.[29] We recognize, moreover, that racialized minority groups in the United States have suffered from the ideology of white supremacy to different degrees and in distinct ways.[30]

Still, we believe that in light of how African Americans have been uniquely oppressed by slavery and Jim Crow segregation from the colonial era through 1965—not to mention similar patterns since then—there are good reasons to foreground the black/white relationship to some extent while insisting that it does not exhaust the racialization of American identity. As Patricia Williams says, "The violently patrolled historical boundary between black and white in America is so powerful that every immigrant group since slavery has found itself assimilated as one or the other, despite the enormous ethnic and global diversity we Americans actually represent."[31]

Racial Writings and Antiracist Rewritings
of the American Republic

To establish a clearer sense of the history to which this book responds, we want to offer a brief sketch of key markers in the racial and antiracist writings and rewritings of America. We understand the racial writing of the republic in terms of the compound of racially coded laws, political and scientific theories, public speeches and declarations, literary works, and public performances that have given a racialized—largely white supremacist—cast to such guiding political conceptions as American, citizenship, freedom, equality, republic, civic virtue, and democracy. Even the terms *America* and *American* are problematic in this regard. Following the voyages of Christopher Columbus and Amerigo Vespucci, these terms not only assigned new names to peoples and places that already had names and identities, but also the United States of America is just one part of the Americas. For our purposes, however, it is appropriate—if somewhat regrettable—that we retain *America* and *American* to designate the United States of America and its citizens precisely because of the role of these particular identities in the racialized history of American Manifest Destiny.[32]

The race problems of the Americas can be traced back generally to Columbus's brutal encounter with the Arawak people of the Bahamas (1493–1502), to Hernando Cortés's equally deadly conquest of the Aztecs of Mexico (1519–21), and to Francisco Pizarro's conquest of the Incas of Peru (1531–35).[33] Racial domination became a central part of American colonial development with the founding of English colonies in Jamestown and New England in the early seventeenth century and with the sale of the first African slaves in Virginia in 1619. Jamestown was established within a so-called Indian confederacy, headed by the chief Powhatan, and eventually the English exterminated Powhatan's people to solidify their own American presence.[34] In the Puritans' Massachusetts Bay Colony, Governor John Winthrop set out a communal vision of "Christian charity," in 1630 that set the tone for much of the subsequent racial writing of America: "Wee must delight in eache other, make others Conditions our owne reioyce together, mourne together, labour and suffer together . . . the Lord will be our God and delight to dwell among vs, as his owne people . . . that men shall say of succeeding plantacions: the lord make it like the New England; for wee must Consider that wee shall be as a City vpon a Hill, the Eies of all people are vpon us."[35] In this spirit, the Puritans justified the taking of Indian land by declaring it legally empty. As Howard Zinn explains, Winthrop maintained that the Indians "had not 'subdued' the land, and therefore had only a 'natural' right to it, but not a 'civil right.' A 'natural right' did not have legal standing."[36]

This pattern of American thought and action led to King Philip's War in 1675–76. This deadly war pitted New England Puritans and their Indian allies (mostly Christian converts) against resisting Wampanoag Indians, led by King Philip, the name the Puritans gave to the Wampanoag chieftain Metacom. In proportion to the size of the population, this was the most fatal war in American history; it nearly decimated the Puritan colonies, and Wampanoag casualties were even greater.[37] In this same era, white Anglo-American colonists enacted the first instance of clear-cut statutory racial discrimination, a Virginia law of 1662 that established a fine against "interracial fornicators." Thereafter a Maryland law of 1681 declared marriages of white women to "Negroes" a "disgrace not only to the English butt allso many other Christian Nations."[38]

Later, in the founding of an independent United States of America, the Declaration of Independence (1776) was silent about slavery and warned of the "merciless Indian savages" even as it asserted, "All men are created equal."[39] The U.S. Constitution (1787) sanctioned slavery with its infamous three-fifths proviso and a stipulation that Congress could not alter its provisions concerning slavery before 1808.[40] In 1790, Congress limited rights of naturalization and citizenship among immigrants to "free white persons."[41] In the nineteenth century, struggles over Negro slavery were exemplified by the Supreme Court's *Dred Scott* decision (1857), in which Chief Justice Roger Taney wrote that Negroes are "so inferior that they had no rights which the white man was bound to respect";[42] the election in 1860 of the Republican Abraham Lincoln as president; the establishment of the Confederacy (1860–61); the Civil War (1861–65); the deadly New York City Draft Riot of 1863, in which Irish-American Catholics lynched free blacks;[43] and Lincoln's Emancipation Proclamation in 1863. The postwar period was marked by the enactment of the Thirteenth, Fourteenth, and Fifteenth Amendments to the U.S. Constitution in 1865, 1866, and 1868, respectively, which were basic to the Reconstruction (1865–77); the establishment of the Ku Klux Klan in 1866; and the Supreme Court's assertion in *Plessy v. Ferguson* (1896) of the "separate but equal" doctrine.[44] *Plessy* upheld the new Jim Crow system of black/white segregation.

Between the 1820s and 1840s, white Americans also enacted other components of their *herrenvolk* republic. For instance, President Andrew Jackson spoke in his first presidential address to Congress as the democratic tribune of the people and, in the same breath, outlined his policy for moving eastern Native Americans west of the Mississippi. In *Worcester v. Georgia* (1832), the Supreme Court declared the Cherokees of Georgia (and by extension every Native American tribe) a "domestic dependent" nation, related to the U.S. government like "a ward to his guardian."[45] The physician and craniologist Samuel George Morton launched an "American school" of white supremacist "race science" in 1839 with his book *Crania Americana*.[46] In the 1840s, white nationalists stated the idea of an American Manifest Destiny.[47] This notion culminated in the U.S. government's annexation of the Mexican territories in the Mexican-America War of 1846–48, the near annihilation of the Plains Indians between 1865 and 1890—capped by the General Allotment (Dawes) Act of 1887 and the massacre at Wounded Knee in December 1890 of more than two hundred Lakota Sioux by the U.S. Seventh Cavalry—and the Spanish-Cuban-American War of 1897, which established the United States as an imperialist power.[48]

The 1840s also saw the rise of a racial Anglo-Saxonism in response to a wave of Irish immigrants. This movement eventually produced a new hierarchy among supposedly distinct white races. Anglo-Saxon elites now held that some supposed white European peoples—Celts, Slavs, Hebrews, Iberians, and Mediterraneans—were unfit for self-government.[49] The same racial logic later materialized in a eugenics-influenced Nordic supremacism in reaction to a new wave of immigrants—mostly from southern and eastern Europe—between 1880 and 1910. It yielded the Johnson-Reed Immigration Act of 1924, which sharply restricted immigration by those deemed members of the unsuitable "European races." The Immigration Act of 1924 also completed "Asiatic" exclusion, including statutory exclusion of Japanese persons, and made all the peoples of the Far East ineligible for U.S. citizenship.[50]

The color lines of the United States between the 1870s and 1963 included a wide array of additional elements, both exclusionary and expansive. The Chinese Exclusion Act of 1882 suspended all Chinese immigration for ten years and forbade the naturalization of Chinese persons already in the United States.[51] In a related series of crucial court cases, from *In re Ah Yup* (1878) to *United States v. Bhagat Singh Thind* (1923), U.S. courts adjudicated claims to naturalization rights by a number of non-Europeans in light of the standing restriction of these rights to "free white persons."[52] Finally, the first sixty-five years of the twentieth century witnessed the following notable developments in the country's racial order, among others: the founding of the National Association for the Advancement of Colored People (NAACP) in 1909 and of the Society of American Indians in 1911; D. W. Griffith's cinematic ode to a Klan-ish America, *Birth of a Nation*, in 1915; the Nineteenth

Amendment to the U.S. Constitution (1920), which prohibited restrictions of suffrage on the basis of sex but did not address obstacles faced by black and Native American women and men; the Indian Citizenship Act of 1924, which established citizenship for Native Americans but without fully securing their voting rights;[53] the Indian Reorganization Act of 1934, which sought, with only partial success, to promote tribal self-government and economic development; the establishment by white property owners' associations of thousands of racially restrictive covenants (sometimes called Caucasian Codes) between the 1910s and 1940s—the era of the "great migration" of millions of African Americans from the South to northern cities;[54] a threatened mass march on Washington by African Americans in 1941, organized by A. Philip Randolph, which pushed President Roosevelt to integrate the war industries; the wartime internment, in 1942, of more than 110,000 Japanese Americans in relocation centers; a series of lawsuits by the NAACP, between the 1930s and 1950s, which led to the Supreme Court's unanimous decision in 1954, in *Brown v. Board of Education*, to overturn the old "separate but equal" doctrine; the Walter-McCarran Act of 1952, which *finally* established that the right of persons to become U.S. citizens "shall not be denied or abridged on the basis of race";[55] and the civil rights movement of the 1950s and 1960s.

Many other acts of resistance to American racism between the 1770s and 1965 gestured toward a nonracist, inclusive America. Among these were the suppressed slave uprising led by "General" Gabriel in Richmond, Virginia, in 1800; Nat Turner's rebellion in Southampton County, Virginia, in 1831, and other slave rebellions; the Seneca Falls Convention for women's rights in 1848, which joined Elizabeth Cady Stanton, Susan B. Anthony, and Frederick Douglass, among others, to declare that "all men and women are created equal"; Harriet Tubman's work on the Underground Railroad from slavery to freedom; the Colored National Conventions of 1848 and 1853; Sojourner Truth's speech at the Fourth National Women's Rights Convention, in New York, in 1853; John Brown's raid on the federal arsenal at Harper's Ferry in 1859; the "trail of tears" march of Chief Joseph and the Nez Perce in 1877; the Ghost Dance of the Lakota Sioux at Wounded Knee in 1890; fleeting efforts at "interracial unity" among late nineteenth-century Populists and the Knights of Labor; and the Harlem Renaissance of the 1920s and 1930s.

Along the way, there has been a wide array of rebellious rewritings of America. Many of these efforts have remained submerged—an invisible republic—for most of this history.[56] Although our present focus is on political thought more narrowly construed, the range of significant texts here includes Native American speeches, stories, and testimonies; slave narratives; David Walker's *An Appeal in Four Articles* (1829); William Lloyd Garrison's launching of the abolitionist newspaper *The Liberator* in 1831; the writings of Martin R. Delaney, Alexander Crummell, Douglass, Wells-Barnett, Anna Julia Cooper, and Du Bois; the anti-imperialist autobiographical sketches of the Yankton Sioux writer and reformer Gertrude Bonnin for the *Atlantic Monthly* in 1900, published under her Lakota name, Zitkala-Sa ("Red Bird"); the poetry of Langston Hughes; the novels and essays of Zora Neal Hurston, Richard Wright, and Ralph Ellison; Billie Holiday's powerful rendition in 1939 of the Jewish schoolteacher Abel Meeropol's antilynching song "Strange Fruit"; the contralto Marion Anderson's performance of "America" and "Nobody Knows the Trouble I've Seen" at the Lincoln Memorial in April 1939; Woody Guthrie's song "This Land Is Your Land," his answer to Irving Berlin's "God Bless America"; the mid-twentieth-century antiracist books of Carey McWilliams, including *Brothers Under the Skin* (1943), *Prejudice: Japanese-Americans* (1944), *A Mask for Privilege* (1948), and *North from Mexico* (1950); the Civil Rights anthem "We Shall Overcome"; the jazz drummer Max Roach's album *Freedom Now Suite* (1960); Martin Luther King Jr.'s "Letter from Birmingham Jail" and "I Have a Dream" speech; and Bob Dylan's anthems of 1962–63, such as "Blowin' in the Wind" and "Only a Pawn in Their Game" (originally, "The Ballad of Medgar Evers").

As we were finishing this book, Barack Obama, a black man (or "mixed-race" person generally regarded as black), son of a white mother from Kansas and a black father from Kenya, was elected the forty-fourth president of the United States by a commanding margin (52.7 percent to 46 percent of the popular vote; 365 electoral votes to 173). This outcome quickly led many people to declare that the United States had overcome its racist past. The *New York Times* reported, "Barack Hussein Obama was elected the 44th president of the United States on Tuesday, sweeping away the last racial barrier in American politics with ease as the country chose him as its first black chief executive." When his victory was declared on election night, President-elect Obama himself remarked, "If there is anyone out there who still doubts that America is a place where all things are possible, who still wonders if the dream of our founders is alive in our time, who still questions the power of our democracy, tonight is your answer."[57] Obama's victory undoubtedly is a historic moment in the racial writing and rewriting of the American republic. Yet the essays that follow indicate a need for circumspection regarding the deep and persisting legacy of U.S. racism and systemic racial inequalities.[58]

Essays and Topics

In speaking to this history, the essays that follow pursue an interdisciplinary approach to the racial writing and rewriting of America. The contributors draw creatively from the fields of U.S. history, American studies, political theory, critical race theory, and gender studies. John Kuo Wei Tchen brings to light the little-discussed role of early American orientalism with respect to Chinese people, things, and ideas in the construction of American national identity. Tchen focuses on the "patrician orientalism" of George Washington and other American revolutionaries who regarded rare consumer goods from China as a mark of distinction and cultured sociability. American patrician orientalism was distinctly American in that, on the one hand, it manifested both admiration for and differentiation from China and the Orient, and, on the other hand, it expressed an American mode of class distinctions that, in opposition to European aristocracy, was embedded in a meritocratic individualist ethic of life, liberty, and happiness. Duchess Harris and Bruce Baum reconsider Thomas Jefferson's legacy through the lens of his sexual relationship with his slave Sally Hemings, with whom he sired children. Harris and Baum pay special attention to the efforts of black-identified Jefferson-Hemings descendants to gain public recognition for having a white president in their family tree.

Laura Janara rereads Alexis de Tocqueville's *Democracy in America* (1835–40), along with a novel by his traveling companion Gustave de Beaumont, *Marie, or, Slavery in the United States* (1835), to illuminate dimensions of Jacksonian-era America that entrenched enduring racism. Janara dissects Tocqueville's separation of Anglo-American egalitarianism from American racism by unearthing his portrait of European American desire for equality *and hierarchy*. In Tocqueville's account, Janara demonstrates, anxiety over democracy's flux generates European American yearning for race privilege as a postaristocratic form of psychic and material security. Tocqueville's

European Americans symbolically fraternalize relations with Native Americans while radically othering Negroes—two distinct psychopolitical dynamics that enable hierarchy amid passion for the idea of equality.

Jerry Thompson addresses the struggles of Mexican Texans against Anglo-American racial nationalism and expansionism into Mexican territory, behind the leadership of Juan Nepomuceno Cortina. In the Cortina War of 1859–60, Cortina led a valiant struggle for racial equality in Texas, becoming a hero to downtrodden Mexicans in Texas. He lost the battle but left an important legacy that is little known in the United States outside of Texas. Catherine Holland takes a novel look at President Abraham Lincoln, avoiding the usual efforts to cast him as either a savior or a cynical demagogue. Holland approaches Lincoln as a statesman who embodies the promise and dangers of the American political tradition. Engaging the legacy of slavery and civil war, she argues, requires deliberate faithlessness to the past to creatively reimagine it.

Cari Carpenter turns to Sarah Winnemucca's revision of America's founding narrative in *Life Among the Piutes: Their Wrongs and Claims* (1883). Carpenter finds in Winnemucca's narrative both an alternative origin story of the United States and a direct challenge to the myth of the vanishing Indian. Winnemucca retells her grandfather's Paiute origin story to give a challenging multigenerational narrative of America. She reinterprets race in America so that *white*, *civilized*, and *citizens* come to signify savagery and broken promises. At the same time, she uses familial rhetoric from her grandfather's story to critique white Americans'—and the U.S. government's—failure to honor kinship responsibilities to the Paiutes.

Patricia Schechter establishes Ida B. Wells-Barnett's place in the intellectual and activist ferment of progressive era America through a reading of her personal narrative, *Crusade for Justice* (1930). Schechter argues that Wells-Barnett's social commitments and sense of self took profound inspiration from religious faith and gave rise to a "visionary pragmatism" that sustained a lifetime of agitation for social justice. Wells-Barnett's visionary pragmatism links the prophetic traditions of African American religion, the intellectual flowering of turn-of-the-century America, and black women's particular legacy of creative resistance under slavery.

Gwendolyn Mink examines the rise of a "republic of white labor" in the late nineteenth century and early twentieth. Focusing on Samuel Gompers, a founder of the American Federation of Labor (AFL), Mink explores the white-dominated labor movement's racist response to intensifying class-based inequalities and white workers' insecurities. Confronted by new immigrants and new and ongoing racialized divisions, organized labor pursued the claims of labor in racially exclusionary ways, epitomized by the AFL's efforts to bring about the passage of the Chinese Exclusion Act of 1882. Thus, Gompers's aim of securing for workers a greater share of the national product was largely an endeavor to create a republic for respectable white workers.

Gary Gerstle considers how Theodore Roosevelt—historian, soldier, rancher, governor, president, and explorer—embodies the contradictions of American nationalism. Roosevelt's ideas and actions epitomize the clash between a civic creed that promises to all Americans the same rights regardless of race, religion, or sex and a racialized Americanism by which white male elites have defined an exclusionary and imperialistic nation informed by notions of racial superiority. Gerstle traces Roosevelt's self-divided and masculinist vision through his epic work *The Winning of the West* (1889–96), his racist ideas about Native Americans, black Americans, Cubans, and Filipinos, his exploits with the Rough Riders, and his New Nationalism program.

Dorothy Roberts examines Margaret Sanger's writings to confront the racial origins of the birth control movement of the early twentieth century in the United States. Roberts explains that feminist ideas about voluntary motherhood were closely connected to and soon superseded in the birth control movement by purportedly gender-neutral goals of family planning and population control. Sanger personifies the birth control movement's mixed legacy: it was meant to liberate women from compulsory childbearing; yet it was seen by many of its white proponents, through a racist and eugenic lens, as a means to control the reproduction of putative inferior races and classes and thus to control the reproduction of certain classes of women.

Joel Olson tackles W. E. B. Du Bois's political theory of race. Olson explains that Du Bois, who is best known for *The Souls of Black Folks* (1909) and his work with the NAACP, developed one of the most systematic political and sociological analyses of the race concept in the history of American social and political thought in the 1930s and 1940s. Olson examines Du Bois's theory of race and of the "public and psychological wages" of whiteness with particular emphasis on his later writings, such as *Black Reconstruction* (1935), *Dusk of Dawn* (1940), and *The World and Africa* (1947).

Allan Punzalan Isaac considers Filipino America identity through the autobiographical novel of Carlos Bulosan, who arrived in the United States in 1930. Bulosan's *America Is in the Heart* (1946) is deeply informed by American imperialism in the Philippines and the construction of the Filipino in the United States as shifting between citizen and alien from the Spanish-American War (1898) to the end of the Second World War and Philippine independence (1946). *America Is in the Heart* considers, through the life of a Filipino migrant worker in the United States, racism and racial and working-class consciousness and the idea of America as a democracy. Bulosan articulates a vision of Filipino nationalist consciousness that counters then-prevailing notions of ethnic assimilationism as well as a critique of U.S. colonialism, class exploitation, and racist violence.

Ben Keppel continues the analysis of mid-twentieth-century America by exploring Lorraine Hansberry's effort to broaden and deepen the American discourse on race during the late 1950s and early 1960s. Keppel explains how, in the wake of the fall of Joseph McCarthy, Hansberry sought to link the American civil rights movement to campaigns in the developing world to replace European colonialism with autonomous nationhood. Her strategy challenged the more visible public approach taken by Ellison and King, both of whom pressed their protests in terms of symbols of Americanism.

Bruce Baum engages James Baldwin's effort in the 1950s and early 1960s to envision an inclusive, nonracist, egalitarian America. Baum focuses on how Baldwin struggles with his own conflicted American identity to frame the central challenge that arises out of the competing visions of American life: that for the U.S. nation-state to approach the promise of an egalitarian America, its people, especially those who have learned to define themselves as white, must squarely confront their feigned innocence concerning the brutal legacy of American racism.

In the afterword George Lipsitz reflects on the historical struggles tracked in this volume in light of the changes in U.S. racial politics in the aftermath of the civil rights movement. Writing fifty-three years after the Supreme Court's epochal decision in 1954 in *Brown v. Board of Education*, which declared legally sanctioned school segregation unconstitutional, Lipsitz finds a decidedly mixed record. While much has changed, people who are not white—particularly African Americans, Native Americans, and Latinos—still face manifestly unequal life chances.[59] Among the most notable features of racial politics in the United States since the mid-1960s have been myriad deliberate, collective efforts by white Americans to "get around *Brown.*"[60] These endeavors, although not seamless or uncontested, effectively have sustained a privileged group position among whites and stalled the progress toward equal justice initiated by the civil rights movement. Consequently, *all* Americans confront an ongoing imperative to right the racial republic.

Notes

Epigraph: Langston Hughes, quoted in Howard Zinn, *A People's History of the United States, 1492–Present*, revised and updated edition (New York: Harper Perennial, 1995), 395–96.

1. James Baldwin, *Nobody Knows My Name: More Notes of a Native Son* (New York: Dell Publishing, 1961), 126.

2. James Baldwin, *The Fire Next Time* (New York: Vintage Books, [1963] 1993), 89.

3. In the spirit of recent critical race theorizing (see note 18), we place "race" in quotation marks here to indicate that it is a socially and politically constructed category and not a biologically meaningful one. Race ideas remain highly consequential, socially and materially, as a basis for racism and racialized social stratification. Racial categories should be understood in this way throughout this book even though the contributors have generally not placed them in quotes.

4. The sociologist Pierre L. van der Berghe uses the term *herrenvolk democracy* to characterize "regimes like those of the United States and South Africa that are democratic for the master race but tyrannical for the subordinate groups." See David R. Roediger, *The Wages of Whiteness: Race and the Making of the American Working Class*, rev. ed. (London: Verso, [1991] 1999), 59. Like Roediger, we prefer to speak of the nineteenth-century United States as a *herrenvolk* republic to call attention to the undemocratic relations that prevailed even among the dominant racialized group.

5. Edmund S. Morgan, *American Slavery–American Freedom: The Ordeal of Colonial Virginia* (New York: Norton, 1975). *Republican* here refers to the tradition of civic republican thought—as in the republicanism of Jefferson and Madison—rather than to the current-day Republican Party.

6. Ibid., 380.

7. Ibid.

8. Ibid., 383.

9. Jefferson championed the writings of English republican thinkers who advocated equality among propertied men but excluded the poor and the idle from their republican visions. See ibid., 382.

10. Racism has been a key feature of modern politics in all Western nation-states. In the United States, however, racism has from the start been fundamentally constitutive of the development of domestic politics. On racism and modern politics more generally, see Charles W. Mills, *The Racial Contract* (Ithaca: Cornell University Press, 1997); Howard Winant, *The World Is a Ghetto: Race and Democracy Since World War II* (New York: Basic Books, 2001); George Fredrickson, *Racism: A Short History* (Princeton: Princeton University Press, 2002).

11. Again, there is a larger story to face about the relationship between race, racism, and ideas of equality. As Fredrickson explains, ideas about race and equality emerged in Europe simultaneously and in mutual interaction with each other during the seventeenth and eighteenth centuries. See Fredrickson, *Racism*, 11–12.

12. Roediger, *Wages of Whiteness*, 12.

13. Ben Keppel, *The Work of Democracy: Ralph Bunche, Kenneth B. Clark, Lorraine Hansberry, and the Cultural Politics of Race* (Cambridge, Mass.: Harvard University Press, 1995), 8.

14. Mark Hulsether, "Evolving Approaches to U.S. Culture in the American Studies Movement: Consensus, Pluralism, and Contestation for Cultural Hegemony," *Canadian Review of American Studies* 23, no. 2 (1993): 1–55.

15. Ibid.

16. Jefferson, Declaration of Independence (1776), in *Free Government in the Making: Readings in American Political Thought*, 3d ed., ed. Alpheus Thomas Mason (Oxford: Oxford University Press, 1965), 131; Samuel Gompers, *The American Labor Movement, Its Makeup, Achievements, and Aspirations* (1914), in Mason, *Free Government*, 658; Theodore Roosevelt, "Speech at Osawatomie, Kansas" (1910), in Mason, *Free Government*, 649–52.

17. We owe the term *race rebels* to Robin Kelley. Kelley uses it to highlight the resistance of black working people who have "struggled to maintain and define a sense of racial identity and solidarity" and whose struggles have generally been "relegated to the margins" of more conventional histories. See Robin D. G. Kelley, *Race Rebels: Culture, Politics, and the Black Working Class* (New York: Free Press, 1996), 4–5.

18. Key works of critical "race" studies include Henry Louis Gates Jr., ed, *"Race," Writing, and Difference*, *Critical Inquiry* 12 (Autumn 1985); Patricia Williams, *The Alchemy of Race and Rights* (Cambridge, Mass.: Harvard University Press, 1991); Roediger, *Wages of Whiteness*; Ruth Frankenberg, *White Women, Race Matters: The Social Construction of Whiteness* (Minneapolis: University of Minnesota Press, 1994); *Critical Race Theory: The Key Writings that Formed the Movement*, ed., Kimberlé Crenshaw, Neil Gotanda, Gary Peller, and Kendall Thomas (New York: New Press, 1995); Lisa Lowe, *Immigrant Acts: On Asian American Cultural Politics* (Durham: Duke University Press, 1996); Mills, *The Racial Contract*; Philip J. Deloria, *Playing Indian* (New Haven: Yale University Press, 1998). Our approach to American nationalism is also informed by recent "constructivist" scholarship on nationalism. See esp. Benedict Anderson, *Imagined Communities* (London: Verso, [1983] 1991); Homi K. Bhabha, ed., *Nation and Narration* (London: Routledge, 1999).

19. Howard Winant explains the notion of racial formation, introduced by Michael Omi and himself, as an approach that "looks at race not only as the subject of struggle and

contest at the level of social structure but also as a contested theme at the level of . . . the production of meanings." *The New Politics of Race: Globalism, Difference, Justice* (Minneapolis: University of Minnesota Press, 2004), 40.

20. See Martin Luther King Jr., "Racism and the White Backlash," in *Where Do We Go From Here: Chaos or Community?* (Boston: Beacon Press, 1968).

21. The stark *herrenvolk* republic, exemplified by the domination of Native Americans and Mexicans and enslavement and then Jim Crow segregation and subordination of African Americans, has been dismantled; but it has been replaced by a more subtle racialized hierarchy that still entails white racialized advantage and the subordination and marginalization, in varying ways, of blacks, Native Americans, Latinos, and Asian Americans. As Stanford Lyman summarizes the new situation, "In America, the toppling of the outer bastion of the white republic's institutionalized racism—legislatively established segregation, 'Jim Crow' laws, and juridically enforced race discrimination—has made its second line of defense—the walls built against job opportunities and occupational advancement—both more visible and less vulnerable to assault." Quoted in David Carroll Cochran, *The Color of Freedom: Race and Contemporary American Liberalism* (Albany: State University of New York Press, 1999), 48.

22. Almost all of the subjects of the essays presented here are public intellectuals who expressed their ideas in part through public speeches and popular journals or in books, articles, novels, and plays that were intended as interventions in the public life of the political community. One partial exception to this is Washington, who, despite his political prominence, is not known for his intellectual contributions.

23. Michael Eric Dyson describes such intellectual whitewashing as "the interpretation of social history through an explanatory framework in which truth functions as an ideological projection of whiteness in the form of a universal identity." See Dyson, "The Labor of Whiteness, the Whiteness of Labor, and the Perils of Whitewashing," in *Audacious Democracy: Labor, Intellectuals, and the Social Reconstruction of America*, ed. Steven Fraser and Joshua B. Freeman (Boston: Houghton Mifflin, 1997), 169. Historical monographs and texts that engage in such whitewashing to a significant degree include the following: Ralph Henry Gabriel, *The Course of American Democratic Thought* (New York: Ronald Press, 1940); Henry Steele Commager, *The American Mind* (New Haven: Yale University Press, 1950); Mason, ed., *Free Government*; Michael B. Levy, ed., *Political Thought in America: An Anthology*, 2d ed. (Chicago: Dorsey Press, 1988); and Kenneth M. Dolbeare, ed., *American Political Thought*, 3d ed. (Chatham, N.J.: Chatham House, 1996). A valuable corrective to these works is S. T. Joshi, ed., *Documents of American Prejudice: An Anthology on Race from Thomas Jefferson to David Duke* (New York: Basic Books, 1999).

24. Considerations of space in the difficult task of putting together anthologies representative of American political thought are undoubtedly part of the problem, but the problem nonetheless remains. Michael Levy's presentation of Jefferson's thought is a good example of this. He includes in his anthology the Declaration of Independence along with several significant letters in which Jefferson elaborates his liberal, republican ideas; but we find little evidence of Jefferson's tortured struggles over race and citizenship. See Levy, *Political Thought in America*, 81–84, 97–101, 138–40, 156–63. Not surprisingly, his selections of Lincoln's writings are a bit more complete in this regard (see ibid., 217–31). Consider also Mason's selections from Roosevelt and Gompers: humanistic excerpts from one of Roosevelt's "New Nationalism" speeches of 1910 ("Whenever the alternative must be faced, I am for men and not for property") and from Gompers's statement, *The Labor Movement, Its Makeup, Achievements, and Aspirations* (1914) ("Working people— and I prefer to say working people and to speak of them as really human beings—are prompted by the same desires, the same hopes of a better life as are other people"). See *Free Government*, 652, 656–57.

25. In this vein, Mason includes an excerpt from Baldwin's essay "Letter from a Region of My Mind," in *Free Government* (876–86), along with a selection from Martin Luther King Jr. but offers nothing from Du Bois. Du Bois fares better in the anthologies edited by Levy (see, *Political Thought in America*, 375–85) and Dolbeare (see *American Political Thought*, 408–21).

26. See Gary Gerstle's defense of this point in his essay below.

27. The Combahee River Collective, "A Black Feminist Statement," in *But Some of Us Are Brave*, ed. Gloria T. Hull, Patricia Bell Scott, and Barbara Smith (Old Westbury, N.Y.: Feminist Press, 1982); Elizabeth Spelman, *Inessential Woman* (Boston: Beacon Press, 1988); and Rose Brewer, "Theorizing Race, Class, Gender: The New Scholarship of Black Feminist Intellectuals and Black Women's Labor," in *Theorizing Black Feminisms*, ed., S. Jones and A. P. A. Busia (New York: Routledge, 1993).

28. Many scholars and popular commentators still focus largely on the black/white divide, often in illuminating ways. See, e.g., Williams, *Alchemy of Race and Rights*; Roediger, *Wages of Whiteness*; Orlando Patterson, *The Ordeal of Integration* (Washington: Civitas/Counterpoint, 1997); David K. Shipler, *A Country of Strangers: Blacks and Whites in America* (New York: Knopf, 1997).

29. There is more to be said regarding, for example, Pacific Islanders (particularly with respect to ongoing struggles for recognition of indigenous Hawaiians), Arab Americans, and ethnic and even racialized divisions among blacks and among whites.

30. George Lipsitz, *The Possessive Investment in Whiteness: How White People Profit from Identity Politics* (Philadelphia: Temple University Press, 1998), chap. 1; and Matthew Frye Jacobson, *Whiteness of a Different Color: European Immigration and the Alchemy of Race* (Cambridge, Mass.: Harvard University Press, 1999).

31. Patricia Williams, "America, Seen Through the Filter of Race: A Conversation on Race," *New York Times*, sec. 4 (July 2, 2000), 11. See also Roediger, *Wages of Whiteness*; and *Toward the Abolition of Whiteness: Essays in Race, Politics, and Working Class History* (London: Verso, 1994); Nikhil Pal Singh, *Black Is a Country: Race and the Unfinished Struggle for Democracy* (Cambridge, Mass.: Harvard University Press, 2004).

32. Michael Rogin, *Fathers and Children: Andrew Jackson and the Subjection of the American Indian* (New York: Knopf, 1975); Reginald Horsman, *Race and Manifest Destiny: The Origins of American Racial Anglo-Saxonism* (Cambridge, Mass.: Harvard University Press, 1981).

33. Peter N. Carroll and David W. Noble, *The Restless Centuries: A History of the American People* (Minneapolis: Burgess, 1973); Zinn, *People's History*, 1–11.

34. Edmund S. Morgan and Marie Morgan, "Our Shaky Beginnings," *New York Review of Books* 54 (April 26, 2007).

35. John Winthrop, "A Modell of Christian Charity," in *Political Thought in America*, 12.

36. Zinn, *People's History*, 13. The Puritans appealed to the Bible, Psalms 2:8 for justification: "Ask of me, and I shall give thee, the heathen for thine inheritance, and the utmost parts of the earth for thy possession" (quoted in Zinn, *People's History*, 14).

37. Carroll and Noble, *Restless Centuries*, 53; Gordon S. Wood, "The Bloodiest War," *New York Review of Books* 46 (April 9, 1998): 41–42.

38. George M. Fredrickson, *White Supremacy: A Comparative Study in American and South African History* (Oxford: Oxford University Press, 1981), 101; Winthrop D. Jordan, *White Over Black: Attitudes Toward the Negro, 1550–1812* (Baltimore: Penguin Books, 1969), 79–80.

39. For more on the Declaration, see the essay by Harris and Baum below.

40. The three-fifths proviso established that each slave would count for three-fifths of a person for the purposes of determining the number of representatives from each state to the U.S. House of Representatives.

41. Jacobson, *Whiteness of a Different Color*, 22.

42. Taney, quoted in Bernard Bailyn, Robert Dallek, David Brion Davis, Donald Herbert Donald, John L. Thomas, and Gordon S. Wood, *The Great Republic: A History of the American People* (Lexington, Mass.: D. C. Heath, 1992), 1:573.

43. Roediger, *Wages of Whiteness*, 148, 150.

44. The Thirteenth Amendment outlawed slavery and involuntary servitude; the Fourteenth declared that no state shall "deprive any person of life, liberty, or property, without due process of the law; nor deny to any person within its jurisdiction the equal protection of the laws"; and the Fifteenth declared that the right to vote cannot be abridged because of race. See Bailyn et al., *Great Republic*, 482.

45. Chief Justice John Marshall, quoted in Peter N. Carroll and David W. Noble, *The Free and the Unfree: A New History of the United States* (New York: Penguin, 1977), 172.

46. Among the other influential works of this school were Josiah Nott and George Glidden, *Types of Mankind* (1854), which went though several printings. See William Stanton, *The Leopard's Spots: Scientific Attitudes Toward Race in America, 1815–59* (Chicago: University of Chicago Press, 1960).

47. The Jacksonian Democrat John L. O'Sullivan wrote, in 1845, that (white) Americans had a "manifest destiny to overspread and to possess the whole of the Continent which Providence has given us for the development of the great experiment of liberty." Quoted in Carl N. Degler, *Out of Our Past: The Forces that Shaped Modern America*, 3d ed. (New York: Harper Colophon Books, 1984), 118.

48. With the Dawes Act, the U.S. government sought to assimilate surviving Native Americans into the national economy by dividing tribal lands into private property allocated to heads of families. See Carroll and Noble, *Restless Centuries*, 352–53; Vine Deloria Jr. and Clifford Lytle, *The Nations Within: The Past and Future of American Indian Sovereignty* (New York: Pantheon, 1984). On Wounded Knee, see Peter Matthiessen, *In the Spirit of Crazy Horse* (New York: Penguin Books, [1983] 1992), 19–20.

49. Jacobson, *Whiteness of a Different Color*, 41–42.

50. Ibid., 82–86; Mae M. Ngai, "The Architecture of Race in American Immigration Law: A Reexamination of the Immigration Act of 1924," *Journal of American History* 86 (June 1999): 80–81. The Nordic and nativist sentiments of this era were expressed in such racist polemics as Madison Grant, *The Passing of the Great Race* (1916), and Lothrop Stoddard, *The Rising Tide of Color Against White World Supremacy* (1920).

51. Bailyn et al., *Great Republic*, 682.

52. The courts initially used the Caucasian category to interpret the phrase "white person," but in *Thind* the Supreme Court dismissed the usefulness of that category when it rejected the claim to whiteness of a high-caste Hindu from Punjab, India. See Ian F. Haney-López, *White by Law: The Legal Construction of Race* (New York: New York University Press, 1996), 2, 223–24.

53. Native Americans were still prohibited from voting in some western states. See Frances Paul Prucha, *The Great Father: The United States Government and the American Indians* (Lincoln: University of Nebraska Press, 1984), 2:794.

54. The U.S. Supreme Court sanctioned these covenants between 1926 and 1948. In 1948, the Court finally ruled that such covenants were "unenforceable as law." See Clement E. Vose, *Caucasians Only: The Supreme Court, the NAACP, and the Restrictive Covenant Cases* (Berkeley: University of California Press, 1967), vii–viii.

55. See Ronald Takaki, "Reflections of Racial Patterns in America," in *From Different Shores: Perspectives on Race and Ethnicity in America*, 2d ed., ed. Ronald Takaki (New York: Oxford University Press, 1994), 223.

56. The idea of the "invisible republic" comes from Greil Marcus's account of the alternative America imagined in Harry Smith's *Anthology of American Folk Music* (1952). Smith's invisible republic, Marcus says, sought to subvert "what, in the 1950s, was known as . . . Americanism. That meant the consumer society, as advertised on TV; it meant vigilance against all enemies of such a society and a determination never to appear as one." Smith's invisible republic was "a mystical body of the republic, a kind of public secret . . . a declaration of a weird but clearly recognizable America within the America of the exercise of institutional majoritarian power." See Marcus, *Invisible Republic: Bob Dylan's Basement Tapes* (New York: Henry Holt, 1996), 96, 125.

57. Adam Nagourney, "Obama Elected President as Racial Barrier Falls," *New York Times* (November 5, 2008), A1.

58. David R. Roediger, "Race Will Survive the Obama Phenomenon," *Chronicle of Higher Education* 55, no. 7 (October 10, 2008) B6–B10.

59. Asian Americans present a complex and internally differentiated grouping—sometimes put forward simplistically as the new "model minority"—whose current positioning demands further specification. See Ronald Takaki, "Race and the End of History," in *The Good Citizen*, ed. David Batstone and Eduardo Mendieta (New York: Routledge, 2001), 81–92; Vijay Prashad, "How the Hindus Became Jews: American Racism After 9/11," *South Atlantic Quarterly* 104 (Summer 2005): 583–606.

60. The U.S. Supreme Court further whittled down *Brown* in *Parents Involved in Community Schools v. Seattle School District No. 1* (2007). In a 5 to 4 decision, the Court invalidated programs in Seattle, Washington, and Louisville, Kentucky, that made modest efforts to maintain school-by-school racial diversity. Justice Anthony Kennedy's concurring opinion left some room for school districts to adopt carefully tailored policies to avoid "racial isolation" and "de facto resegregation in schooling." Nonetheless, the decision hobbles efforts to overcome the legacy of racism and racialized inequality in U.S. schools. See Linda Greenhouse, "Justices, 5–4, Limit the Use of Race for School Integration," *New York Times* (June 29, 2007), A1, A20.

George Washington

Porcelain, Tea, and Revolution

On the evening of July 9, 1776, impassioned New York citizens and Continental soldiers pulled down the two-thousand-pound gilded statue of King George III on Bowling Green, breaking off its head and mutilating its nose. In the months to come, Manhattan, a half-evacuated trading port, would be the scene of the next battle of the Revolutionary War. General George Washington made plans for the city's defense.

At the same time, under Washington's personal supervision, his housekeeper, Mrs. Mary Smith, proceeded to furnish his New York home. Carefully kept accounts and receipts reveal the purchase of mahogany knife cases, a carpet, a damask tablecloth, a feather bed, pillows, a tureen, eight porcelain mugs, two dozen plates, and other miscellany. The pro-British Burling Slip merchants Frederick and Philip Rhinelander supplied numerous imported creamware dishes, sauceboats, plates, and fluted bowls, including three even more costly china bowls. And the Bayard Street retailer George Ball sold "burnt china cups & saucers" and other tea service items to the household.[1] During this time the general and Mrs. Washington kept up "a high level of comfort in dining and furnishings," maintaining a "tolerably genteel" table.[2] By September, miscalculations forced Washington's inexperienced troops to retreat. At great expense and trouble the general's household was packed up and reestablished at the Morris-Jumel Mansion in Haerlem Heights.

What explains General Washington's seemingly extraordinary desire for luxury in the midst of America's war for independence? It would be easy to caricature his material wants at this moment of battle. This enigmatic anecdote, however, opens up fresh insights into the founding generation's efforts to formulate a national identity. While these historical details may appear trivial to traditional interpretations of early American history, they illustrate how the Founding Fathers and mothers of the United States used tea, porcelains, and other representations of China to construct their new nation. These practices contributed to the racialization of the American republic and played a key role in the making of a hybrid Anglo-American identity. For elite white men, concepts of freedom, happiness, property, individuality, rational self-interest, and despotism were part of ongoing debates about how one tamed wild passions, harnessed them via self-cultivation, produced wealth, and became a gentleman without overindulging in luxuries and becoming "effeminate" and "corrupt."

"To Fix the Taste of Our Country Properly"

While based in West Point in 1779, Washington gave detailed instructions on which officers, staff, and surgeons should be issued what supplies. Tea was to be distributed as follows: "Fifty pounds of the best quality for future disposal: one pound of the best kind to each General Officer; half a pound of the same to each field officer and head of a staff department and a quarter of a pound pr. man of the remainder to any other officer of the army who shall apply."[3] The general's careful deliberations on the apportioning of teas exemplified his proper role as a patriarch rewarding his officers. His insistence on having Chinese tea sets or Wedgwood Queensware reminded him and his officers, in the heat of battle, of his status and authority. Such luxury items were scarce during war, and their rarity made Washington's role in distributing tea all the more significant symbolically.[4]

Before the war, Washington was well aware of the divide between the haves and the have-nots. In Virginia common people ate their meals from a communal family bowl, often using their hands to scoop out the food. In more settled areas the poor were more likely to eat their porridge with spoons. Wealth was measured throughout the century by the number of chairs one owned, whether one had a frame bed, or whether one lived in a dwelling of more than one room.[5] For those aspiring to differentiate themselves from the practices of most Americans, learning the proper use of such "instruments" as knives, forks, and spoons, which signified luxury and elegance, became important. Washington worked tirelessly at uplifting himself from his humble origins to the status of landed gentry—as distinct from farmers, whom he called the "grazing multitude."[6] His tea-drinking and porcelain-collecting habits embodied these efforts. They further embodied the contradictory crosscurrents of the emergent Anglo-American revolutionary culture. Washington strove to be both a proper British gentleman and an American revolutionary.

In 1755 Washington made his first order for Chinese porcelains. Sending three hogsheads of tobacco, he prevailed upon the London "Chinaman" Richard Washington to choose a set of goods "agreable to the present taste" and "good of their kind." (Significantly, eighteenth-century British porcelain merchants, male and female, were called Chinamen and Chinawomen, and their china was sold in china shops.) Introduced by a fellow planter, Washington had to place his trust in this unknown merchant. Desperately hoping to be treated fairly, Washington emphasized their shared surname. "I should be glad to cultivate the most intimate corrispondance with you, not only for names-sake but as a friend, and shall endeavour in all things to approve myself worthy your Regard."[7] Such was the nature of the British empire that a Virginia planter was at the mercy of a British shopkeeper.[8]

When they couldn't get the authentic goods, Europeans and some Americans copied them "after the Chinese taste." The French term *chinoiserie* referred to the seventeenth- and eighteenth-century fashion for European-made imitations of Chinese goods. These were the creations of craftsmen who had no firsthand experience of the distant and highly romanticized "Cathay." Gold-embroidered tapestries of small people living in a willow-patterned world, elaborate gardens with "gossamer pavilions," architecture with pagoda-styled roofs, faux porcelains, fantastic latticework, fanciful stage sets, faux variations of lacquered furniture, and various other decorative notions formed the material expression of this European orientalism.[9]

Once elected president, George and Martha Washington moved into the first presidential palace at Pearl and Cherry streets in New York. George Washington wrote the New York merchant Gouverneur Morris, who was in Paris, asking him to shop for stylish porcelains.[10] Morris wrote back, "You will perhaps exclaim that I have not complied with your Directions as to Economy, but you will be of a different Opinion when you see the Articles. I could have sent you a Number of pretty Trifles for very little Cost, but . . . your Table would have been in the Style of a petite Maitresse of this City, which most assuredly is not the Style you wish." Morris's use of the gendered and classist phrase "the Style of a petite Maitresse" convinced Washington to accept a grander role: "I think it of very great importance to fix the taste of our Country properly, and I think your Example will go so very far in that respect. It is therefore my Wish that every Thing about you should be substantially good and majestically plain; made to endure."[11]

For a new nation in which the majority of people still lived in humble dwellings and possessed modest material belongings, Chinese commodities signified what the sociologist Pierre Bourdieu has termed "distinction."[12] Upwardly striving Americans wanted not just tea sets, porcelains, and tea. As the historian Richard Bushman has illustrated, such desires also led citizens to adopt housing styles designed to show their wealth and accommodate more and more personal belongings. Multistoried houses with hallway stair entry areas and separate rooms for entertaining, dining, cooking, and living came to set a new standard for genteel living.[13] The tasteful display of these passionately coveted things from the "Orient" and the "Indies" (and elsewhere in the non-European world) distinguished one moneyed space from the other.

Corrupting Virtues and Revolutionary Passions

While Washington coveted Chinese luxuries, other revolutionaries argued that consumption of luxuries corrupted virtue. While many New Yorkers emulated and envied the wealth and refinement of Chinese court culture, some radicals urged a boycott of all foreign luxuries. They argued, with little support, that Americans could make their tea from local flora. The love of luxuries from China and the Indies came to represent the antithesis of Anglo-American republican virtue—such things were deemed addictive and corrupting. Earnest moralists read and took to heart the observation of the English radical Catharine Macaulay in a New York edition of her address to the people of Britain in 1775, that a "long succession of abused prosperity" lured the empire into a "ruinous operation by the Riches and Luxuries of the East."[14] The British novelist Tobias Smollet wrote, "Roman Commonwealth of old" and other civilizations were ruined because "Luxury and Profuseness" from the Orient "led the Way to Indigence and Effeminacy; which prepared the Minds of the People for Corruption; and Corruption for Subjection; as they have constantly succeeded one another, and will do so again, in the same Circumstances, in all Countries, and in all Ages."[15] Benjamin Franklin worried about new dependencies. In the *Columbia Magazine* he stated, "One is astonished to think of the number of vessels and men who are daily exposed in going to bring tea from China, coffee from Arabia, and sugar and tobacco from America: all commodities which our ancestors lived very well without."[16] Indeed, many believed the East India Company and the new financial order were ruining "old England."[17]

The procommerce political philosopher David Hume disagreed. He acknowledged that "all the Latin classics . . . are full of these sentiments, and universally ascribe the ruin of their state to the arts and riches imported from the East." The belief in corrupting "Grecian and Asiatic luxury," however, "mistook the cause of the disorders," which really proceeded from an "ill model'd government" and the "unlimited extent of conquests."[18] For now the desire for Oriental goods superseded the threat of "Oriental despotism."

Indeed, the right to easy access to desired Chinese consumer goods threatened to overwhelm radical boycott positions. The freedom to consume such foreign items as teas, to wear what one wanted, or to set one's table with porcelains had been subject to a long tradition of social controls in England. Such actions led to the organization of a popular revolt, or, as T. H. Breen notes, created a unifying issue for private consumers to rally around.[19] Boston merchants urged their customers not to buy British goods, sloganeering: "Save your money and you can save your country."[20] The New York Sons of Liberty resolved an even more dramatic position during the tea boycott: tea drinkers threatened "the liberties of America."[21]

Nevertheless, American boycotters gained their radical goals largely because the smuggling of teas continued unabated. In practice, Americans often appropriated without controls consumables deemed foreign and therefore taboo. Tea smuggled by Americans became acceptable to consume, while British East India Company tea was not. Freedom, in part, was defined as the unfettered access to the "baubles of Britain." After all, it was the British Crown's augmentation of the East India Company's power to monopolize the consumption of Chinese goods that precipitated the various tea boycotts. During the New York Tea Party, held months after the Boston protest, one of the leaders of the Sons of Liberty, Alexander McDougall, also known as "Hampden," wrote to his "Fellow Citizens" in self-consciously Lockean terms. "The chief end of all free government, is the protection of Property, from Injuries without it." He conceived of property "in the large sense, in which Mr. Locke uses it, as comprehending Life, Liberty, and Estate," and he asserted propertied male citizen's "natural liberty" and the right to "defend themselves" against "the control and Tyranny of others"—ergo the right to rebel against the despotic authority King George had bequeathed to the East India Company. As long as Americans worked hard for their material objects of desires, why should they not have the unfettered right to trade and consume Chinese luxuries?[22]

Elite Community Building

Chinese goods were not used simply to satisfy materialist desires, however. For Gouverneur Morris's fellow New Yorkers, the culture of consuming and giving luxury objects became intrinsic to the formation of a merchant-led patrician elite. Rituals of using, giving, and passing on Chinese objects were a means of community building. As the elite practice of separating the workplace from the home became more commonplace in late eighteenth-century America, women became responsible for "raising the standards of the quality of domestic life in the household, raising the standards for rearing and educating children, and assuming the moral guardianship of all family members and even of society as a whole."[23] With the assistance of servants and slaves, elites came to employ the home as a vehicle for cultivating genteel moral virtue. Chinese objects of distinction were critical to this process. Most notably, teatime and the family dinner were turned into secular rituals in which social interactions among family, friends, and guests could take place.

Teatime, in contrast to time ordinary folk spent in the common taverns (which John Adams described as "the eternal haunt of loose disorderly People"), represented a social space where one could demonstrate one's skills at the art of conversation with American women who displayed their "Wit," good "Sense," and "Virtue."[24] Performed according to British and Conti nental standards, the serving of tea required having the proper "Tea Geer," which included the teapot, cups, saucers, tea table, caddie spoon, tea caddie, and other items. The more stylish the "equipage" the more refined the server.[25] In private homes proper and improper norms of interaction between the genders were transacted. Adams complained of a coarse woman who embarrassed some "shoe string fellows that never use Tea" about the awkward manner in which some people behaved at a tea she had held. While scolding the indiscreet woman, Adams did not challenge the firmly entrenched attitude that one's skills at having tea revealed one's sophistication and pedigree.[26] Indeed, in this Anglo-American world the lack of such refinement brought on derision. Patriarchal disapproval sanctioned those who did not conform and kept proper women in their place, while displays of refinement merited compliments and reinforced chains of acceptable social relationships.

Women had a more intimate, memory-keeping relationship to these Chinese things than men. They were largely responsible for developing and maintaining bonds of sentiment. The giving of valued gifts became an important means by which networks of sentiment were woven, a shared sphere of meanings, power, and hierarchy. Sentimental values were consolidated between the givers and the receivers. In effect, the process of giving helped to reinforce the authority of certain traditional core values.[27] This paradox of "keeping-while-giving" can be amply demonstrated by the manner in which New York patricians used their most prized porcelains. Important events in life were marked by the giving of gifts to bring those with established wealth and the nouveau riche together into a shared civic society.

A Chinese enameled punch bowl given by the Schuyler family to Alexander Hamilton and the Schuylers' daughter Elizabeth in 1780 to commemorate their marriage, for example, signified acceptance of Hamilton into the family and its social circles. The marriage (and bowl) marked Hamilton's rise in New York society. The Schuylers' closest friends and associates (often kin) were the Hudson Valley Knickerbocker elite: the Delanceys, Livingstons, Van Rensselaers, and Van Cortlandts. A year later, General Washington offered Hamilton command of a battalion, and the following year he was appointed Continental receiver of taxes and admitted to the New York bar.[28]

Perhaps the most important role of such valued gifts was their intergenerational effect. Elite families created a time and an environment for young people to become children. Their familial obligation as children was to learn and practice a world of behaviors and knowledge that would perpetuate their family's wealth and status. Children's specially inscribed objects and toys, miniaturized from adult scale, helped to acculturate children in their relations to Chinese objects. Not only were porcelain sets passed down from generation to generation, but children were quickly socialized into the ritualistic behavior associated with the objects. For example, Mary Clinton, the daughter of DeWitt Clinton's brother, owned a matching blue-and-white tea set with her initials monogrammed into the design. Indeed, Chinese porcelains were so much a part of the adult world that Susan

Watkins's handmade dollhouse dating back to 1834 prominently displayed a tiny Chinese blue-and-white platter and tea set in the dining room.[29]

Through the medium of the dollhouse and the tiny play porcelains, parents and grandparents were communicating their desire that their daughters and granddaughters be properly cultured. If the patrician boy's obligation to his family was to master the constantly destabilizing world of commodities and the symbolic knowledge necessary for that work, the patrician girl's obligation was to master the conversion of such alienated things into a world of stable and meaningful human relationships that would provide the family with a sense of secure identity. In this way Chinese export porcelains became Americanized through family crests, designs, and added sentimental meanings.

For this Anglo-American society the range of objects reflecting the social self became quite broad. For Washington it certainly included his land, slaves, house, and the material embodiment of his service as a general and president. For Hamilton, his sense of self included his achieved ambitions. And for Watkins it probably included her dollhouse and her relationship to her grandparents. These possessions became so inalienable to one's personal sense of self, William James pointed out in another context, that their loss represented far more than the actual material object, for "there remains, over and above this, a sense of the shrinkage of our personality, a partial conversion of ourselves to nothingness."[30] By implication, the loss of access to such sentimentalized objects, from the Orient and elsewhere, was an important concern.

How Did China Become Wealthy?

The founding generation of European Americans sought to abstract lessons from what had been written about China's Confucian-based civilization. They were fascinated by extant translations of the great sage's linkage of personal virtue with the affairs of the state.[31] The maxim that the morality of a civilization's patriarch-leader was responsible for the general well-being and wealth of his nation appealed favorably to revolutionists and republicans alike. The Jesuit priest Jean Baptiste Du Halde's influential book *The General History of China* credited such centralized moral and civil authority for the creation of the Grand Canals, the Great Wall, the civil service system, and national taxation and was represented to have benevolently managed natural resources in balance with national trade.[32] In addition, the well-regarded writings of François Marie Arouet de Voltaire, François Quesnay, and associated political economists (now referred to as Physiocrats) celebrated China as a stable, prosperous agricultural civilization that should be emulated in the West.[33]

Such books and thinkers had a significant influence on the ways in which Franklin and Jefferson, both of whom had spent time in Paris, thought about how to make the new nation prosper. Franklin, for example, regularly noted a wide range of useful Chinese flora, fauna, crafts, inventions, and practices adoptable in America, including windmills, mulberry trees and silk production, rhubarb, rice cultivation, papermaking, and central heating.[34] The printer-philosopher-inventor's penchant for parables illustrated his transcultural uses of knowledge about Chinese. He reinforced the Protestant values of collective hard work by citing the following saying from "a certain Chinese Emperor": "I wil, if posible, have no Idlenes in my Dominions; for if there be one Man idle, some other Man must sufer Cold and hunger."[35] Indeed, in the introduction to the first volume of Franklin's American Philosophical Society journal was the indicative passage, "Could we be so fortunate as to introduce the industry of the Chinese, their arts of living and improvements in husbandry . . . America might become in time as populous as China."[36]

Jefferson, who owned a copy of Du Halde's book, spoke authoritatively about a Chinese play and planned on having a miniaturized Chinese pavilion (modeled after one in Kew Gardens in London) and Chinese temple built for his treasured garden in Monticello.[37] More significantly, however, was Jefferson's translation of Count Destutt de Tracy's *Treatise on Political Economy*. A central argument of this book, which Jefferson believed "should be . . . in the hands of every American citizen," was an exposition on the connection between virtuous individual will and its salubrious social effects.[38] Extending the Physiocrats' interest in Confucian moral statecraft, de Tracy linked utilitarian moral virtue with individual will and individual will with happiness, as defined by possessing property.[39] In this sense, French thinkers translated Confucian philosophic ideals into a pragmatic Lockean-like theory for generating individual and national wealth, and Jefferson became the school's major advocate in the United States.

In contrast to Washington's love of porcelains, Franklin's practical curiosity, and Jefferson's sociophilosophical bent, Hamilton thought about

China primarily as part of the global exchange of resources and goods. He paid careful attention to Malachy Postlethwayt's *The Universal Dictionary of Trade and Commerce.*[40] The following entry was typical of Hamilton's notes:

Asia.

Productions; all those in Europe with the adition of many either in greater abundance than there or not produced there at all—

There is a great abundance of diamons pearl coral gold silver copper, iron, sulphur red earth, salt-petre, allum quicksilver, potter's earth (of which is made the porcelain) raw silk cotton, tea, sage, coffee, nutmegs, mace cloves cinnamon pepper, indigo china-root, aquila-wood, rhubarb, musk, vermilion, sticklack borax, *lapis laxuli* Dragon's blood, cubebs [a pepper from Java] frankincense, saffron myrrh, manna, ambergrease and many other of the valuable drugs and gums.[41]

Such notations not only marked what any given nation produced but also what access they had to the Indies market and what made them wealthy.[42] Rates of exchange and equivalencies, what he called "political arithmetic," fascinated Hamilton. He wrote notes on the relative values of gold to silver in Europe and China, the labor needed to maintain a "hundred in all the necessities of life," and what America as the newcomer to global trade might offer to these markets.[43]

Murphy's *The Orphan of China*

In addition to the circulation of goods and books, cultural productions, such as plays, spectacles, and events, became important vehicles for the construction of American nationalism and foreign others. The New York performances of *The Orphan of China* offer unique insights into how this process worked.

The Orphan of China, a tragic play by the British playwright Arthur Murphy, was based on earlier adaptations of a Chinese opera. In 1787 it was staged at the John Street Theatre, one of the nation's first and most important stages.[44] The following lines opened the New York production:

Enough of Greece and Rome. The exhausted store
Of either nation now can charm no more . . .

On eagle wings the poet of to-night
Soars for fresh virtues to the source of light,
To China's eastern realms; and boldly bears
Confucius' morals to Britannia's ears.[45]

The fact that *The Orphan of China* played at the John Street Theatre in New York before, during, and after the Revolution is significant. Despite the political divides between colonial Tories, British soldiers, and revolutionary patriots, the piece commanded continuing interest among them all. Indeed, they shared many cultural values.[46]

The original play, *Zhaoshiguer*, is considered by Chinese scholars to be a minor operetta that was written around 1330 by the Yuan Dynasty writer Chi Chun-hsiang.[47] Nevertheless, its translation by the French Jesuit Father Premare gave it significant visibility in the West. Jefferson recommended the work to his brother-in-law as one of the classics of Chinese literature.[48] Though the opera was accepted as an authentic Chinese work, Premare in effect transformed it into a European tragedy. As this minor Chinese opera entered European intellectual circles, it was constantly retranslated, reinterpreted, and rewritten.

Intellectuals used various versions of *The Orphan of China* to support different European concerns, ranging from the attempt to articulate formal universal principles of successful drama to more political matters.[49] Bishop Richard Hurd, for example, thought he found conclusive evidence in Premare's translation of *Zhaoshiguer* of universal common sense. Surely, Hurd argued, if such an isolated and ancient culture as China could realize these rules, "what effects must it not have in more enlightened countries and times, where the discipline of long experience, and criticism (which is improved common sense) come in to the assistance of the poet?"[50] Such arguments both praised and belittled Chinese civilization.

The 1797 published version of Murphy's play reveals his attitudes toward China in a prologue and epilogue. While emphasizing the radical Whig preoccupation with the enlightened responsibilities of governance, he told his public to "set your hearts at rest" because the British government and people were far superior to the Chinese.[51] In British cosmopolitan culture China was losing its luster as "an exotic land of wonder" and wisdom and taking on the new cast of a "provincial empire eager to clasp the British constitution to its breast."[52] As the British empire expanded during this era, other empires looked less impressive and novel, and more arrogant attitudes gained currency.

In late eighteenth-century New York City, by contrast, China had not yet lost its attraction. As a minor and peripheral city of the British empire, New York still welcomed what London considered out of fashion. This context explains the success of Murphy's play. The play's periodic staging nevertheless warrants a deeper explanation. How could it please both British soldiers of an occupation army and American revolutionaries?

The Orphan of China simultaneously allowed for a critique of the British monarchy, gaining the legitimacy of Chinese civilizational precedent for American values, and for a reconnecting of the United States culturally to an Anglo-Saxon cultural tradition. In the American context, this interpretation easily justified the rebellion of republicans over monarchists. Revolutionaries could enjoy *Orphan* as a play about the universal striving for republican virtue. Self-sacrifice for a common good was neither simply an American invention, nor simply part of the claimed Greco-Roman heritage of good Anglo-Saxons; it was also a universal truth, demonstrated by this play from a far different culture.

While such uses of Chinese cultural artifacts aligned China with Western notions of republican virtue, a damaging and countervailing message was emerging, one that echoed the radical tea boycotters on the corrupting dangers of Oriental goods. As long as China represented Confucian antiquity, it could be extolled as one with Western Enlightenment traditions. Yet as British imperial power rose, the China of contemporary geopolitics was viewed as outdated, again subject to foreign rule. Overzealous monarchs in China were despotic, whereas "people's hearts" supported British monarchs. [53] Debt-ridden Americans, however, could ill afford such an imperious British attitude. For them China was still a place to be admired and envied, a source of luxuries and the hoped-for savior of the American economy. At the same time, growing familiarity would soon breed contempt. European and Anglo-American theater both appropriated and subjugated Chinese difference into a realm of exoticized contrasts—for now an Orientalist otherness to be idealized and emulated. Murphy's epilogue articulated what would become an American refrain about China: "They all are crippled in the tiny shoe." [54] The gentry practice of binding women's feet, thought to be ultrafeminine and erotic (and a means of patriarchal control), was used to symbolize all of China. In this view, Chinese monarchs and by inference all Chinese men were de facto tyrants.

Patrician Orientalism

Having different dispositions, members of the founding generation used Chinese and other exotic goods and ideas in various ways. Washington sought distinction through his export porcelains and Queensware. McDougal created a more radical, democratic America in revolt against tea and despotism. Hamilton sought wealth through marriage and political arithmetic. Generations of Schuyler women gave valued gifts to forge bonds of sentimentality. Generations of Johns Street Theatre–goers used *The Orphan of China* to sort out their feelings toward mother England, monarchy, and revolution. Although each use of Orientalism differed, such various practices wove together an everyday life that helped to define an independent occidental identity emulating China and drawing upon British patrician culture while not being too closely tied to either. Such patrician Orientalism both helped to formulate order and hierarchy for a commonweal elite and was sometimes used to challenge the status quo. This elite culture embodied an underlying consensus that the trade of goods and ideas with the empire of China would foster the distinction, independence, development, wealth, and governance of the new nation.

Perhaps this complex patrician orientalism was best embodied by Gouverneur Morris. In addition to promoting an exemplary taste for the national elite, he helped to formulate the nation's early policy toward China. In 1783, he wrote a letter to the secretary of Congress supporting a trade scheme of Robert Morris, his business partner. "Exchange for the superfluities of the East" should be promoted, he wrote, to "prevent the Europ Powers from draining us as they now do of our Specie."[55] He presented the establishment of the China trade as an act of patriotism, part of nation building.

The late eighteenth-century usage of the term *exchange* was part of the lexicon of terms associated with the rise of capitalism and international trade. The word originally implied the reciprocal bartering of goods for goods, whereas money given for goods constituted a sale. The ability to trade goods freely, in barter or with specie, denoted calculated mutual self-interest at work—assumed to be "fair bargains struck between . . . free individuals."[56] Fundamentally different things had to be made equivalent in the negotiation process. And as evidenced by Washington's constant anxieties with his London Chinaman, "unequal exchange is intrinsic to the exchange process itself."[57]

For the process of trade to work, it was believed the natural and man-made resources of the Orient should be freely open to exchange. The term *superfluities* connoted excess from what was necessary, a superabundance.[58] The wealth of merchants and of the nation, therefore, was contingent on either the taking over of established trade routes to the richest Asian lands and empires from European rivals or the finding of new routes.[59] Adam Smith proposed that a rising nation's surpluses must then be "sent abroad and exchanged for something of which there is a demand at home."[60] Demand drove exploration, wars, and the establishing of trade ports. By 1776 the British East India Company's trade with Canton, only one port in glorious China, was surpassing all the trade of all the Indian ports on the Arabian and China seas combined.[61] The rapacious quest for trade advantages and the taste for tea and other refinements became ways of measuring a nation's greatness.[62]

Gouverneur Morris's words carried meanings that exemplified how patrician Americans understood and assessed themselves, their propertyless brethren, and all people, ideas, and things related to China, the Indies, and other parts of Asia. Morris was articulating a complex set of socioeconomic exchanges. The foreign exchange of goods between individuals, peoples, and nations was understood within the daily domestic negotiation of social relationships. Those wanting upward mobility and more access to "the baubles of Britain" and the luxuries of China pressed for a loosening of the controls exercised by elites. At the same time, revolutionaries sought to reestablish a society of order and deference. Both proponents and critics of the republican court and republican simplicity implicated Chinese goods and ideas in some way or another. Luxury goods and ideas from China and in the style of China were imbued with symbolic meanings and were integral to the formulation of a new American individual and nation. Before the Revolution, these beloved things became part of the driving force for social, political, and economic change. After the Revolution such expectations propelled the consumer republic to seek its own trade routes. The solution to postwar malaise would be to trade directly with China.

In these ways the question of what Chinese and American elites wanted from their trade relations was a key to early American wealth. The question of how China became wealthy was a key to how cultural nationalists formed their mythos of American destiny. Modernity was born of this new civilization, rising phoenix-like from the ashes of old despotic civilizations.

Notes

1. Franklin Knight, *Monuments of Washington's Patriotism Containing a Fac Simile of His Public Accounts Kept During the Revolutionary War, June 1775–June 1783* (Washington: Trustees of Washington's Manual Labour School and Male Orphan Asylum, 1844) 4:471.

2. Susan Gray Detweiler, *George Washington's Chinaware* (New York: Harry N. Abrams, 1982), 65.

3. George Washington, *The Writings of George Washington from the Original Manuscript Sources, 1745–1799*, ed. John C. Fitzpatrick (Washington: United States Government Printing Office, 1931–44) 16:321.

4. By 1763, the British entrepreneur Josiah Wedgwood had pioneered a lead-glazed faux porcelain earthenware that was popular among the British aristocracy and inexpensive enough to be affordable to the middle classes. Detweiler, *Chinaware*, 53–54, 57, 62.

5. Alexander Hamilton, *Gentleman's Progress: Itinerarium of Dr. Alexander Hamilton*, ed. Carl Bridenbaugh (Chapel Hill: University of North Carolina Press, 1948), 8. See also Richard L. Bushman, *The Refinement of America: Persons, Houses, Cities* (New York: Alfred A. Knopf, 1992), 76.

6. Gordon S. Wood, *The Radicalism of the American Republic* (New York: Alfred A. Knopf, 1982), 27.

7. George Washington to Richard Washington, December 6, 1755, George Washington Papers, Manuscripts Division, Library of Congress.

8. T. H. Breen, "'Baubles of Britain': The American and Consumer Revolutions of the Eighteenth Century," *Past & Present* 119 (May 1988): 73–104.

9. Hugh Honour, *Chinoiserie: The Vision of Cathay* (New York: Harper and Row, 1961), 5–8; Dawson, *Chinese Chameleon*, 106–31; and Ellen Paul Denker, *After the Chinese Taste: China's Influence in America, 1730–1930* (Salem, Mass.: Peabody Museum of Salem, 1985), 1–8.

10. Washington, *Writings*, 30:443–45.

11. Morris (Paris) to GW, January 24, 1790, George Washington Papers, Manuscripts Division, Library of Congress, vol. 22 (Commercial Letters).

12. Pierre Bourdieu, *Distinction: A Social Critique of the Judgement of Taste* (Cambridge, Mass.: Harvard University Press, 1984), 1–7.

13. Bushman, *Refinement*, 110–22.

14. Gordon S. Wood, *The Creation of the American Republic, 1776–1787* (New York: Norton, 1969), 36; Catharine Macaulay, *An Address to the People of England, Scotland, and Ireland, on the Present Important Crisis of Affairs* (London: E. and C. Dilly, 1775), 9.

15. Tobias Smollet, no. 56, July 29, 1727, cited in John Sekora, *Luxury: The Concept in Western Thought, Eden to Smollet* (Baltimore: Johns Hopkins University Press, 1977), 84.

16. *Columbia Magazine* 4 (April 1790): 245–48.

17. Sekora, *Luxury*, 84. Rodris Roth, "Tea-Drinking in Eighteenth-Century America: Its Etiquette and Equipage," in *Material Life in America, 1600–1860*, ed. Robert Blair St. George (Boston: Northeastern University Press, 1988), 440; William H. Ukers, *All About Tea* (New York: Tea and Coffee Trade Journal Company, 1935), 389.

18. David Hume, "On Luxury," in *Political Discourses* (Edinburgh: A. Kincaid and A. Donaldson, 1752), 32–33; *Race and the Enlightenment*, ed. Emmanuel Chukwudi Eze (Oxford: Blackwell, 1997), 5, 29–33.

19. Breen, "Baubles of Britain," 86–87. See Edmund S. Morgan and Helen M. Morgan, *The Stamp Act Crisis: Prologue to Revolution* (Chapel Hill: University of North Carolina Press, 1953); and T. H. Breen, "An Empire of Goods: The Anglicization of Colonial America, 1690–1776," *Journal of British Studies* 25 (1986): 467–99.

20. Charles M. Andrews, "Boston Merchants and the Non-Importation Movement," *Trans. of the Colonial Society Massachusetts* 19 (1916–17): 92.

21. "New York Sons of Liberty Resolutions on Tea," Nov. 29, 1773, in *Documents of American History*, ed. Henry Steele Commager (Englewood Cliffs, N.J.: Prentice-Hall, 1988) 1:70.

22. *New York Journal*, Oct. 14, 1773.

23. Diana di Zerega Wall, "At Home in New York: Changing Family Life Among the Propertied in the Late Eighteenth and Early Nineteenth Centuries" (Ph.D. diss., New York University, 1987), 253, 255.

24. John Adams, *Diary and Autobiography of John Adams*, ed. L. H. Butterfield, (Cambridge, Mass.: Belknap Press of Harvard University Press, 1961–1966), 1:129.

25. On British women's uses of the tea table, see Elizabeth Kowaleski-Wallace, *Consuming Subjects: Women, Shopping, and Business in the Eighteenth Century* (New York: Columbia University Press, 1997), 19–72.

26. J. Adams, *Diary* 2:113–14, 386–87. Having "a dish of tea" was also the subject of satire regarding materialistic excess. See John Smith, "A Little Teatable Chitchat, a la mode; or an ancient discovery reduced to modern practice," 1781, in *Dramas from the American Theatre, 1762–1909*, ed. Richard Moody (Cleveland: World, 1966), 9–10.

27. Annette B. Weiner, *Inalienable Possessions: The Paradox of Keeping-While-Giving* (Berkeley: University of California Press, 1992), 6–12.

28. Jacob Ernest Cook, *Alexander Hamilton* (New York: Charles Scribner, 1982), 1–8, 18–19; Saul K. Padover, *The Mind of Alexander Hamilton* (New York: Harper, 1958), 31.

29. See Nancy Cott, "Notes Toward an Interpretation of Antebellum Childrearing," *Psychohistory Review* 7, no. 4 (1973): 20; Bernard Wishy, *The Child and the Republic: The Dawn of American Child Nurture* (Philadelphia: University of Pennsylvania Press, 1967), 181.

30. William James, *The Principles of Psychology* (New York: Henry Holt, 1890), 293.

31. A. Owen Aldridge, *The Dragon and the Eagle: The Presence of China in the American Enlightenment* (Detroit: Wayne State University Press, 1993), 23–46.

32. Father Du Halde's influential four-volume study was one of the few books about China circulating in the European American colonies and the United States during the eighteenth century. Jean Baptiste Du Halde, *The General History of China, containing a Geographical, Historical, Chronological, Political and Physical Description of the Empire*

of China (London: John Watts, 1736). On the early American interest in Confucianism, see Aldridge, *Dragon*, 23–46.

33. Aldridge, *Dragon*, 144–60. Also see Lewis A. Maverick, *China a Model for Europe* (San Antonio: Paul Anderson, 1946).

34. Benjamin Franklin, *The Papers of Benjamin Franklin*, ed. Leonard W. Labaree (New Haven: Yale University Press, 1959–78), 6:77; "Poor Richard Improved, 1765," 12:11–12; 16:200; 17:107; 18:188; 19:268; 19:317; and 19:323. American Philosophical Society, *Transactions* 3 (1793): 8–10.

35. Franklin, *Papers*, 21:173.

36. American Philosophical Society, *Transactions* 1 (1768): xix.

37. E. Millicent Sowerby, *Catalogue of the Library of Thomas Jefferson* (Washington: Library of Congress, 1952–59), 1:132–38; and Frederick Doveton Nichols and Ralph E. Griswold, *Thomas Jefferson, Landscape Architect* (Charlottesville: University Press of Virginia, 1977).

38. Letter to Mr. Joseph Milligan, April 6, 1816, in *The Life and Selected Writings of Thomas Jefferson*, ed. Adrienne Koch and William Peden (New York: Random House, 1944), 663.

39. Count Antoine Louis Claude Destutt de Tracy, *A Treatise on Political Economy*, trans. Thomas Jefferson (New York: A. M. Kelley, 1970), 35–36, 46, 71–72.

40. Alexander Hamilton, *Alexander Hamilton's Pay Book*, ed. E. P. Panagopoulos (Detroit: Wayne State University Press, 1961), 4–5.

41. Ibid., 36–37.

42. Ibid., 45.

43. Ibid., 4, 42–43.

44. Robert M. Dell and Charles A. Huguenin, "Vermont's Royall Tyler in New York's John Street Theatre: A Theatrical Hoax Exploded," *Vermont History* 38, no. 2 (Spring 1970): 105.

45. William Whitehead, Esq., Poet-Laureat, Spoken by Mr. Holland, quoted in Arthur Murphy, *The Orphan of China, A Tragedy, as Performed at The Theatre-Royal, Drury-Lane* (London: George Cawthorn, 1797), xiii.

46. George C. D. Odell, *Annals of the New York Stage* (1931; reprint, New York: AMS Press, 1970), 1:135, 199, 201, 242; William Purviance Fenn, *Ah Si and His Brethren in American Literature* (Peiping [Beijing]: College of Chinese Culture, 1933), xxvi, 101; Chen Shou-yi, "The Chinese Orphan: A Yuan Play," *Tien Hsia Monthly* 3, no. 2 (September 1936): 114.

47. S. Chen, "Orphan," 89–115. The Wade-Giles transliteration of the Chinese is *Chao-shih-ku-erh*, translated as "The Little Orphan of the House of Chao."

48. Aldridge, *Dragon*, 21, 95.

49. For historical context, see Allardyce Nicoll, *A History of Late Eighteenth-Century Drama, 1750–1800* (Cambridge: Cambridge University Press, 1927), 335.

50. Cited in S. Chen, "Orphan," 93, 96–97, 109. Also see Appleton, *Cycle*, 84.

51. Murphy, *Orphan*, 88–89.

52. Appleton, *Cycle*, 88–89.

53. Murphy, *Orphan*, 89.

54. Ibid.

55. Gouverneur Morris to Charles Thomson, the Secretary of Congress, December 30, 1783, *Charles Thomson Papers*, Library of Congress.

56. *The Compact Edition of the Oxford English Dictionary* (OED) (Oxford: Oxford University Press, 1971), s.v. "exchange."

57. William M. Reddy, *Money and Liberty in Modern Europe: A Critique of Historical Understanding* (Cambridge: Cambridge University Press, 1987), 64–65, 88, 199. Count Destutt de Tracy defined *society* as "purely and solely a continual succession of exchanges." Destutt de Tracy, *Treatise*, xvi, 6.

58. OED, s.v. "superfluities."

59. Lars Magnusson, *Mercantilism: The Shaping of an Economic Language* (London: Routledge, 1994), 6.

60. Adam Smith, *The Wealth of Nations* (London: Penguin Books, 1970), 472.

61. Holden Furber, *Rival Empires of Trade in the Orient, 1600–1800* (Minneapolis: University of Minnesota Press, 1976), 2, 7, 17, 24, 127, 330.

62. Immanuel Wallerstein, *The Modern World System* (New York: Academic Press, 1974), 132.

Jefferson's Legacies

Racial Intimacies and American Identity

In his *Notes on the State of Virginia* (1787), Thomas Jefferson wrote, "The whole commerce between master and slave is a perpetual exercise of the most boisterous passions, the most unremitting despotism on the one part, and degrading submissions on the other."[1] Recent evidence indicates that Jefferson—a slave owner who was by turns a Virginia state legislator and governor, the principal author of the Declaration of Independence, ambassador to France, secretary of state, vice president, and president—himself pursued such "boisterous passions" with respect to his slave Sally Hemings (1773–1835). The story of Jefferson and Hemings, Stephanie Camp notes, represents for Americans "the crime and seduction of miscegenation; the ambiguities of Black and white racial identities and meaning; the coexistence of prejudice and power with family, intimacy, and sex."[2]

We reconsider Jefferson's legacy through the lens of his master-slave sexual intimacy with Hemings, highlighting the politics of Jefferson's personal relationship with black America. This relationship is a reminder of how intertwined the lives of white people and black people were in the making of this nation, even as leading politicians, scholars, and racists long advanced fictive accounts of the nation as essentially white. Jefferson's basic contradictions concerning equality, slavery, and "race" are now well known. As the author of the idea that "all men are created equal" (in the Declaration) and a champion of religious liberty, he helped to construct the myth of a universalistic civic national identity despite how Americans' individual destinies have been shaped by racial and ethnic ascriptions.[3] A critic of slavery, he maintained one of Virginia's largest slave populations, asserted "negro" racial inferiority, and doubted that free blacks could live harmoniously with whites.[4] On top of all this, he, like many other white slave owners, lived out the secrets and lies of American white supremacism and white nationalism in the most personal way.

"What is important historically about the Hemings-Jefferson affair," Winthrop Jordan suggests, "is that it has seemed to so many Americans to have mattered."[5] We are particularly concerned with the ways in which the Hemings-Jefferson affair has mattered to many Americans: how it was first publicized in 1802; how it has been discussed by historians in the United States and by Jefferson's biographers; and how it recently has been debated in new ways in light of DNA tests, publicized in 1998, that point to Jefferson's paternity of Hemings's children. Two competing views of the Hemings-Jefferson affair open a window on how race, gender, and sexuality have shaped American national identity. Leading historians and Jefferson's biographers, chiefly white men, have long dismissed rumors of a Jefferson-Hemings sexual relationship. This stance has betrayed unwarranted protectiveness of Jefferson's innocence specifically and of white American innocence more generally. In contrast, many of Jefferson's descendants who have been identified as African American exhibit a proprietary bearing toward their lineage that suggests a kind of possessive investment in their own whiteness.[6]

We are especially interested in the struggles that the black descendants of Hemings and Jefferson have undergone in their quest to gain public recognition *as* Jefferson descendants. These struggles exemplify the vexed place of black Americans within the traditional American national narrative. Owing to the whitewashing, the racial whiteness, of the founding story of the American republic, African Americans have found it difficult to reinstate their role in an honest accounting of this history.[7] While black people have continually been denied their full political, social, and economic rights and standing as Americans, they have fought against their exclusion both directly—from slave rebellions to the civil rights movement and beyond—and indirectly—by asserting their ongoing contribution to U.S. history. The descendants of the relationship between Jefferson and Hemings are part of the much larger but long obscured history of power-laden sexual intimacy between black and white Americans.

Acknowledging Hemings's standpoint—or at least the ways in which it has been erased—is crucial to decentering the white supremacist and masculinist aspects of Jefferson's legacy. Because Hemings's voice has been silenced, below we discuss the offspring of another white male and black female relationship, one that occurred later in U.S. history: Essie Mae Washington-Williams, the daughter of the segregationist senator Strom Thurmond and his family's black maid.

Jefferson's America

Although Jefferson's America deeply shaped the contemporary United States, the two are vastly different places. The U.S. population in 1790, according to the first national census, was 3,929,214. Native Americans were not included, but 700,000 African American slaves were, and so were about 60,000 free blacks. Approximately 90 percent of the free white population came from the British Isles, mostly from England. People of German origin were the next largest group. About 250,000 more European immigrants arrived from 1783 to 1815, when the overall population rose to nearly 9 million. More than 200,000 new African slaves were brought into the country between 1790 and 1810, although the official ending of the slave trade in 1808 slowed their importation. Jeffersonian America was overwhelmingly rural, with a few small urban centers. Westward expansion was strong, and domestic manufacturing was just beginning.[8]

Jefferson hoped the country would remain primarily agrarian rather than become dominated by urban "panders of vice." "I think our governments will remain virtuous for many centuries," he wrote in 1787, "as long as they remain chiefly agricultural; and this will be as long as there shall be vacant lands."[9] He sought by means of the Louisiana Purchase (1803) to maintain a virtuous republic of white yeoman farmers, his exclusionary "Empire of Liberty." This expansionist vision excluded African Americans and involved aggressive efforts to move the Native American tribes that inhabited the Louisiana Territory further west. Jefferson was also hesitant to extend rights of self-government to the Creoles of Louisiana.[10]

Jefferson racially wrote the republic quite literally. In drafting the Declaration of Independence (1776), he crafted one of the country's formative documents. As Jamaica Kincaid says, "America begins with the Declaration of Independence, the most important clue to the character of Americans as a people." The document conveys strains of American idealism and self-righteousness.[11] In his preliminary draft of the Declaration—in a passage the Continental Congress deleted—Jefferson condemned the king of England, George III, for supporting the slave trade: "He wages cruel war against human nature itself, violating its most sacred rights of life and liberty in the persons of a distant people who never offended him, captivating and carrying them into slavery in another hemisphere."[12]

Jefferson's starkest contradictions concerned his relationships with black Americans and slavery. "The leisure that made possible his great writings on human liberty," Richard Hofstadter observes, "was supported by the labors of three generations of slaves."[13] Jefferson promoted equality but held that black people were racially deficient. He speculated about racial kinship between European Americans and Native Americans, thinking that Native Americans could be civilized for American citizenship; yet he perceived an intractable racial divide between white Americans and black slaves.[14] In *Notes on the State of Virginia*, he said, "I advance it . . . as a suspicion only, that blacks, whether originally a distinct race, or made distinct by time and circumstances, are inferior to the whites in endowments of body and mind. It is not against experience to suppose that different species of the same genus, or varieties of the same species, may possess different qualifications."[15] Jefferson doubted the two races could coexist peacefully if the slaves were emancipated because of the "deep rooted prejudices entertained by the whites; ten thousand recollections, by the blacks, of the injuries they have sustained; new provocations; the real distinctions which nature has made; and many other circumstances." Accordingly, he outlined his thoughts about colonizing "negroes" "to such place as the circumstances of the time should render proper."[16] As Andrew Burstein explains, Jefferson "frequently used the word harmony in his political prescriptions for national union; but racial harmony was impossible for him to project. . . . Yet he held views that comported with those of most of his white neighbors and the other proper Virginia gentlemen."[17]

Jefferson was sufficiently self-critical, however, to acknowledge doubt about blacks' inferiority. In 1791, in a letter to Benjamin Banneker, a self-taught black mathematician and astronomer who had sent Jefferson a letter criticizing his race ideas, Jefferson wrote, "No body wishes more than I do to see such proofs as you exhibit, that nature has given to our black brethren, talents equal to those of the other colors of men, and that the appearance of a want in them is owing merely to the degraded condition of their existence."[18] In 1809 he reiterated to Henri Gregoire that "no person living wishes more sincerely than I do, to see a complete refutation of the doubts I have myself entertained and expressed on the grade of understanding allotted to [negroes] by natures." He had conveyed his doubts in *Notes* "with great hesitation" and based on "personal observation on the limited sphere of my own State."[19]

Still, Jefferson remained reluctant to embrace black rights and pessimistic about coexistence between whites and free blacks after emancipation. After 1787 he refrained from publicly expressing his antislavery views.[20] He also limited his endorsement of individual rights and republican politics when faced with the slave revolution in Haiti, which began in 1791 and led to Haiti's independence in 1804. As president he withheld diplomatic recognition of the Haitian revolutionaries and even encouraged France to reinvade. "He saw Haiti," Joyce Appleby says, "more as a threat to Southern slavery than as a beacon of freedom."[21]

In 1829, three years after Jefferson's death, David Walker, a free black man, highlighted the racial duplicity of Jefferson's legacy in *Appeal to the Colored Citizens of the World*. Walker noted how Jefferson combined his avowal of equality with degrading claims concerning the capabilities of African Americans:

> Has Mr. Jefferson declared to the world, that we are inferior to whites, both in endowments of our bodies and our minds? It is indeed surprising that a man of such great learning, combined with such excellent natural parts, should speak so of a set of men in chains. . . .
>
> Do you know that Mr. Jefferson was one of as great characters as ever lived among whites? See his writings of the world, and public labours for the United States of America. Do you believe that the assertions of such a man, will pass away into oblivion unobserved by this people and the world? If you do you are much-mistaken. See how the American people treat us—have we souls in our bodies? . . .
>
> See your Declaration Americans!!! Do you understand your own language? Hear your language, proclaimed to the world, July 4, 1776—"We hold these truths to be self evident—that ALL MEN ARE CREATED EQUAL!"[22]

Walker struck at the basic contradiction in Jefferson's thought but did not address how Jefferson lived this contradiction in his personal life.

Sally Hemings's America

Allegations of the existence of a sexual relationship between Jefferson and Sally Hemings have a long history. Sally and her brother James, both slaves of Jefferson, were the children of Betty Hemings, a slave, and Jefferson's father-in-law, John Wayles. Sally, called Dashing Sally because of her beauty and Dusky Sally because of her racial identity, therefore, was a half-sister to Jefferson's wife, Martha, who died in 1782.[23] In 1787, Sally, at the age of fourteen, accompanied Jefferson's nine-year-old daughter Mary to Paris, where Jefferson was an American minister.[24] Back home at Monticello, his plantation in Virginia, Jefferson distanced himself, physically and psychically, "from the fact that he owned other human beings." He kept his slaves, aside from the fair-skinned Hemings family, "living and working out of sight."[25] Meanwhile, it is now almost certain that he pursued a long-term sexual relationship with Sally, and he kept most of the Hemings family as slaves until his death.[26]

Conflicting accounts of Jefferson and Hemings over the years betray competing political investments in Jefferson. The first public mention of the relationship was by the unscrupulous journalist James Callender in 1802. Callender, a former associate of Jefferson's with an axe to grind, wrote that Jefferson had a slave concubine in the "African Venus" Hemings: "By this wench Sally our president has had several children."[27] Although anti-Jefferson Federalists made much of this charge (fig. 1), Jefferson evaded it and was reelected in 1804.[28] In 1873, Madison Hemings, a son of Sally who had been freed by Jefferson's will, stated in an Ohio newspaper that he and four siblings (one lived for only a short time) were the children of Jefferson and Hemings.[29]

Despite this, Jan Ellis Lewis and Peter Onuf explain, most of Jefferson's biographers and the historians who have weighed in on the Jefferson-Hemings story, especially white ones, "have either insisted that a liaison was either impossible or highly unlikely or declared themselves agnostics on the issue."[30] Dumas Malone, the author of a celebrated six-volume biography of Jefferson, maintained that the idea that Hemings was Jefferson's mistress was "virtually unthinkable in a man of Jefferson's moral standards and habitual conduct." That some of Hemings's children "strikingly resembled Jefferson" was likely owing to the paternity of Jefferson's nephew, Peter Carr.[31] Merrill Peterson maintained in 1970 that "unless Jefferson was capable of

FIGURE 1 "A Philosophic Cock," James Akin. Hand-colored aquatint. Newburyport, Massachusetts, ca. 1804. Courtesy American Antiquarian Society. Reprinted in Joseph J. Ellis et al., *Thomas Jefferson: Genius of Liberty* (New York: Viking Studio, in association with the Library of Congress, Washington, D.C., 2000), 90.

slipping badly out of character in hidden moments at Monticello, it is difficult to imagine him caught up in a miscegenous relationship."[32] Joseph Ellis acknowledged in *American Sphinx* (1997) that Jefferson "was present at Monticello nine months prior to the birth of each of Sally's children." Nonetheless, he concluded that "the likelihood of a liaison with Sally Hemings is remote." Jefferson insulated himself from "both sex and slavery."[33] Likewise, when the Irish writer Conor Cruise O'Brien dwelt on the Hemings-Jefferson story to discredit Jefferson in *The Long Affair* (1996), the American historian Bernard Bailyn responded that "the prospect of Jefferson's leaping into bed with Sally is much more exciting to O'Brien than it ever was to Jefferson."[34]

Having a greater appreciation of oral history, many black Americans, including African American scholars, have long believed the stories passed down from Madison Hemings and others concerning a sexual relationship of Jefferson and Hemings.[35] Regarding Madison's recollections, Annette Gordon-Reed, an African American and the author of the first extended scholarly study of the Hemings story, notes that until recently a "black man and former slave's version of life at Monticello was squarely pitted against not only the cult of Jefferson, but also the separate and distinct cult of the Jefferson scholar." When the white female biographer Fawn Brodie defended Madison's story in a book in 1974, more traditional Jefferson scholars disparaged her work. Gordon-Reed comments, "It could not have gone unnoticed that a white woman was using the words of a black man to say that a group of white males did not know what they were talking about."[36] Brodie herself discerned a continuing scholarly sanctification of Jefferson. Scholars like Peterson and Malone "glorify and protect [Jefferson] by nuance, by omission, by subtle repudiation."[37]

Brodie's treatment of Sally Hemings was a marked departure from previous discussions. Her innovation, Gordon-Reed points out, "was to treat Sally Hemings . . . as a human being and to make full use of her humanity."[38] The African American novelist Barbara Chase-Riboud radicalized this approach in *Sally Hemings* (1979), in which she imagined Hemings as "a person whom one could believe that Jefferson could have loved."[39] Gordon-Reed raises perhaps the most provocative question of all these writers: "Might not Sally Hemings have thought being the mistress of a slave master a suitable role?"[40]

Gordon-Reed notes that scholarly discussion has generally started from the assumption that any Jefferson-Hemings relationship "would have involved a degree of force." She acknowledges that the idea that Hemings might have welcomed Jefferson's advances could be disturbing for both whites and blacks. Yet she complicates the picture of a strictly coercive relationship: "[Sally] was a young woman whose grandmother had been the mistress of a white man. Her mother had been the mistress of another white man, a plantation owner, Sally's father. Historians attribute her family's special position at Monticello to her mother's relationship with John Wayles. Although her mother had not derived the ultimate benefit from that relationship—Wayles did not free the family—it had allowed Elizabeth Hemings and her children to live better and have more opportunities than the rest of Jefferson's slaves." Social hierarchies within the slave system were evident at Monticello, and Hemings males "were treated more like white servants than like black slaves."[41] In fact, in Jefferson's reading of Virginia law, the children he had with Sally were potentially white: "Our canon considers two crosses with pure white, and a third with any degree of mixture, however small, as clearing the issue of the negro blood." Since the status of such children depended on their mother, they would remain slaves unless their master freed them. Yet once a male slave of this description was emancipated, Jefferson said, "he becomes a free *white* man, and a citizen of the United States to all intents and purposes."[42] Part of Jefferson's thought here, Peter Onuf explains, was that when his "children passed into the white world, all connections with their father—and their previous servile condition—would be erased."[43] They would become free whites with no evident Jefferson kinship.

Still, Gordon-Reed's question about how Sally might have regarded being Jefferson's mistress cannot be answered definitively. Sally had her own story, but apart from Madison Hemings's memoir we have little access to it.[44] Evidence from the subtle ways in which other slave women, such as Harriet Jacobs, negotiated the gendered power dynamics between master and slave suggests that Hemings may not have been merely a pawn of Jefferson's whims. In *Incidents in the Life of a Slave Girl* (1861), the first slave narrative written by a female, Jacobs (also known by her pen name, Linda Brent) reveals that she consciously chose as her lover a white man who was not her master in order to improve her social and economic status. She also employed verbal combat, or "sass," in self-defense against her master's advances.[45] On the basis of Jacobs's example, Clarence Walker suggests that Hemings "may have used sex to get her children's freedom."[46]

This line of reasoning is speculative, however. As a black woman and a slave, Hemings had "nothing to fall back on; not maleness, not whiteness, not ladyhood."[47] Even if Sally had reasons, given her circumstances, to accept being the mistress of a slave master, further questions arise. What should we make of descendants of Hemings and Jefferson who are publicly regarded and self-identify as black and who actively seek public acknowledgment of their Jeffersonian lineage? For white Americans, recognizing Jefferson's moral ambiguity may challenge their sense of American innocence. For black Americans, we suggest, establishing a familial connection to this prominent Founding Father confirms the duality of their American experience.

Monticello

These conflicting views were evident in the recent "fight for Monticello." Soon after the evidence from DNA testing was published in *Nature* in October 1998, several members of the Jefferson-Hemings family had their first meeting on *The Oprah Winfrey Show*. One of Jefferson's white descendants, Lucian Truscott IV, invited his Hemings cousins to the next annual Jefferson family reunion at Monticello in May 1999. Michele Cooley Quille attended that Monticello gathering to present the dying wish of her father, Robert H. Cooley III, to be buried at Monticello. Cooley, a faculty member at Johns Hopkins University, had died suddenly on July 20, 1998. The Monticello Association, consisting of lineal descendants of Jefferson, denied her request because the DNA evidence wasn't yet published.[48] The Cooley family represents a part of black America that wants recognition for having "a President in the family."[49] In February 2001, the Cooley family attended a session of the General Assembly of Virginia to witness the passing of a resolution that publicly acknowledges the growing body of evidence that Jefferson and Hemings had children together. Two months later, President George W. Bush invited the Jefferson and Hemings families to the White House for a celebration of Thomas Jefferson's 258th birthday. In July 2003, about 150 Hemings family descendants gathered for a reunion at Monticello (fig. 2).[50]

The scholarship on Jefferson has changed since the DNA findings were released in 1998. The Jefferson-Hemings relationship has since been acknowledged by the *William and Mary Quarterly*, the National Genealogical Society, and, in January 2000, the Thomas Jefferson (Memorial) Foundation, which owns Monticello.[51] Nevertheless, in May 2002 the Monticello Association voted against admitting descendants of Sally Hemings into their organization, concluding that there was not sufficient evidence to prove Jefferson fathered Hemings's children. Then, on February 24, 2003, the Thomas Jefferson Foundation revised its position regarding the children of Sally Hemings: "Although the relationship between Jefferson and Sally Hemings has been for many years . . . a subject of intense interest to historians and the public, the evidence is not definitive, and the complete story may never be known. The Foundation encourages our visitors and patrons, based on what evidence does exist, to make up their own minds as to the true nature of the relationship."[52] Thus, even strong scientific

FIGURE 2 Jefferson-Hemings Family Get-Together, 2003. From James Dao, "A Family Get-Together of Historic Proportions," *New York Times*, Monday, July 14, 2003, A9. Photo by Willie J. Allen Jr. / The New York Times / Redux.

evidence butts up against white racial resistance to a broadened understanding of American nationhood that includes black Americans as members of a founding family.

As we have noted, divergent interpretations of Jefferson's relationship—popular and scholarly—have largely divided along racial lines, white commentators often being protective of Jefferson's putative innocence and black commentators being more inclined to accept the Hemings oral history. One of the reasons we became interested in the black descendants of the Jefferson family is their desire to be recognized. That desire has a direct bearing on the experience of Duchess Harris. As an African American born in 1969, in the midst of Black Power, Harris's first popular culture memory is of the television miniseries *Roots*. She has found it difficult to imagine why black Americans would have a possessive investment in their whiteness. Furthermore, she is fair-skinned and has been told her entire life that her mother's family descended from Alexander Spotswood (1676–1740), the royal colonial lieutenant governor of Virginia (1710–22). It never occurred to Harris that the lieutenant governor might have loved anyone in the family or that she should celebrate her Spotswood heritage. Granted, Spotswood did not write the Declaration of Independence, become president, or die on the Fourth of July; however, some of her family members spend their reunions reminding the youngest generation to have pride because they are Spottswoods (his black descendants added a *t*). Until the Jefferson DNA announcement, she had thought her family odd for celebrating its familial tie with prominent white Americans.

A Senator in the Family

What does it mean when black Americans assert their place in the American national narrative through sexual relationships of white men and black women that were often coercive? The African American sociologist Orlando Patterson has said that learning of Jefferson's relationship with Hemings made him feel "less alienated from [Jefferson], as I suspect will most African-Americans eventually. He is part of the family, a family with a ghastly, contradictory past."[53] While Patterson's family metaphor is problematic, the Jefferson-Hemings relationship does make Jefferson a more sympathetic figure for some African Americans (and some other Americans). Still, Patterson's remark does not fully answer the question, and the contemporary story of Essie Mae Washington-Williams (b. 1925) suggests another answer. Washington-Williams tells her story in her memoir *Dear Senator* (2005).[54] Her father was Strom Thurmond (1902–2003), the famous white segregationist politician from South Carolina; her mother was Carrie Butler (b. 1909), the Thurmond family's sixteen-year-old black maid. Late in 2003, Washington-Williams reported that although her mother never said whether her sexual relationship with Thurmond was consensual, she herself had a good relationship with her father. On December 15, 2003, six months after Thurmond's death, a lawyer for the Thurmond family confirmed his paternity of Washington-Williams, then seventy-eight years old.[55] Unlike the Jefferson family, the Thurmond family had known of Essie Mae's existence all along.

Because of Thurmond's segregationist politics the disclosure that he had fathered a black woman caused a stir.[56] When Essie Mae Washington went to college in the 1940s Thurmond was a relatively liberal Democratic governor of South Carolina. He increased social spending, pushed to improve black schools, and chose not to obstruct a decision by the federal judge J. Waties Waring to allow blacks to vote in primaries. But when President Harry Truman integrated the armed forces in 1948 and backed federal laws against lynching, the poll tax, and racial discrimination, Thurmond organized other southern politicians against an erosion of states' rights.[57]

This activity led to Thurmond's presidential run in 1948 as the head of the States' Rights Party, the Dixiecrats. He claimed that segregation laws were "essential to the racial protection and purity of the white and Negro races alike."[58] Thurmond came in third behind the Democrat Truman and the Republican Thomas Dewey but won four states, 1.1 million votes, and 38 electoral votes. In 1954, he was elected to the U.S. Senate as a Democrat from South Carolina and continued his fight against black civil rights. In 1956, he organized the infamous Southern Manifesto, which called the Supreme Court's school desegregation ruling of 1954 a "clear abuse of judicial power." In 1957, he set the Senate record for filibustering with a twenty-four-hour and eighteen-minute speech intended to prevent a vote on a civil rights bill backed by the administration of Dwight Eisenhower.[59]

By 1964, Thurmond had joined the Republican Party and supported Barry Goldwater for the presidency. With the Democrats increasingly becoming aligned with civil rights politics, his move signaled a major shift in American politics. Beginning with Richard Nixon's presidential campaign in 1968, the Republican Party, with Thurmond's support, began to appeal to white southern conservatives, and the formerly Democratic south began turning Republican. Thurmond later downplayed his segregationist past and became the president pro tempore of the Senate when Republicans took control of that body in the 1980s. He retired at the age of one hundred.[60]

Given Thurmond's segregationist record, Washington-Williams's connection to him is telling. She recently explained that she "highly respected him, and he respected me, and he never once said anything about 'Let's not talk about this to other people.'" For many years, however, she chose not to tell people that Thurmond was her father because he was a segregationist: "I didn't want people to know that was my father. So I didn't want to talk about it."[61]

Despite Thurmond's controversial political career, Washington-Williams, who lived in Compton, California, was one of his biggest fans: "My father was going to the Senate, where he could do the whole nation some good. I wanted to go see him, and I wanted to take Julius [her husband] with me. . . . We had a TV, a dishwasher, a view of the Hollywood sign in the distant hills, and three beautiful children. Plus my father was a senator. Was this not the American Dream come true?"[62] Washington-Williams admits,

"There were many occasions when I felt deeply embarrassed for him and for myself."[63] She criticizes his political activity during 1954 and 1955, the time of *Brown v. Board of Education* and the Montgomery bus boycott, and laments his comment in 1956 that "'outside agitators' . . . were out to destroy 'the harmony which had existed for generations between white and Negro races.'" He also called white southerners "the greatest minority in the nation," but she nonetheless accepted his invitation to visit him in Washington in 1956.[64] She described the end of her visit with Thurmond: "He gave me another envelope and a big hug and kiss and had his driver take us back to Union Station and see us onto the train. He had given us several thousand dollars this time. Whatever he stood for, however he segregated me from his real life, I couldn't help but like having a senator for a father."[65]

Not many black scholars have commented on Washington-Williams's memoir. There may be several reasons for this silence. She is an elder in the black community, and perhaps people do not wish to disrespect her. Many African Americans have white men in their families who never acknowledged them or gave them money; Thurmond did both for Essie Mae. Because of Thurmond's support, Washington-Williams is more advantaged than many of her peers. Her son Ronald is an emergency room physician whose medical school education Thurmond paid for; her son Julius Jr. is a bus operator for Seattle's Metropolitan Transit Authority; her daughter Monica is the director of a battered women's shelter, Polly's Healing Center; and her daughter Wanda founded her own information technology consulting business. In 2005 (when her memoir was published), raising four children who became gainfully employed would fulfill what it means to live the American dream.

Jefferson's Legacies, White American Debts

Washington-Williams's pride in her father sheds light on why so many of Jefferson's black descendants are proud to have a president in their family. These stories also illuminate the possessive investment that some black-identified Americans have in their white lineage in both personal and political registers.[66] Just as Thurmond fathered members of a black middle class, so did Jefferson.

One of Jefferson's more convoluted legacies is the material and cultural capital—including access to racial whiteness—he passed on to Sally Hemings's children. He freed all of Hemings's children. Following his promise to Sally that her children would be freed at the age of twenty-one, her oldest children, Beverley (a son) and his sister Harriet, were allowed to leave Monticello in 1822, the year Harriet turned twenty-one. (Beverley had turned twenty-one two years earlier.) By the terms of Jefferson's will (he died on July 4, 1826), Madison and Eston Hemings were freed, after ostensibly serving as apprentices until they attained their majority to their uncle, the carpenter Johnny Hemings. At Jefferson's extraordinary request, the brothers were given permission by the Virginia legislature in 1826 to remain in the state after winning freedom.[67] (A law of 1806 had decreed that emancipated slaves had to leave Virginia within a year.) That the Hemings children's freedom was tied to their coming of age suggests that Jefferson thought of Sally Hemings as his "substitute wife."[68] Jefferson freed no other slave in this fashion. Furthermore, Harriet Hemings was the only female slave Jefferson ever freed.[69]

Madison Hemings referred to his parents' relationship as the treaty of Paris—a treaty of sexual commerce—with Jefferson promising lenient, indulging treatment in return for sexual favors.[70] The Hemings children and their descendants gained tangible benefits from this sexual commerce, although until recently this did not include recognition as Jeffersons. As Lucia Stanton explains, "Jefferson gave Madison Hemings what few sons of slave women received—a skilled trade, if not an education, and the freedom to pursue it for his own benefit."[71] At the same time, Madison's children and grandchildren remained in Ohio, where he had moved and "were bound by the restricted opportunities for blacks at the time."[72] Meanwhile, Harriet, Beverley, and Eston Hemings passed into the white world. They traded the burdens of hiding the black side of their family tree for the benefits of racial whiteness. For instance, Eston and his wife, Julia, moved to Ohio in 1852, passed into whiteness, and changed their family name to Jefferson. Their daughter Anna married and lived as a white woman; their sons Beverly F. Jefferson and John Wayles Jefferson became successful businessmen, and their "grandsons even exceeded the success of [their] sons."[73]

More recently, Shannon Lanier, an African American–identified descendant of Hemings and Jefferson, has spoken proudly of what he inherited from both Hemings and Jefferson while noting divisions in his extended family. In *Jefferson's Children* (2000), Lanier, who was twenty years old at the time, says, "From Sally and Madison I inherited the stories that were handed down—my oral history—and a strong sense of family. From Jefferson, I inherited an insatiable love of learning and a belief that we are all created equal. Although Jefferson was one of the founders of the United States, his family is not yet united, because many of the descendants of Jefferson and his wife, Martha, still refuse to acknowledge as family the descendants of Jefferson and his slave Sally Hemings."[74] Like many Hemings-Jefferson descendants, Lanier has been more fortunate than many other African Americans. At the same time, his remarks, and the efforts of other black Jefferson descendants to gain public recognition *as Jeffersons*, speak to continuing struggles of African Americans for equal recognition *as Americans*.

Given the respective places of Jefferson and Hemings at Monticello and in the formation of the country, perhaps it is not surprising that Jefferson's black descendants would celebrate their Jeffersonian lineage, despite its racist elements. Their Jeffersonian whiteness gives them a kind of epic American identity they don't get through their blackness. More generally, the Jefferson-Hemings story indicates the kind of reparations white America still owes to black (and Native) America. Many people who oppose reparations fear that black America is looking for a check. The idea is broader and deeper than that, however. As Manning Marable says, "'reparations' means 'to repair,' 'to make whole again.' The 'double consciousness' of Americans of African descent first described by W. E. B. Du Bois, the age-old chasm between our identification with this country and our cultural affinity toward the Black diaspora of Africa, cannot be bridged until there is a final rendezvous with our own history. That is why, ultimately, the demand for Black reparations is not fundamentally about the money."[75]

The black descendants of Jefferson and Thurmond received either whiteness, a measure of freedom, money, some belated public recognition (of a sort), or all of the above. Thus, they gained material and symbolic advantages that most black Americans have not received. Yet along with other black Americans they still have not received true reparations. This must include the establishment of full equality, politically, socially, and economically.[76] It also calls for rewriting U.S. history to address black peoples' experiences of racial and sexual political oppression, including the fraught role of black-white racial intimacy in the construction of the American national identity.

Notes

1. Thomas Jefferson, *Notes on the State of Virginia*, in *Thomas Jefferson: Writings*, ed. Merrill D. Peterson (New York: Library of America, 1984), 288.

2. Stephanie M. H. Camp, "Sally Hemings and Thomas Jefferson," *Mississippi Quarterly* 53 (spring 2000): 275.

3. Richard Hofstadter, *The American Political Tradition* (New York: Vintage Books, 1974), 22–55; David Hollinger, "The Ethno-Racial Pentagon" (1995), in *Race and Ethnicity in the United States: Issues and Debates*, ed. Stephen Steinberg (Malden, Mass.: Blackwell, 2000), 197.

4. Gordon S. Wood, "Ghosts of Monticello," in *Sally Hemings and Thomas Jefferson: History, Memory, and Civic Culture*, ed. Jan Ellen Lewis and Peter S. Onuf (Charlottesville: University of Virginia Press, 1999), 21 (hereafter *Sally Hemings*).

5. Winthrop Jordan, "Hemings and Jefferson: Redux," in *Sally Hemings*, 50.

6. The point is that *whiteness* operates as a form of social capital for those persons racialized as white. See George Lipsitz, *The Possessive Investment in Whiteness* (Philadelphia: Temple University Press, 1998), chap. 1.

7. James Sidbury, "The Construction of Race in Republican America," in *A Companion to the American Revolution*, ed. Jack P. Green and J. R. Pole (Malden, Mass.: Blackwell, 2000), 610–16.

8. Reginald Horsman, *The New Republic: The United States of America 1789–1815* (Essex, England: Longman/Pearson Education, 2000), 9–10, 88–89; Peter N. Carroll and David W. Noble, *The Restless Centuries: A History of the American People* (Minneapolis: Burgess, 1973), 132.

9. Jefferson, quoted in Hofstadter, *Political Tradition*, 38.

10. Joyce Appleby, *Thomas Jefferson* (New York: Henry Holt, 2003), 65, 106–10.

11. Jamaica Kincaid, "The Little Revenge of the Periphery," *Transition*, no. 73 (1998): 70–71.

12. "Declaration by the Representatives," in *Jefferson: Writings*, 22.

13. Hofstadter, *Political Tradition*, 23.

14. Catherine A. Holland, "Notes on the State of America: Jeffersonian Democracy and the Production of a National Past," *Political Theory* 29 (April 2001): 199ff.

15. Jefferson, *Notes*, 270, 266–67.

16. Ibid., 264.

17. Andrew Burstein, *Jefferson's Secrets: Death and Desire at Monticello* (New York: Basic Books, 2005), 131.

18. Letter to Benjamin Banneker, August 30, 1781, in *Jefferson: Writings*, 982.

19. Letter to Henri Gregoire, February 25, 1809, in *Jefferson: Writings*, 1202.

20. Sean Wilentz, "Life, Liberty, and the Pursuit of Thomas Jefferson," *New Republic* (March 10, 1997), 40.

21. Appleby, *Jefferson*, 78–79; Burstein, *Jefferson's Secrets*, 125–26. Gary Wills, following Jefferson's Federalist critics, provocatively calls Jefferson the "Negro President" because he won the Electoral College vote in the presidential election of 1800, and thus the presi-

dency, over John Adams partly due to the three-fifths clause of the Constitution. Under this clause slaves were counted as three-fifths of a person in allocating representation and electoral votes among states. Adams won more popular votes, but Jefferson, Wills explains, "received eight more votes than Adams in the Electoral College, [and] at least twelve of his votes were not based on the citizenry that could express its will but on the blacks owned by Southern masters." See Gary Wills, "The Negro President," *New York Review of Books* 50 (November 6, 2003): 45.

22. Walker, quoted in Cornel West, *Democracy Matters: Winning the Fight Against Imperialism* (New York: Penguin, 2004), 47–48.

23. Annette Gordon-Reed, *Thomas Jefferson and Sally Hemings: An American Controversy* (Charlottesville: University of Virginia Press, 1997), 1; Merrill Peterson, *Thomas Jefferson and the New Nation: A Biography* (New York: Oxford University Press, 1970), 81.

24. Gordon-Reed, *Thomas Jefferson*, 160, 24.

25. Wilentz, "Life, Liberty," 40.

26. DNA evidence, when joined with other historical evidence, leaves Jefferson as "the only serious candidate" for paternity of Hemings's children. See Fraser D. Neiman, "Coincidence or Causal Connection? The Relationship between Thomas Jefferson's Visits to Monticello and Sally Hemings's Conceptions," *William and Mary Quarterly*, 3d ser., 57 (January 2000): 199 n. 3.

27. James Callender, "Our President Again," *Richmond Recorder*, September 1, 1802, excerpt in *Sally Hemings*, 260, 259; Gordon-Reed, *Thomas Jefferson*, 59–63.

28. Peterson, *Thomas Jefferson*, 706–9; Appleby, *Jefferson*, 75.

29. Gordon-Reed, *Thomas Jefferson*; Lucia Stanton, "The Other End of the Telescope: Jefferson through the Eyes of His Slaves," *William and Mary Quarterly*, 3d ser., 57 (January 2000): 140–44.

30. Lewis and Onuf, "Introduction," in *Sally Hemings*, 2.

31. Dumas Malone, *Jefferson the President: First Term, 1801–1805* ((Boston: Little Brown, 1970), 214, 497–98.

32. Peterson, *Thomas Jefferson*, 707.

33. Joseph J. Ellis, *American Sphinx: The Character of Thomas Jefferson* (New York: Knopf, 1997), 305–6. Ellis has since acknowledged the probability of the relationship. See Joseph J. Ellis, "Jefferson: Post-DNA," *William and Mary Quarterly*, 3d ser., 57 (January 2000): 125–38.

34. Conor Cruise O'Brien, *The Long Affair: Thomas Jefferson and the French Revolution, 1785–1800* (Chicago: University of Chicago Press, 1996); Bernard Bailyn, "Sally and Her Master," *Times Literary Supplement*, November 15, 1996, 4.

35. Venetria K. Patton and Ronald Jemal Stevens, "Narrating Competing Truths in the Thomas Jefferson–Sally Hemings Paternity Debate," *Black Scholar* 29, no. 4 (1999): 8–15.

36. Annette Gordon-Reed, "'The Memories of a Few Negroes': Rescuing America's Future at Monticello," in *Sally Hemings*, 239.

37. Fawn M. Brodie, *Thomas Jefferson: An Intimate History* (New York: W. W. Norton, 1974), 30.

38. Gordon-Reed, *Thomas Jefferson*, 159.

39. Ibid., 182. The black writer William Wells Brown addressed the Jefferson-Hemings story in his novel *Clotel; or, the President's Daughter* (1853). See Clarence Walker " 'Denial is Not a River in Egypt,' " in *Sally Hemings*, 193.

40. Gordon-Reed, *Thomas Jefferson*, 164.

41. Ibid.

42. Jefferson to Francis C. Gray, March 4, 1815, quoted in Peter S. Onuf, "Every Generation Is an 'Independent Nation': Colonization, Miscegenation, and the Fate of Jefferson's Children," *William and Mary Quarterly*, 3d ser., 57 (January 2000): 166. In *Notes*, Jefferson doubted that a freed black slave could "mix with, without staining the blood of his master"; and in the 1770s, Jefferson supported laws banishing from Virginia any white woman who bore "a child by a negro or mulatto." See Jefferson, *Notes*, 270; Paul Finkelman, "Jefferson and Slavery: 'Treason Against the Hopes of the World,' " in *Jefferson's Legacies*, ed. Peter S. Onuf (Charlottesville: University Press of Virginia, 1993), 195.

43. Onuf, "Independent Nation," 166.

44. Lewis and Onuf, "Introduction," 9.

45. Joanne M. Braxton, *Black Women Writing Autobiography: A Tradition Within a Tradition* (Philadelphia: Temple University Press, 1989), 34; Walker "Denial," 190.

46. Walker "Denial," 190.

47. Paula Giddings, *When and Where I Enter: The Impact of Black Women on Race and Sex in America* (New York: William Morrow, 1984), 15.

48. Shannon Lanier and Jane Feldman, *Jefferson's Children: The Story of One American Family*, introd. by Lucian K. Truscott IV (New York: Random House, 2000), 43–44.

49. Byron W. Woodson Sr., *A President in the Family: Thomas Jefferson, Sally Hemings, and Thomas Woodson*, foreword by Michele Cooley-Quille (New York: Praeger, 2001). The Woodson family's claims to Jefferson lineage were called into question by the recent DNA evidence. See Walker, "Denial," 193.

50. James Dao, "A Family Get-Together of Historic Proportions," *New York Times*, July 14, 2003, A9.

51. Ibid.

52. See http://www.monticello.org/plantation/hemingscontro/hemings-jefferson_contro .html (accessed May 2006).

53. Orlando Patterson, "Jefferson the Contradiction," *New York Times*, November 2, 1998, A27.

54. Essie Mae Washington-Williams and William Stadiem, *Dear Senator: A Memoir by the Daughter of Strom Thurmond* (New York: Regan Books, 2005).

55. Ibid., 218.

56. In at least one way this stir was rather muffled. The media ignored the likelihood that Thurmond violated the law against statutory rape in his sexual relationship with Carrie Butler. See Kimberlé Crenshaw, "Was Strom a Rapist?" *The Nation* 278 (March 15, 2004): 5–7.

57. Ibid., 132–37; Adam Clymer, "Strom Thurmond, Foe of Integration, Dies at 100," *New York Times*, June 27, 2003, A1, A22.

58. Quoted in Washington-Williams, *Dear Senator*, 134.

59. Ibid., 170–75.

60. Clymer, "Strom Thurmond," A1, A22.

61. Tavis Smiley Archives, Friday, January 28, 2005, http://www.pbs.org/kcet/tavissmiley/archive/200501/20050128_transcript.html#1.

62. Washington-Williams, *Dear Senator*, 168.

63. Ibid., 170.

64. Ibid., 170–71.

65. Ibid., 173.

66. Washington-Williams, who has sought to join the Daughters of the Confederacy and the Daughters of the American Revolution, is perhaps a somewhat extreme example of a larger phenomenon. See Tavis Smiley Archives, Friday, January 28, 2005, http://www.pbs.org/kcet/tavissmiley/archive/200501/20050128_transcript.html#1.

67. Burstein, *Jefferson's Secrets*, 116.

68. Ibid., 325.

69. Lucia Stanton and Dianne Swann-Wright, "Bonds of Memory: Identity and the Hemings Family," in *Sally Hemings*, 179; Stanton, "Other End," 142–43.

70. Burstein, *Jefferson's Secrets*, 163.

71. Stanton, "Other End," 143.

72. Stanton and Swann-Wright, "Bonds of Memory," 169.

73. Ibid., 168–69; Beverly Gray, "Sally Hemings," in Lanier and Feldman, *Jefferson's Children*, 37–39.

74. Lanier and Feldman, *Jefferson's Children*, 11.

75. Manning Marable, *The Great Wells of Democracy: The Meaning of Race in America* (New York: Basic Civitas, 2002), 251–52.

76. Ibid., 252.

Tocqueville and Beaumont, Brothers and Others

In the 1830s, Alexis de Tocqueville and Gustave de Beaumont made their famous voyage through the United States; each subsequently wrote about the "race" relations there.[1] Many scholars have found Tocqueville to be inattentive to inequality in American democracy.[2] Indeed, revealing his interest in France, an ethnically homogeneous polity, Tocqueville opens his chapter entitled "Three Races" by proclaiming that "these topics are like tangents to my subject, being American, but not democratic" (DA 316). Similarly, Beaumont often separates U.S. democracy from American race relations. He writes that while "a great number of writers . . . have remarked that the laws of the United States guarantee an equality which is not found in reality . . . I found not only political equality . . . I could see social equality everywhere, in money matters, in the professions, in all their customs" (M 226–27; see 98–100, 230). However, Tocqueville's and Beaumont's portraits illustrate how European Americans, in subordinating Indians and blacks, produce not a politically and socially egalitarian democracy situated amid an otherwise racist society and culture but a social state internally structured—psychologically and materially—by inegalitarian relations with non-Europeans.[3] In fact, they show that racism in the United States is entwined by psychological affinity with dynamics central to both a democratic social condition in general and European Americans' postaristocratic, postcolonial condition in particular. What is more, Tocqueville's and Beaumont's European Americans exercise two distinct means of managing relations with non-Europeans: while they (i) *fraternalize* relations with Indians, they (ii) *absolutely differentiate* themselves from blacks. As historians have been showing, in early American history "the racial distinction between Indian bodies and white bodies remained far less certain than that between blacks and whites."[4] That said, Tocqueville's and Beaumont's texts also reveal that by the 1830s, the time of their visit, European Americans had begun reimagining Indians as absolute others as well, a reversal they would increasingly enact throughout the nineteenth century.[5]

Separation Anxiety

In *Marie*, Beaumont's French protagonist Ludovic describes the broad historical transition from aristocracy to democracy that so preoccupied Tocqueville: "When I was born, a social order which had existed for fifteen centuries had just crumbled. . . . A new world was rising upon the wreckage of the old; spirits were restless, passions fired, minds in travail; the face of all Europe was changing—opinions, customs, laws were swept into a whirlwind" (M 25). Seeking lessons for France, Tocqueville analyzes European aristocracy as prolegomenon to French and American democracy. He presents it as a fixed chain of authority that organized serfs, servants, nobles, and God. Relations of noblesse oblige combined with elaborate rules of manner, and legal class distinctions conveyed one's place in a seemingly eternal order of mutuality that fostered a sense of security, determinacy, and certainty at the same time it permitted the individual no escape from its dictates (DA 13, 14). *Democracy in America* conveys how the transition from aristocracy to democracy signifies release from such structure into flux, as "in ages of democracy all things are unstable," including the "human heart" (DA 582, see 9–20, 460, 478, 498).

The transition away from aristocracy is central to the ethos of modern democracy. Located in his French and American democracies' governing mentalities is an ambivalent array of what Tocqueville calls *les passions*. These passions include resentment of aristocracy's hierarchical subjugations and, in the United States, of the heavy hand of empire. The emergent democracy of the North in the United States is driven by a yearning for liberty beyond the humiliating clutches of an oppressive class society and imperial dictates. But this new freedom also brings ambivalence about what it means to separate from that familiar world of security and determinacy as order and guaranteed modes of belonging and social differentiation give way to uncertainty. While Beaumont's Anglo-Americans feel "profound enmity" toward England, so too are they filled with "filial piety which holds colonies to the mother country long after they have become free" (M 218). Even as *Democracy in America* locates in Anglo-Americans an overt, principled quest for liberty and equality, it illustrates a covert companion desire for the comforts and predictability of hierarchy.[6] Tocqueville says that American society "had no infancy, being born adult," but the extent to which this new society is adult hinges on its emerging out of Europe, as American democracy "sprang full-grown and fully armed from the midst of the old feudal society" (DA 303, 375, see 279).[7] Tocqueville's work illustrates that the Anglo-Americans' psychic transition away from aristocracy and empire and toward democratic flux constitutes a world-historic moment of separation anxiety. To recover a sense of the lost order and certainty that once guaranteed everyone a defined place in society's chain, new forms of social differentiation are established. In the democratic North, alongside the prevailing passion for the idea of equality, subterranean cultural anxiety and yearning for predictable structure combine fatefully with other psychodynamics in U.S. democracy to entrench a racist culture.

Indian Brethren and a Founding Fratricide

Early in *Democracy in America*, Tocqueville configures the relationship between the aristocratic and emergent democratic social states as metaphorically that of mother and child. How do we understand a man's nature? "Go back; look at the baby in his mother's arms. . . . Only then will you understand the origin of the prejudices, habits, and passions which are to dominate his life. The whole man is there, if one may put it so, in the cradle. Something analogous happens with nations" (DA 31). Tocqueville thus treats (maternal) European aristocracy as a formative site for emergent (child) modern democracy—as its "point of departure." True to this trope, he repeatedly characterizes England (and sometimes Europe, more generally) as *la mère-patrie* to the United States.[8] He describes the French and U.S. revolutions as birthing processes and posits the U.S. colonies as coming to birth (*naître*) and growing (*grandir*) such that U.S. democracy and society are variously in states of infancy, childhood, and adolescence.[9] Beaumont similarly remarks upon European Americans' "cradle" and the fact that they were "surrounded at birth by the light of the age of maturity" (M, 106, 107, 57, 95). Tocqueville adds that England-as-mother has given birth to "two main branches of the great Anglo-American family," the modified aristocratic southerners and their democratic republican "brothers in the North" (DA 355, see 34).

In adopting familial imagery to characterize sociohistorical phenomena, Tocqueville and Beaumont reflect prevailing discourses. In colonial America, loyalists cast themselves as "immature offspring" who willingly ceded their powers to the legitimate mother authority of England. The revolution-aries transvaluated these familial symbols to recast England as a tyrannical mother who threatened to destroy her offspring: "We have been told 'that Britain is the mother and we are the children, that a filial duty and submis-sion is due from us to her,'" wrote John Adams. Now, he urged, it was time these children reject this mother and her illegitimate powers.[10] But as Mi-chael Rogin argues, texts and art from the period suggest that, in addition to these unambiguous passions for and against England's imperial author-ity, there existed even among revolutionaries a subterranean fear over the prospect of separating from this discursively maternalized site. After all, England was not merely a tyrannical empire, but also a familiar source of material and psychic comfort for a people struggling to establish itself in a harsh, unfamiliar territory. For Rogin, anxiety over the loss of England-as-mother is evident in the revolutionaries' positing of liberty as a substi-tute maternal figure.[11] In Tocqueville and Beaumont, nature serves the Eu-ropean Americans as a mother figure alternative to England.[12] Beaumont's Ludovic rhapsodizes that the "old earth of America" is now "pregnant at last with a civilized future" (M 103). Tocqueville signifies North America as "the yet empty cradle [berceau]" for "those English colonies."[13] The cradle is traditionally a female purview, but it also marks distance between child and mother's breast, so that for Tocqueville's United States, the American continent wins for colonists distance from imperial England.

In Tocqueville's writings, this symbolic familial drama expands to in-clude indigenous Americans, echoing the standing European American habit of fraternalizing relations with Indians. Early on, European Ameri-cans posited Native Americans as the original offspring of a maternalized nature. The U.S. chief administrator of Indian affairs from 1816 to 1830 sug-gested that the "earth was their mother, and upon its lap they reposed."[14] But if nature's lap was already occupied, how could European Americans secure her as their source of comfort and security? Struggling to establish the meaning of their relations with Native Americans and to claim land, European Americans expanded the circulating, discursive family drama by imagining Indians as their symbolic brothers. Now Indianized, Euro-pean Americans could claim the ancient land. So "American rhetoric filled the white-Indian tie with intimate symbolic meaning. Indians were, every treaty talk insisted, our 'friends and brothers.'"[15] While fraternalization re-flected Enlightenment principles of universalism, it also worked to fulfill

European Americans' "forbidden white longing" for aboriginal American status for which they envied Indians.[16] Most richly in the Jacksonian era of rigorous genocide, fraternalization of Native Americans rhetorically concealed state-sanctioned violence against them.

Tocqueville deploys this same fraternal imagery, but critically, in a manner that reflects his Christian presumption of human equality and reveals the corruption lacing European American deployment of the metaphor. He imagines U.S. democracy as marked by an emergent familial "design" and "the time must come when there will be in North America one hundred and fifty million all," like siblings, "equal one to the other, belonging to the same family, having the same point of departure, the same civilization, language, religion, habits, and mores, and among whom thought will circulate in similar forms and with like nuances" (DA 412). He knows the Indians are to be tragically purged by their "white brothers" from this growing democratic family because mastery is the aim: "The American people *see* themselves marching through wildernesses, drying up marshes, diverting rivers, peopling the lands, and subduing nature" for agricultural settlement (DA 337, 485; see M 116). Out of the American cradle springs a "nation of conquerors."[17]

Tocqueville records that in the wilderness at Saginaw, he and Beaumont encountered a community of "thirty people, men, women, old people, and children." He describes this community as "a scarcely formed embryo [*embryon à peine formé*], a growing seed entrusted to the wilds, which the wilds must fertilize."[18] Embedded deep in nature, this embryo is an original hybrid of social factors—French Canadians, European Americans, Indians, and "half-castes."[19] Again Tocqueville posits a violent family drama. While "several exiled members of the great human family have met together in the immensity of the forests . . . they cast only looks of hatred and suspicion on one another."[20] In this wilderness, European Americans take Indians "by the hand in brotherly fashion [*fraternellement*]" to "lead them away to die far from the land of their fathers."[21] Though the "American goes to the church, where he hears a minister of the Gospel repeat to him that men are brothers" and the "Indian occasionally casts a stoic glance on the dwellings of his European brethren [*ses frères d'Europe*]," the two are in "contest."[22] Tocqueville is certain of the outcome, as when "Providence" placed the Indians amid the coveted "riches of the New World," it "seems to have granted them a short lease only."[23]

What does Tocqueville's fraternal metaphor reveal about the European American violence? Distinguishing democratic from aristocratic modes of brotherhood, he says that while aristocratic primogeniture meant the eldest "becomes the chief and to a certain extent the master of his brothers," in democracy "children are perfectly equal" (DA 588; but see M 228). Apparently, then, although the Indian was the "first and legitimate master of the American continent," the terms of democracy dissolve his exclusive rights to it.[24] Accordingly, John Quincy Adams insisted that Indians could not be permitted an exclusive claim to the "exuberant bosom of the common mother."[25] But within the democratic family life of Tocqueville's Anglo-Americans, "there is no cause for friction" because brothers have "a common origin" and "no peculiar privilege distinguishes them" (DA 588, 589). This is not the sort of brotherhood the Anglo-Americans feel for Indians: rather, envy over the Indians' prior attachment to nature breeds brutality. As Beaumont's Nelson reports, "The land [the Indians] occupied formerly, from which they have been thrown out, had . . . been given to them 'forever.' Their new haven will be respected just so long as it does not excite the envy of their enemies" (M 140). In Tocqueville's schema, such envy is also democratic. He theorizes the prevalence of envy in democracy as the "debased" rather than "manly" version of the governing passion for the idea of equality (DA 57). Observing European Americans' unrelenting pursuit of material wealth, he argues that in democracy, unlike aristocracy, "the poor conceive an eager desire to acquire comfort, and the rich think of the danger of losing it." Members of the middle class "have enough physical enjoyments to get a taste for them, but not enough to content them" (DA, 530–31). The middle-class American is "aware of dominating positions near him"; he is filled "with distress, fear, and regret" as he chases wealth with "feverish ardor" (DA 536–37). European Americans are pressed by anxious jealousy beyond sharing the land equally with Indians, toward acts of "tyranny" and "oppression" that reduce the Indians to an "inferior position" (DA 317, 318). Historically, President Andrew Jackson told the Chickasaws that their "white brothers" wanted the land they occupied, and, if they did not surrender it, he would not protect them from their white brothers' desires.[26]

Tocqueville's analysis illuminates how democracy's prevailing ideology— love for the idea of equality—can lead to rampant materialism and legitimation of inegalitarian wealth holdings. He argues that every society boasts its own "code of honor"—the norms that sustain its peculiar internal social structures. In democratic America, the prevailing code of honor is "love of money" (DA 616–21; see M 106, 36, 34), rendered honorable to ensure conditions peculiarly required by the American experiment: the "exploitation" and the "clear[ing], cultivat[ion], and transform[ation of] the huge uninhabited continent" (DA 616–17, 621, 284). However, Tocqueville also associates this acquisitiveness with democratic individualism, which renders inhabitants blind to collective goods and the needs of their fellow inhabitants. Such pathology undergirds the new economy, wherein workers "no longer belong to [themselves]," and owners are "like the administrator[s] of a huge empire." This "industry" "may in turn lead men back to aristocracy" (DA 555, 556); in Beaumont's novel, "aristocracy" already exists in U.S. democracy, in which "the factory is the manor; the manufacturer the overlord; the workers are the serfs" (M 106). The seizing of Indian land is driven by these same democratic and American dynamics.

Rogin argues that in the eighteenth century impassioned charges against England enabled colonists not only to stir popular revolution against the empire, but also to repress fears of violence in American democracy in favor of exaggerated ideas of American innocence.[27] After 1776, though, England was less available to play scapegoat for ills still unfolding in the United States. How, then, to manage guilt and shame for the murder of Indian "brethren"? In this same historical period, there appeared the figure of the "American Adam," representative of American exceptionalism and marker of a putatively novel lineage of humanity forging new beginnings in the American "Eden."[28] The fact that this metaphorical Adam went unaccompanied by a symbolic Eve or an Indian brother pressed the idea that the founding of the United States was innocent and good, invoking no fall from grace or consequential expulsion from the garden. This circulating idea of new beginnings reverberates in Tocqueville's description of American democracy as an "embryo" that "gestates" in the wilderness. However, like Herman Melville's guileless youngster Billy Budd, who commits murder, Tocqueville's America is conceived partly through violent acts. Seeing in America impending greatness born in part of symbolic fratricide, Tocqueville insists, "no man can entirely detach himself from the past" (DA 48): haunting the cultural unconscious of his Anglo-Americans are systematic atrocities committed against imagined brothers.

As Tocqueville critiques European American fraternalization of Indians, he was aware that this rhetoric was being transmogrified into expressions of white supremacy. On one hand, Christian theology had posited in the European imagination all peoples as descendants, first, of Adam, then of Noah; early English settlers saw it as "self-evident" that they "were from a common stock" with Indians.[29] Natural philosophy "stressed an underlying, universal human similarity, one to which English interpretations of North America deferred from the 1550s to 1640s."[30] Europeans *wanted* to believe in such kinship with Indians: for one thing, colonizers had "to combat the apprehension that new climates would damage or destroy English bodies."[31] Later, such thinking was reinforced by Enlightenment views of universal human reason and monogenesis; conveying such meaning himself, Tocqueville describes Indians as members of "the great human family" (DA 29). On the other hand, the effects of European disease on Indian mortality (see DA 318) encouraged Anglo-American colonists, fearful of epidemics, to "adjust the terms of natural philosophy" to claim "that the native peoples were less resistant to disease and that their susceptibility was natural to their bodily constitution"; hence, the production of a novel (though still nonracial) idiom of essentially different bodies.[32] Colonists eventually speculated even that Indians were not indigenous to America and thus unsuited to it. These moves reassured Europeans that God meant for them to have America.[33] In Tocqueville's travel essays, an Anglo-American, echoing Locke, reports that "God, in refusing the first inhabitants the capacity to become civilized, has destined them in advance to inevitable destruction. The true owners of this continent are those who know how to take advantage of its riches."[34]

Still, if "no man can entirely detach himself from the past," European Americans know they have violated imagined brothers. Tocqueville hints that beneath European Americans' energetic appeals to legality, philanthropy, and "great principles of morality," guilt circulates (DA 339). Reginald Horsman concurs: "The white Americans of Jacksonian America . . . wanted a clear conscience. If the United States was to remain in the minds of its people a nation divinely ordained for great deeds, then the fault for the suffering inflicted in the rise to power and prosperity had to lie elsewhere."[35] Historically, nascent anti-Indian racialism collided with the fact of the European slave trade—an activity increasingly endorsed by intellectual and scientific arguments for innate racial inequality.[36] By the 1830s, the slavery-endorsing racist logic infused European American conceptualizations of Indians, and Indians were no longer common humanity but rather "'permanently other.'"[37] Tocqueville reminds us, however, that they were part of that embryo in Saginaw—part of the genesis of U.S. democratic society and culture.[38] One wonders, then, whether bonds of symbolic brotherhood are too insubstantial to fend off competing drives to dehumanize, or whether they may themselves portend violence. Tocqueville's European Americans use "fraternity" to emulate Indians to win title to the land. Tocqueville is horrified that, because "fraternity" invokes not just commonality but Christian brotherly love, it was also used to submerge the realities of European American violence; he himself uses "fraternity" to critique the genocide. At the same time, in its story of Cain's attack on Abel, the Judeo-Christian tradition warns that brotherhood is potentially violent. Tocqueville's portrait suggests that imagined intimacy in a shared world of limited resources, combined with the envy characteristic in democracy, can constitute grounds for violent contest and conquest.

Othering in America

While European Americans initially emphasized their sameness to Indians, David Brion Davis argues that "one can trace a continuity of negative and dehumanizing images of black Africans from medieval Muslims to fifteenth- and sixteenth-century Iberians and on to sixteenth- and seventeenth-century northern Europeans and Euro-Americans."[39] By the eighteenth century, the new anthropologists and naturalists were categorizing people into a hierarchy of races delineated by putatively inherited physiological and mental characteristics—a move that legitimized European colonization and enslavement of non-European peoples.[40] Tocqueville and Beaumont illustrate the impact of this modern slavery on the "passions," "mores" and "opinion" of the democratic U.S. North.

Tocqueville argues that "in antiquity the slave was of the same race as his master and was often his superior in education and enlightenment. . . . Freedom once granted, they mingled easily" (DA 341). But "in the modern world," the "ephemeral fact of servitude is most fatally combined with the physical and permanent fact of difference in race. Memories of slavery disgrace the race, and race perpetuates memories of slavery" (DA 341, see 342, 319). Tocqueville suggests that physical appearance is a definitive marker of identifiable racial "origin[s]" that performs in America as a "visible and indelible sign" of subjugation (DA 341, 342). Beaumont concurs: "American society, with its Negroes, is in a totally different situation from the ancient slave-owning societies. The color of American slaves changes all the consequences of liberation. . . . In vain will the blacks receive their liberty; they will still be regarded as slaves" (M 6, but see 198–99). "Perpetuat[ing] the memory of his servitude," the black's color will prevent the "mingling of the two races" (M 63; see 214, 243).

In the U.S. North, democratic public opinion serves as racism's ready vehicle (DA 341; see M 77). For Tocqueville, democratic society's mores are governed by the deep powers of public opinion and potentially by majority tyranny (DA 89, 248–76, 393–96). The manly independence of spirit that enables the aristocrat to stand apart from the pressures of society is supplanted in democracy by the individual's weakness; aristocracy's confidence in an élite is replaced by confidence in the public (DA 643, 435, 641). Amid the relative uncertainty, mobility, and leveled authority of democracy, public opinion stands in as a new composite authority whose guidance comforts, offsetting the burden of individual sovereignty. The power of public opinion is then amplified as it infiltrates law and public institutions (DA 253–54, 436). Tocqueville laments, "When a man or a party suffers an injustice in the United States, to whom can he turn?" Not to public opinion, legislatures, executives, police, juries, or even judges, governed as they are by the majority.[41] Beaumont's Ludovic agrees: "'The people who hate the Negroes are those who make the laws; it is they who appoint the magistrates . . . the people, with its passions, is the ruler'" (M 77; see 93).

Nor is there much chance of inspiring a just response within the democratic public. Distracted by pursuit of wealth, individuals fail to form distinct views (DA 436, 642–43). For potential dissenters, "the sense of their isolation and impotence at once overwhelms them" (DA 643, see 258, 644). Desiring to marry Marie, an apparently white woman but with remote African ancestry, Beaumont's Ludovic finds himself "'faced by that prejudice, powerful, inflexible, widespread in all classes, which dominates America, with no voice raised against it; crushing its victims without reserve, pity, or remorse.'" Marie's father explains that the American keeps the "blood of his forebears pure" by "stigmatiz[ing]" members of the other "two races," even when their "color can no longer be seen." The tyranny of this opinion begins to work on Ludovic himself so that "'when I saw, in the free states, the black population covered with disgrace perhaps worse than slavery; all people of color branded by public contempt, overwhelmed with abuse, more degraded by shame even than by misery: then I felt terrible conflicts stir within me'" (M 71, 63).

So both Tocqueville and Beaumont explain racism in the democratic North in terms of public opinion's prejudice against the "indelible" mark of color, tied as it is to American slavery. But the point of Beaumont's story about Marie is that color is *not* an indelible mark. His novel illustrates a dimension of American racism that his and Tocqueville's express racialism misses: how the idea of racial difference-as-hierarchy is posited by the institution of racial slavery and subsequently sustained culturally by public opinion even when difference in color is physiologically unapparent. Beaumont recalls an outing to a Baltimore theater where he observed that whites were allotted the first balcony, mulattoes the second, and Negroes the third. He noticed a woman in the second balcony "whose complexion, of perfect whiteness, proclaimed the purest European blood." Puzzled, he questioned the man beside him, who reported that the woman was "colored" because "'local tradition has established her ancestry, and . . . she had a mulatto among her forebears.'" Spotting another woman in the first balcony whose face "was very dark," Beaumont was told, "'She is white; local tradition affirms that the blood which flows in her veins is Spanish'" (M 5, see n.). The tragedy in Beaumont's novel is that the Frenchman Ludovic falls in love with Marie, who is apparently white; Ludovic must be told that more than a century before, her mother's family line "'had been soiled by a drop of black blood'" (M 55). Ludovic wants to marry Marie, but her father forbids it, ironically emphasizing a color difference that does not exist: "'If you contemplated reality with *a less prejudiced eye*, you could not endure *the sight*, and you would realize that a white man can never marry a woman of color.'"[42] Ludovic rages back: "'You sun-browned white men will bow your heads before the lily whiteness of the colored girl'" (M 67). In this dialogue, whiteness is exalted, and Ludovic attacks the injustice of racism when "the color can no longer be seen" (M 63). But the text unveils how not substantive markers of difference but a publicly guarded idea of race categories propels radical othering.

Fear of Falling

Tocqueville argues that "humanity, justice, and reason stand above [majority rule] in the moral order. . . . The majority recognizes these limits and if it does break through them, that is because, like any man, it has its passions and, like him, may do evil knowing what is good" (DA 395–96). Tocqueville and Beaumont show racism "breaking through" moral limits to mollify Anglo-Americans' passions stirred by the flux and leveling of democracy itself. Despite the Anglo-Americans' desire to separate from England-as-authority, they remain anxiously attached to it as a source of prestige. Amid what Tocqueville calls the mediocrity produced by the idea of equality, the Anglo-Americans mark their difference from other American inhabitants to produce a privileged "racial" identity.

Tocqueville says the *bois-brulés*—the offspring of Indians and French Canadians[43]—constitute the "real link between the European and the Indian." Likewise, in some places in the United States, "European and Negro blood are so crossed" that "one can really say that the races are mixed, or rather that there is a third race derived from those two" (DA 356). However, "of all Europeans, the English have least mingled their blood with that of Negroes"; and there are "infinitely fewer [mulattoes in the United States] than in any other European colony"—a fact Tocqueville attributes to Anglo-Americans' "pride of origin." "The white man in the United States is proud of his race," imagined as "English," and is therefore "proud of himself" (DA 356, 357). Beaumont shows that England "inspires very pronounced feelings of jealousy in all Americans. However, . . . one sees that at the same time they are proud of their descent from so great a nation as England" (M 218). They "childishly value the antiquity of their origin and the nobility of their forebears. There are those who will endlessly reiterate their genealogies; sometimes they will stretch the truth to prove their illustrious descent."[44] With the Anglo-Americans' "political institutions and social conditions not permitting them to take titles of nobility, they cling by every possible means to trivial aristocratic distinctions" (M 229). The desire of northern Anglo-Americans to claim noble-like status is enabled by southern racial slavery, which has already demarcated (even imagined) skin color as the mark of natural hierarchy. Beaumont's Anglo-Americans easily fulfill their passion to be of a "privileged class" because their "white skin" has been lent the "mark of nobility" (M 231). They guard this privilege: "As long as the freed Negroes show themselves submissive and respectful to the whites . . . they are assured of support and protection. . . . But as soon as they announce their claims to equality the pride of the whites is aroused, and the pity inspired by misfortune gives way to hatred and scorn" (M 243).

In European aristocracy, the rich "can hardly imagine anything different" from their material comforts, which are "by no means the aim of their existence; they are just a way of living." The poor are accustomed to their deprivations and are comforted by lifetime bonds with the upper classes, which feel a duty toward them. Tocqueville contrasts this psychic security with the insecurity felt in democracy, which transformed weblike social relations into atomizing individualism and stimulated acquisitive desire (DA 530, 531). The idea of equality presses people to want as their just democratic deserts what their neighbors have: "One must not blind oneself to the fact that democratic institutions most successfully develop sentiments of envy in the human heart" (DA 198). Meanwhile, social flux in democracy threatens loss, further feeding desire to secure status and wealth to reassure inhabitants that they will not be left in a relatively inferior and vulnerable position (DA 57, 503–04). But the tantalizing promise of democratic equality "ever retreats before them without getting quite out of sight" (DA 538). So the assurance is fleeting, and there remains a haunting urge to secure ever more wealth and inviolable prestige (see M 106, 116). In Tocqueville's and Beaumont's U.S. democracy, the psychodynamics of envy, desire, and materialism native to democracy potently utilize the ideas of U.S. slavery to secure inviolable white status in that democracy.

Consider also how Tocqueville distinguishes between racism in the South and the democratic North. He observes that in the southern states where slavery still existed, "less trouble is taken to keep the Negro apart: . . . people are prepared to mix with them to some extent; legislation is more harsh against them, but customs are more tolerant and gentle." The white master does not fear "lifting the slave up to his level, for he knows that when he wants to he can always throw him down into the dust" (DA 343; see M 72). "Abolition of slavery in the South would increase the repugnance felt by the white population toward the Negroes" (DA 357, see 343). That is, "the southern American has two active passions which will always lead him to isolate himself: he is afraid of resembling the Negro, once his slave, and he is afraid of falling below the level of his white neighbor" (DA 357).

This fear of assimilating and falling is stronger yet among whites in the democratic North. Tocqueville's New Englanders had generally "belonged to the well-to-do classes at home," and their tradition of comfort, education, and status inculcated in them an enlightened interest in communal equality, but also a love of moderate privilege and fear of flux that could undo such standing (DA 35). So in the North, the more legal race hierarchy is dissolved, the more "white northerners shun Negroes" because they are "frightened by an imaginary danger" (DA 357, see 343). Beaumont's Ludovic observes that in the North, "'where equality of all is proclaimed, the whites keep their distance from the Negroes, so as not to be confused with them; they avoid them with a sort of horror, . . . maintaining by custom the distinction which the law no longer makes'" (M 72).

The specter for whites of falling to some unknown middling position to which blacks rise entices them to hold blacks at an unbridgeable distance. This othering guarantees northern whites a property in their whiteness that cannot be lost, unlike other forms of postaristocratic property, which are susceptible to the new democratic flux. So blacks signify for this privileged race that which they fear becoming but, in their racialized world, cannot become. This explains why, later, white working-class Americans increasingly offered allegiance to white owning classes rather than to fellow workers of color. For Ludovic, "'Everywhere there exists hostility between the rich and the proletariat; however, the two classes are not separated by any insurmountable barrier; the poor become rich, the rich poor.'" In contrast, "'when the American crushes the black population with such contempt, he knows that he need never fear to experience the fate reserved for the Negro'" (M 74). So Tocqueville's and Beaumont's white American democracy and Negro undercaste are two sides of the same coin: the Negroes and Europeans are "bound one to the other without mingling; it is equally difficult for them to separate completely or to unite" (DA 340). For one of Beaumont's characters, American racism "'is doubtless unjust; but it is essential to the very dignity of the [white] American people'" (M 63, 64, 65, 62).

American Democracy and Imperialism

Tocqueville and Beaumont reveal a European American struggle, in the face of blacks increasingly endowed with formal rights, to secure *European-ness* (as whiteness) as a kind of aristocratic heritage. Meanwhile, in gazing upon Indians as the first occupants of American land, European Americans reject Europeanness to seize native *Americanness* to claim land. Out of democratic envy and greed for security, colonists repel and murder Indians while projecting guilt onto them (M 229), eventually transforming these fraternalized Indians into othered "red blacks."[45] Out of these same

democratic psychodynamics and by way of tyrannical democratic public opinion, northern European Americans win from blacks inalienable
privilege.

Do these two American strategies to familialize and to cast as "other" op-
erate today? Radical differentiation of humans within the European American social state remains evident in the country's unresolved struggle with
ongoing immigration and the legacy of slavery. European Americans continue to identify with native Americanness to other newcomers to America.
In U.S. actions abroad, alongside othering, Americans also deploy imagery
of intimate bonds.[46] Just as Tocqueville and Beaumont illustrate the super-
ceding of symbolic fraternalism by racist othering, one should examine
U.S. actions abroad carried out under the rubrics of the Monroe Doctrine,
Manifest Destiny, and the call to spread democracy to uncover how discursive appeals to intimate relations may rhetorically conceal violent and
expropriating drives.

Notes

For insights, thanks to Bruce Baum, reviewers at *Political Theory*, Mary Dietz, Stephen
White, Duchess Harris, August Nimtz, and Pamela Leach. This essay appears in full in
Political Theory (December 2004).
1. Beaumont's novel readily presents his own voice; some chapters and the appendices
are explicit commentary. See Gerard Ferguson's introduction to Beaumont's *Marie, or,
Slavery in the United States*, trans. Barbara Chapman (1958; reprint, Baltimore: Johns
Hopkins University Press, 1999), ix; and George Wilson Pierson, *Tocqueville in America*
(Baltimore: Johns Hopkins University Press, 1996), 522. Beaumont's *Marie* is hereafter
cited with the abbreviation "M."
2. For example, Rogers M. Smith, "Beyond Tocqueville, Myrdal, and Hartz: The Mul-
tiple Traditions in America," *American Political Science Review* 87 (September): 549–66;
William Connolly, "Tocqueville, Territory and Violence," *Theory, Culture, and Society* 11
(1994): 19–40; Mark Reinhardt, *The Art of Being Free: Taking Liberties with Tocqueville,
Marx, and Arendt* (Ithaca: Cornell University Press, 1997), chaps. 2, 3. See Alexis de
Tocqueville, *Democracy in America*, trans. George Lawrence (1966; reprint, New York:
Anchor Books, Doubleday, 1969), 316, 356; Beaumont, M, 98–100, 137, 226–27; Roger
Boesche, ed. *Alexis de Tocqueville: Selected Letters on Politics and Society* (Berkeley: Uni-
versity of California Press, 1985), 69–73, 297–99, 343–45, 347. Tocqueville's *Democracy in
America* is hereafter cited with the abbreviation "DA."
3. European Americans did not benefit equally. See, for instance, Noel Ignatiev, *How the
Irish Became White* (New York: Routledge, 1995).
4. Alan Taylor, "Blood and Soil," *New Republic* 225 (October 8, 2001): 49.

5. David Brion Davis, "The Culmination of Racial Polarities and Prejudice," *Journal of the Early Republic* 19 (Fall 1999), 760.

6. See Laura Janara, *Democracy Growing Up: Authority, Autonomy, and Passion in Tocqueville's* Democracy in America (Albany: SUNY Press, 2002).

7. Ibid., 59–65.

8. Tocqueville, DA / *De la démocratie en Amerique I* (Paris: Garnier-Flammarion, 1981), 33/88, 34/88, 39/94, 40/95, 40/96, 76/139, 112/183, 76, 139, except see 408/536, 507.

9. Tocqueville, DA / *La démocratie I*, on birth and growth, 26/78, 34/88, 44/100, 50/106, 114/184, 162/240, 166/246, 176/258, 259 twice, 240/334, 271/371, 385, 412, 714. DA / *De la démocratie en Amerique II* (Paris: Garnier-Flammarion, 1981), 505/121, 590/130. See Janara, *Democracy*, chap. 2.

10. In Michael Paul Rogin, *Fathers and Children: Andrew Jackson and the Subjugation of the American Indian* (New York: Vintage Books, 1976), 25.

11. Ibid., 24, 30.

12. See Janara, *Democracy*, chap. 2.

13. Tocqueville, DA, 30, 26, see 25, 26, 283; *La démocratie I*, 84. See Tocqueville, "Fortnight in the Wilds," 383, 382; and "Journey to Lake Oneida," 344, both in *Journey to America*, trans. George Lawrence (New York: Anchor Books, 1971).

14. In Rogin, *Fathers and Children*, 114.

15. Ibid., 5, 6.

16. Ibid., 210.

17. Tocqueville, "Fortnight," 364.

18. Ibid., 395; Alexis de Tocqueville, *Voyage en Amérique*, ed. R. Clyde Ford (Boston: D. C. Heath, 1909), 66.

19. Tocqueville, "Fortnight," 391.

20. Ibid., 395.

21. Tocqueville, DA, 339; *La démocratie I*, 452.

22. Tocqueville, "Fortnight," 354; *Voyage en Amérique*, 68.

23. Tocqueville, DA, 30; see "Fortnight," 351, 364, 393, 394, 396; Beaumont, M, 137.

24. Tocqueville, "Fortnight," 351, 393; see Rogin, *Fathers and Children*, 6.

25. In Rogin, *Fathers and Children*, 6.

26. Ibid., 192.

27. See ibid., 27, 28.

28. Terence Ball, "The Myth of Adam and American Identity," in *Reappraising Political Theory* (Oxford: Oxford University Press, 1995).

29. Karen Ordahl Kupperman, "Presentment of Civility: English Reading of American Self-Presentation in the Early Years of Colonization," *William and Mary Quarterly* 54:1 (January 1997): 193.

30. Joyce C. Chaplin, "Natural Philosophy and an Early Racial Idiom in North America: Comparing English and Indian Bodies," *William and Mary Quarterly* 54:1 (January 1997): 230.

31. Ibid, 239–40.

32. Ibid, 230, 232, 231.

33. Ibid, 249, 250, 244, 248.

34. Tocqueville, "Fortnight," 354.

35. Reginald Horsman, *Race and Manifest Destiny: The Origins of American Racial Anglo-Saxonism* (Cambridge, Mass.: Harvard University Press, 1981), 190.

36. Davis, "Culmination," 762, 767; see also his "Constructing Race: A Reflection," *William and Mary Quarterly* 54:1 (January 1997): 11, 16.

37. Kupperman, quoted in Davis, "Constructing Race," 14; see Horsman, *Race and Manifest Destiny*, chap. 10.

38. Beaumont writes of Saginaw, "One can find in the heart of the wilderness the very character of a nation" (157).

39. Davis, "Culmination," 767. But Morgan claims that blacks in America were initially treated like European indentured servants, not as permanent slaves: Edmund S. Morgan, *American Slavery, American Freedom: The Ordeal of Colonial Virginia* (New York: Norton, 1975).

40. See Seymour Drescher and Stanley L. Engerman, eds., *A Historical Guide to World Slavery* (Oxford: Oxford University Press, 1998); Ivan Hannaford, *Race: The History of an Idea in the West* (Washington: Woodrow Wilson Center Press, 1996), xii.

41. Tocqueville, DA, 252. On "Negroes" prevented from exercising voting rights in Pennsylvania, 252 n. 4; see 343. Beaumont comments on this and the New York race riots of 1834 (M, 215, 245–51).

42. Beaumont, M, 57, emphasis added.

43. Tocqueville, "Fortnight," 362.

44. Beaumont, M, 228–29.

45. David R. Roediger, *The Wages of Whiteness: Race and the Making of the American Working Class*, rev. ed. (1991; London: Verso, 1999), 22; Horsman, *Race and Manifest Destiny*, 2, 3, 205.

46. See Rubin Westin, *Racism in U.S. Imperialism: The Influence of Racial Assumptions on American Foreign Policy, 1893–1946* (Columbia: University of South Carolina Press, 1972), 43.

"The Sacred Right of Self-Preservation"

Juan Nepomuceno Cortina and

the Struggle for Justice in Texas

Less than three decades after Stephen F. Austin rode into San Antonio de Béxar, the Stars and Stripes was unfolded over a vast area from the Rio Grande to the Pacific. As Anglo-Americans proclaimed their Manifest Destiny to control North America, Mexicans living in areas such as Texas were forced into a new political and legal system that proved difficult and often traumatic for them to adjust to. The triumph of Manifest Destiny and the accompanying racial contempt of the victor for the vanquished would at times become unendurable to many of those who were expected to become docile, law-abiding citizens of the Republic of Texas and, after 1845, of the United States.[1] But there was resistance to this undeterred tide of westward expansion and the accompanying concept of white racial superiority.

Decades before Mexican American civil rights leaders in Texas such as José Tomás Canales struggled to end Texas Ranger and vigilante oppression of Mexican Texans and Nicasio Idar established La Gran Liga Mexicanista to protest lynching and discrimination and José Ángel Gutiérrez struggled to establish the Raza Unida Party, there was Juan Nepomuceno Cortina (1824–94).[2] Wheras Canales, Idar, and Gutiérrez worked within the existing political system, Cortina resorted to armed rebellion. The renowned Texas folklorist J. Frank Dobie has called Cortina "the most striking, the most powerful, the most insolent, and the most daring as well as the most elusive Mexican bandit, not even excepting Pancho Villa, that ever wet his horse in the muddy waters of the Río Bravo."[3] Cortina was much more than a bandit, however. A powerful force for racial equality in Texas, he campaigned tirelessly, often at the end of a gun barrel, for an end to the abuse of

Mexican Texans. Although largely illiterate and marked by immense contradictions, Cortina rose to great political and military heights and became a hero to many poor, disfranchised Mexicans in Texas.

At the time of Cortina's birth in Camargo in 1824, his father, Trinidad Cortina, was alcalde (mayor) of the town. Cortina's great-great-great-grandfather Blas Maria de la Garza Falcon (1712–67) was captain of the presidio of Cerralvo, Nuevo León, Mexico, on the far northeastern edge of the Spanish empire, when he was given permission to establish the village of la Villa de Santa Ana de Camargo. His great-grandfather Jose Saldivar de la Garza was given the large (261,276 acres) Potrero del Espiritu Santo (Pasture of the Holy Ghost) land grant in 1772, in what is now south Texas.

Cortina fought the Texas Rangers, the U.S. Army, the Confederate Army, and French imperialists. Like Nathaniel Bacon and Daniel Shays, he was one of the few individuals in the history of the United States to have a war named after him. What came to be known as the Cortina War of 1859–60 started as a personal feud but evolved into a struggle against Anglo-American racial nationalism and expansionism. In the end, Cortina would lose the fight, and the wounds opened by American expansion would endure well into the next century. Yet his life and struggle remain enshrined in Mexican American popular culture as a symbol of militant resistance to Anglo oppression and racism.

Living under the long and bitter legacy of the Alamo, Goliad, and San Jacinto coupled with the resounding victory of the U.S. Army during the Mexican War (1846–48), Mexicans in Texas became second-class citizens. The stunning racial myth of the Alamo would endure for decades.[4] But it was not as much the myth as how the truth came to be used that was so damaging. Mexicans were not only racially inferior, many Anglo Texans insisted, but also cruel, cowardly, and treacherous. As a consequence, they came to be treated cruelly. Ridiculing the treaty that ended the Mexican War, Cortina never acquiesced to the new complexities of social and political inequality north of the Rio Grande. "I never signed the Treaty of Guadalupe Hidalgo," he would defiantly proclaim.[5]

Cortina watched in the decade following the Mexican War as racialized confrontation and conflict engulfed the southern part of the Lone Star State. In September 1854, the citizens of Seguin on the Guadalupe River east of San Antonio announced that Mexicans of the *peón* class could neither enter nor reside in Guadalupe County. Residents in Austin then publicly accused twenty Mexican Texans, or Tejanos, of stealing horses and declared that Mexican laborers would be forcibly expelled from the capital. Shortly thereafter, representatives from eight counties in south-central Texas met at Gonzales to discuss the threat Tejanos were posing to the institution of slavery. It was rumored, but never confirmed, that Mexican Texans were assisting slaves in their flight to Mexico by way of an underground railroad. Two years later, in 1856, authorities in Colorado and Matagorda counties evicted their Mexican Texan populations. West of San Antonio, Uvalde County prohibited all Mexicans from passing through the county without a passport.

In 1857, the so-called Cart War erupted between whites and Mexican teamsters, or *carreteros*, in the area between San Antonio and the gulf coast. Here Tejano and Mexicano teamsters had traditionally eked out a living by hauling merchandise from the port of Indianola to San Antonio and the interior of the state. When Tejano teamsters undercut rates by rival Anglos along the road, the Anglos, partly inspired by racist Know-Nothing propaganda, launched a campaign of lawless acts of terror against their competitors. Hoping to gain control of the growing trade, Anglo freighters, wearing masks fashioned from gunnysacks, not only destroyed carts belonging to Mexicans but also confiscated and pillaged their cargoes. As many as seventy Tejanos and Mexicanos were said to have died in the violence as their wagon trains were robbed and destroyed. The Cart War inflamed racial prejudices to the point that citizens in Goliad County warned that any Mexican who committed a crime in their county would be swept "from the face of the earth."[6] On the Rio Grande frontier, Cortina watched as a number of Mexicans were gunned down in Brownsville, and their deaths went largely unnoticed by Anglo-dominated law enforcement officers. As ethnic tensions accelerated, a member of the Texas House of Representatives went so far as to introduce a bill in the state legislature that would establish peonage in the state.

By this time, Cortina had become a leader in the eyes of many of the poor class of Mexicans on both sides of the border by participating in the rough-and-tumble politics of south Texas while at the same time serving in the Mexican militia. He was sometimes employed as a "striker" at local elections, hired to take many of the lower-class Mexican Americans to the polls on election day and show them how to vote. One Brownsville resident remembered him as "an influential man in elections" and someone who was "treated with a great deal of leniency."[7] From the politics of the Lower

Rio Grande Valley, he learned that intimidation was an accepted political tactic and that the party with the most money, guns, alcohol, and promises of spoils could control Brownsville and Cameron County. Although composing a majority of the population in the Lower Rio Grande Valley, Mexican Texans were rarely elected to office, and when they were the individuals chosen were usually subservient to the dominant Anglo political and economic establishment. Only in 1853, when two Tejanos were selected as county commissioners in Cameron County, did the Mexican Texan majority come close to holding any meaningful power in county politics. Petit and grand juries, highly politicized instruments of intimidation, rarely included Tejanos.[8]

Within two years of the town's establishment in 1848, Brownsville had grown to a population of twenty-five hundred and had the second busiest post office in Texas. Although the community and county had several wealthy merchants and stockholders, the vast majority of the population was poor Tejanos and Mexicanos. Huddled in small *jacales*, or shacks, on the outskirts of town and nearby ranches and small farms, they subsisted on the barest of necessities, cooking outdoors on an open hearth most of the year and sweltering in the unbearable summer heat. Called *pelados* (penniless nobodies), they were the poorest of the poor. They dressed in rags and were easily distinguishable from the Anglos and upper-class Mexicans, such as Cortina, who dressed in fancy, colorful garments. Treated badly, they grudgingly endured the bitter racial discrimination that became a way of life in Brownsville. In 1856, the Brownsville *American Flag* admitted that "Americans [i.e., Anglo-Americans] have at times committed offenses which . . . have been overlooked, but which, if committed by Mexicans would have been severely punished."[9]

Ironically, the Cortina War, as noted, started not as a struggle for justice or equality but as a personal feud between Cortina and a man named Adolphus Glavecke.[10] Although Cortina and Glavecke had known one another since Cortina was a teenager, and the two had rustled cattle and horses together, a deep mistrust developed. Glavecke had become a legal and financial advisor to Cortina's mother, a Rasputin-like influence whom Cortina came to strongly resent. Cortina also became leery of Glavecke's connections to the corrupt Brownsville legal establishment. In particular, he was upset with the way Glavecke and a local judge handled the estate of his deceased aunt.[11] In the growing feud, Glavecke used his influence with a Cameron County grand jury to have Cortina indicted for rustling cattle.[12] As a consequence, Cortina came to refer to Glavecke as "infamous and traitorous," the "author of a thousand misdeeds," and he swore to kill him on sight.[13]

In the spring of 1859, one of Brownsville's leading citizens, Charles Stillman, claimed fifteen to twenty Mexicans of "bad character" had been driven away from the Nueces River and were camped at Rancho San José "occupied by one Cortina."[14] At about the same time, the U.S. Army decided to abandon its forts on the Rio Grande, including Fort Brown at Brownsville, and transfer the garrisons to the western frontier to fight Indians. Now that the border was unprotected by the military, "Mexican armed soldiers, highwaymen, and Indians" would invade the area, the Brownsville merchant elite warned, but their protests fell on deaf ears.[15] Cortina came to realize that, with the military gone, the situation on the border was dramatically altered.

In an atmosphere of uncertainty Cortina rode into Brownsville on July 13, 1859. He was thirty-five-years old at the time and in the prime of life. Following his indictment for cattle stealing, he had come to town heavily armed and accompanied by friends at his side. While sitting at a popular coffeehouse and bar on Market Plaza, Cortina watched as City Marshal Robert Shears attempted to arrest a Mexican who was said to have been drunk and who was accused of abusing a local restaurateur. When the man became defiant, Shears began viciously pistol whipping him, before attempting to drag the man off to jail. Recognizing the man as having once worked for his mother, Cortina made the fateful decision to intercede. "Why do you ill treat this man?" he reportedly asked. "He answered me insolently," Cortina recalled years later, "and then I punished his insolence and avenged my countrymen by shooting him with a pistol and stretching him at my feet."[16] Shears claimed that Cortina fired first when his back was turned. What is certain is that Shears was struck by a second shot that ripped into his left shoulder, the bullet exiting through his back.[17] With the marshal lying in the street bleeding, Cortina swung the elderly *vaquero* up behind him on his horse and galloped out of town "amidst the stupor of the Yankees and the enthusiastic hurrahs of the Mexicans."[18]

As the tension-filled summer of 1859 passed into fall, Cortina was indicted for attempted murder.[19] Tired of the racism that permeated Brownsville, of the duplicity of county public officials, and of the corruption of the legal establishment and fearing he might be arrested or killed, Cortina concluded he had to give up any hope of making a life in Texas and decided to cast his future with his native Mexico. But matters in Brownsville still continued to preoccupy his thoughts. Unforgiving, he remained adamant about killing Adolphus Glavecke and even Marshall Shears.

In early September, Cortina made another fateful decision. Before departing from Matamoros with the Mexican military, he would take his revenge on Glavecke and his other enemies by raiding Brownsville. After taking part in a delayed celebration in Matamoros commemorating Mexico's independence, early in the morning of September 28 he led some seventy raiders into the dung-splattered and darkened streets of the town. Soon the sounds of pistol and rifle fire echoed through the night, and shouts of "Viva Cheno Cortina," "Viva la República," and "Mueran los Gringos" (Death to the Gringos) rang out.[20]

The town was caught completely by surprise. In command of the situation, Cortina posted sentinels on the corners of the main street with orders to shoot anyone attempting to resist or interfere. "No man could have appeared on the streets with arms without being shot down," an observer recorded.[21] "Organized resistance," a local priest recalled, "was out of the question. . . . The Americans, terror-stricken, had only time to look for hiding places."[22] As the raid continued, a number of Brownsville's Tejanos joined Cortina. Although the Cortinistas killed five men and took guns, ammunition, liquor, and several horses, there was no attempt at wholesale plunder. In fact, several times during the raid, Cortina told Mexicans not to fear him, that he had come to Brownsville only to kill "bad Americans."

With his raid on Brownsville, Cortina had become one of the first to strike at a racist system many Mexicans on the border found demeaning and immoral. In the months that followed, debate would center around exactly who the raiders were and where they had come from. Fifty-four of the Cortinistas, most of them from Mexico, were identified by the Cameron County grand jury that investigated the raid. To the grand jury, the raid Cortina had led was an "invasion of American territory by armed Mexicans."[23] The Mexican Border Committee that was sent to investigate problems on the Rio Grande in 1873 concluded, however, that the majority of the Cortinistas were from the United States.[24]

From Rancho del Carmen, his mother's ranch on the river nine miles above Brownsville, on Friday, September 30, 1859, Cortina, very much in the Mexican tradition, issued a *pronunciamineto* attempting to rationalize the Brownsville raid. Printed in English and Spanish and distributed on both sides of the river, the proclamation was addressed to the "inhabitants of the State of Texas, and especially to those of the city of Brownsville."[25] Since Cortina was largely illiterate, the author of the proclamation remains somewhat of a mystery. Speculation has centered around a prominent, well-educated sympathizer and newspaper editor in Matamoros, Miguel Perez.[26] Admitting that he had ridden into Brownsville to kill Glavecke and a few others, Cortina said he was also acting against the criminality of "a multitude of lawyers, a secret conclave" clearly intent on "despoiling the Mexicans of their lands."[27] Glavecke was only part of a "perfidious inquisitorial lodge to persecute and rob us without any cause."[28] Inspired by the "sacred right of self-preservation," Tejanos under his leadership would defend themselves to the death.[29]

As Cortina sat in camp at Rancho del Carmen, Brownsville remained in a state of panic. Several citizens, including the town's leading merchants and public officials, hastily formed a committee of safety for protection. Fearful of a second attack, some inhabitants obtained eighty thousand bricks from a local brickyard and used them to construct barricades, while chains were stretched across the main streets leading into town. But a large part of the Mexican population was in sympathy with Cortina, so few came forth to man the barricades and stand guard.

The committee of safety also scribbled out a petition to Gov. Richard Hardin Runnels pleading for help. Copies were sent to army headquarters at San Antonio and to President James Buchanan. Leading men of "very low character," Cortina had, "in a most brutal and ruthless manner," killed a number of citizens and mutilated their bodies in a "beastly" way, it was reported. With an "extraordinary influence" over men of "low character," the wily Cortina had "succeeded in [in]ducing into his service persons who have hitherto been regarded as good people."[30] Joined by recruits from as far away as the Nueces River, he was threatening to "lay the town in ashes" and plunge south Texas into a vicious guerrilla war.

With every able-bodied man under arms, day and night, the citizens were desperate for "prompt, ample, and efficient" protection. In particular, they wanted federal troops back on the border. Many remained dazed at how "a single Mexican outlaw" with "several hundred desperate, lawless and licentious beings," could create such turmoil by holding an entire region of the Lone Star State in his grasp.[31] Many in Austin and in Washington, D.C., also wondered how an illiterate "Mexican bandit" could capture an entire town.

The explosive situation on the Rio Grande might well have faded into the footnotes of history had not another incident stoked the coals of the valley's burning racial animosities. Early on the morning of October 12, a posse led by Sheriff James Browne rode upriver toward Rancho del Carmen where they captured Tomás Cabrera, who was recognized from the September 28 raid as Cortina's chief lieutenant. Cabrera was brought into town and imprisoned. The sixty-year-old Cabrera was one of Cortina's closest friends, the two having ridden together since before the Mexican War.

Learning that Cabrera had been captured, Cortina promised to "lay the town in ashes" if he were not released.[32] With *Cortinistas* firing shots into Brownsville in open daylight, panic once again gripped the community. If the citizens would promise not to prosecute him and release Cabrera, Cortina said "he would withdraw his men and leave the country." Convinced there could never be peace in Cameron County until he was killed or driven across the river, authorities in Brownsville organized and armed a small militia called the "Brownsville Tigers." Marching on Rancho del Carmen, the militia was decisively defeated by Cortina and 300 *Cortinistas*, however. Fleeing in panic, the militia even abandoned two small artillery pieces.[33]

Two days later, from his forward camp downriver from his mother's ranch, Cortina sent a letter to Brownsville saying he did not wish to attack the town for fear of hurting "many persons who are faultless." If his enemies in Brownsville were not turned over to him, however, he had "sufficient force and artillery to batter down the houses."[34] With his men visible from the town's barricades, and the boom of the captured cannon echoing every morning promptly at six a.m., a chilling, somewhat unnerving atmosphere settled over the town.

In the days and weeks following the fight at Rancho del Carmen, word spread that Cortina had been victorious, and recruits of all ages continued to ride and walk into his camp. Many recruits came from Mexico, while others arrived from the small ranches and farms on the Texas side of the river. Sixty men broke out of jail in Ciudad Victoria, the capital of Tamaulipas, and made their way north to the border to join Cortina.[35] A band of thinly-clad Tampacaus Indians from near Reynosa also reached his camp.[36] A few of the recruits were mounted and armed while others arrived only with the clothes on their back. All were attracted to the charismatic leader and most shared a hatred of the oppressive *gringos*.

In the weeks that followed, Cortina's popularity continued to grow as he built a small army at Rancho del Carmen. At the same time, the *Cortinistas* began plundering many of the Anglo owned ranches and farms along the Rio Grande.[37] At the head of 1,500 sombrero-crowned angry Mexicans, Cortina was even reported to be within fifteen miles of Goliad. There was little doubt, the Indianola *Courier Bulletin* reported, that all the Mexicans in Goliad County had joined Cortina in revenge for the killings in the Cart War. Flying the Mexican flag, Cortina was determined to push the *gringos* all the way to the Colorado River. Others said he would stop only at the Sabine.[38]

By the first week of November 1859, news of the Cortina War had spread north across the Nueces River to San Antonio, Austin, and to Washington. Many Texans who were already alarmed by the news of John Brown's raid on Harper's Ferry, Virginia, appeared certain that Cortina was coming north from the border to liberate the slaves in Texas and murder the Anglos in their beds. Many Anglo Texans harbored bitter recollections of another Mexican army that had marched across the Rio Grande in 1836.

Encouraged by his continued success, Cortina issued a second *pronunciamiento* from Rancho del Carmen on November 23, 1859. Similar to the first proclamation, it was fiery, full of anger, and it was designed to appeal to the poor and politically dispossessed. Although the document emphasized many of the same ideas as the first, it was evident in the second proclamation that Cortina was more confident and aware that he was addressing a larger audience. He now perceived himself as the spokesman and defender of all "Mexican Inhabitants of the State of Texas."[39] The loss of land, either through legal manipulation and chicanery, or through threats and intimidation, must be avenged. The impunity with which Anglos had killed Mexicans in Brownsville and Cameron County could not go unanswered. Moreover, the racism and arrogance of the newcomers who had come to the border like "flocks of vampires in the guise of men," must be halted forthwith.[40] "Many of you have been robbed of your property, incarcerated, chased, murdered, and hunted like wild beasts," he angrily reminded all Mexicans in Texas.[41]

The *pronunciamiento* was published in Spanish in Matamoros and later translated and reprinted as a broadside by the office of the Brownsville

American Flag, where it was simultaneously rebutted. The broadside referred to Cortina as an "arch-murderer and robber" and a "Christian Comanche." According to the *American Flag*, the document was little more than a "collection of balderdash and imprudence." Cortina had, nevertheless, "banded together an imposing army," most of them citizens of Mexico, who were "levying war against the State and Union," and "flying a foreign flag . . . on American soil."[42]

As frightening news from the border spread north, Texas Rangers were soon on the march. From the mail Cortina had intercepted as well as from a network of spies, informers, and sympathizers, he knew the Rangers were to rendezvous in Brownsville, and he prepared to ambush them in the chaparral north of town. "He knew more about what was going on outside of Brownsville than we did," one citizen confessed.[43] On the morning after the arrival of the first Rangers in Brownsville, Cortina was spotted "with a troop . . . estimated at 200 men, marching down the main road toward the city."[44] The barricades were hastily manned and Cortina retreated. That night, Tomás Cabrera was dragged out of the jail by the Rangers and hanged by a frenzied mob in Market Square. "Who did it, is not known," the Corpus Christi *Ranchero* announced.[45] Another source would only say that "an unknown and lawless mob" was responsible.[46] Although they denied any involvement in the hanging, it was later confirmed the Rangers were responsible. There would be hangings and executions of other Mexicans in the months that followed, further inflaming racialized relations on the border.

On the edge of the Palo Alto Prairie, not far from the old Mexican War battlefield just north of Brownsville, the *Cortinistas* decisively defeated a small company of Rangers. In the chaparral, Cortina, who was said to be "mounted on a beautiful paint horse," carefully positioned his men and one of their captured artillery pieces. As the Rangers approached, the *Cortinistas* retreated into the dense underbrush and sprang their trap. In a vicious firefight that lasted for thirty minutes, three of the Rangers were killed and four wounded.[47]

The day after the Palo Alto fight, the bodies of the dead Rangers were found stripped and mutilated. In retaliation, the Rangers rode to Santa Rita, a small Mexican Texan village about two miles from Cortina's camp, where they were joined by more Rangers and forty "Brownsville Tigers." After burning several *jacales*, the Rangers and their allies agreed they would attack Cortina and drive him into Mexico.[48] Some proclaimed they were determined to "exterminate Cortina." Within sight of Cortina's main camp, they were met by a "galling fire of round shot, grape and canister" and after concluding that Cortina was too "strongly entrenched and fortified," the Rangers beat a hasty retreat. In confusion and "hotly pressed by Cortina and his followers," they fled to the safety of Brownsville.[49]

The next day, the Rangers again moved out to do battle. One mile above Rancho del Carmen, again in sight of Cortina's camp, it was decided that since Cortina had between 350 and 500 men, it would be "imprudent to attack the enemy in his fortifications."[50] Retreating again to Brownsville, more than 100 of the Rangers left the border for points north. The remainder of the Rangers waited for reinforcements. The Cortina War had become a no-holds-barred, vicious guerrilla war that was quickly spinning out of control.

On November 13, 1859, ten days before Cortina issued his second *pronunciamiento*, the United States Army decided to move against him when Maj. Samuel Peter Heintzelman, a hard-nosed, thirty-three-year veteran of the army, received orders directing him to march for the border.[51] Arriving in Brownsville from San Antonio on December 15, 1859, Heintzelman, took 165 bluecoat regulars and 125 Rangers and moved upriver to meet Cortina. Two miles beyond Rancho del Carmen, at a small ranch called La Ebonal, the *Cortinistas* made their stand. With the regulars and Rangers advancing through the dense chaparral, Cortina's men launched a counterattack crying out "*Gringos! Viva Cortina!*" But the superior firepower of the bluecoats sent them reeling as eight of Cortina's men lay dead on the field.[52] The exact number of dead was difficult to determine since several men had been blown to pieces. It was later learned that Cortina, with 200 of his men, had not been in the fight but at Los Indios, north of Brownsville. There he was hoping to ambush other Rangers he had learned were on their way to Brownsville.[53]

As Cortina retreated upriver with his small army, the decisive battle of the Cortina War came at Rio Grande City on December 27, 1859. With the regulars rushing forward to support the Rangers, the *Cortinistas* fled through the small town. As Cortina abandoned the field, many of his men escaped along the river road leading upriver to Roma, while others ran for the river. So hastily was Cortina's retreat that he abandoned all his records, including lists of the names of his men. Outgunned and outmaneuvered, he lost at least sixty men killed out of a total force of 600. Fifteen Rangers were wounded while none of the regulars were lost.

Although Cortina's small army was badly battered at Rio Grande City, small bands of *Cortinistas* remained active on the Rio Grande. In February 1860, it was alleged that Cortina attacked the steamboat *Ranchero* at Rancho La Bolsa above Brownsville. In retaliation, the Rangers crossed the river into Mexico and a vicious firefight erupted with at least 100 *Cortinistas* in which several of Cortina's men were killed and wounded, and Cortina himself escaped glancing gunshots.[54] The details of exactly what happened at *La Bolsa* were not learned for several weeks largely due to misinformation by the jingoistic *Brownsville Flag*. In reality, the *Ranchero* had not been attacked but had been caught in crossfire between the *Cortinistas* on the south bank of the Rio Grande and the Rangers and regular cavalry on the Texas bank. Following the fighting, the Rangers torched *Rancho La Bolsa* and pursued Cortina into the interior.

With the coming of the Civil War, Cortina again appeared on the border when he invaded Zapata County and attacked the county seat of Carrizo on May 22, 1861. Decisively defeated by a small Confederate army from Laredo, he lost seven men in the fray, while eleven other *Cortinistas* were captured and either hanged or shot as bandits.[55] Retreating into the Mexican interior again, Cortina joined the Mexican army. A man of many colors, he cooperated briefly with the Imperialists before he proclaimed for the republic and appointed himself governor of Tamaulipas. In early 1867, as a general in the Mexican Army of Benito Juarez, Cortina was at the colonial city of Querétaro for the surrender of the Imperialist army and the execution of Maximilian. Again Cortina returned to the border only to be blamed for masterminding the theft of thousands of head of livestock in south Texas. William Steele, Texas adjutant general, claimed that Cortina was in control of a border army of no fewer than two thousand "armed adherents."[56] Once again Texas Rangers moved into the area, indiscriminately hanging Mexican Texans and invading Mexico. By 1871, the border violence had become so intense that it threatened to drag the two republics into war, and both countries sent commissions of investigation to the region. Although the U. S. Commission amassed a mountain of incriminating evidence implicating Cortina in the cattle raids, the Mexican Commission largely exonerated him.[57] Subsequent American diplomatic pressure would lead to Cortina's arrest by President Sebastián Lerdo de Tejada in 1875 and his removal to Mexico City, where he was imprisoned and then placed under house arrest. Eleven months later, Cortina issued a *pronunciamiento* at the village of Azcapotzalco on the outskirts of Mexico City, in which he threw his support behind Gen. Porforio Diaz and the *Porfiristas*. After fleeing from the capital, he again returned to the border. But in the struggle for power in Tamaulipas, Gen. Servando Canales had Cortina arrested, court-martialed, and when found guilty, he was ordered before a firing squad.[58] He was eventually sent to Mexico City, however, and placed in the military prison of Santiago Tlatelolco. Released under house arrest, Cortina remained in Central Mexico for sixteen years until his death at Atzcapozalco on October 30, 1894.

The mere mention of Cortina's name in Texas today brings instant recognition from librarians, archivists, and historians. Middle school students read of his daring 1859 raid on Brownsville and his defeat of the Texas Rangers. In the Tejano community, lively *corridos* recall his daring deeds. College students and scholars continue to debate his legacy. He shot the Brownsville marshal, ambushed Texas Rangers, captured the United States mail, battled the United States Army, harassed the Confederate Army, ambushed French Imperialists, attacked Mexican liberals, and fought anyone else who dared get in his way. He defied one Mexican president, revolted against a second, and fell victim to the political intrigues of a third. He never learned to read and only with difficulty could he write his name but he rose to political and military heights of which the more literate could only dream. Perhaps even more important was that through all the sound and fury that was the history of Texas and Mexico, he brought a sense of dignity and pride to many of the poor and dispossessed Mexicanos and Tejanos on both sides of the Rio Grande.

Notes

1. Reginald Horsman, *Race and Manifest Destiny: the Origins of American Racial Anglo-Saxonism* (Cambridge, Mass.: Harvard University Press, 1981), chaps. 11–12.

2. Arnold De León, *Mexican Americans in Texas: A Brief History* (Arlington Heights, Illinois: Harlan Davidson, 1993), 56–57, 88, 114, 127–33.

3. J. Frank Dobie, *A Vaquero of the Brush Country* (Austin: University of Texas Press, 1985), xii.

4. See Timothy M. Matovina, *The Alamo Remembered: Tejano Accounts and Perspectives* (Austin: University of Texas Press, 1995).

5. Brownsville *Daily Ranchero*, August 1, 1871.

6. Quoted in Arnoldo de Leon, *They Called Them Greasers, Anglo Attitudes toward Mexicans in Texas, 1821–1900* (Austin: University of Texas Press, 1983), 82.

7. W. W. Nelson, Indictments by the 12th District Court (Brownsville), Spring, 1859, Sam Houston Papers, Texas State Archives.

8. Jerry Thompson, *Juan Cortina and the Texas-Mexico Frontier, 1859–1877* (El Paso: Texas Western Press, 1994), 1–2.

9. Brownsville *American Flag*, August 20, 1856.

10. At different times Glavecke had served as tax assessor-collector, county commissioner, alderman, and deputy sheriff. Commissioners Court Minutes (1848–62), Cameron County Clerk's Office; Brownsville; Minutebook I (1850–59), 123, 346–47, City Secretary's Office, Brownsville; and List of Candidates Qualifying, September 14, 1854, Cameron County, Record Group 307, Texas State Archives, Austin, Texas.

11. *Antonio Tijerina vs. Adolphus Glavecke*, Minutebook B, 398–99, 577–79, District Clerk's Office, Brownsville, Texas.

12. Adolphus Glarvke [*sic*] Affidavit, January 16, 1860, *Difficulties on the Southwestern Frontier*, 36th Cong., 1st sess., no. 52, 65. Hereafter referred to as DSF.

13. Proclamation! Juan Nepomuceno Cortinas to the Inhabitants of the State of Texas, and especially those of the city of Brownsville, September 30, 1859, DSF, 70–71.

14. Charles Stillman Affidavit, January 18, 1860, *Hostilities on the Rio Grande*, 36th Cong., 1st sess., no. 21, 15–16. Hereafter referred to as HRG.

15. F. W. Latham, et al., to John B. Floyd, March 9, 1859, DSF, 12–14.

16. Juan N. Cortina, To the Public, September 9, 1875, *Texas Frontier Troubles*, 44th Cong., 1st sess., no. 343, 118. Hereafter referred to as TFT.

17. Robert Shears Affidavit, January 14, 1860, HRG, 17.

18. Juan N. Cortina, To the Public, September 8, 1875, TFT, 118.

19. *State v. Juan Nepomocino [sic] Cortina*, et al., Cause no. 394, 395, and 396. Minutebook B, District Clerk's Office, 78, 92.

20. Grand Jury Report, November 11, 1859, DSF, 93. For an overview of the Cortina War, see, Jerry Thompson, ed., *Fifty Miles and a Fight: Major Samuel Peter Heintzelman's Journal of Texas and the Cortina War* (Austin: Texas State Historical Association, 1998).

21. Unsigned Letter, *New Orleans Picayune*, October 10, 1859, quoted in DSF, 39–40.

22. P. F. Parisot, *The Reminiscences of a Texas Missionary* (San Antonio: Johnson Brothers, 1899), 97.

23. Grand Jury Report, January 18, 1860, Washington Daniel Miller Papers, TSA. Three of the raiders, Juan Vela, Florencio Garza, and Vicente García, were later caught on the wrong side of the Rio Grande, found guilty of first degree murder in the deaths of Robert Johnson and Viviano García, and hanged on June 22, 1866. Another *Cortinista*, Evaristo Rómulo, had been hanged in January 1861. Jerry Thompson and Lawrence T. Jones III, *Civil War & Revolution on the Rio Grande Frontier: A Narrative and Photographic History* (Austin: Texas State Historical Association, 2004), 115–17.

24. Brownsville *American Flag*, October 8, 1859.

25. Cortina Proclamation, September 30, 1859, Letters Received, Adjutant General's Office, Record Group 94, National Archives, Washington, D.C.

26. R. Fitzpatrick to Lewis Cass, January 4, 1860, Matamoros Despatches, RG 59, NA.

27. Cortina Proclamation, September 30, 1859, AGO, RG 94, AGO.

28. Ibid.

29. Ibid.

30. Henry Webb, et al., to Hardin R. Runnels, October 2, 1859, DSF, 21–22.

31. Ibid.

32. S. P. Heintzelman to John Withers, March 1, 1860, TFT, 4.

33. Israel B. Bigelow, letter, October 23, 1859, in *Galveston News*, quoted in DSF, 47–48.

34. Juan Nepomuceno Cortina, letter, October 26, 1859, DSF, 69–70.

35. Heintzelman notes from the Brownsville *American Flag*, extra, October 25, 1859, Heintzelman Papers, Library of Congress.

36. Grand Jury Report, January 8, 1860, Miller Papers, TSA.

37. Affidavit of William D. Thomas and Nathaniel White, November 6, 1859, DSF, 49–50.

38. Indianola *Courier*, November 12, 1859.

39. Cortina Proclamation, November 23, 1859, DSF, 79.

40. Ibid.

41. A week later, the *pronunciamiento* was also printed verbatim in the Corpus Christi *Ranchero*. Brownsville *American Flag*, November 26, 1859; Corpus Christi *Ranchero*, December 3, 1859.

42. Broadside, November 26, 1859, in LR, AGO, RG 94, NA.

43. Unsigned Affidavit, Heintzelman Papers, LC.

44. Ibid.

45. Corpus Christi *Ranchero*, November 26, 1859.

46. W. P. Reyburn to F. A. Hatch, November 21, 1859, DSF, 67.

47. Wm. G. Tobin to H. B. Runnels, November 27, 1859, Houston Papers, TSA; Corpus Christi *Ranchero*, November 26, 1859.

48. Tobin to Runnels, November 27, 1859, Houston Papers, TSA.

49. Corpus Christi *Ranchero*, December 3, 1859.

50. Tobin to Runnels, November 27, 1859, Houston Papers, TSA.

51. Thompson, ed., *Fifty Miles and a Fight*, 119.

52. Ibid. See also Heintzelman to Washington, December 16, 1859, HP.

53. Heintzelman Journal, December 16, 1859, HP, LC; Stephen B. Oates, ed., John Salmon Ford, *Rip Ford's Texas* (Austin: University of Texas Press, 1963), 364.

54. Ford, *Rip Ford's Texas*, 285–86.

55. Jerry Thompson, *Mexican Texans in the Union Army* (El Paso: Texas Western Press, 1986), 6–7.

56. Wm. Steele to Richard Coke, July 1, 1875, TFT, 152.

57. "Report of the United States Commissioners to Texas," *Depredations on the Frontiers of Texas*, 42nd Cong., 3rd sess., no. 39, 1–63; *Reports of the Committee of Investigations Sent in 1873 by the Mexican Government to the Frontier of Texas* (New York: Baker & Godwin, 1875), 127–63.

58. Thompson, *Juan Cortina*, 93.

"Shoot Mr. Lincoln"?

> It is a curious truth . . . that an unschooled nineteenth-century American politi-
> cian named Abraham Lincoln . . . has turned out to be among the most revered
> of the human beings who have ever walked this earth. . . . Except for religious
> figures, he has had few superiors on the short list of the most admired . . . of
> humankind. Among his countrymen, I believe, he has . . . no equal. There he
> stands: tall, homely, ready to make a self-deprecating joke, stretching higher
> than the greatest of his countrymen, an unlikely figure among the mighty of
> the earth.
>
> —WILLIAM LEE MILLER

> An increasing number of scholars, hooked beyond redemption on the warm and
> comforting myths of The Immaculate Emancipation . . . are circling the wagons
> around a new and improved version of the old myth, suggesting that Lincoln
> was converted at the last moment . . . or that he said all those terrible things
> about . . . Black deportation because he wanted to get elected to office, like any
> other red-blooded American. Worse, far worse is the fact that few historians . . .
> deal with Lincoln and the Civil War historically . . . as an unfolding process and
> *an open wound* that is still festering and poisoning the body politic.
>
> —LERONE BENNETT JR.

> People are funny about they Lincoln shit. Its historical. People like they histori-
> cal shit in a certain way. They like it to unfold the way they folded it up. Neatly
> like a book. Not raggedy and bloody and screaming.
>
> —SUZAN-LORI PARKS

There is perhaps no figure in American history, with the possible exception of Thomas Jefferson, whose reputation enjoys a greater range of
celebration and censure than Abraham Lincoln's. He is hailed as a national
hero who emancipated the slaves and saved the Union; condemned as a

hypocrite who, while opposing chattel slavery, envisioned the end of the race question as hinging on black deportation; labeled a cynical political operator who exploited white racism to promote his political career; or, in a recent hybrid of these, he is admired as a politically savvy idealist who consciously manipulated proslavery Americans' worst vice—their unapologetic racism—as a means of achieving the abolitionists' greatest objective—the complete elimination of slavery.[1] This essay takes a different tack. Rather than view Lincoln as savior, demagogue, or virtuous manipulator, I read him as a figure in whom the complex legacies of the American political tradition coalesce, a figure who inhabits the fissures and tensions of this tradition, a good son of Founding Fathers. Reflecting on Lincoln, then, entails reflecting on the legacy of that founding and, beyond that, on the dangers that spring from too close an embrace of the national patrimony of the United States. If, as I will suggest here, fidelity to this past turns national destiny into perpetual tragedy, then perhaps engaging the legacy of slavery and civil war requires a calculated and deliberate faithlessness, a performative politics that reinhabits the past and, by staging it differently, resists reproducing it.

Lincoln's Moment

Abraham Lincoln appeared on the national scene in a transformational moment, when existing agreements that sought to resolve slavery through territorial containment were no longer secure and Americans grappled to reconcile increasingly incommensurable positions with respect to the South's peculiar institution. Throughout the 1830s and 1840s, the growing abolitionist movement repositioned slavery as a moral evil, shattering the modus vivendi liberalism of sectional compromise and calling for northern secession from the Union to purify itself of this national sin.[2] When *Dred Scott* enabled slaveholders to relocate their households, with their slaves, to free states and territories, and the Kansas-Nebraska Act overturned the Missouri Compromise, the tenuous balancing act of the early republic collapsed altogether. Lincoln confronted a political landscape torn asunder by its twin commitments to the doctrine of property in the self and a popular sovereignty that in many places countenanced chattel slavery. Earlier American statesmen had negotiated this tension by racializing the republic, reserving both the franchise and the activities of self-governance to white citizens. In the absence of the legally sanctioned buffer of sectionalism, Lincoln argued during his senatorial campaign of 1858, sharp divisions among white citizens made conflict over the terms of national unity inevitable. And it is precisely here, on the question of the political ground of nationhood, where we encounter the many Lincolns who now populate our libraries and bookstores.

In Dwight Anderson's formulation, Lincoln was "a man divided, torn by conflicting obligations to the Declaration of Independence and the Constitution, resolved to become the instrument of national salvation."[3] Patterning his early political vision on the strong nationalism of the Federalist Party, Lincoln in two of his earliest political speeches—the address to the Young Men's Lyceum of Springfield in 1838 and the U.S. House speech condemning the Mexican War a decade later—takes up issues of national significance that explicitly recall George Washington's Farewell Address and its cautions about the dangers of sectional faction. Where Washington had warned of the perils to the young republic posed by charismatic leaders who excited "geographical discriminations,"[4] Lincoln's Lyceum address warned against the "mobocratic spirit" of proslavery vigilantism, calling for "reverence for the laws" and fealty to national institutions.[5] A decade later, on the floor of the U.S. House of Representatives, Lincoln chided President James Polk for having waged unlawful war against Mexico on the basis of misleading and constantly shifting justifications. He called on the president to account for his actions, to abjure the tactics of the lawyer that "employ . . . every artifice to work round, befog, and cover up," and to act in ways appropriate to his office: "Let him answer fully, fairly, and candidly. Let him answer with facts and not with arguments. Let him remember he sits where Washington sat, and so remembering, let him answer as Washington would answer."[6]

Lincoln invoked Washington to reaffirm the constitutional spirit of 1787, extolling government institutions as bulwarks against factional disorder. Yet his speech in the House did not win the accolades he hoped it might. Stung by congressional indifference and his constituents' ridicule (the citizens of Illinois strongly supported the Mexican War), Lincoln entered a prolonged period of despondency, giving up his House seat and withdrawing from national political life for some years. The period appears to have been one of a sort of political conversion. By the time he resurfaced in 1858 as a candidate in the Senate race against Stephen Douglas, Lincoln's emphasis had shifted away from territorial compromise and popular sovereignty (which

Douglas advocated in the hope of deferring the slavery question to local jurisdiction) toward the conviction that slavery was a moral wrong and that a nation divided on a question of moral fundamentals could never be politically stable. "When he finally emerged from his moratorium," Anderson suggests, "he did so with a revolutionary vengeance, identifying himself not with Washington . . . but with Jefferson. By aligning his personal resentments against constitutional fathers with the injustice of Negro slavery, Lincoln discovered in the Declaration of Independence a means of liberation for both himself and the slave."[7]

Significantly, Lincoln embraced the Declaration as an uncorrupted substitute for a Constitution that had left the institution of chattel slavery intact and thus frustrated him in its agnosticism with regard to moral principles. For Lincoln, the Declaration figured as a more complete original by comparison with an incomplete copy, the Constitution. In his speech at Springfield, he berated Douglas for having misrepresented his (Lincoln's) purported "disposition to make negroes perfectly equal with white men in social and political relations." Clarifying, Lincoln insisted, "I adhere to the Declaration of Independence. If Judge Douglas and his friends are not willing to stand by it, let them come up and amend it. Let them make it read that all men are created equal except negroes. Let us have it decided, whether the Declaration of Independence, in this blessed year of 1858, shall be thus amended."[8]

However, if his embrace of Jefferson enabled Lincoln to recognize how the institutionalization of chattel slavery undermined democratic ideals, this moral universalism did not involve reimagining African Americans as full and equal citizens. On the contrary, Lincoln's turn to Jefferson also entailed the embrace of Jefferson's white nationalism, of branding slavery as a moral wrong—a violation of natural freedoms—while stopping short of insisting upon full equality.[9] Famously joking in a campaign speech in Chicago in 1858 about "that counterfeit logic which presumes that because I do not want a negro woman for a slave, I do necessarily want her for a wife," Lincoln went on to suggest that it was Douglas, not he, who promoted racial mixing by endorsing the right of the residents of the territories to own slaves. "The Judge regales us," he said, "with the terrible enormities that take place by the mixture of the races; that the inferior race bears the superior down. Why, Judge, if we do not let them get together in the territories they won't mix there."[10] Weeks later, in Ottawa, Lincoln reiterated his convictions about the wrongs of slavery while reaffirming the virtues of a racially segregated republic:

> I have no purpose to introduce political and social equality between the white and the black races. There is a physical difference between the two, which in my judgment will probably forever forbid their living together upon the footing of perfect equality, and inasmuch as it becomes a necessity that there must be a difference, I . . . am in favor of the race to which I belong, having the superior position. . . . But I hold that notwithstanding all this, there is no reason in the world why the negro is not entitled to all the natural rights enumerated in the Declaration of Independence, the right to life, liberty, and the pursuit of happiness.[11]

Instead of Anderson's depiction of Lincoln as a "man divided," then, we might more accurately think of him in slightly altered terms, not as someone torn between conflicting principles so much as one who embodied an American liberalism that found coherence only through the displacement of racial equality. For the architects of the Constitution, this meant displacing the race question onto the states and maintaining national unity through the legal apparatus of sectionalism. For abolitionists, this meant an embrace of formal equality between the races as a substitute for substantive equality in the conduct of everyday life. Lincoln's newfound Jeffersonianism, however, was less a moral conversion than a political one, a search for a political ground that would preserve the Union now that sectional compromise had collapsed.

History itself would force Lincoln to return to his earlier theme of constitutional unity, this time refigured through his engagement with Jeffersonian racial democracy. With the establishment of the Republican Party as the explicitly antislavery party, the threat of secession shifted from the abolitionists of the North to the slaveholding states of the South, forcing Lincoln, on a speaking tour in the East in early 1860—less than three months before being nominated as the Republican candidate for president—to return to the theme of preserving the Union. In a speech at the Cooper Institute in New York City in February, he reiterated Washington's insistence on sectional containment: "Less than eight years before Washington [warned against sectional faction], he had . . . approved and signed an act of Congress enforcing the prohibition of slavery in the Northwestern Territory." However, this time Lincoln placed the legal framework of sectional compromise in the service of Jeffersonian schemas for state-initiated emancipation, deportation, and colonization of former slaves outside the territorial boundaries of the United States: "In the language of Mr. Jefferson, uttered many years ago, 'It is still in our power to direct the process of emancipation and deportation peaceably, and in such slow degrees as that the evil will wear off insensibly; and [slaves'] places be, *pari passu*, filled up by free white laborers.'"[12]

With the secession of South Carolina in December 1860, Lincoln's hope for the gradual atrophy of the institution of chattel slavery met with the realities of civil war. However, throughout the war, he continued to seek solutions that would avoid immediate abolition. No period in his presidency illustrates this fact better than the months between March 1862 and January 1863, during which Lincoln grappled with the implications of emancipation. In early March 1862, the president recommended to Congress a measure guaranteeing compensation to states that would voluntarily emancipate slaves and abolish slavery. Though it passed, it did so with overwhelming opposition from Democrats and border-state unionists, who threatened to withdraw their support from the Union cause.[13] Lincoln wavered under this pressure, and in May revoked a military order emancipating slaves in South Carolina, Georgia, and Florida.[14] By July, Lincoln had become convinced that no form of emancipation—compensated or uncompensated, gradual or immediate—would gain the assent of the slave states, and he drafted the Emancipation Proclamation. As Gideon Welles, Lincoln's secretary of the navy, explained a decade later, the president had arrived at the conclusion that emancipation was not simply a moral but also "a military necessity, absolutely essential to the preservation of the Union. We must free the slaves or be ourselves subdued. The slaves were undeniably an element of strength to those who had their service, and we must decide whether that element should be with us or against us."[15] On July 22, Lincoln presented his initial draft of the Emancipation Proclamation to the full cabinet but was persuaded by Secretary of State William H. Seward that the measure would have greater impact if he postponed public announcement until after the Union's military success was more secure. That security came with the Union victory at Antietam on September 17. Five days later, Lincoln met with his cabinet to discuss the matter once again, this time signing the Proclamation, which went into effect on January 1, 1863.[16]

In the midst of these efforts, however, Lincoln continued to argue for the ultimate necessity of a white republic. The first president to address a delegation composed entirely of African Americans, he met with leaders of the free African American community of the District of Columbia at the White House on August 14. Lincoln acknowledged to them that slavery was "the greatest wrong inflicted on any people," but also enjoined them to consider the inequities that even free blacks suffered in the United States: "Even when you cease to be slaves, you are yet far removed from being placed on an equality with the white race. You are cut off from many of the advantages which the other race enjoys. The aspiration of men is to enjoy equality with the best when free, but on this broad continent not a single man of your race is made the equal of a single man of ours." Pointing to the "evil effects" of slavery on white citizens as well as on slaves, Lincoln offered the war as an example: "See our present condition—the country engaged in war!—our white men cutting one another's throats . . . then consider what we know to be the truth. But for your race among us there could not be war, although many men engaged on either side do not care for you one way or the other. Nevertheless, I repeat, without the institution of Slavery and the colored race as a basis, the war could not have an existence. It is better for us both, therefore, to be separated." Having effectively blamed African Americans for the war, Lincoln then invited his guests to contemplate emigration, proposing federal support for the establishment of a colony of emancipated African Americans in Central America. Such a colony would open the door, he suggested, to voluntary emancipation, enabling slaveholders to free their slaves secure in the knowledge that, once free, African Americans would not remain in the United States.[17]

Civil War

Shortly after the Emancipation Proclamation took effect, the painter Francis Bicknell Carpenter set about to produce a painting representing the cabinet meeting in which Lincoln introduced his draft. For six months in early 1863, Carpenter was "turne[d] . . . loose" in the White House to complete his work, eventually entitled *First Reading of the Emancipation Proclamation of President Lincoln*.[18] As he executed his studies for the painting, he drew members of the cabinet into conversation about the Proclamation, their interpretation of its significance, and their thoughts on the war. In the midst of one such conversation with the president, Carpenter reported, Lincoln launched into a discussion of Shakespeare's tragedies. Lincoln was fascinated with *Hamlet*, which he planned to see in production with Edwin Booth in the title role that evening.[19] However, the president's imagination was caught up less with Hamlet's indecision as with his stepfather Claudius's guilt at the murder of his brother. Reflecting on the permanence of guilt, Lincoln intoned the king's soliloquy from the play's third act:

> O, my offense is rank, it smells to heaven,
> It hath the primal eldest curse upon't,
> A brother's murther. Pray can I not,
> Though inclination be as sharp as will. . . .
> My fault is past, but, O, what form of prayer
> Can serve my turn? "Forgive me my foul murther"?
> That cannot be, since I am still possess'd
> Of those effects for which I did the murther:
> My crown, mine own ambition, and my queen.
> May one be pardon'd and retain th'offense?[20]

Claudius's despair stems from his conviction that repentance is futile as long as he retains the profit gained through his crime. Lincoln's appreciation of such despair suggests an appreciation of his own tragic position as well as of the impossibility of escaping it. In presiding over a war that tore the nation apart so that it might be made whole, Lincoln has, like Claudius, participated in a national fratricide. Yet with Union victory now imminent, with both the abolition of slavery and the reunification of the nation at hand, repentance was beyond reach.

"The essence of tragedy," Helen Bacon has written, "is the moment of concentrated awareness of irreversibility, of that which nothing can undo, in the light of which life, for any survivors on stage and off, including the audience, will henceforth be lived."[21] Lincoln survived Lee's surrender at Appomattox by a matter of mere days, and it is the nation rather than its Civil War president that lives out its consequences. Even today, Americans live with and within the terms of a military settlement that left intact one of the central sources of the conflict. Citizens of the United States inherit a unified nation in which slavery is a thing of the past, but they also inherit a political tradition that retains the ideal of a white republic as the unacknowledged, unstable foundation of public freedom and social equality. The question that tragedy asks, then, is one not only about America's past, but also about its future. Can a legacy be both curse and gift?

Nearly a century and a half after Union victory, the Civil War continues to hold Americans in its thrall. Refought in immensely popular Hollywood movies and independent documentary series, it has given rise to the new genre of the "edutainment" film. As historical narratives by Shelby Foote and James McPherson and a fictionalized account by Charles Frazier climb to the top of bestseller lists, it has become a gold mine for the publishing and motion picture industries.[22] Museums and rural automobile and urban walking tours of Civil War sites anchor economic revitalization programs in Cincinnati, Chattanooga, and Richmond. An estimated forty to sixty thousand Americans attend Civil War artifact swap meets and participate in battle reenactments each year in places as likely as Gettysburg, Pennsylvania, and as unlikely as Santa Cruz County, California. Major reenactments, like that of Gettysburg, attract corporate funding from PepsiCo and Salomon Smith Barney.[23] Efforts by the Disney Corporation to build a Civil War theme park near a Virginia battleground were scrapped only after sustained protests from historians and local residents that an amusement park would trivialize the very history to which Disney claimed to give voice.

Not least, an NAACP boycott of South Carolina called to protest the flying of the Confederate battle flag over the State House interjected the Civil War into the presidential primary of 2000. In an ironic twist of history, the Democratic contenders unanimously denounced the flag, while those seeking the nomination of the party of Lincoln refused to do so. Senator John McCain of Arizona issued a statement: "As to how I view the flag, I understand both sides. Some view it as a symbol of slavery. Others view it as a symbol of heritage. Personally, I see the battle flag as a symbol of heritage." For his part, then–Texas governor George W. Bush promoted a solution that echoed Stephen Douglas's position on slavery. "The governor has a position, and his position is that the people of South Carolina can figure the issue out," announced a campaign spokeswoman a few days after fielding criticism of a Bush fundraiser held on the grounds of a former slaveholding plantation outside Charleston.[24]

Early in the twenty-first century, "America's most popular war"[25] has become a form of mass national theater. This is strange theater, for it combines the genuine political anguish suggested by the flag controversy with the more casual entertainment of movies and auto tours. And while battle reenactments would appear to break a spectatorial relationship between past and present by transforming consumers of history into actors, there is also a sense in which the inhabiting of historical scripts can make one feel caught within one's own past, unable to envision anything other than its eternal repetition. Like Lincoln's embrace of Claudius, Americans' embrace of history, even as tragedy, may imply that there is little they can do to address history's open wounds in the present except live in and with the legacy of the past.

But I want to suggest that this national tragedy might also serve a radically different purpose, that the public might break free of the spectatorial trap of historical literalism. In closing, I want to approach this possibility via a different sort of tragedy, a racially self-conscious rewriting of Lincoln that reimagines him not as a white president but as a black man.

Black Republican?

Throughout his national political career, Lincoln was dogged by an epithet the Democrats' used to revile him: black Republican. Rumors were circulated during the presidential campaign of 1860 that "his real name is Abraham Hanks. He is the illegitimate son by an [*sic*] man named Inlow from a Negress named Hanna Hanks."[26] Throughout 1862–63, *Punch Magazine* featured a series of political cartoons that depicted an African American Lincoln. In one, published in 1862, this black Lincoln is a card sharp playing his last card over a keg of gunpowder. That card is a (black) spade bearing the face of a black man (fig. 1).[27]

Such representations were, of course, forthright efforts to undermine Lincoln's credibility by depicting him as a political outsider who inhabited founding traditions only to distort them. But we might ask, what effect could the imaginative refiguration of Lincoln as African American have, not simply in Lincoln's era, but in the present, as the nation experiences something of a Civil War renaissance in which sectional antagonism is reborn as mass theater? This is at least one of the questions posed by the playwright Suzan-Lori Parks in two works, *The America Play* and *Topdog/Underdog*, both of which ask if and how history might be inherited differently.

Parks's *The America Play* (1993) takes place in an American history theme park described as "A great hole. In the middle of nowhere."[28] In it, a

ABE LINCOLN'S LAST CARD; OR, ROUGE-ET-NOIR.

FIGURE 1 African American Lincoln. Cartoon by Sir John Tenniel, from *Punch Magazine*, October 18, 1862.

black man whose character is named "The Foundling Father as Abraham Lincoln," but who refers to himself as the "Lesser Known" and who bears a striking resemblance to the Civil War president, fashions a successful career portraying Abraham Lincoln. Dressed in frock coat and stovepipe hat, he occupies the stage to recite the president's best-known speeches while audience members throw rotten food at him. Successful, he takes his show on the road, and someone remarks that "he played Lincoln so well that he ought to be shot." "It was as if the Great Man's footsteps had been suddenly revealed," and the Lesser Known redesigns his act. Instead of making speeches, the new act features him seated in a rocking chair in a darkened box as if watching a play on stage, his back turned to his own audience: "The public was invited to pay a penny, choose from the selection of provided pistols, enter the darkened box and 'Shoot Mr. Lincoln.' The Lesser Known became famous overnight."[29]

Less than a decade later, another African American Lincoln made his appearance in Parks's Pulitzer Prize–winning *Topdog/Underdog*. This play tells the story of two adult brothers named Lincoln and Booth who as children were abandoned by their parents. Lincoln survived to adulthood by running a lucrative street game of three-card monte; Booth became a thief. After his partner was shot and killed by an angry mark, Lincoln abandoned the game and got a job, "a sit down job. With benefits."[30] Like the Lesser Known of *The America Play*, this Lincoln has found work in an arcade, where, dressed in whiteface, beard, and stovepipe hat, he sits with his back to customers who choose a pistol, approach him, and shoot. Unlike the Lesser Known, however, this Lincoln is not on his way up, but down. He has squandered an inheritance of five hundred dollars left by his father. His wife has left him, and Lincoln has moved into his brother's one-room apartment. Day after day, he earns his keep by reenacting the presidential assassination.

For his part, the jobless Booth fills his days by waiting for life to happen. This is not a passive, but an active, enterprise. He is determined to revive Lincoln's three-card monte game for himself, and he obsessively practices throwing the cards. He is also courting an old girlfriend, Grace—"She's in love with me again but she don't know it yet"—and has bought an engagement ring a half size too small so that, once it's on her finger, she won't be able to remove it.[31] In the game and in the romantic fantasy of Grace, Booth invests his hopes of self-mastery. But he lacks his brother's understanding of the game and throws the cards awkwardly; Grace keeps standing him up, and he can't find an opportunity to propose.

When Lincoln loses his arcade job—displaced by a wax dummy who requires neither wages nor benefits—Booth persuades a drunken Lincoln to help him learn the card game, proposing that they return to the streets together. However, Booth's inability to grasp the finer points of the game, it turns out, is a function of his idealism. He has mistaken a game of deception for a game of skill, having placed his faith in a different con, that of an illusory meritocracy in which hard work is rewarded. Humiliated, he brags that Grace has proposed to *him* and tells his brother that he'll have to move out so she can move in. He notices that Lincoln carries a roll of cash and figures out that his brother has already resurrected his game, alone. Removing from its hiding place an old nylon stocking with money knotted in the toe, Booth discloses to Lincoln his own inheritance, left to him by their mother, and boasts that he never spent it. He challenges Lincoln to a game of three-card monte, and they set Booth's inheritance as its stakes. Lincoln throws the cards. Booth chooses the red heart over the black spade and loses. When Lincoln pulls a knife to cut the knotted stocking, Booth pulls a gun on his brother. As they argue, Booth reveals that, frustrated by Grace's continuing disinterest, he has killed her. Booth pulls the trigger and kills Lincoln, then picks up the cards and throws them, poorly, yelling "My *inheritance*. You stole my *inheritance*, man. That aint right. That aint right and you know it. You had yr own. And you blew it. You *blew* it, motherfucker! I saved mine and you blew yrs. Thinking you all that and blew yr shit. And I *saved* mines."[32] His illusions of a fair game shattered, the play ends as Booth takes up Lincoln's body in his arms, sobbing.

Topdog/Underdog might be read as a Civil War reenactment of a decidedly different sort. There is no donning of blue and gray costumes, no muskets, no cannon fire. This is not a war between the states so much as a modern American rewriting of classical tragedy, the two brothers investing their faith in different contemporary incarnations of the Civil War president. Booth is the idealist who persistently mistakes cons for honest games. He inhabits an America ruled by the image of Lincoln as the Great Emancipator. His carefully crafted self-image of working-class domesticity is belied by his career as a thief and his murder of Grace, yet he holds fast to his inheritance, bound tightly in his mother's stocking. He invests his faith in playing by the rules—"Sometimes we will win, sometimes they will win. They fast they win, we faster we win"[33]—and resorts to violence when the rules play him. His brother, by contrast, inhabits an America remade in the image of a cynical president who exploited a citizenry's worst vices to promote his political career. Parks's Lincoln embraces the con—whether that of three-card monte or the arcade game—and he, too, is betrayed by it. His career as the president is cut short when he is replaced by a wax dummy, in much the same way he replaced a white man when he took the job, paid less for his work than his predecessor had been. And his skill in the con game of three-card monte ultimately kills him.

These brothers have been shaped by a history that also abandons them. Thus, survival in the America that Parks's counternarrative of American freedom evokes is a street game, and from their respective efforts to remain true to the past—Lincoln's reenactment of a presidential assassination, the constancy of Booth's hope that history will be set aright if he can learn to throw the cards well—comes only violence. The actor Jeffrey Wright, who performed the role of Lincoln in the play's initial New York runs, has posed the critical question: "The play is perched on top of an historical inevitability. Suzan talks about it as an existential question. At the end of the play, is their destiny fulfilled, or were they supposed to do something different and they missed?"[34] Put in more national terms, we might ask, Is Lincoln's legacy of unity and resentment America's destiny, and violence its inevitable fulfillment? Or is there another course that might be taken, one that addresses the past without reenacting it by imagining the nation's future differently? The play does not offer solutions, but by placing race at the center of the drama, by treating the historical legacy of a white republic as a con game equally for those who reject the rules and for those who strive to fulfill them, it demands nonetheless that Americans grapple with the question of their inheritance.

For her part, Parks put it somewhat differently, discussing the pull of the Civil War president on her own imagination and on the national imagination more generally: "It's like Lincoln created an opening with that hole in his head. We've all passed through it into now, you know, like the eye of a needle. Everything that happens, from 1865 to today, has to pass through that wound."[35] This notion of having to "pass through" Lincoln's wound is worth pausing over, for it suggests at least two possibilities. First, it points to the significance of Lincoln's legacy in contemporary America: the past is an inescapable component of the present, it exerts force in and through the present, and Americans cannot survive if they remain oblivious to its enduring power. Yet the effort—the activity—required to "pass through" Lincoln's wound might also be construed as pointing to the transformative potential of the past, to the opportunities posed in and by the present of inhabiting the past(s) differently. In *Topdog/Underdog*, both brothers are caught up in and reenact different aspects of Abraham Lincoln's legacy, and neither survives the experience. To be sure, this tragedy will not save Americans any more than it saves Parks's characters. But it might enable them to acknowledge the pull that the past exerts upon them, its capacity to shape them in its image, and perhaps to break its hold. The tragedy of Lincoln's legacy is the opening through which all Americans must pass, but it also might be the occasion for reimagining, rewriting, and reembodying the racialized republic.

Notes

Epigraphs: William Lee Miller, *Lincoln's Virtues: An Ethical Biography* (New York: Alfred A. Knopf, 2002), xi; Lerone Bennett Jr., *Forced Into Glory: Abraham Lincoln's White Dream* (Chicago: Johnson Publishing, 2000), ix; Suzan-Lori Parks, *Topdog/Underdog* (New York: Theatre Communications Group, 2002), 52. Parks's line is spoken by the brother named Lincoln. Because Parks's departures from standard English are deliberate, I will not follow the convention of acknowledging misspellings, "[*sic*]," as I quote from her work.

1. The hybrid variant is developed in James Oakes, *The Radical and the Republican: Frederick Douglass, Abraham Lincoln, and the Triumph of Antislavery Politics* (New York: W. W. Norton, 2007).

2. See, for example, William Lloyd Garrison, "The Great Crisis," *The Liberator*, December 29, 1832.

3. Dwight G. Anderson, *Abraham Lincoln: The Quest for Immortality* (New York: Alfred A. Knopf, 1982), 199.

4. "Farewell Address," *The Writings of George Washington*, ed. John C. Fitzpatrick (Washington: United States Government Printing Office, 1940), 35:223.

5. "Address Before the Young Men's Lyceum of Springfield, Illinois," *The Collected Works of Abraham Lincoln*, ed. Roy P. Basler et al. (New Brunswick: Rutgers University Press, 1959), 1:111, 112. All further quotations from Lincoln are taken from this collection, abbreviated hereafter as *Collected Works*. Lincoln alludes here to two recent mob actions: first to the lynching of an African American man in St. Louis, and second to the lynching of the abolitionist Elijah Lovejoy, the editor of the *Alton Observer* (Illinois), whose editorial condemnation of the St. Louis lynch mob turned the mob's attention on himself. For further detail, see Miller, *Lincoln's Virtues*, 129–39.

6. "Speech in the United States House of Representatives on the Mexican War," *Collected Works*, 1:438, 439.

7. Anderson, *Abraham Lincoln*, 7.

8. "Speech at Springfield, Illinois," *Collected Works*, 2:519–20.

9. For more on the racial dimensions of Jefferson's imagination of the American nation, see Catherine A. Holland, *The Body Politic: Foundings, Citizenship, and Difference in the American Political Imagination* (New York: Routledge, 2001); also, Catherine A. Holland, "Notes on the State of America: Jeffersonian Democracy and the Production of a National Past," *Political Theory* 29, no. 2 (April 2001): 190–216.

10. "Speech at Chicago, Illinois," *Collected Works*, 2:498.

11. "First Debate with Stephen A. Douglas at Ottawa, Illinois," *Collected Works*, 3:16. See also Lincoln's eulogy of the Declaration delivered in his "Speech at Lewistown, Illinois," *Collected Works*, 2:546–47.

12. "Address at Cooper Institute, New York City," *Collected Works*, 3:537, 541.

13. 12 Stat. 617.

14. 12 Stat. 1264.

15. Gideon Welles, "The History of Emancipation," *The Galaxy* 14 (December 1872): 842–43.

16. 12 Stat. 1268.

17. "Address on Colonization to a Deputation of Negroes," *Collected Works*, 5:372.

18. For a complete account, see F. B. Carpenter, *Six Months at the White House with Abraham Lincoln: The Story of a Picture* (New York: Hurd and Houghton, 1866). The brief passage quoted here appears on 20.

19. Ibid., 51–52.

20. William Shakespeare, *Hamlet*, act 3, sec. 3, lines 36–56 *passim*.

21. Helen Bacon, "Aeschylus," in *Ancient Writers*, vol. 1, ed. T. James Luce (New York: Charles Scribner, 1982), 108.

22. Shelby Foote, *The Civil War: A Narrative* (Alexandria, Va.: Time-Life Books, 1998); James M. McPherson, *Battle Cry of Freedom: The Civil War Era* (New York: Ballantine Books, 1988); Charles Frazier, *Cold Mountain* (New York: Atlantic Monthly Press, 1997).

23. Mary Delach Leonard, "The Civil War: A Blood Feud We Can't Get Out of Our Blood," *St. Louis Post-Dispatch*, March 12, 2003, E1; "Playing at War: Re-enactors Head to Roaring Camp," *Marin Independent Journal*, May 15, 2003.

24. Anne E. Kornblut, "Bush Attempts to Sidestep S.C. Racial Politics: No Stand on Confederate Flag," *Boston Globe*, January 13, 2000, A1.

25. Catherine Watson, "Civil War Is the Most Popular in an Ever-Growing Hobby," *Minneapolis Star-Tribune*, August 31, 2003, 8G.

26. Quoted in David Herbert Donald, *Lincoln Reconsidered: Essays on the Civil War Era* (New York: Vintage, 2001), 18.

27. See Herbert Mitgang, "The Art of Lincoln," *American Art Journal* 2, no. 1 (1970): esp. 5–8.

28. Suzan-Lori Parks, *The America Play and Other Works* (New York: Theatre Communications Group, 1995), 158.

29. Suzan-Lori Parks, *The America Play*, 164.

30. Suzan-Lori Parks, *Topdog/Underdog*, 53.

31. Ibid., 10.

32. Ibid., 110.

33. Ibid., 22.

34. Quoted in Don Shewey, "This Time the Shock Is Her Turn Toward Naturalism," *New York Times*, July 22, 2001, sec, 2, 1.

35. Quoted in Joshua Wolf Shenk, "Beyond a Black-and-Lincoln," *New York Times*, April 7, 2002, sec. 2, 5.

Sarah Winnemucca and the Rewriting of Nation

In the first chapter of Sarah Winnemucca's *Life Among the Piutes: Their Wrongs and Claims* (1883), the author's grandfather Truckee tells his community that the Paiutes were originally composed of two dark and two white children. When a vicious quarrel ensued between them, their parents insisted that they separate. Truckee claims that the whites who arrive in the area during the 1840s are the returning descendants of these white brothers, and so their appearance is cause for celebration: "'My white brothers,—my long-looked-for white brothers have come at last!'"[1]

Given the dynamic nature of origin stories, it is not surprising that Winnemucca's grandfather, especially when faced with the arrival of an unknown people, modified Northern Paiute stories to explain the whites' appearance. In this essay I present *Life Among the Piutes* as an alternative origin story of the United States: one that departs from both the conventional Anglo-American narrative of the republic and the myth of the vanishing Indian. In retelling her grandfather's story, Winnemucca (fig. 1) at once preserves his vision and exposes its limitations. Presenting her grandfather's enduring loyalty to the whites and her more cautious response to them, Winnemucca offers a kind of multigenerational narrative of America that challenges those that are more frequently told.[2] Neither entirely idealistic nor defeatist, her narrative is an important retelling of America's national origins.

As one of the first American Indian writers to be published, Winnemucca was a pivotal figure of national narration in the 1800s and continues to be so today. In the second half of the nineteenth century she was involved with Anglo-Indian negotiations, policy, and warfare; at the beginning of the twenty-first century her likeness was chosen for one of the two statues to represent Nevada in the nation's Capitol.[3] Her interventions in Anglo-American narratives of the United States are a crucial site for the consideration of alternatives to America's traditional origin story, in which a group

FIGURE 1 Sarah Winnemucca
(1844–91). Nevada Historical Society.

of oppressed Europeans find a new home and purpose in "enlightening" the "savages" of the so-called New World.

What would it mean for scholars of American studies to take seriously this vision of siblings reunited after an initial conflict? Or to imagine the Americas as land owned by Indians, with "white children" returning not for the intended joyous reunion but for an unlawful seizure of that land? How does the template of the family change conventional Anglo interpretations of the American republic—and what it means to be American?[4] *Life Among the Piutes* offers a complex reinterpretation of race, so that *white*, *civilized*, and *citizens* signify savagery and broken promises. In turn, the familial rhetoric of her grandfather's origin story is a means of critiquing whites'—and the U.S. government's—failure to live up to certain kinship responsibilities implicit in this particular Paiute origin story.[5]

CARI M. CARPENTER   113

In a blistering account of the United States, Winnemucca speaks directly to the white reader, both drawing from and revising her grandfather's origin story:

Oh, for shame! You who are educated by a Christian government in the art of war; the practice of whose profession makes you natural enemies of the savages, so called by you. Yes, you, who call yourselves the great civilization; you who have knelt upon Plymouth Rock, covenanting with God to make this land the home of the free and the brave. Ah, then you rise from your bended knees and seizing the welcoming hands of those who are owners of this land, which you are not, your carbines rise upon the bleak shore, and your so-called civilization sweeps inland from the ocean wave; but, oh, my God! leaving its pathway marked by crimson lines of blood, and strewed by the bones of two races, the inheritor and the invader; and I am crying out to you for justice,—yes, pleading for the far-off plains of the West, for the dusky mourner, whose tears of love are pleading for her husband, or for their children, who are sent far away from them. Your Christian minister will hold my people against their will; not because he loves them,—no, far from it,—but because it puts money in his pockets. (207)

Here Winnemucca incorporates the very words Anglo Americans use to articulate their Americanness in order to expose the hypocrisy of this vision: "Plymouth Rock" and "home of the free and the brave" are included to show how far removed these "citizens" are from such lofty ideals. The familial language of her grandfather's narrative remains, but this time it is used to mark the difference between the "civilized" invader who is motivated not by kinship but by monetary reward, and the rightful "inheritor" who grieves for her spouse and children. The inheritor—the lawful owner—is a Northern Paiute; the invader is the returning, disobedient (and perhaps disowned) sibling. Winnemucca's use of shame is reminiscent of Truckee's origin story, in which the father asks his children before separating them, " 'Why are you so cruel to each other?' " (7). The children hang their heads: " 'They were ashamed' " (7). In shaming the white reader, Winnemucca mobilizes an emotion that is closely linked to a sense of moral obligation and a desire for others' approval. As a consequence, the reader is implicated in a complex network of familial responsibilities. Citizenship is in turn reformulated as the reward of membership that is attained not through one's skin color or language, but one's goodness to others.

....

Winnemucca heard her grandfather's version of the origin story as a young girl, when white men, seeking land and gold, began to enter Northern Paiute territory. Born around 1844, she spent her childhood among the Northern Paiutes—the Numa, as they call themselves—in the arid stretch of the Great Basin now known as Nevada. As a member of the Cui-ui Eaters, a band named after an ancient fish in Pyramid Lake, Winnemucca grew up in a nomadic community that depended on hunting, gathering of pine nuts, and fishing. Her mother, Tuboitony, was the daughter of Truckee, a distinguished Paiute leader, and Sarah's father was often referred to as Chief Winnemucca.

Around the age of twelve, when Winnemucca worked as a housekeeper and companion for various white families, she became fluent in both Spanish and English. Returning to Pyramid Lake in 1866, she discovered that because she could speak and write English she was expected to serve as a go-between for the white and Paiute communities, which were increasingly at odds. Upon her arrival, military officials asked her to urge her father to bring his people to the reservation. As an interpreter for the military and the white agents who ran the reservations, Winnemucca was one of the few Paiutes who could support herself financially in a time when tribes were increasingly exploited by whites. But the position of translator came with certain disadvantages: as a mediator between whites and Paiutes, she was vulnerable to accusations of betrayal from either side. Her relationship to the familial narrative of the nation, then, was all the more charged.

Voicing mixed feelings about her grandfather's relationship to the whites, Winnemucca seems to share his surprised disappointment in them at the same time that she suggests his optimism is naïve. As she notes, "But he was disappointed, poor dear old soul!" (6). Winnemucca portrays her grandfather, and his version of this origin story, as well meaning but ultimately misguided. Yet in the following paragraph she notes that she can "imagine his feelings, for I have drank [*sic*] deeply from the same cup" (6). In this sense she both identifies with her grandfather's worldview and distinguishes it from her own. In pronouncing, "How good of him to try and heal the wound, and how vain were his efforts!" Winnemucca leaves it rather unclear whether she is critiquing his unrealistic optimism or the whites' disregard of their familial obligations to American Indians (7). Truckee affirms his commitment to the whites on his deathbed, when he makes a white man promise that he will send Sarah and her sister to live briefly with a white family in California. In this sense, he continues the kinship vision of his origin story, placing his grandchildren in the custody of white "caretakers."

Truckee's story—or, more accurately, Sarah Winnemucca's version of it—both adopts and revises other Paiute origin stories that tell of antagonistic siblings who are ultimately separated. Many of the alternative versions focus not on "dark" and "white" brothers (a distinction that seems particularly tied to Anglo conceptions of race as skin color) but on figures who go on to create other tribes. Nellie Shaw Harnar (who, incidentally, questions the preeminence of the Winnemucca family in Northern Paiute history) tells of a quarrelsome brother who is sent to California, where he engenders the Pitt River Indians. Another brother goes to Owen's Valley, creating the Southern Paiutes, or Pe tah neh quad. According to this narrative, Salt Lake was formed from the tears of the Stone Mother who was left behind.[6] John Wesley Powell, who collected ethnographic information about the Northern Paiutes in the second half of the nineteenth century, records a story of Pi-aish, who married a woman named Pa-ha. Their two sons began to fight so much that Pi-aish caused a great fog to settle over the land, separating the boys forever. Later, when Pi-aish felt the land was overpopulated, he caused another fog so that people were lost and scattered "and all the world was settled."[7] Another story, "The Tracks of the Creator," tells of the father Gray Wolf (Nümüna), who sends his quarreling children away.[8] Similarly, "The Creation of the Indians" describes four children who fight until their father pricks each in the leg and sends them in different directions. Upon the death of the parents and children, they reunite. That is, the story claims, "how the Indians started."[9] In many of these narratives others are regarded not as aliens but as long-lost relatives who one day may return.

The origin story related in *Life Among the Piutes* is also linked to Northern Paiute tales of the cannibal Nümüzo´ho, a figure who represents the nation's ability to incorporate potentially destructive elements for its benefit. These stories describe his decimations of the community and its eventual resolve to destroy him. Forging a dramatic victory over the famous cannibalist, Eagle, Owl, and Badger roast him in a pit: "When he was cooked, they took him out; when those Cannibals were tender, they took them out. They cleaned their teeth. They took out the meat they had been eating. Coyote cleaned their teeth. He made people alive again from the meat he took from their teeth."[10] In a powerful reversal, it is the cannibal who is eaten—and who therefore sustains the community. Reminiscent of Leslie Marmon Silko's contemporary novel *Ceremony*, these narratives are empowering in that they present the destructive force as something created by, and under the power of, an American Indian community.

In each of these stories, the whites' (mis)behavior is explained and dealt with in Paiute terms. The story "White Men Are Snakes" declares that Anglos engage in disreputable actions because they were once snakes: "That's why the white people took everything away from the Indian; because they were snakes. If that snake hadn't been on the tree, everything would have belonged to the Indian. Just because they were snakes and came here, the white people took everything away. They asked these Indians where they had come from. That's why they took everything and told the Indians to go way out in the mountains and live."[11] Most poignantly, "The True Beginning of the Earth" speculates that the whites act as they do, upsetting the natural order of things, because they "don't know about the beginning of this earth."[12] The Indian speaker's fear of the whites is thus based on the whites' ignorance rather than on their superiority.[13]

Winnemucca's rhetoric is all the more compelling in that it frames whites' actions as a disappointment to her grandfather. When she recounts her childhood fears that whites would eat her, thus reversing the usual native-as-cannibal motif, she declares, "Oh, can any one imagine my feelings *buried alive*, thinking every minute that I was to be unburied and eaten up by the people that my grandfather loved so much?" (12). Two taboos at the heart of culture—cannibalism and incest—converge as Winnemucca, describing the whites as family members, shares the horrifying image of eating one's own relatives. This interpretation works on two levels, suggesting her bifurcated audience: it is both an indication to whites of their barbarity and, in borrowing from the cannibalism theme of origin stories, a Paiute-centered take on this encounter.

It is tempting to read Winnemucca's term "Great Father" in reference to the president of the United States as a disturbing one that reinforces the paternalism with which whites treated American Indians in the nineteenth century. Yet if we examine this and other familial terms through the lens of Winnemucca's revision of her grandfather's origin story, it becomes possible to see them as her means of critiquing whites' misconduct and, accordingly, their violation of this familial/national narrative. As Winnemucca states, "We call all good people father or mother; no matter who it is,— negro, white man, or Indian, and the same with the women" (39). By honoring familial obligations, one earns authority and respect. Her words echo Truckee's origin story: "[The father] said to them, 'Have I not been kind to you all, and given you everything your hearts wished for? You do not have to hunt and kill your own game to live upon. You see, my dear children, I have the power to call whatsoever kind of game we want to eat; and I also have the power to separate my dear children, if they are not good to each other'" (7). Someone like Samuel Parrish, the agent of Malheur Reservation whom the Paiutes come to trust and admire for his fair dealings with them, is described as "our Father." The term "my children," which Parrish uses to refer to Paiutes on the reservation, may in fact be Winnemucca's version of his words rather than those he actually said; that is, she might have inserted them into her retelling of his speech in order to honor his membership in their community (106). On the other hand, Parrish could have used this phrase to indicate his understanding of and respect for the Paiutes' conception of nationhood. Likewise, Winnemucca's description of herself as "mother" can be read as her assertion of authority: as she declares at one point, "'Tell [the Northern Paiutes] I, their mother, say come back to their homes again'" (182). To regard such terms as titles of honor bestowed upon those whites who live up to their obligations (and so are recognized as members of a familial community) requires, of course, acknowledging Native Americans' agency and self-definition rather than focusing on how they were viewed by whites.

Winnemucca also rewrites racial language so that a word like *white* refers not to skin color but to one's betrayal of family or, by extension, one's nation. In this sense, Winnemucca distinguishes the soldiers, whom she generally finds more trustworthy than other colonists, from whites: "Brother and my people always say 'the white people,' just as if the soldiers were not white, too" (86). This distinction allows her to maintain a sense of family that is based not exclusively on genetic or biological factors but on an individual's fulfillment of certain moral obligations. In being good, a white person loses his whiteness in some sense and is honored as a member of the Paiute family and nation. In contrast, she describes a cruel Anglo woman as white: "Dear reader, this is the kind of white women that are in the West. They are always ready to condemn me" (168). Directing her words to a white woman reader, Winnemucca presents her with the opportunity—and the challenge—to prove her goodness and, accordingly, her departure from these "white women." The powerful position of whiteness is framed as what the reader (if she is indeed "dear" and "good") is *not*: a striking rhetorical move that challenges and denaturalizes Anglo-American racial hierarchies. American Indians themselves aren't necessarily admirable in Winnemucca's account: she distinguishes between those who are "good," the "hostiles," and, sarcastically, "the civilized." Particularly shameful are Egan and Oytes, who betray their Indian communities and in so doing enact a certain whiteness.

This parallel between whiteness and the betrayal of one's family is further evident in Winnemucca's petitions, some of which are included in *Life Among the Piutes*. As one petition to Congress states, "And especially do we petition for the return of that portion of the tribe arbitrarily removed from the Malheur Reservation, after the Bannock war, to the Yakima Reservation on Columbia River, in which removal families were ruthlessly separated, and have never ceased to pine for husbands, wives, and children, which restoration was pledged to them by the Secretary of the Interior in 1880, but has not been fulfilled" (247). The U.S. government's policies are thus described as violations of American Indian families. Again, whites are reprimanded for their failure to honor the familial agreement among Native Americans and between Indians and Anglos. In similar terms Winnemucca ultimately appeals to President Rutherford B. Hayes, calling on him as a "'husband and father'" to consider the horror of being forcibly separated from his wife and children (246). Reframing the U.S. president in terms of his familial status rather than his political position, Winnemucca suggests that he and the American Indians are equals: both would be devastated if they were separated from their family members. The image of familial separation she presents in the petition also serves as a sharp contrast to that of her grandfather's origin story, in which separation is a justified punishment for wrongdoing. In the case of the Malheur Reservation, the U.S. government, acting unlawfully as the father, divides families for no good reason.

This centering on the Northern Paiute family is particularly poignant in Winnemucca's chapter "Domestic and Social Moralities," which can be read as a kind of conduct manual. Winnemucca makes clear throughout the chapter that the Paiutes embrace a lifestyle whites could learn from. The chapter begins with the assertion, "Our children are very carefully taught to be good" (45). They learn immoral habits like swearing not only from each other but from whites. It is difficult not to hear the sarcasm in the following comparisons between whites and Northern Paiutes: "We don't need to be taught to love our fathers and mothers," she declares, implying that whites, on the other hand, do (45). When she later asserts, "It is always the whites that begin the wars," Winnemucca holds whites responsible for violating the peaceful reunion (51). Marshalling such evidence of the Paiutes' morality, Winnemucca uses it to bolster their nation: "We have a republic as well as you. The council-tent is our Congress, and anybody can speak who has anything to say, women and all" (53). Here the conventional use of sentimental language as a means for the civilized whites to educate the savage Indian is reversed; the Paiute family—and nation—is equal to that of the white reader. Just as the family she envisions is strengthened, so too is her republic, a word that to an Anglo-American reader would have connoted a virtuous, egalitarian political unit. Winnemucca goes so far as to suggest that the Northern Paiute republic is even more egalitarian than the United States, for "anybody can speak . . . women and all."

While I am uncomfortable with any neat distinction between Anglo and Indian conceptions of family—those, for example, that would see Anglos as strictly exclusionary and Indians as entirely tolerant of difference—it is important to acknowledge a difference between how Winnemucca is evoking family and how she believes it is envisioned by her opponents. Consider the following passage:

> Alas, how truly our women prophesied when they told my dear old grandfather that his white brothers, whom he loved so much, had brought sorrow to his people. Their hearts told them the truth. My people are ignorant of worldly knowledge, but they know what love means and what truth means. They have seen their dear ones perish around them because their white brothers have given them neither love nor truth. Are not love and truth better than learning? My people have no learning. They do not know anything about the history

of the world, but they can see the Spirit-Father in everything. The beautiful world talks to them of their Spirit-Father. They are innocent and simple, but they are brave and will not be imposed upon. They are patient, but they know black is not white. (258–59)

Winnemucca strategically portrays her people in terms of a firm distinction with which the nineteenth-century white reader would be familiar: the allegedly unlearned Indian versus the educated white person. The last two sentences, however, complicate this distinction: the Northern Paiutes "are brave and will not be imposed upon . . . they know black is not white." Recast in familial terms, relations between whites and Paiutes are marked by Anglo neglect of their kinship responsibilities. Winnemucca thus severs goodness, whiteness, and learning—concepts intricately linked in conventional sentimentality—to assert the Paiutes' dignity. Without (familial) love, she claims, there is no truth. And so the all-knowing Anglos are reduced to ignorance.

....

With its focus on the issues of familial loyalty and betrayal, *Life Among the Piutes* can be read not only as an alternative origin story of the United States, but also as a direct challenge to the myth of the inevitable disappearance of the Indian. The putative vanishing of American Indians, a common narrative in the nineteenth-century United States, is reminiscent of that of the "successful translator" whom Lawrence Venuti describes in *The Translator's Invisibility*: one who becomes invisible in the process of translation: "The translator remains subordinate to the author of the original work . . . the originality of translation lies in self-effacement, a vanishing act, and it is on this basis that translators prefer to be praised."[14] Venuti's descriptions of translation as it exists within contemporary Anglo-American culture are reminiscent of colonization: he describes it in terms of "intervention," "uniformity," "identification," "weird self-annihilation," "marginal status," "ambiguous legal definition," "imbalance," "exploitation," "domesticating revision," and "ethnocentric violence."[15] This juxtaposition of the colonizing project and "inevitable" violence in translation makes me uneasy because of the prominent myth of the colonization of the Americas as inevitable and thus somehow justified.[16] But Venuti's project, which is "to make the translator more visible," is one that antiracist and anticolonialist forces can surely embrace. Indeed, if the "vanishing Indian" has particular resonance with the "vanishing translator," the Indian who refuses to disappear must be equally compelling.

If the translator's goal is to be as invisible as possible, Winnemucca—as an interpreter—existed in tension with an origin story that keeps Northern Paiutes at the center. Yet she manages to refuse the disappearance expected of the translator/Indian. In one intriguing scene, she reads a letter that she is asked to transmit from a corrupt agent to another white man. Although she acknowledges that reading the letter is a "wicked thing," she delights in it, for it validates her suspicion of the agent's corruption (135). By keeping the letter, she intervenes in this transaction—insisting on her presence. In this role, Winnemucca has a rare ability to produce meaning for white and Paiute audiences—and for the readers of her self-narrative, all of whom are dependent upon her translation. Instead of disappearing in the process of linguistic exchange, Winnemucca asserts herself as an interpreter and as an American Indian; to borrow Venuti's terms, she refuses linguistic self-annihilation.[17]

The Paiutes' complicated relationship to the English language is embodied in Truckee's "white rag friend," a letter written by General John Charles Frémont, an early white explorer of the area. The letter commends Truckee's performance in the Mexican-American War. His amiable relations with whites are evident in the name Frémont gives him: "Captain Truckee." According to Winnemucca, this word signifies "all right" or "very well" in her language (9). Truckee believes that the power of the letter rests in its ability to speak: " 'This is my friend. . . . Does it look as if it could talk and ask for anything? Yet it does. It can ask for something to eat for me and my people' " (43). For Truckee, the note is not simply a symbol of their friendship; it is an object so valuable that he insists on being buried with it. As he tells the Paiutes, " 'Just as long as I live and have that paper which my white brothers' great chieftain has given me, I shall stand by them, come what will. . . . Oh, if I should lose this, . . . we shall all be lost' " (22). His sense that he and the other Paiutes will be lost without this English message suggests their dependence on it. Indeed, the English words are so powerful that he fears they speak too much, that they have a voice of their own. When a group of Mexicans who are enemies of the whites visit his camp, he remarks, " 'I am not going to show them my rag friend, for fear my rag friend will tell of me'" (28). Although the paper allows him to travel through white territory and acquire food, it also has the potential to deceive him by speaking in his place. The paper, which Truckee kisses "as if it was really a person," thus becomes another figure of white betrayal (22). One could argue that in the act of presenting the letter, Truckee becomes the successful—and thus annihilated—translator, for he has transmitted this message from one white man to another without intervening in it.

Yet it would be too simplistic to argue that Truckee is entirely effaced by the white rag friend, for it carries with it a history of his relations with whites and a record of his service in the Mexican War. Indeed, the letter is powerless without Truckee's wise management of its distribution. He also intervenes in this transmission of meaning by insisting that it be interred with him. In other words, he takes it out of circulation, claiming it as his own. As Gillian Brown argues in another context, "As this extension of the proprietor into his or her valued articles, property reflects and represents the individual; as emblems of their owner, cherished things ratify the individual sovereignty of their proprietors."[18] Likewise, rather than eradicating Truckee, the paper attests to his personhood.

Aware that her position as an interpreter places her in danger of either being betrayed or being seen as a betrayer, Winnemucca distinguishes herself from interpreters like the "half-breeds," who are willing to say anything for the right price (91). Some of these half-breed traitors are her relatives and so enact a very personal, familial betrayal: "I am sorry to say these Indian interpreters, who are often half-breeds, easily get corrupted, and can be hired by the agents to do or say anything" (91). According to her, those who occupy this intermediary position between whites and Paiutes lack the desire or even the ability to determine what they will and will not say; transmitting commands from whites to the Paiutes, they are the conduit of colonial control—and, accordingly, betrayers of the family. Conscious of her own intermediary position, Winnemucca tries to imagine a space in which she is not simply a voice box for her Anglo-American employers, a space where she can evaluate and manipulate the language she speaks. Winnemucca experiences an increasing tension between being loyal to her white employers and speaking her own voice. She is careful to account for and condemn the one occasion when she accepted money for a deceptive purpose: to help whites move her people to the Malheur Reservation.

Recounting her motivation, she remembers thinking, "'[White people] make money any way and every way they can. Why not I? I have not any. I will take it.' So I did, for which I have been sorry ever since,—many times" (217). Once again, whiteness is defined in terms not only of individual greed but of the betrayal of one's community.

A later scene indicates the degree to which whites coerced Winnemucca into speaking (or, in this case, not speaking in a particular way) as well as her struggle to resist that coercion. When an Anglo-American agent declares he will pay her only if she does not communicate the contents of a letter from the U.S. government to the Northern Paiutes, she responds, "I did not promise, and went away. I did not say anything for five or six days" (235). Silence, perhaps the most effective form of resistance a translator can exert, has the potential to mark her complicity with the corrupt agent or, on the other hand, to excuse her from participating in this exchange.

It is as a spokesperson for whites that Sarah Winnemucca both endangers and ultimately secures her familial—and national—loyalty. Her salary as an interpreter for whites, for example, helped finance her lectures on the government's exploitation of the Paiutes. After having served as an interpreter for various white men, Winnemucca began to lecture on the East Coast. Her visit culminated in a meeting with President Hayes in 1880. During Winnemucca's stay, her right to deliver speeches is challenged by several government officials, one of whom tells her not to lecture. He refuses to allow her to speak with the reporters—to "talk on" some of the most powerful papers in existence. Knowing that her every word is being scrutinized, Winnemucca makes sure the officials are in hearing distance when she informs her father and brother of her plans to lecture—just to make the government representatives angry.

When the Paiutes ultimately accuse Winnemucca of betraying them for failing to read the letter she received from the president, her response poignantly illustrates her commitment to the familial model of Truckee's origin story. Standing before the group, she holds the paper over her head in a defiant gesture, declaring, "'I have suffered everything but death to come here with this paper. I don't know whether it speaks truth or not. You can say what you like about me. You have a right to say I have sold you. It looks so. I have told you many things which are not my own words, but the words of the agents and the soldiers. I know I have told you more lies than I have hair on my head. I tell you, my dear children, I have never told you my own words; they were the words of the white people, not mine.' " (236) Her remarks provoke several questions. To what degree does Winnemucca's admission that her words are the whites' lies and false promises compromise the credibility of her own speaking voice? Does her entire narrative then become a medium for white discourse? Is there no space outside of white discourse—white subjectivity—from which she can speak?

If the successful translator eradicates his or her own existence by perfectly reproducing the original, the resistant translator produces a text that is not an exact copy. In Venuti's words, "By producing the illusion of transparency, a fluent translation masquerades as true semantic equivalence when it in fact inscribes the foreign text with a partial interpretation, partial to English-language values, reducing if not simply excluding the very difference that translation is called on to convey."[19] Winnemucca accomplishes the kind of resistance Venuti calls for by reminding the Northern Paiutes of her role in the translation. As she tells her community, "It is not my own making up; it came right from him, and I will read it just as it is, so that you can all judge for yourselves" (236). She thus inserts a distinction between her "own words" and "the words of the white people," making her own position visible. In the final sentence, she returns authority to the Paiutes, declaring that now they are aware of the duplicity of the whites' language, they can judge it for themselves. Her speech has a powerful effect on her audience, who begs her forgiveness for having accused her of lying. By translating whites' words but at the same time pointing out the distinction between these words and her own, she demonstrates the failed repetition: the (literal) white lie. While she translates the message as it is written, she shows that the whites' words do not mean what they say, thus exposing the falsity of the original text.

Although Noreen Lape maintains that Winnemucca "cannot disengage herself from the false language forced upon her by the White government," I contend that she effectively intervenes in the translation, refusing—like the narrative itself—to be effaced.[20] Throughout the narrative, Winnemucca reminds the reader that her speech is prompted not only by her white employers, but also by the Paiutes' requests that she speak to the U.S. government on their behalf. As she recalls, "Very late in the fall my people came again . . . and once more they asked me to talk for them. I then told them I would do what I could" (139). She echoes this sentiment a few pages later: "Then they all asked me if I would go if they would give me the money to go with. I told them I would only be too happy to do all I could in their behalf, if they wanted me to" (146). Since her authority within the Northern Paiute community is jeopardized the moment she is suspected of not speaking for her people, she regains this authority by declaring, "I have said everything I could in your behalf, so did father and brother" (236). As the returning family member, Sarah Winnemucca pledges her fidelity to this family, to this nation, and to the origin story itself. Imperfect translation thus becomes a means for her to write her own loyalty and, accordingly, her (and their) survival.

Notes

1. Sarah Winnemucca Hopkins, *Life Among the Piutes: Their Wrongs and Claims* (1883; reprint, Reno: University of Nevada Press, 1994), 5. "Piutes" is a misspelling in the original edition; the proper spelling is *Paiute*. Although Hopkins, the name of Winnemucca's last husband, is included in the original edition, I follow most critics in referring to her simply as Sarah Winnemucca. As a child she was known as Thocmetony.

2. Although Penelope Kelsey also sees Winnemucca's narrative as a testament to indigenous nationhood, she reads it specifically as an instance of Native American literature's "continual exclusion from the writing of—and about—the American Renaissance." See Kelsey, "Natives, Nation, Narration: Reading Roanoke in the Renaissance," *ESQ* 49, nos. 1–3 (2003): 152–53.

3. In March 2001, the Nevada legislature passed a bill in support of the Sarah Winnemucca statue. The artist Benjamin Victor was chosen to design the bronze statue, and the Nevada Women's History Project raised the necessary funds. The statue was installed in the U.S. Capitol in March 2005.

4. Although *family* might seem limited as a political term, especially when aligned with *nation*, I would argue that it is only so within a cultural context that sees family units as biologically based, nuclear units: a conception rather incompatible with the Northern Paiute communities of Winnemucca's time.

5. Ethnologists have noted that Northern Paiutes in the precontact period formed bands on the basis of resource availability that could be dismantled and reformed with relative flexibility. Accordingly, leaders gained their positions through their ability to maintain the community's respect. As Martha C. Knack and Omer C. Stewart claim, "Theirs was a way of life rooted in the nature of the plants and animals of the land and in the small social groups which spent their entire lives together within the same circle of relatives and friends, a thinly populated world full of uncertainty, unpredictable food, and potential starvation. In response to this, the people had spread out over the land and developed a strong ethic of hospitality to visitors and kinsmen, no matter how distantly related nor how long unseen." See Knack and Stewart, *As Long as the River Shall Run: An Ethnohistory of Pyramid Lake Indian Reservation* (Berkeley: University of California Press, 1984), 28.

6. Nellie Shaw Harnar, *The History of the Pyramid Lake Indians 1843–1959 and Early Tribal History 1825–1834* (Sparks, Nev.: Dave's Printing and Publishing, 1974).

7. Quoted in D. D. Fowler and C. S. Fowler, eds., *Anthropology of the Numa: John Wesley Powell's Manuscripts on the Numic Peoples of Western North America, 1868–1880*, Smithsonian Contributions to Anthropology 14 (Washington: Smithsonian Institution Press, 1971), 221.

8. "The Tracks of the Creator," in *Coyote Was Going There: Indian Literature of the Oregon Country*, ed. Jarold Ramsey (Seattle: University of Washington Press, 1977), 231.

9. "The Creation of the Indians," in *Coyote Was Going There*, 236.

10. "Nümüzo´ho Plays Ball," in *Coyote Was Going There*, 250.

11. "White Men Are Snakes," in *Coyote Was Going There*, 258.

12. "The True Beginning of the Earth," in *Coyote Was Going There*, 259.

13. Given that many of the American Indian tales and origin stories in print are products of interactions between (usually white) ethnographers and American Indians of the nineteenth century and early twentieth, their sources must always be considered. I include these stories not as transparent accounts of Paiute beliefs but as documents that present myriad, multilayered reflections of the knowledge about particular American Indian communities that is created in specific cultural contexts. "The Tracks of the Creator" comes from an article by W. L. Marsden, a white man who lived near an Oregon Paiute community. The other stories appear in Isabel T. Kelly's "Northern Paiute Tales," which she compiled during the summer of 1930 while visiting several Paviotso (Northern Paiute) bands. See Kelly, "Northern Paiute Tales," *Journal of American Folklore* 51, no. 202 (Oct.–Dec. 1938): 363–437. For another account of origin stories that explains the arrival of the whites, see A. LaVonne Brown Ruoff, "Reversing the Gaze: Early Native American Images of Europeans and Euro-Americans," in *Native American Representations: First Encounters, Distorted Images, and Literary Appropriations*, ed. Gretchen M. Bataille (Lincoln: University of Nebraska Press, 2001), 198–223.

14. Lawrence Venuti, *The Translator's Invisibility: A History of Translation* (1995; reprint, London: Routledge, 2002), 4.

15. Ibid., 2–21.

16. Ibid., 19.

17. Ibid., 8.

18. See Gillian Brown, *Domestic Individualism: Imagining Self in Nineteenth-Century America* (Berkeley: University of California Press, 1990), 42. Granted, Brown goes on to argue that in the context of Harriet Beecher Stowe's *Uncle Tom's Cabin*, the personhood of Tom and other characters is limited by their slave status.

19. Venuti, *Translator's Invisibility*, 21.

20. Noreen Groover Lape, "'I would rather be with my people, but not to live with them as they live': Cultural Liminality and Double Consciousness in Sarah Winnemucca Hopkins's *Life Among the Piutes: Their Wrongs and Claims*," *American Indian Quarterly* 22 (Summer 1998): 266.

PATRICIA A. SCHECHTER

The Politics of the Possible

Ida B. Wells-Barnett's *Crusade for Justice*

Ida B. Wells-Barnett (1862–1931) became an international figure in Anglo-American reform and a celebrated heroine for African Americans through her courageous and outspoken leadership against lynching in the United States during the 1890s. Antilynching reform remains her best-remembered achievement, and the newspaper image of her from those years as the crusading Miss Ida B. Wells dominates her legacy today. This imprint, however, represents a mere fragment of Wells-Barnett's life and accomplishments. She achieved professional distinction as a journalist in the 1880s, founded and ran a social settlement, the Negro Fellowship League, in Chicago from 1910 to 1920, taught Sunday school for over thirty years, married and raised a family of four children, and even ran for elected office in 1930. Wells-Barnett's autobiography, *Crusade for Justice*, somewhat reinforces the idea that her work before 1900 against mob violence was the most important and exciting in her life, and most historians and popular commentators have followed suit. But in probing the text as a whole and situating the story it tells in its own shifting literary and media contexts, I reveal a rich and challenging portrait of black women's intellectual and social life. In so doing, I want in this essay to challenge the containment strategies that have silenced black women and undermined their work in American society.[1]

Crusade for Justice: The Autobiography of Ida B. Wells tells the story of how Wells-Barnett came to her antilynching calling, how she carried out that calling, and how she maintained the work in the face of increasing political isolation. Its drama of physical movement and personal transformation draws on themes found in American slave narratives and Christian conversion narratives. In a critical departure from these traditions, however, Wells-Barnett dispenses with the central organizing plots of both genres as developed by African American women, namely, finding freedom, finding God, and finding one's mother.[2] Although Wells-Barnett does not worry out loud about her soul or her mother in *Crusade for Justice*, the narrative takes on full meaning only in relationship to faith and to the legacy of slavery, especially to her slave mother, a set of concerns that weighed heavily on her and the women of her generation.

The autobiography divides roughly into three parts: birth, youth, and early womanhood in Mississippi and Tennessee (1862–92); travels in England and across the United States during the early antilynching campaign (1892–95); and her long, productive, if unevenly successful, years in Chicago (1895–1919). Rather than claim authority over slavery, the archetypal black experience of the nineteenth century, the preface to *Crusade for Justice* instead stakes out a special claim to the Reconstruction era, to "the facts of race history which only the participants can give" from the "time of storm" immediately after the Civil War.[3] As the story of this child of Reconstruction unfolds, it appears that her mother's legacy is assured and that her challenge is to find surrogate fathers.[4] In Wells-Barnett's case, orphanhood, marriage resistance, and personal notoriety created unusual possibilities and challenges for working out her destiny as a freedwoman. The lack of a living father created special burdens and uneasy opportunities in her life; self-naming and self-protection emerge as the key markers in her struggle for safety and security.

When Wells-Barnett wrote in the late 1920s, the freedwoman's story was not a full-blown literary convention. To articulate its complexity, she used at least three different narrative voices: testifying as Iola, speaking as Exiled, and reassessing as a parable teller.[5] These voices correspond to sections in *Crusade for Justice*. In the opening eight chapters, Wells-Barnett testifies to conditions in the South that led her to oppose lynching in the African American Christian tradition of personal witnessing. The second section—nearly half the book but covering barely three years of her life—describes her early antilynching work, especially her time in Great Britain, as a phase of exile from the South and the United States. In this middle section, the author's contemporary voice is literally exiled from the text, and the story is told largely through reprinted newspaper articles from the 1890s. Seven chapters and numerous inserts consist of reprinted letters, press clips, and travelogues written some thirty years earlier. This documentary, scrapbook approach suggests that Wells-Barnett's voice from the 1920s needed bolstering; the narrative's concluding chapters explain why. This final section describes her years in Chicago in moralistic parables of personal frustration, political betrayal, and only occasional success in which God or fate vindicates her efforts. Taken together, the voices of *Crusade for Justice* articulate a politics of the possible for African American womanhood between the end of Reconstruction and the beginning of the Great Depression, a path charted by an orphan who, in the mid-1880s, picked up a pen and renamed herself Iola.

Testifying

The drama of the narrative's first section turns on achieving control over language, personal reputation, and physical safety, issues of prime historical moment to postbellum African American women. These issues are linked to the legacy of slavery. The most vivid details of slavery concern the violent treatment of Wells-Barnett's female kin, specifically her mother and paternal grandmother. Her mother, Lizzie Warrenton Wells of Virginia, "used to tell us how she had been beaten by slave owners and the hard times she had as a slave."[6] Her father, Jim Wells of Mississippi, never forgave his former mistress for having "stripped and whipped" his slave mother in anger (Jim's father was his master). "I have never forgotten those words," wrote Wells-Barnett. "I cannot help but feel what an insight into slavery they give."[7] From this history of violence toward slave women and of women's resistance to physical and sexual assault, Wells-Barnett built her own story toward a powerful statement of identification for women of the next generation.[8]

When, in 1891, a minister of the African Methodist Episcopal (AME) church in Vicksburg, Mississippi, questioned Wells-Barnett's virtue, she confronted him to defend her name and her slave mother's memory: "I wanted him to know at least one southern girl, born and bred, who had tried to keep herself spotless and morally clean as my slave mother had taught me." In this act she not only defended herself but also "vindicated the honor of the many southern girls who had been traduced by lying tongues."[9] Like her slave mother's fertility and sexuality, a freedwoman's reputation was an intimate yet public matter over which she had limited control. *Crusade for Justice* also suggests that writing was a crucial means of self-defense and self-affirmation. The autobiography describes Wells-Barnett's writing for the newspaper the Memphis *Free Speech*, which was owned by African

Americans, as an outlet for her to "express the real 'me.'"[10] This "real 'me'" emerged under the pen name Iola. Pen names were fairly common among black women journalists of the period because they offered a shield against the prejudice so easily flung at them.

Capped by the confrontation with the Vicksburg minister, the first section of *Crusade for Justice* portrays the movement of a "southern girl, born and bred" from the shocks of childhood loss and the paralysis of sexual slander to the effective, wage-earning words of a mature adult. Wells-Barnett's private diary from her Memphis years reveals an added layer of this movement. Since women were not empowered to defend their sexual reputations, Wells-Barnett turned to God: "O my Father, forgive me, forgive me. Humble the pride exhibited [by her vow not to forget the slanders against her] and make me thy child."[11] The autobiography testifies less about God's saving grace or heaven-sent trials and more about public struggles and practical strategies for survival. Stressing the public spheres of press, court, and pulpit, *Crusade for Justice* is written to fire "race pride" in "our youth."[12] The diary records Wells-Barnett's private struggle with God; the narrative provides a survival guide for making freedom real for African Americans, particularly African American women.

Having established command over language and over her reputation, Wells-Barnett reaches the major turning point of the autobiography. The lynching of three black male shopkeepers in Memphis in March 1892 functions as a conversion experience. The event, Wells-Barnett wrote, "changed the whole course of my life."[13] The Memphis lynching sealed her turn to protest much as the hanging of the Haymarket anarchists in 1886 moved the young Emma Goldman to lifelong radicalism.[14] The event also advanced Wells-Barnett's thinking about lynching, confirming that the cry of rape of white women used to justify lynching was an excuse to "keep the race terrorized and 'keep the nigger down.'"[15] The triple lynching and subsequent attack on the *Free Speech* office for a critical editorial she wrote on lynching also prompted her to leave the South permanently. Finally, the lynching gave the aspiring writer in Ida B. Wells a story to tell.

Talking Through Tears

Telling the story of lynching outside the South posed another set of challenges for Wells-Barnett concerning personal reputation and the tenuous social status of unmarried black women. The middle section of *Crusade for Justice* highlights the moral support and funds Wells-Barnett received from African American women in the North as well as the guiding, fatherly protection delivered by the elder statesman among African Americans, Frederick Douglass. The delicate means by which she secured their support is symbolized in this section by scenes of talking through tears, tears that once immobilized her early in life. By talking through tears, Wells-Barnett carried out a demanding public performance while keeping femininity visibly in play before her audiences.

After denouncing lynching in the press in May 1892, Wells-Barnett left Tennessee for the relative safety of the North, first Philadelphia and then New York. She found a welcoming African American community in Brooklyn, whose organized women seemed particularly eager to adopt her and the cause of antilynching. The schoolteacher Maritcha Lyons and the journalist Victoria Earle Mathews likely saw in Wells-Barnett and the possibility of restarting *Free Speech* in the North a way to expand their ongoing community work, efforts which included public school desegregation and relief of needy children.[16] In the narrative's words, the members of women's clubs in New York, led by Lyons and Mathews, formed "a solid array behind a lonely, homesick girl who was an exile" for speaking out against lynching.[17] Wells-Barnett dedicated her first antilynching pamphlet, *Southern Horrors*, to the "Afro-American women of New York and Brooklyn." She cited their "race love, earnest zeal and unselfish effort," shown especially at a testimonial dinner for Wells-Barnett in October 1892 that raised the funds to pay for the pamphlet's publication.[18]

The testimonial, which attracted African American women from Boston and Philadelphia, blended gestures from religion, theater, and politics into a ritual naming ceremony and a great show. Wells-Barnett's name literally was in lights with *Iola* illuminated on the dais by gas jets. Down South, Wells-Barnett defended the name of "the many southern girls traduced by lying tongues." Up North, club women adopted her and the cause. In addition to cash, Wells-Barnett was presented with a "gold brooch in the shape of a pen, an emblem of my chosen profession" and a symbol of the power of words. The pin was inscribed with the word *Mizpah*, a place-name from the Hebrew bible meaning "lookout," christening her with a new identity and mission from scripture.[19]

Crusade for Justice identifies the Brooklyn testimonial as the occasion of Wells-Barnett's first "honest to goodness" address, a signal moment in her life. She cried during her presentation but, despite her "streaming face," she continued to speak with a steady voice. The narrative attributed her tears to feelings of "loneliness and homesickness" summoned by recounting the Memphis lynching and called these tears an uncharacteristic "exhibition" of "woman's weakness." "Whatever my feelings I am not given to public demonstrations," she said. For their part, the women in the audience assured Wells-Barnett that she had not "spoiled things" by the "breakdown." The tears, she reported, "made an impression. . . . *favorable to the cause and me.*"[20] A man in the audience, a relative of Douglass, told Wells she "could not have done anything more effective" than cry to win over that New York crowd.

Wells-Barnett's confession at this point—"I had no knowledge of stage business"—was not quite the case. In Memphis, she had performed public readings, organized and acted in a dramatic club, and even been scouted by New York talent agents. The northern press had already noted her ambition to be a "full-fledged journalist, a physician, or an actress."[21] Tears probably signaled that she felt comfortable to express emotion before African American audiences. The image of tears moving silently down her face as she continued her speech without interruption is rich with other meanings. Tears could be an intuitive, "natural" expression of right feminine feeling, proof of her status as female victim (and survivor) in her community. The image of Wells-Barnett talking through tears also conveys verbal competence hard-won and tested by faith. Tears were much more acceptable for a proper lady than anger or its cousin, sarcasm, for which she was also well known. And tears worked.

Talking through tears also captures the particularly fraught quality of middle-class black women's participation in the public sphere. *Crusade for Justice* highlights Douglass's role in this difficult task. Wells-Barnett and Douglass first crossed paths at lectures in Washington, D.C., in mid-1892, began a correspondence, and eventually collaborated on several projects. A letter of endorsement Wells-Barnett requested and received from Douglass became the preface to her pamphlet *Southern Horrors.* "Brave woman!" Douglass declared. "You give us what you know and testify from actual knowledge. You have dealt with the facts with cool, painstaking fidelity and left those naked and uncontradicted facts to speak for themselves."[22] In her role as critic, Wells-Barnett relied on Douglass to vouch for both her facts and her virtue, the status of one being inextricable from that of the other. Like the incident at Vicksburg when the minister questioned her virtue, she needed public verification by a reputable male figure in order to function in the public sphere.[23] British reformers directly prevailed upon Douglass for a public letter bearing "testimony to the character of Miss Wells and the truth of her statements" about lynching.[24] Wells-Barnett carried Douglass's letter around England and used it regularly, like a shield. For example, when an English reporter asked, "Do you really mean all that your article implies [about the South]?" Wells-Barnett responded, "Frederick Douglass knows that what I say is true" and handed the man the letter.[25] Douglass's letter bolstered her reputation, and club women shored up her spirit and finances, but neither could completely protect her from bodily harm. Back in New York, Wells-Barnett was assaulted on the Fulton Ferry in the summer of 1894 by a pair of white toughs who had heard "about the crusader and her alleged traducing of Southern women."[26]

No one in *Crusade for Justice* receives more appreciation than Douglass, whose death scene Wells-Barnett recounts in detail and whom she praises as "the greatest man that the Negro race ever produced on the American continent."[27] Wells-Barnett was in Kansas City when she learned of his passing in February 1895, and she wrote a letter of acknowledgment in the press. She stated, "It was to me the saddest hour of my life, save that when I knew I was an orphan, when I realized that not only the noblest man of our race was gone, but my best friend and strongest supporter . . . the blinding tears will not let me . . . narrate a tenth part of his personal goodness to me and his help to the cause."[28] Douglass's death was another occasion for talking through tears, for exhibiting strength amidst adversity, and for a public demonstration of feminine bona fides, in this case, the vocation of grieving. The letter claimed both a useful political genealogy and a unique emotional bond, linking private feeling with public service, religious duty with practical politics. That Douglass's death created a virtual second orphaning was scarcely an exaggeration. In the preceding three years, with the support of Douglass and black club women, Wells-Barnett accomplished the most creative and daring work of her life, work that would seal her reputation for the next century.

Exiled

The period between May 1892, when Wells-Barnett left Memphis, and June 1895, when she settled permanently in Chicago, receives more attention than any other in *Crusade for Justice*. Throughout the historical record, the events of these years, especially her British lecture tours, echo as the high point of her life. Her travel abroad involved two visits, in 1893 and 1894. Before her second trip, Wells-Barnett secured an opportunity to publish letters written from Britain in a widely read Chicago newspaper, the *Inter-Ocean*, and a series of these appears in the autobiography. As much as the letters, Wells-Barnett's pen name from this period, Exiled, expressed the peripatetic quality of her life and her experiment with the politics of the possible in the public sphere.

"Exiled" artfully revisioned historical subjectivity for southern freedwomen by linking their contemporary political dilemmas with the predicament of their African and enslaved foremothers, who also endured extreme dislocation and violence. Exiled-as-victim made for acceptably feminine politics by deflecting individual heroics and identifying the actions of wrongdoers. Exiled-as-survivor (like orphanhood) allowed Wells-Barnett to claim unusual amounts of both autonomy and support from her community. Unlike her orphanhood, Wells-Barnett's exile was not accidental, but political. Exile was punishment for her opposition to lynching. In the context of African American Christianity, Exiled also connected Wells-Barnett to the larger African American community, for whom a key metaphor of self-identification was the biblical story of Exodus and the continuing exile in the Americas of people of African descent.[29] As an example of the politics of the possible, Exiled expressed black women's and the black community's situation in the United States in 1892 and, by naming it, created a space for its transformation.

Of particularly liberating potential was the ability of Exiled to depart from the bodily aspects of race and sex that ordered Victorian identity and labeled black women deviant. The meaning of Exiled derived from power and place, not nature; the symbolics of Exiled concerned citizenship and religion and deflected some attention from the body. Exiled could appear in print as an androgyne critic of indeterminate race and gender, affording Wells-Barnett a degree of literary license.[30] However, the space opened up on paper by Exiled contracted before live audiences. As was the case for black abolitionist women, Anglo-American audiences expected to discern or read Wells-Barnett's authority, identity, and, to some extent, her argument through her skin. Such readings by whites relied on the plantation slave stereotypes of black woman as "mammy" or "Sapphire," as asexual menial or supersexed wench.[31] When Wells-Barnett moved from the press to the podium, she encountered a politics of authenticity once rooted in the slave experience but now, in freedom, also linked to the body and skin color.

Crusade for Justice suggests that despite her cold facts, her press clippings, and her political exile, Wells-Barnett's body became an exhibit for her arguments about the South. The British keyed skin color to credibility. A London hostess stated that Wells-Barnett's success abroad would have been much greater had she been a "few shades blacker."[32] This comment appears in *Crusade for Justice* within a few paragraphs of the author noting what "an absolutely new thing" it was to be in England, where people did not seem to notice "the color of the skin."[33] Wells-Barnett was trying to impress her readers in the 1920s with the social freedom she found abroad, but in the 1890s color consciousness and commentary on her "odd racial composition" figured regularly in British publications.[34] Wells-Barnett was announced in London as a "Coloured Woman in the Pulpit," and the charge that her mixed heritage somehow tainted her point of view caused her to bristle in an interview: "Taint, indeed? I tell you, if I have any taint to be ashamed of in myself, it is the taint of *white* blood!"[35] "Exiled" resisted the negative position, or even the nonsubjectivity, assigned to black women in American culture. England offered, alternately, a chance to play up blackness or to straddle the color line, sometimes uncomfortably.[36]

In the context of sexual objectification and skin-color consciousness, Wells-Barnett's platform personae before audiences in England suggest a muting of her body language consistent with the physical displacement evoked by Exiled. British listeners remarked repeatedly on her composure at the podium, familiar as many were with the comic and rough flamboyance of blackface minstrelsy then popular in English music halls.[37] Rather than risk teary declamations while under such visual scrutiny, Wells-Barnett masked passion and feeling in order to avoid the charge of unrestraint or immorality that so easily attached to African American women. Wells-Barnett was probably aware of and perhaps played to the sculptural feminine ideal for actresses, derived from Greek art and statuary, which dominated the London stage in those years.[38] One British supporter vividly described her speaking style: "She spoke with a cultivated manner with great simplicity & directness & with a burning intensity of feeling well-controlled. It was the most convincing kind of speaking—it sounded intensely genuine & real. There was no attempt at oratories, no straining after effects."[39] Audiences remarked on her "quiet and unimpassioned but earnest and forcible" delivery as well as her "avoidance of all oratorical tricks, and her dependence upon the simple eloquence of facts."[40] Her style won rave reviews: "She spoke with singular refinement, dignity and self-restraint, nor have I ever met any other 'agitator' so cautious and unimpassioned in speech," noted the London *Christian Register*. "But by this marvelous self-restraint itself," the article went on, "she moved us all the more profoundly." [41] Wells-Barnett herself highlighted the effectiveness rather than the cost of such restraint. If at this moment the theatrical ideal for women was a kind of frozen beauty, her powerful stage presence held audiences fast. "I spoke an hour and a half" in Bristol, Wells-Barnett wrote to the *Inter-Ocean* in 1894, "and not a person in that vast audience moved."[42]

Parables

Slave narratives end in freedom. Spiritual autobiographies climax with salvation and the doing of God's work. Anglo-American Victorian life stories typically close with marriage for women or with public success for men. Striking a much more modern note, *Crusade for Justice* ends or, rather, fails to properly end, with a series of redundant, unresolved parables of crisis in Wells-Barnett's authority. The final section of the autobiography contrasts the international success and visibility of the antilynching years with the local, usually unrecognized, and sometimes thwarted struggles of the Chicago decades. This denouement points back to the spiritual autobiographers, since Wells-Barnett's inability to fulfill her calling at home alludes to Jesus' saying in Luke that "no prophet is acceptable in his own country."[43] The parable-like stories of the final section contain another religious reference, since Jesus taught in parables. Wells-Barnett also describes drawing strength for her Chicago community work from the example of Jesus' ministry among sinners.[44] The parables' message of frustration and disappointment further implicates faith since misunderstanding is the portion of prophets in Christian tradition.

The parables, probably written in 1929–30, also capture a troublesome aspect of community organizing, namely, the ways in which social struggles sometimes turn on the attitude of the individuals who are closest by. This tendency carried special significance for African American women who risked the charge of "betraying the race" for turning criticism toward the community, especially toward men.[45] Three parables in the narrative's final section especially capture Wells-Barnett's complex story of loyalty and betrayal, endurance and frustration, self-possession and social embeddedness, all of which touch back on the narrative's founding parable, the Vicksburg incident. One concerns Ida B. Wells's marriage in 1895 to Ferdinand Lee Barnett. The other two parables involve clergy who reject her initiative in political protest, first in 1894 upon her return from England and again in 1919 in the wake of the Chicago race riot.

The chapter bridging Wells-Barnett's return to the United States from abroad describes a gathering of AME church ministers in Philadelphia. During the summer of 1894, she traveled across the country speaking against lynching, collecting antilynching resolutions, and organizing local communities to keep up the fight. In Philadelphia, however, clergy raised a note of protest. After her address to the group, a minister objected "on the ground that they ought to be careful about endorsing young women of whom they knew nothing—that the AME church had representative women who ought to be put before the public and whom they could endorse unhesitatingly." After a moment of amazement and stunned silence that again points to the immobilizing potential of male moral judgment, Wells-Barnett found her words. She dispensed entirely with the idea that she even needed the clergy, relying directly on God instead. "Why gentlemen," she recalled saying, "I cannot see why I need your endorsement. Under God I have done work without any assistance from my own people. And when I think that I have been able to do the work with his assistance that you could not do, if you would, and you would not do if you could, I think I have a right to feeling of strong indignation."[46] Setting the tone for the entire final section of the narrative, she described the ministers' response in this scenario as emblematic, as "the beginning of a great deal of the same sort that I received at the hands of my own people" which inhibited the fight against lynching.[47]

About a year after the Philadelphia incident, Wells-Barnett found herself exhausted, "physically and financially bankrupt," from the antilynching crusade. "Thus it seemed to me that I had done my duty," she explained and, unable to return to the South for fear of violence, she settled in Chicago.[48] There, in June 1895, she married Barnett, a lawyer and editor of the Chicago *Conservator* newspaper. Antilynching-as-Exiled proved extremely taxing both politically and emotionally. The autobiography does not discuss the marriage proposal or engagement but tellingly refers only to "the offer of a home of my own" from Barnett.[49] Nearing the age of thirty-three,

Wells-Barnett perhaps could depend less comfortably on surrogate fathers for protection. Douglass's death in February of that year had eliminated a major source of emotional and political support.

In the autobiography's parable of her marriage, Wells-Barnett highlights her community's negative reaction to her engagement, using irony and a bit of sarcasm to explore the politics of work and marriage for black women. She described the public as "more outspoken because of the loss to the cause than they had been in holding up my hands when I was trying to carry a banner," alluding again to the idea of exile, specifically Moses' leadership of the Israelites in battle in the book of Exodus.[50] "Strange as it may seem," she continued, "my people . . . seemed to feel that I had deserted the cause, and some of them censured me rather severely in their newspapers for [marrying]."[51] Susan B. Anthony also rebuked Wells-Barnett for her "divided duty" between home life and a "special call" for "special work."[52]

As contemporary black feminist scholars have argued, women like Wells-Barnett viewed marriage and family as compatible with both wage labor and public efforts for community benefit. *Crusade for Justice* suggests that this view found critics within black communities as well as among white suffragists.[53] The marriage parable also implies, however, that Barnett supported such a politically engaged partnership. Because one person or couple could not end lynching, Wells-Barnett continued her political work as a married woman and mother and strongly backed a protest organization, the Afro-American Council, which was revitalized in 1899 to pursue civil rights agitation. "So despite my best intentions," she wryly concludes this parable on marriage, "when I got back home to my family [after the first council meeting in Rochester, New York] I was again launched in public movements."[54]

After working for a quarter century in "public movements" in Chicago, Wells-Barnett, in the penultimate chapter of the autobiography, describes an emotional climax in a series of challenges to her leadership. The scene is her resignation from a newly formed local Protective Association, organized in the aftermath of the bloody Chicago race riot of July 1919. In a disagreement with the association's clergy-dominated leadership, Wells-Barnett resigned after making an "impassioned speech" that changed none of the ministers' minds.[55] When she put her membership card on the table and turned to leave, the words "Good-bye" and "Good riddance" followed her out of the room.[56] Back in 1894, she had left the Philadelphia ministers sitting "with their mouths open" as she proudly walked out of their meeting. In 1919, it was Wells-Barnett who left the room silenced, "tears streaming down" her face. Unable to talk through her tears this time, the scene points to a severe crisis of authority and intense personal suffering. In this scenario, partisan calculation trumped the politics of the possible. The autobiography offered a justification after the fact: "I never went back to a meeting of the so-called Protective Association and very soon it became a thing of the past."[57]

The Chicago parables suggest that the access to audiences and publication that Wells-Barnett garnered through witnessing as a "southern girl, born and bred" or through testifying as Exiled eroded in the years after 1895. Once a special place, the South, and her exile from it offered a unique public persona and a distinctive if tenuous social authority. Wells-Barnett was an exotic specimen to the British; foreign news that "our Iola" brought back from abroad was exciting to African Americans, many of whom had never left their hometowns in the United States. In Chicago, by contrast, Wells-Barnett became one among many contending for the crumbs of white patronage, the loyalty of African American voters, and an economic foothold on the city's segregated South Side. Wells-Barnett's community-building efforts, her continued investigative reporting on racial violence, and her party politicking in Chicago were all important resistance work. The final section of her narrative stresses political reversals that were difficult, if not impossible, to answer either with the facts of lynching, personal testimony about conditions, or the invocation of God's authority. Solving social problems required money and votes, both of which were withheld from all U.S. women citizens until late in Wells-Barnett's lifetime.

In this context, the association of Wells-Barnett with Joan of Arc merits special attention. She chose the image of Joan of Arc to frame the writing of her *Crusade for Justice*. The preface to the narrative opens with a description of a Young Women's Christian Association gathering at which a young woman identifies Wells-Barnett with Joan of Arc but cannot say why.[58] Joan symbolized youthful, God-inspired female daring, an image that clung to Wells-Barnett in the public's imagination long after her marriage and the birth of her children and the headline-grabbing days of the early antilynching crusade. It was apt because it captured Wells-Barnett's ability to transgress gender norms to make a religious and political point. Yet the same preface to the narrative closes with the parent-like dedication of the narrative to "our youth." "It is therefore for the young people who have so little of our race's history recorded that I am for the first time in my life writing about myself."[59] Throughout the text, *Crusade for Justice* refuses to simply settle or choose between the religious heroine and the devoted mother, affirming instead the freedom to be either or both.

Conclusion

Crusade for Justice records Ida B. Wells-Barnett's at first faltering, then deft engagements with stereotypes and expectations about black women and her bold, sometimes angry conflicts with these expectations. In middle-class African American settings, gender expectations often were most salient and made serious demands on the body, as in talking through tears. Security in her slave mother's legacy as well as father-daughter mentoring relationships, epitomized by that with Frederick Douglass, were crucial to securing Wells-Barnett's public presence. For their part, white people in the North, South, and abroad laid their own stage cues and trip wires. In nearly all settings, however, negative presumptions about black women created nearly impassible barriers for those who did not position themselves as a chaste and obedient wife, mother, or daughter.

A religiously directed sense of her own possibility allowed Wells-Barnett to be a rebellious Joan of Arc who was also a nurturing Sunday school teacher, a role model for youth, and a devoted mother. As Exiled, Wells-Barnett did not just play upon the world stage but rewrote the script, grounding her sense of self and service in religious tradition and communal understandings of history. More than any other of her public identifications, Exiled abandoned the dominant culture's racist demand for bodily fixity around the coordinates of sex, race, and place. Some black critics obliged the demand for fixity, even celebrated it, as in Anna Julia Cooper's proud identification as "A Black Woman from the South" in her well-known collected essays, *A Voice from the South*. Cooper memorably figured the honor of the "whole *Negro race*" in the "quiet, undisputed dignity" of black womanhood, turning on its head the stereotype of "the black woman bringing down the black man."[60] As Exiled, Wells-Barnett remapped social possibilities by abandoning her place, be it the repressive South or ladylike quiet, and by challenging others to join her. *Crusade for Justice* describes how as the southern girl Iola, as Exiled, and as a modern Joan, Ida B. Wells engaged the theatricality of modem life and politics,, marked then as now by struggle around sex, race, and place in U.S. society.

Notes

1. For a fuller treatment and background materials, see Patricia A. Schechter, *Ida B. Wells-Barnett and American Reform, 1880–1930* (Chapel Hill: University of North Carolina Press, 2001).

2. Compared to the writings of Anna Julia Cooper, Wells-Barnett's autobiography has been relatively neglected by scholars of African American literature. See V. P. Franklin, *Living Our Stories, Telling Our Truths: Autobiography and the Making of the African-American Intellectual Tradition*, and Joanne M. Braxton, *Black Women Writing Autobiography: A Tradition within a Tradition* (Philadelphia: Temple University Press, 1989), 102–38. For other treatments of Wells-Barnett's ideas, see Hazel V. Carby, *Reconstructing Womanhood: The Emergence of the Afro-American Woman Novelist* (Cambridge, Mass.: Harvard University Press, 1987), and Joy James, *Transcending the Talented Tenth: Black Leaders and American Intellectuals* (New York: Routledge, 1997).

3. Ida B. Wells-Barnett, *Crusade for Justice: The Autobiography of Ida B. Wells* (Chicago: University of Chicago Press, 1970), 4–5.

4. Hortense V. Spillers, "'The Permanent Obliquity of an In(pha)llibly Straight': In the Time of the Daughters and the Fathers," in *Changing Our Own Words: Essays on Criticism: Theory in Writing by Black Women*, ed. Cheryl A. Wall (New Brunswick: Rutgers University Press, 1989), 127–49.

5. According to Frances Smith Foster, Wells-Barnett's *Crusade for Justice* does not fit the two dominant modes of postbellum African American autobiography, those focusing on childhoods spent in slavery and those telling "black success stories" in freedom. Foster, *Written by Herself: Literary Production by African American Women, 1746–1892* (Bloomington: Indiana University Press, 1993), 117–30.

6. Wells-Barnett, *Crusade for Justice*, 9.

7. Ibid., 10.

8. Elsa Barkeley Brown, "Negotiating and Transforming the Public Sphere: African American Political Life in the Transition from Slavery to Freedom," *Public Culture* 7 (Fall 1994): 106–46.

9. Wells-Barnett, *Crusade for Justice*, 44–45.

10. Ibid., 31.

11. Diary of Ida B. Wells, December 19, 1885, Ida B. Wells Papers, Regenstein Library, University of Chicago.

12. Wells-Barnett, *Crusade for Justice*, 5.

13. Ibid., 31, 47.

14. Emma Goldman, *Living My Life* (New York: New American Library, 1977), 10.

15. Wells-Barnett, *Crusade for Justice*, 64.

16. On New York black women, see Hallie Quinn Brown, *Homespun Heroines and Other Women of Distinction* (New York: Oxford University Press, 1988).

17. Wells-Barnett, *Crusade for Justice*, 79.

18. Wells, *Southern Horrors: Lynch Law in All its Phases*, in *Selected Writings of Ida B. Wells- Barnett*, compiled by Trudier Harris (New York: Oxford University Press, 1991), 15.

19. Wells-Barnett, *Crusade for Justice*, 80; Detroit *Plaindealer*, October 21, 1892.

20. Wells-Barnett, *Crusade for Justice*, 80 (emphasis added).

21. Wells Diary, February 25, 1886; Washington *Bee* quoted in the New York *Freeman*, December 12, 1885.

22. Quoted in Wells, *Southern Horrors*, 15. On Douglass, see William S. McFeely, *Frederick Douglass* (New York: W. W. Norton, 1991).

23. Ida B. Wells to Frederick Douglass, June 3, 1894; May 6, 1894; Frederick Douglass to Reverend Aked, May 22, 1894, Frederick Douglass Papers, Library of Congress.

24. Frederick Douglass to Rev. Dr. Clifford, May 22, 1894, reprinted in the New York *Age*, July 5, 1894 (citation courtesy of Paul Lee).

25. [London] *Daily Chronicle*, April 28, 1894.

26. New York *Sun*, August 1, 1894.

27. Wells-Barnett, *Crusade for Justice*, 232. For Douglass's death scene, see 74–75.

28. Indianapolis *Freeman*, March 30, 1895.

29. Albert J. Raboteau, "African Americans, Exodus, and the American Israel," in *African-American Christianity: Essays in History*, ed. Paul E. Johnson (Berkeley: University of California Press, 1994), 1–17.

30. Susanne Kaeppler, *The Pornography of Representation* (Minneapolis: University of Minnesota Press, 1986), 155–57.

31. Nell Irvin Painter, *Sojourner Truth: A Life, A Symbol* (New York: W. W. Norton, 1996), 138–42.

32. Wells-Barnett, *Crusade for Justice*, 214–15.

33. Ibid., 212.

34. *Christian World*, March 15, 1894; Charles F. Aked, "A Blot on a Free Republic," *Review of the Churches* 9 (May–October 1894): 97. See also *Daily Chronicle*, April 28, 1894.

35. Westminster *Gazette*, May 10, 1894.

36. At one point Wells agreed to assist a British physician researching "the relative mortality from tuberculosis between [among] those of mixed blood." New York *Age*, July 21, 1894 (citation courtesy of Paul Lee).

37. Douglas Lorimer, *Colour, Class and the Victorians: English Attitudes to the Negro in the Mid-Nineteenth Century* (Leicester: Leicester University Press, 1984), 82–91.

38. Gail Marshall, *Actresses on the Victorian Stage: Feminine Performance and the Galatea Myth* (Cambridge: Cambridge University Press, 1998).

39. Catherine Impey to Albion Tourgee, June 24, 1893, Albion Tourgee Papers, Chatauqua Historical Society, Westfield, New York.

40. Chicago *Inter-Ocean*, April 9, 1894; Manchester *Guardian*, May 9, 1894.

41. *Christian Register*, April 12, 1894.

42. Wells-Barnett, *Crusade for Justice*, 156.

43. Luke 4:24.

44. Wells-Barnett, *Crusade for Justice*, 358.

45. Nell Irvin Painter, "Hill, Thomas, and the Use of Racial Stereotype," in *Race-ing Justice: En-Gendering Power: Essays on Anita Hill, Clarence Thomas, and the Construction of Social Reality*, ed. Toni Morrison (New York: Pantheon, 1992), 200–14.

46. Wells-Barnett, *Crusade for Justice*, 222.

47. Ibid., 222–23.

48. Ibid., 238.

49. Ibid.

50. Exodus 17:8–16

51. Wells-Barnett, *Crusade for Justice*, 241. See also Fannie Barrier Williams, "Illinois," *Woman's Era* (June 1895): 5; "Ida Wells Married," *New York Times*, June 28, 1895.

52. Wells-Barnett, *Crusade for Justice*, 255.

53. Deborah Gray White, "The Cost of Club Work, The Price of Black Feminism," in *Visible Women: New Essays on American Activism*, ed. Nancy Hewitt and Suzanne Lebsock (Urbana: University of Illinois Press, 1993), 247–69.

54. Wells-Barnett, *Crusade for Justice*, 256.

55. "Committee Appointed," *Chicago Defender*, August 30, 1919.

56. Wells-Barnett, *Crusade for Justice*, 408.

57. Ibid., 408.

58. Ibid., 3. See also Painter, *Sojourner Truth*, 261.

59. Wells-Barnett, *Crusade for Justice*, 4.

60. Anna Julia Cooper, *A Voice from the South: By a Black Women from the South*, ed. Mary Helen Washington (New York: Oxford University Press, 1988), 31.

GWENDOLYN MINK

ABRIDGED BY BRUCE BAUM

Meat vs. Rice (and Pasta)

Samuel Gompers and the Republic of White Labor

Organized labor has played a key role in struggles for workers' rights and social justice in the United States. At the same time, labor often has mobilized in racially exclusionary ways, mirroring and reinforcing broader American racism. Samuel Gompers, a cigar unionist and the first president of the American Federation of Labor (AFL) from 1886 until his death in 1924, epitomized these two tendencies. He championed the populist and Progressive Era project of extending American prosperity to the working class. "The working people," he said in 1914, "will never stop in their efforts to obtain a better life for themselves, for their wives, for their children, and for all humanity. The object is to obtain complete social justice."[1] Yet despite his appeal to "all humanity," Gompers rallied the AFL to racist political action against Chinese immigrants, effectively advancing a racially exclusive republic of white labor.

Rather than pursuing a broader unionism and the wider interests of the working class, Gompers's AFL represented a small fraction of the working class while it claimed jurisdiction over the whole. Organized labor's job-conscious focus—manifest in the AFL's efforts to protect and improve the wage-earning status of workers rather than escape from that status—was not unique to unionism in America. In the United States, however, job consciousness and unionism became distinctively suffused with ethnic and race consciousness. Trade unionism was thus consolidated on the basis of both craft and caste. Indeed, the AFL, which spoke as the only organized representative of the working class until the rise of the Congress of Industrial

Organizations (CIO) in the 1930s, made antagonisms *within* the class—and hence the interests of its white worker constituency—preeminent.

This intraclass mobilization was first worked out around the issue of anti-Chinese legislation. The first sustained and dramatic instance of union politicization on the basis of labor market pressures occurred in California when white workers in San Francisco mobilized against the Chinese.[2] From the mid-1870s a profound racial and nativist strain would be at the political core of trade unionism.

Although the presumed Chinese menace was geographically contained, the anti-Chinese movement must be viewed in a national context. It invigorated national union solidarity and endowed traditional job- and organization-conscious unionism with a coincident race consciousness. It produced a union logic whereby old labor—native-born and northwest European—distinguished itself from new immigrants on the basis of its conformity with liberal tradition, values, and structures. It provided a solvent for the tension between union voluntarism and ethnic partisanship. By 1896 these developments had prepared the way for a connection between union and political party that sent old labor and new immigrants along separate electoral paths. And by the following year these developments had placed a class-neutral but group-charged demand for restricted immigration at the heart of the trade union political agenda.

In several crucial respects, then, anti-Chinese agitation in California foreshadowed a more general trade union nativism. A mixture of economic, racial, and national arguments against the Chinese soon gave old labor organizational and political defenses to use against new immigration from Europe.[3] Within the labor movement, "class feeling" fell to "race feeling," but the coincidence of episodic booms in the San Francisco labor movement and action against the Chinese suggested to labor leaders that race feeling was an important source of solidarity within old labor.[4] The interaction of race feeling and union feeling encouraged the internal (organizational) development of old labor. One reason it did was that among the trades supposedly invaded by the Chinese in San Francisco was the cigar industry. In addition to being well organized in the East, the cigar trade was among the leaders in the labor movement. Convinced by colleagues in San Francisco that "unless protective measures [are] taken, it is evident that the whole industry [will] soon be 'Chinaized,'" eastern cigar makers joined the anti-Chinese crusaders in the West. As Gompers recalled in his autobiography, the Chinese problem was "an element in deciding the cigar makers to give early and hearty endorsement to the movement for a national organization of labor . . . for the help of all wage earners was needed in support of Chinese exclusion."[5]

The Chinese presence helped define the political goals of old labor as well. The issues of race and labor market were created by unregulated immigration and demanded an unambiguous political remedy: pass a law. Winning passage of a law, however, extended bread-and-butter unionism into the political sphere. The solution to the Chinese problem lay with Congress, so labor's anti-Chinese campaign nationalized union politics. The nationalization of the trade union movement in the 1870s and 1880s thus coincided with its politicization. The trade union movement's political goal, moreover, had enormous and enormously negative consequences for class-based labor politics in the United States.

Background of the Anti-Chinese Movement

When a working class coalesced in San Francisco in the late 1860s, it inherited a tradition of antagonism toward the Chinese that had first found expression in the mining frontier.[6] By 1867 the Chinese issue had become central to California workers as well as to astute politicians in the state. Between 1860 and 1870 the population of San Francisco grew from 57,000 to almost 150,000.[7] Several developments gave the Bay Area labor market nearly one-third of the state's population. First, declining yields in the mines after 1865 sent thousands of white miners into the city looking for work. Second, the construction of the transcontinental railroad enabled 50,000 people to migrate overland in 1868 and 1869, most of them to San Francisco. Third, with the completion of the railroad in 1869, another 10,000 white and Chinese former railroad workers moved to San Francisco to find work. Fourth, as the mining communities folded the Chinese relocated in San Francisco; by 1871 one of every three workers in the city was Chinese. Fifth, the California population was disproportionately male; the overwhelming majority of those who settled in San Francisco entered the labor market, and by 1871 there were four workers for every job.[8] Finally, employers stepped up their efforts to recruit new workers.[9]

These pressures on the labor market did not develop in a political vacuum. The state and capital (mainly the railroads) seemed to be in league behind the expansion of the labor market, chiefly through the continuing entry of Chinese.[10] The Burlingame Treaty of 1868 between the United States and China seemed to invite the Chinese, and the arrival of some twenty-two thousand new Chinese immigrants in San Francisco between 1868 and 1871 encouraged white workers to identify joblessness and wage reductions with the Chinese presence. Workers were aroused against further Chinese incursions when the Southern Pacific Railroad announced that it intended to rely on Chinese labor in its projected railroad construction.[11] The immediate consequences of the Bay Area's population boom were the reduction of wages and the extension of the working day combined with the pressure of unemployment. Because the Chinese were a highly visible segment of the San Francisco labor force (13.2 percent in 1870), white workers tended to blame the Chinese, whom whites regarded as racially and culturally different, for the unfavorable wages and working conditions.[12]

Race consciousness, as an expression of labor market anxieties, was prefigured by the race-conscious political heritage of the California mining frontier and the race-conscious political heritage of the antebellum and Civil War working class. In this regard, the composition of San Francisco's white working class is relevant: the city's population was nearly 50 percent foreign-born. Of the white immigrant population, 41 percent were born in Ireland; of the white working population, 25 percent were Irish born.[13] The Irish (and German Catholics) had themselves been targets of nativists in the East, so a new rationale was required before they could become carriers of nativist unionism. But that rationale was already there, in the political lineage that tied most Irish to the Democratic Party. That lineage descended from the Jacksonian producer ethic through urban party systems to Democratic conceptions of race and equality. Both their Democratic heritage and their experience with anti-Catholic nativism separated most Irish from Republicanism, especially from its weakest component—the assertion of equality for blacks. Irish Democratic sympathies had been expressed in wartime elections in New York and Pennsylvania; Irish race hostilities had been demonstrated in the New York draft riots of July 1863.[14]

In San Francisco, therefore, a significant segment of the white working class carried a political heritage that interacted easily with race-conscious mobilization against Chinese labor competition. The interaction of race consciousness and job consciousness, Democratic affinities and unionism, gave the union movement a new racial rationale for nativism, following which former victims of nativism would themselves become nativists. Race consciousness was an important precondition for how white labor articulated its anxieties over the labor market. Race dissolved the antebellum antinativist consensus among old-stock Catholic workers after the Civil War. The Chinese issue was the vehicle for that dissolution; the organizational and political consolidation of old labor against new immigrants was the result.

The Anti-Chinese Movement, 1870–80

After 1870 direct competition from Chinese labor in two critical industries spurred workers to organize around the Chinese issue. The cigar makers and the boot and shoe workers brought anti-Chinese nativism to the forefront of unionism. Workers in both trades were affiliated with vigorous national unions—the Cigar Makers' International Union and the Knights of St. Crispin. Moreover, at a time when workers were seeking someone to blame for unemployment and wage cuts, eastern members of both trades endorsed the anti-Chinese maneuvers of California's workers because cheap Chinese labor jeopardized the national market position of eastern products. Both trades were, in fact, objectively affected by Chinese labor.[15]

In the spring of 1870 the Knights of St. Crispin launched the first of a series of campaigns that would culminate in Kearneyism (see below). The Knights demanded from their employers both a wage increase and the elimination of Chinese labor from the industry. Anticoolie clubs joined the Knights and other trade unions in the first Anti-Chinese Convention of California. White workers marched through San Francisco waving placards denouncing the Chinese: "Women's Rights and No More Chinese Chambermaids," "Our Women Are Degraded by Coolie Labor," "American Trade Needs No Coolie." Committees of unemployed workers were sent from shop to shop to demand the ouster of the Chinese, and boycotts were organized against Chinese-made goods. By August 1870 the Anti-Chinese Convention had condemned the coolie system, urged the immediate abrogation of the Burlingame Treaty, demanded an end to Chinese immigration, denounced public officials who employed Chinese, and opposed the permissive policies that enabled steamship companies to recruit Chinese immigrants.[16]

Eastern labor groups meanwhile sponsored anti-Chinese rallies in Boston and New York City, and various commentators in the East aroused anxieties about the Chinese threat. In the New York *Tribune*, for example, Henry George indicted the "long-tailed barbarians" for "making princes of our capitalists . . . and crushing workers into the dust." He predicted that "in every case in which Chinese comes into fair competition with white labor, the whites must either retire from the field or come down to the Chinese standard of living."[17]

George's prediction was immediately germane to the cigar industry. Of all the trades in San Francisco, cigar manufacture was the most severely affected by Chinese labor: of eighteen hundred cigar makers in 1870, some 91 percent were Chinese. The wages of cigar makers in California, because of the lower cost of Chinese labor, averaged 10 percent less than in twenty other states. As a result, eastern cigar makers—notably Samuel Gompers and Adolphe Strasser, president of the Cigar Makers' International Union—defended the anti-Chinese posture of their colleagues in California and actively involved themselves in the exclusion movement.[18]

Aside from grooming Gompers for leadership of the AFL, the most durable contribution of white cigar makers to trade unionism grew out of their efforts to reassert control over the cigar-making trade. In 1874 cigar makers revived and refashioned the union label as a certificate of white labor.[19] Chinese-made goods could not bear the union label, which facilitated boycotts, white trade unionism, and anti-Chinese nativism. By 1880 the cigar-making industry in San Francisco had been forced to reduce the proportion of Chinese in the workforce to 33 percent. The linkage of union label, white labor, and union shop revealed the organic connection between nativism and trade unionism.[20]

By 1875 anti-Chinese nativism had gripped the white working class in San Francisco, partly because of trade union campaigns against the Chinese and partly because of new pressures on the labor market following the eastern panic of 1873. California was spared the immediate economic crisis created by the panic, but between 1873 and 1875 it was forced to absorb 154,300 overland migrants who moved west—mostly to San Francisco—to escape the depression in the East.

The economic problems generated by unemployment were aggravated by mining stock panics in 1875. Meanwhile the period 1873–76 saw the largest influx of Chinese immigrants in California's history—seventy-three thousand in all. Despite the obvious abundance of white labor created by overland migration, the California Immigrant Union argued in 1875, "Chinamen are a necessary evil at present, for the reason that most of the young men of our state and newcomers generally, will not work for small wages.

As soon as this is remedied by an importation of Eastern and European labor . . . the employment of Chinese will gradually be diminished." When a financial and industrial crisis finally hit California in 1876–77, white workers blamed the Chinese, and Chinese exclusion was presented as a precondition for economic revival.[21]

The Democratic Party played the Chinese card to win control of California in 1867 and to secure that control in 1876. During 1876, Democratic candidates passionately denounced the Chinese, demanded restrictions on Chinese immigration and deportation of resident Chinese, and advocated changes in the Burlingame Treaty.[22] Nationally the Democratic platform forcefully denounced the Chinese based on their putative racial inferiority and (racially determined) inability to assimilate.[23] As the party out of power during the 1860s, the Democratic Party worked well as a vehicle of protest. But in the 1870s, when the depression inflamed the antagonism of white workers toward Chinese, the Democrats were in power. As part of California's political establishment the Democratic Party was compromised as a conduit for the worker discontent unleashed by depression, especially when it had not delivered relief from the Chinese.[24]

White workers, particularly the unemployed, were thus ripe for independent political mobilization. During the summer of 1877 Denis Kearney aroused their mass opposition to the Chinese in sandlot rallies that shook San Francisco.[25] In August, Kearney formed the independent Workingmen's Party landownership of California, which aimed to "extirpate the Chinese"; its constituency united white workers with elements of the middle class, chiefly small property holders like Kearney himself.[26]

It is doubtful Kearney was committed to any political program beyond Chinese exclusion. He was only marginally connected to earlier trade union struggles against the Chinese, and, indeed, some have maintained that he saw the anti-Chinese movement merely as an opportunity to embark on a political career.[27] Still, he won a mass following almost instantly when he inveighed against the Chinese. Though neither a labor leader nor a workingman in any class sense, Kearney powerfully articulated the labor market anxieties of white labor in class-neutral terms. He thereby helped redirect conflict between labor and capital into group-charged competition in the political arena.

Kearney's Workingmen's Party gave political focus to nearly ten years of working-class agitation against the Chinese.[28] Speaking for its working-class nativist base, the party's first platform promised to rid the country of the Chinese, to wrest government from the rich (that is, the railroads who recruited Chinese workers), to destroy the power of wealth through taxation, to elect only Workingmen to public office, and to mark as public enemies all employers of the Chinese.[29] In addition, officers of the party issued a manifesto: "We have made no secret of our intentions. . . . Before you and the world, we declare that the Chinamen must leave our shores. We declare that white men, and women, and boys, and girls, cannot live as the people of the great republic should and compete with the single Chinese coolies in the labor market."[30]

The Democratic Party would eventually redirect this anti-Chinese insurgency into its own channels. But initially the established parties collaborated in order to squelch the Workingmen's movement. When the Workingmen began running candidates and winning elections—as they did in the spring of 1878—Republicans and Democrats formed bipartisan slates to consolidate their electoral power against the Workingmen. The Workingmen's Party also came into conflict with unions late in the spring of 1878. Kearney was able to retain control of the movement, but his refusal to compromise with union labor generated conflicts between union and party that eventually restored unionism, and later the Democratic party, to the organizational center of anti-Chinese nativism.[31]

The Workingmen were largely responsible for the decisions made at the state's constitutional convention in June 1878, both because their movement had called for the convention and because they dominated the proceedings in a coalition with the small, farmer-based Grangers.[32] Although the convention was dominated by representatives of workingmen, the new constitution, according to Henry George, "entrenched vested rights—especially in land—more thoroughly than before, and interposed barriers to future radicalism . . . which it will require almost a revolution to break through. It was anything but a workingmen's constitution."[33] Indeed, what was in good measure a "Workingmen's constitution" disenfranchised fragments of the working class and politically institutionalized the group bias of urban white labor. For George, the Chinese presence had once been symptomatic of the monopoly problem. Now, however, the anti-Chinese obsession of politicized workers seemed to play directly into the hands of monopoly. As George now reasoned, labor politics built around the race question was ultimately a distraction. It prevented workers from coming to terms with the fundamental questions of landownership and the shrinking opportunity for individual enterprise.

But for the Workingmen, the Chinese question was fundamental, so the new constitution was a Workingmen's constitution: It contained at least eight anti-Chinese provisions. It forever barred the Chinese from voting, denied the Chinese access to employment on public works projects, and prohibited corporations from hiring Chinese. Among other things, it also empowered the legislature to impose conditions for Chinese residence and removal and to discourage or prohibit Chinese immigration.[34] During the convention debate speech after speech betrayed the extent to which the economic rationale of anti-Chinese nativism had been subsumed by popularly held racial prejudice. One speaker argued that the Chinese race would destroy white civilization: "If clover and hay be planted upon the same soil, the clover will ruin the hay, because clover lives upon less than the hay; and so it is in this struggle between the races. The Mongolian race will live and run the Caucasian race out."[35]

Drawing strength from the popularity of the anti-Chinese cause, the Workingmen broadened their political efforts. In San Francisco's municipal elections in 1879 the party elected Workingmen to a number of offices, most important that of the city's new mayor. In the same election Workingmen offered an "Against Chinese Immigration" entry on the statewide ballot; it was approved by a vote of 150,000 to 900.[36] After the elections of 1879, however, the Workingmen's Party dissipated rapidly.

Most Workingmen, especially the Irish among them, had been and still were basically Democrats.[37] Defection to an independent party at the local level could coexist with general Democratic identification, especially in a fledgling urban party system.[38] Still, such electoral insurgency was usually short-lived because the Democratic Party typically made itself accessible to the influence of local labor. Sustained extra-Democratic mobilization was even more difficult within the national party system, where it required a complete break with intense partisanships based in bitter Civil War experience. Irish-Democratic solidarities in particular were deep and of long standing because of the party's Jacksonian message, its shield against anti-Catholic nativists, and, in older urban centers, its capture of Irish partisanship through management of patronage and control of naturalization and electoral ritual.[39] Meanwhile, Democrats within the Workingmen's Party moved in 1880 to redirect the anti-Chinese movement into Democratic institutions, and Kearney was ultimately forced to retire from politics.

Democrats, Unions, and the Yellow Peril

The Democratic Party profited enormously from the dissolution of the Workingmen's Party. But along with the Republican Party, it benefited even more from the experience of the Workingmen's movement. Kearneyism demonstrated the power of the labor vote. It also showed that the labor vote could be harnessed without conceding class-charged, labor-specific demands such as the regulation of hours and wages. As a result, both parties were quick to espouse the anti-Chinese catechism after the state's constitutional convention. California Republicans pursued Chinese exclusion in Congress, and in 1880 the national Republican platform included an anti-Chinese plank. Yet Republicans outside California were uncertain nativists. Principled Democratic anti-Chinese nativism was more credible. California Democrats formed a majority in the State Assembly behind stringent policies toward Chinese residents, while the national Democratic Party dominated a majority in Congress behind Chinese exclusion bills.

For the Republicans, anti-Chinese nativist rhetoric was electorally necessary in California. For the Democrats, the anti-Chinese shibboleth was also electorally necessary—especially if the Democratic Party was to hang on to the labor vote.[40] For the Republicans, the Chinese issue was divisive: steamship companies and railroads had invested heavily in Chinese immigration, and abolitionist and radical Republicans believed that at the core of anti-Chinese nativism lay race prejudice.[41] The Democrats found anti-Chinese nativism easier to embrace. Though the Democratic Party had long sheltered white immigrants against anti-Catholic nativism, its advocacy of ethnoreligious liberalism was not connected to racial liberalism. As long as the Chinese stood in analogy to blacks rather than to old-stock immigrant groups, anti-Chinese nativism did not engage ideological controversy within the Democratic Party. The Chinese–black analogy was prominent in the debate over Chinese exclusion, among abolitionist and radical Republicans as well as among Democrats. In New York City the *Tribune* assailed Democratic race analogies: "If there is despicable prejudice anywhere in this land, of which all decent men are heartily ashamed, the Democratic party has not failed to appeal to that prejudice."[42] By 1880 the Chinese issue had moved to the center of national politics.

Economic recovery facilitated the absorption of most white workers into the Democratic Party in California. It also revitalized trade unionism in San Francisco, where early in 1880 several unions launched an anti-Chinese effort that signaled the emergence of a consolidated trade union movement. Late in 1881 the Representative Assembly of Trades and Labor Unions, or Trades Assembly, headed by Frank Roney, commissioned a statistical study of the Chinese position in industry. The Committee on Chinese Statistics of the Trades Assembly produced a report that, while relatively restrained in racial and cultural commentary, was strident in its view of the impact of the Chinese on the labor market: "The trades that have suffered the most are the cigarmakers, tailors, boot and shoemakers. . . . We find [the Chinese] employed . . . as laborers in almost every department of industry."[43] The report went on to document the adverse effect of Chinese labor on wages. As a whole, however, the survey data showed that Trades Assembly unionists were affected only marginally by Chinese competition in the labor market, with the important exceptions of cigar making, shoemaking, and the sewing trades. Still, anti-Chinese sentiment was a powerful impulse among San Francisco trade unionists.

The anti-Chinese activities of the Trades Assembly were productive: by 1882, forty-nine unions had been organized in San Francisco, all but two of which were affiliated with the city federation. Thirty-one of them had been established only after the Kearney agitation had mobilized workers.[44] Until controversy over passage of the Chinese Exclusion Act erupted in the spring of 1882, moreover, trade union economic action tended to be the vehicle through which anti-Chinese goals were pursued.

The Trades Assembly also appealed to union solidarities beyond San Francisco by sending representatives to the founding convention of the AFL to rally eastern workers behind anti-Chinese legislation.[45] That such appeals were heard became clear in 1882 during the national debate over the Chinese Exclusion Bill. Three thousand workers in Philadelphia demonstrated in favor of the measure during the congressional phase of debate and petitioned the House of Representatives to "remove a menace to the welfare of American Workingmen."[46] And when the Republican president Chester Arthur vetoed the bill, eastern workers attended mass protest meetings and adopted resolutions condemning the veto and demanding an end to Chinese immigration.[47]

In San Francisco, the Trades Assembly responded to President Arthur's veto by redoubling its efforts to win immigration controls. Unions undertook more explicitly political action because of the Republican administration's reluctance to concede a restrictive immigration policy.[48] Within a few days of the presidential veto the Trades Assembly called a convention to reaffirm labor's united front against the Chinese. This anti-Chinese resolve was abruptly co-opted, however, when President Arthur signed a revised Chinese exclusion bill into law on May 6, 1882.

As the restrictions began to be felt in 1883, agitation quietly subsided, and the Trades Assembly withered away. Further, the ebbing of that controversy permitted the limitations of craft unionism to surface explicitly. The fear George had expressed in 1880 proved real: labor had been first distracted and later immobilized by its obsession with the Chinese issue. Indeed, not only had potentially radical segments of labor been stymied, but the career of trade unionism in San Francisco, too, seemed to depend on the salience of the Chinese issue.

Still, the quiet produced by the Chinese Exclusion Act was only temporary. As the Chinese themselves began to strike and to unionize, anti-Chinese nativism was resurrected among both workers and small manufacturers and entrepreneurs, who were most seriously threatened by Chinese labor organization. Some white trade unions became stronger: the national Cigar Makers' International Union, for example, formerly eclipsed by the local White Cigar Makers' Association, made its presence in San Francisco permanent in 1884. A less direct result was that resurgent anti-Chinese nativism—particularly in reaction to the incomplete achievements of the Chinese Exclusion Act and in anticipation of the struggle to extend the act in 1892—was complemented by the militant national labor struggles of the mid-decade. The synergism of these two struggles reinvigorated the union movement in San Francisco. By 1900 San Francisco was a closed-shop town.

Anti-Chinese nativism was likewise a building block of national trade union politics. In its early years the AFL tried to promote racial inclusiveness with regard to blacks,[49] and it did not articulate a coherent opposition to new European immigration until the late 1880s. At its founding convention in 1881, however, the AFL enlisted in the anti-Chinese crusade. In his testimony before the Senate committee investigating relations between labor and capital in 1883, Gompers spoke stridently against the Chinese.[50] The AFL campaigned for Chinese (and later Japanese) exclusion in openly racist terms, denouncing "Mongolians" for bringing "nothing but filth, vice and disease" and for degrading "our people on the Pacific Coast to such a degree that could it be published in detail the American people would in their just and righteous anger sweep them from the face of the earth."[51] A few years later the AFL would publish a pamphlet written by Gompers and Herman Guttstadt, whose title conveniently summarizes the federation's attitudes: *Meat vs. Rice: American Manhood vs. Asiatic Coolieism: Which Shall Survive?*

As the AFL perfected its racial arguments against the Chinese, its formal racial liberalism toward blacks gave way to racial prejudice. The AFL not only submitted to Jim Crow within its ranks, but also began to reason that blacks were racially unsuited for union membership. As Gompers would say before the end of the century, "Those peculiarities of temperament such as patriotism, sympathy, etc., . . . are peculiar to most of the Caucasian race, and . . . also make an organization of the character and complexity of the modern trade union possible."[52]

Race analogies and race theory brought race logic into the core of trade unionism; meanwhile the labor-market anxieties that gelled around Chinese immigration placed immigration-centered labor-market remedies alongside race logic at the core of the AFL's political agenda. There race and labor market issues interacted, ultimately rationalizing race-principled union opposition to the unrestricted immigration of other groups of workers who, like blacks, were not "union material" and who, like the Chinese, posed a hazard to the economic and cultural integrity of the republic. As Gompers insisted in 1905, "The caucasians" (by whom he seems to have meant old labor) "are not going to let their standard of living be destroyed by negroes, Chinamen, Japs, *or any others.*"[53] This interaction of race, labor market, and immigration would form the cornerstone of the exclusionary unionism and politics practiced by the AFL.

Race and the Development of Labor Politics

In the mid-1880s union labor set about consolidating itself as the organizational representation of the working class. This move brought it into collision with capital, in the courts and in the workplace, and with rival representatives, chiefly the Knights of Labor. But it also brought union labor into collision with a rapidly expanding stratum of workers whose cheap labor and green hands were reminiscent of the Chinese. This conflict between old labor and new immigrants pushed union labor into the national political arena because the national government controlled immigration policy.

Of course there were differences between the Chinese and the new European immigrants. For one thing, southern and eastern Europeans came in much greater numbers than the Chinese, and they soon composed dramatic proportions of the industrial labor force. For another, new European immigrants enjoyed the privilege of suffrage as the Chinese had not; they were seen as an important presence in electoral politics. Rather than broaden and diversify the American labor movement, however, the economic and political presence of the new European immigrants only hardened the nativist resolve of union labor. Exclusionist craft unionism was the organizational manifestation of this resolve, while narrow interest politics became its political expression.

Nativism was intimately tied to the development of unionism and labor politics: it cemented craft rigidity, limited the privilege of organization to a minority of workers, and was the first issue to link the economic interest of workers to their collective effectiveness in the political process. Focused initially on the Chinese but later generalized as a response to southern and eastern European immigrants, nativism further politicized old labor as union labor. This joining of organizational, labor market, and race anxieties along boundaries within the working class represented an explosive political mixture, threatening the bonds of traditional partisanship that dominated the politics of the Gilded Age. Ultimately, the Democratic Party's speedy appropriation of union nativism and its delivery of Chinese exclusion pushed labor nativists toward an appreciation of positive state intervention, if on a limited scale. As union labor recognized these lessons, so the party system recognized that union labor was an interest to be reckoned with.

The interaction of race and union interest eventually brought the AFL within the orbit of the Democratic Party. The Democratic path to union nativism would be slightly less rocky than the proimmigration path that dominant forces in the Republican Party ultimately followed. The historic Democratic defense of old-stock immigrants against the anti-Catholic nativism of Whigs, Know-Nothings, and Republicans made nativism as such a problematic principle for Democrats to embrace. The equally historic Democratic defense of race thinking, however, mediated this difficulty. The race implications of Chinese immigration, which Democrats were quick to stress, allowed Democrats to differentiate between defense of the ethnoreligious and political habits of *immigrants* and opposition to the effects of *immigration* on race and the labor market. This differentiation eventually allowed the Democratic Party to remain a shelter from anti-Catholic and antiradical nativism while accommodating union nativism.

By the turn of the century, contradictions within the parties with respect to immigration would be largely resolved. The Republican position would express procapitalist, proimmigration interests, while the Democratic position would reflect nativist union sympathies. Meanwhile, the anxieties of old labor concerning organizational efforts and the labor market had hardened its race logic. The concerns of union labor over union building and job consciousness would be quite wittingly funneled through the sieve of racial nativism. Gompers defended union labor's support for immigration restriction in 1902, saying, "This regulation will exclude hardly any of the natives of Great Britain, Ireland, Germany or Scandinavia. It will exclude only a small proportion of our immigrants from North Italy. It will shut out a considerable number of South Italians and Slavs and others equally or more undesirable or injurious."[54] Racial protection of society and the labor market would be the first bond in the forging of a tie between unions and Democrats in the election of 1896 and after.

Notes

Abridged from Gwendolyn Mink, *Old Labor and New Immigrants in American Political Development: Union, Party, and State, 1875–1920* (Ithaca: Cornell University Press, 1986), chap. 3.

1. Samuel Gompers, *The American Labor Movement: Its Makeup, Achievements, and Aspirations* (1914), in *Free Government in the Making: Readings in American Political Thought*, ed. Alpheus Thomas Mason, 3d ed. (New York: Oxford University Press, 1965), 657.

2. Alexander Saxton, *The Indispensable Enemy: Labor and the Anti-Chinese Movement in California* (Berkeley: University of California Press, 1971). My discussion follows many of Saxton's insights.

3. Ibid., 273–79; and A. T. Lane, "American Trade Unions, Mass Immigration, and the Literacy Test 1900–1917," *Labor History* 25 (winter 1984): 5–25.

4. See Frank Roney, *Frank Roney, Irish Rebel and California Labor Leader: An Autobiography* (New York: AMS Press, 1931), chaps. 4–5.

5. Samuel Gompers, *Seventy Years of Life and Labor* (New York: E. P. Dutton, 1919), 1:217.

6. Cf. Saxton, *Indispensable Enemy*, chap. 3; Mary Roberts Coolidge, *Chinese Immigration* (New York: Arno Press, [1909] 1969); Hubert Howe Bancroft, *Works*, vol. 38 (1887); and Carl C. Plehn, "Labor in California," *Yale Review* 4 (1896): 410.

7. U.S. Bureau of the Census, Ninth Census, *Population* (1872), 1:5.

8. Lucille Eaves, *History of California Labor Legislation* (Berkeley: University of California Press, 1910), 3; Elmer Sandmeyer, *The Anti-Chinese Movement in California* (Urbana: University of Illinois Press, 1939), 17.

9. Eaves, *California Labor Legislation*; Coolidge, *Chinese Immigration*, 6, 350; Ira Cross, *History of the Labor Movement in California* (Berkeley: University of California Press, 1935), 61.

10. The railroads were long identified as the importers of Chinese contract labor. Legislation to enforce such contracts triggered the first cries for Chinese exclusion in the spring of 1852. See *Daily Alta California*, March 10, 21, April 12, May 4, 1852.

11. Coolidge, *Chinese Immigration*, 30; Cross, *Labor Movement*, 64.

12. Ninth Census, *Population*, 768

13. Ibid., 347, 768.

14. See Joel Silbey, *A Respectable Minority: The Democratic Party in the Civil War Era, 1860–1868* (New York: Norton, 1977); Eric Foner, *Free Soil, Free Labor, Free Men: The Ideology of the Republican Party before the Civil War* (New York: Oxford University Press, 1970), 231; and James F. Richardson, *The New York Police: Colonial Times to 1901* (New York: Oxford University Press, 1970), 130–42. According to Richardson, the draft riots erupted as a consequence of social and labor market conditions, including competition between Irish and black workers. The rioters were generally lower-class Irish. The riots were at one level probably class acts but at another fraught with race feeling.

15. In 1870 the labor force in the boot and shoe industry was 19 percent Chinese-born, 26 percent Irish-born, 18 percent German-born, and 3 percent British-born. Twenty percent was U.S.-born, though presumably many of this group were children of old-stock immigrant groups. Ninety-one percent of the labor force in cigars and tobacco was Chinese. Statistics compiled from the U.S. Census of 1870 in Coolidge, *Chinese Immigration*, 359.

16. Sandmeyer, *Anti-Chinese Movement*, 47–48.

17. Henry George, "The Chinese on the Pacific Coast," *New York Tribune*, May 1, 1869, 1, 3.

18. Coolidge, *Chinese Immigration*, 359, 366; Gompers, *Seventy Years*, 216–17; Samuel Gompers and Herman Guttstadt, *Meat vs. Rice, American Manhood vs. Asiatic Coolieism: Which Shall Survive?* (1902).

19. Saxton, *Indispensable Enemy*, 74.

20. California *Assembly Journal*, 23d sess. (1880), 78; E. R. Spedden, "The Trade Union Label," Johns Hopkins University *Studies*, ser. 28, no. 2, 89 n. 1.

21. Cross, *Labor Movement*, 69; Sandmeyer, *Anti-Chinese Movement*, 16–17; Coolidge, *Chinese Immigration*, 354

22. Sandmeyer, *Anti-Chinese Movement*, 49.

23. Kirk H. Porter and Donald B. Johnson, *National Party Platforms, 1840–1960* (Urbana: University of Illinois Press, 1961), 50, 54.

24. James Bryce, *The American Commonwealth* (New York: Macmillan, 1910), 2:449.

25. San Francisco *Examiner*, July 24–28, 1877.

26. Roney, *Frank Roney*, 300; Ralph Kauer, "The Workingmen's Party of California," *Pacific Historical Review* 13 (September 1944): 278–91.

27. Roney, *Frank Roney*, 271.

28. Cf. Eaves, *California Labor Legislation*, 33.

29. Kauer, "Workingmen's Party," 280.

30. Quoted in Cross, *Labor Movement*, 98.

31. See Hubert Howe Bancroft, *History of California* (1887), 7:358; San Francisco *Examiner*, October 30, 1877; *Evening Bulletin*, November 5, 1877; Kauer, "Workingmen's Party," 282.

32. Kauer, "Workingmen's Party," 283–84; Theodore H. Hittell, "Observations on the New Constitution," *Overland Monthly* 1 (January 1883): 34–41; Eaves, *California Labor Legislation*; Henry George, "The Kearney Agitation in California," *Popular Science Monthly* 17 (August 1880?): 446; and Eric Foner, "Class, Ethnicity, and Radicalism in the Gilded Age: The Land League and Irish-America," in *Politics and Ideology in the Age of the Civil War*, ed. Eric Foner (New York: Oxford University Press, 1980), 150–201.

33. George, "Kearney Agitation," 446.

34. Eaves, *California Labor Legislation*, 37; Carey McWilliams, *Factories in the Field* (Boston: Little, Brown, [1939] 1944), 3. Affected corporations successfully challenged the anti-Chinese clauses of the new constitution in the courts. See *In Re Tiburcio Parrott*, 6; Sawyer, 349–89.

35. See *Debates and Proceedings of the Constitutional Convention of California* 2 (1881): 700–704.

36. Cross, *Labor Movement*, 123; Kauer, "Workingmen's Party," 287.

37. Roney, *Frank Roney*, 303–04.

38. Steven P. Erie, "The Organization of Irish-Americans into Urban Institutions: Building the Political Machine, 1840–1896," paper delivered to the American Political Science Association (1983); Martin Shefter, "The Electoral Foundations of the Political Machine: New York City, 1884–1897," in *The History of American Electoral Behavior*, ed. Joel Silbey, Allan G. Bogue, and William H. Flanigan (Princeton: Princeton University Press, 1978), 263–99.

39. Lee Benson, *The Concept of Jacksonian Democracy* (Princeton: Princeton University Press, 1961); Paul Kleppner, *The Cross of Culture: A Social Analysis of Midwestern Politics, 1850–1900* (New York: Free Press, 1970); Clifton Yearley, *The Money Machines: The Breakdown of Reform of Governmental and Party Finance in the North, 1860–1920* (Albany: State University of New York Press, 1972); Amy Bridges, *A City in the Republic* (Cambridge: Cambridge University Press, 1984), chap. 5.

40. In April 1882 the *New York Tribune* commented that the Democratic Party hoped to become strong in California through hatred of the Chinese.

41. *Daily Alta California*, March 4, 1882, 1, March 9, 1882, 1; Saxton, *Indispensable Enemy*, 133–37.

42. Quoted ibid., April 19, 1882, editorial, 2.

43. Quoted in *Daily Alta California*, January 8, 1882, 1; Saxton, *Indispensable Enemy*, 169.

44. Saxton, *Indispensable Enemy*, 160.

45. Actually, to the founding of the Federation of Organized Trades and Labor Unions, the immediate predecessor of the AFL.

46. Quoted in *Daily Alta California*, March 18, 1882, 1.

47. lbid., April 15, 27, 1882.

48. Republicans in California were embarrassed by the veto; Californians generally were enraged. See *Daily Alta California*, April, 1882, 1.

49. Until the late 1890s the AFL denied charters to unions whose constitutions explicitly denied membership to blacks. Probably the most famous controversy arising from this policy involved the National Machinists' Association, whose union constitution drew the color line. Though the AFL (notably Gompers) helped organize a separate union that did not include a color bar in its constitution, it (and Gompers) acquiesced in a compromise that transferred the point of discrimination from the constitution to individual admission decision. Bernard Mandel, "Samuel Gompers and Negro Workers, 1866–1914," *Journal of Negro History* 40 (1955): 34–60.

50. U.S. Senate, Committee on Education and Labor, *Relations between Capital and Labor*, Hearings (1885), 1:280–82.

51. AFL *Proceedings* (1893), 73.

52. *American Federationist* 5 (1898): 269–71.

53. Samuel Gompers, "Talks on Labor," *American Federalist*, September 1905, 636–37 (emphasis added). Saxton argues that "the phrase 'any others' . . . actually contained a major significance. It referred to the so-called new immigration from southern and eastern Europe." Alexander Saxton, "Race and the House of Labor," in *The Great Fear: Race to the Mind of America*, ed. Gary B. Nash and Richard Weiss (New York: Holt, Rinehart, and Winston, 1970), 15.

54. Gompers, AFL *Proceedings* (1902), 21–22.

Theodore Roosevelt and the Divided

Character of American Nationalism

Any examination of American nationalism must, sooner or later, contend with its contradictory character. On the one hand, it offers a civic creed promising all Americans the same individual rights irrespective of color, religion, or sex. On the other hand, American nationalism has long harbored racial ideologies that define the United States and its mission in ethnoracial ways and have sought to prove American racial superiority through economic might and military conquest.

This essay explores the contradictory character of this nationalism. It does so not by identifying groups such as the National Association for the Advancement of Colored People (NAACP) and the Ku Klux Klan (KKK) that espoused one principle or the other, but by examining how the two principles often coexisted in the minds of single individuals. No individual better illustrates this phenomenon than Theodore Roosevelt, a historian, dude rancher, civil service commissioner, police commissioner, governor, soldier, president, explorer. Few figures of any age have matched his devotion to the American nation or his influence on the form and content of American nationalism. Regardless of the task Roosevelt was carrying out, the office he had assumed, or the adventure he had undertaken, he was always looking for ways to strengthen the American nation and intensify the nationalist ardor of the American people.

Roosevelt's nationalism expressed itself as a combative and unapologetic racial ideology that thrived on aggression and the vanquishing of savage and barbaric peoples. From the perspective of that ideology, it was vital that Americans cultivate their racial superiority and expel or subordinate the racial inferiors in their midst. Yet Roosevelt also located within American nationalism a powerful civic tradition that celebrated the United States as a place that welcomed all people, irrespective of their nationality, race, and religious practice, as long as they were willing to devote themselves to the nation and obey its laws.[1] Moreover, Roosevelt loved the idea of America as a melting pot—a crucible—in which a hybrid race of many strains would be forged. Mixing of this sort, Roosevelt believed, had created and would sustain American racial superiority. His affection for the melting pot expressed, too, the personal delight he took in crossing social boundaries and meeting diverse groups of people.

Most of the time Roosevelt found ways to reconcile his commitments to the racial and civic traditions of American nationalism. He disciplined his celebration of hybridity by insisting that certain kinds of boundary crossing would damage the racially superior character of the American nation, and he expended much effort to explain why blacks, in particular, could not participate in America's great melting pot. But Roosevelt's efforts at reconciliation were not always successful. In particular, his commitment to the civic tradition sometimes filled him with anxiety and uncertainty about America's racial order and caused him to violate that order in sensational and politically damaging ways. The civic and racial traditions, in other words, sometimes pulled Roosevelt in such different directions that he could not easily encase them both within the national identity he was laboring so hard to create. Building the American nation from such contradictory materials turns out to have been exceptionally difficult political and personal work.

Roosevelt never stopped trying to reconcile his civic and racial beliefs or to construct his nation, as his extensive writings amply attest. Nor did he ever question the need to build a nation. But the sheer arduousness of his nation-building efforts allows one to glimpse the problem of trying to yoke divergent human aspirations to a nationalist ideal. Roosevelt celebrated racial conquest but also admired certain forms of racial mixing; he prized social order as a paramount political good but also thirsted for adventure and the thrill of the unexpected and the chaos that so often accompanied it. The very complexity of his strivings, in other words, may have rendered one nation too limiting a space for personal exploration and aspiration. The case of Roosevelt suggests that the desire to escape or to transcend the nation lurked not only in the minds of international migrants, such as the Italian sojourners about whom Donna Gabaccia writes, but in the minds of leading nationalists themselves.

Roosevelt's Racialized Nation

In the late nineteenth century, nationalist ideologies grounded in race strengthened their hold on the peoples of many countries, including those of the United States. These were the years of a remarkable global capitalist expansion. Societies in disparate geographic and cultural regions were interpenetrating each other, their peoples looking variously for work, raw materials, markets, and, at least the missionaries among them, souls ripe for salvation. The resulting jostling of peoples, often under adverse economic conditions—poverty-level wages among workers, production costs that exceeded revenues among farmers, the eclipse of small business by corporations—generated fears of social disintegration and a tendency to blame misfortune on social contamination. Groups within every industrial society began calling for racial purity as a way of strengthening their nations and of overcoming the problems that capitalist development had thrust upon them. International competition intensified, as nations sought to prove their economic, military, and racial superiority.

In the United States one can detect the growing prestige of racial ideologies in the victory over Spain in 1898 and in the acquisition of Spanish colonies in the Caribbean Sea and the Pacific Ocean. The war generated national unity, becoming an occasion when seemingly intractable divisions—between North and South, capital and labor, native-born and immigrant—were at least momentarily overcome. But such unity depended on the reinvigoration of America's racial nationalist tradition. In the new American territories of the Philippines and Puerto Rico, the indigenous peoples were declared racially inferior and thus incapable of handling the responsibilities of American citizenship. At home, the formal subjugation of the African American population in the South through Jim Crow allowed white southerners to believe that "their" nation had finally been redeemed. White westerners associated national greatness with their campaigns to "cleanse" their cities and states of Chinese and Japanese influence. A belief in the superiority of the American "race" underlay these efforts at racial exclusion and subordination. Drawing on internationalist and allegedly scientific racialist discourses, themselves the product of the modern age of capital, white Americans found the essence of their race in its Anglo-Saxon, English-speaking, or simply white character.[2]

In the 1880s, Theodore Roosevelt had turned his intellectual talents to identifying the historical origins of this American race and to tracing how it made itself the greatest English-speaking race the world had ever known. That was the purpose of his epic work, *The Winning of the West* (1889–96), most of which focused on the conquest and settlement of the American West by people of European origin.[3]

If for Karl Marx history was the history of class conflict, for Roosevelt it was the history of race conflict, of the world's various races struggling for supremacy and power. The history of racial conflict, in Roosevelt's eyes, pointed in the direction of civilization and progress: more often than not, the higher, civilized races triumphed over the lower, savage or barbaric ones. But this tendency was not an iron law; there had been reversals—the Dark Ages being the most notable—when the forces of barbarism had overwhelmed the citadels of civilization. No race, no matter how civilized its people or how superior their mental ability, could afford to become complacent about its destiny. Racial triumph came only to those peoples willing to fight for it. Success in battle required the cultivation of manly, warlike, even savage qualities: physical toughness and fitness, fearlessness, bravery, single-mindedness, ruthlessness. Thus, Roosevelt found the formative experience of the American race neither in the godly Puritans who settled New England, nor in the virtuous farmers of the mid-Atlantic states who diligently worked the land, nor even among the Boston, New York, and Philadelphia merchants who made great fortunes by acquiring and trading the continent's abundant resources. Rather, he found it in the backwoodsmen who bravely ventured forth into the wilderness to battle the Indians and clear the land. The backwoodsmen, in Roosevelt's eyes, like the Germans who had invaded Britain and fashioned a super-Teutonic race there, were warriors above all, and their primary task was not placid husbandry but relentless war against the savage Indians who claimed the lands as their own. Roosevelt had no use for Frederick Jackson Turner's view of the frontier as a sparsely inhabited place awaiting cultivation by diligent bands of husbandmen. "A race of peaceful, unwarlike farmers," Roosevelt argued, "would have been helpless before such foes as the red Indians, and no auxiliary military forces could have protected them or enabled them to move westward. . . . The West would never have been settled save for the fierce courage and the eager desire to brave danger so characteristic of the stalwart backwoodsmen."[4]

Roosevelt loathed the savage red man but admired him, too, for his bravery, cunning, and, most of all, ferocity. The backwoodsman achieved his greatness as a result of the battles he fought to subdue the Indian foe. Roosevelt regarded the conquest of the Indians and the winning of the West as "the great epic feat in the history of our race." The relentless westward march was "a record of men who greatly dared and greatly did, a record of wanderings wider and more dangerous than those of the Vikings; a record of endless feats of arms, of victory after victory in the ceaseless strife waged against wild man and wild nature."[5] The war to exterminate the Indian created the Americans.

That war, Roosevelt believed, had set in motion a critical assimilatory process, one that fashioned a single American people out of many European races. The backwoodsmen, according to Roosevelt, were primarily the descendants of two British races, the Scotch-Irish and the English, but included in their ranks significant numbers of Germans, Huguenots, Hollanders, and Swedes. Although those distinct so-called racial groups were still conscious of their differences when they arrived in the wilderness, they became oblivious to them within the lifetimes of the first settlers. "A single generation, passed under the hard conditions of life in the wilderness," Roosevelt wrote, "was enough to weld [them] together into one people." And so, "long before the first Continental Congress assembled, the backwoodsmen, whatever their blood, had become Americans, one in speech, thought, and character." "Their iron surroundings," Roosevelt continued, "made a mould which turned out all alike in the same shape." Here, for the first of many times, Roosevelt referred in a positive way to the melting pot origins of the American people.[6]

But Roosevelt included in his American brew only races emanating from Europe. What to do, then, with non-European races residing on American soil? Roosevelt did not worry much about the proper place of Indians in the nation, for the savage wars with the Americans had culminated in their expulsion or extermination. But he was troubled by the place and role of blacks. Roosevelt regarded the importation of African slaves to the North American continent as a racial and national catastrophe. The European races who conquered America, Roosevelt intoned, "to their own lasting harm, committed a crime whose short-sighted folly was worse than its guilt, for they brought hordes of African slaves, whose descendants now form immense populations in certain portions of this land." Those "hordes" could never truly be assimilated into American society: the distance separating them from the white races was simply too great. Neither could they provide the proud savage foe against whom American warriors defined their race and peoplehood, for the Africans were already a bowed and conquered people when they arrived, forced to obey their masters' every command. Regrettably, the black man could "neither be killed nor driven away." He had to be found a place in the nation. But where? Giving blacks an equal place would violate the racial order of things, while hemming them into a subordinate status vitiated the American commitment to democracy and equal opportunity.[7]

Roosevelt blamed this dilemma not on his heroic backwoodsmen, but on the "trans-oceanic aristocracy" of the seventeenth century and eighteenth that had allegedly created and sustained the international slave trade. The racial crime committed by those aristocrats had already triggered one national disaster, the Civil War, that almost destroyed the mighty nation the backwoodsmen had so painstakingly and courageously built. And even emancipation, an act Roosevelt heartily supported, provided no simple cure to the race problem because Negroes, he believed, would not take well to democracy, a form of government that depended on a self-control and mastery that only the white races had attained. As president, Roosevelt struggled to devise what were, in his eyes, decent remedies to the race problem. But he always regarded the Negro as an indelible black mark on the white nation that had so gloriously emerged in the mid-eighteenth century, a constant reminder of America's racial imperfection, of an opportunity compromised by the nefarious dealings of corrupt, antidemocratic, and immoral aristocrats. There would never be, Roosevelt once conceded in private correspondence, a true solution to "the terrible problem offered by the presence of the negro on this continent."[8]

The 1890s: Crisis, War, and Nationalist Renewal

The Winning of the West brims with confidence. But even as he was writing this treatise Roosevelt was beset by worry that past achievements had set in motion processes that could yet ruin the American race. By the early 1890s, the wild frontier of the eighteenth century had vanished, and the Indians had been routed. The conquest of the West and the invention of democracy had triggered technological and cultural revolutions that were rapidly making America into an urban, industrialized society. While the backwoodsmen had set the changes in motion, their very success had forced them to the margins of American society. Roosevelt worried that America, as a result, would lose its racial edge. "A peaceful and commercial civilization," he wrote, "is always in danger of suffering the loss of the virile fighting qualities without which no nation, however cultured, however refined, however thrifty and prosperous, can ever amount to anything."[9]

Everywhere Roosevelt spotted signs of racial degeneration: in an overly refined elite that had abandoned "the strenuous life" for the effete manners and habits of European aristocrats; in a falling birth rate among this same elite, an unmistakable sign to Roosevelt that the vigor of this mighty race was slipping; in the impoverished urban masses whose loyalty to the nation was questionable and whose growing involvement in lawless strikes Roosevelt regarded as signs of barbarism; in a society so preoccupied with material gain and "ignoble ease" that it no longer knew how to pursue the heroic life. In short, the unique, racially superior civilization the backwoodsmen had assiduously created was in danger of going the way of Rome, brought low by opulence, complacency, effeminacy, and military collapse.[10]

Roosevelt conceived of his personal life as a crusade against the enervating effects of excessive civilization. He was determined to excel at hunting and ranching, to develop the qualities that made the Scotch-Irish backwoodsmen such a vigorous race. His two wives and six children were ample demonstration of his virility and, he hoped, an example that other members of his race would emulate. He preached against the complacent life, whether that of the beggar content to live off charity or of the railroad tycoon obsessed with counting his money. He called repeatedly for the pursuit of a "higher life" of glory, as achieved by George Washington, Abraham Lincoln, and Ulysses S. Grant. Each of those heroes had distinguished himself during war, and Roosevelt believed that true eminence would elude him until he, too, had proved his worth on the battlefield.[11]

Just as he expected his program for a strenuous life to bring him personal greatness, so Roosevelt believed that an emphasis on muscular and racialized nationalism would reinvigorate America. By the early 1890s he had cast his lot with Adm. Alfred Thayer Mahan and other imperialists who argued that the United States should vie with Britain, France, Germany, Russia, and Japan for territory, military might, and world power. Social Darwinists to the core, the imperialists believed that America had to prove itself the military equal of the strongest European nation and the master of the lesser peoples of Asia, Africa, and Latin America. Hankering for a fight, they strove to turn emergent power struggles in the Caribbean and the Pacific into armed confrontations. Fights with barbarian races abroad could replace the fight with the savage Indians at home and thus keep Americans racially fit. As Roosevelt declared in 1897, "No triumph of peace is quite so great as the supreme triumph of war." The imperialists' opportunity came in 1898, when the explosion of the battleship *Maine* in Havana harbor set Spain and the United States on the path to war.[12]

At the first opportunity, Roosevelt resigned as assistant secretary of the navy to accept the lieutenant colonelcy of the First Volunteer Cavalry, soon to be immortalized as the Rough Riders. More than twenty thousand men applied for the one thousand available places, and Roosevelt filled a majority of the ranks with cowboys, hunters, and prospectors from the West and Southwest—men who bore the closest resemblance to his fabled backwoodsmen. "They were a splendid set of men," Roosevelt would later write, "tall and sinewy, with resolute, weather-beaten faces, and eyes that looked a man straight in the face without flinching." "In all the world," he added, "there could be no better material for soldiers than that afforded by these grim hunters of the mountains, these wild rough riders of the plains." Having come from lands that had been "most recently won over [from the savage Indians] to white civilization," these men were among the few remaining Americans who still possessed the ferocity, the independence, and the war-making skills of the Kentucky backwoodsmen.[13]

Just as the predominately Scotch-Irish backwoodsmen had benefited from the admixture of minority streams from France, Germany, and elsewhere, so the quality of the Rough Riders was enhanced by the inclusion of complementary American strains. Most important were the fifty men, most of them athletes, who had come from Harvard, Princeton, and Yale universities and who, in Roosevelt's eyes, possessed a worldliness and a capacity for leadership that many of the rowdy southwesterners lacked. Roosevelt chose an equal number of Indians (segregated in their own company), a few of pure blood but most a disciplined mixture of red and white. He selected a smattering of Irishmen and Hispanics, at least one Jew, one Italian, four New York City policemen, and a group "in whose veins . . . blood stirred with the same impulse which once sent the Vikings overseas." Like the frontier, the regiment created the conditions for a carefully regulated process of racial mixing, one meant to generate the finest possible American fighting force.

Three cups of southwesterners, a leavening tablespoon of Ivy Leaguers, a tablespoon of Indians, and a sprinkling of Jews, Irish, Italians, and Scandinavians yielded, in Roosevelt's eyes, a sterling, all-American regiment.[14]

The inclusion of even limited numbers of Indians, Jews, and Italians made the regiment more diverse than the bands of backwoodsmen who had conquered the West had been—a sign, perhaps, that Roosevelt was becoming more liberal in his racial attitudes than he had been when he wrote *Winning of the West*.[15] Yet Roosevelt was not prepared to welcome every racial type into the Rough Rider crucible: he had neither sought nor accepted any black or Asian American volunteers, demonstrating once again his conviction that the inclusion of the "most inferior" racial ingredients would pollute the American brew. The melting pot continued to depend for its success as much on exclusion as on inclusion.[16]

The Rough Riders quickly achieved a camaraderie that, in Roosevelt's eyes, justified his efforts to regulate the racial mixing. The Ivy Leaguers brought civility to a regiment full of rowdy spirits, while the roughness and physicality of the southwesterners compelled the elite easterners to abandon their aversion to hard and disagreeable labor. The regiment somewhat uneasily absorbed the few Irishmen, Italians, and Jews, giving them affectionate though belittling nicknames such as Sheeny Solomon and Pork-chop. The social equality Roosevelt encouraged also shaped relations between officers and enlisted men. Roosevelt craved a close relationship with his troops. He got to know each of his thousand men by name, greeted them with waves rather than formal salutes, bought them beer after a long march, took his sergeants to dinner at a restaurant reserved for the army's top brass, and commandeered officers' rations for his enlisted men. Here was a way for him to re-create a frontier environment, where social distinctions and rank counted for little. A man was judged for his ability as a man, and that was all.[17]

Roosevelt wanted his regiment to shine. Using all of their organizational abilities and influence in Washington, Roosevelt and his superior, Col. Leonard Wood, made sure the Rough Riders were among the first troops to disembark at Daiquirí, Cuba, in June 1898 and to begin marching toward the expected engagement with Spanish troops in the heavily fortified hills east of Santiago. The Spanish, as it turned out, were in no mood for a long war and gave up after only three weeks and four battles. But the Rough Riders played important roles in three of the four—Las Guásimas, Kettle

Hill, and San Juan Hill—and came home military heroes. Roosevelt, by muscling his way to Cuba, had literally willed his regiment to the battlefield and to glory.[18]

It had taken considerable propaganda to turn the light-complexioned and highly cultured Spanish enemy into the dark and savage foe, but the American tabloids, led by the Hearst and Pulitzer papers, proved equal to the task. These newspapers fed American civilians and troops a steady diet of sensational stories about atrocities the Spanish had committed against the freedom-loving Cubans, and they focused on the sinister Catholicism of the Spanish as a way of explaining to their Protestant nation the autocratic, ruthless character of Spanish rule. Visually, the Spanish were often depicted in the simian form that Americans used to portray the races they most despised.[19]

The Rough Riders' first encounter with Spanish troops seemed to confirm the Spaniards' savage racial nature. The Americans had expected to meet the Spanish in a civilized engagement on an open field of battle, but instead they were ambushed in heavily forested terrain at Las Guásimas. The battle revealed that the Spanish army had adopted the guerrilla maneuvers favored by their Cuban adversaries, an intelligent adaptation of military tactics to the Cuban terrain and foe that the Americans would come to respect. But initially it seemed to Roosevelt and others steeped in frontier lore that at Las Guásimas they had encountered a savage enemy. Roosevelt's recounting of the battle resembled the narratives he had written about eighteenth-century Indian attacks in the Kentucky backwoods. Victory came to the Rough Riders, in Roosevelt's telling, because they demonstrated the same pluck, resourcefulness, and courage as the Kentucky backwoodsmen. And just as the tough conditions of the American wilderness had welded the frontiersmen, "whatever their blood," into one superior people, so too the rough encounter at Las Guásimas had forged the motley Rough Riders into a truly American shape.[20]

Las Guásimas was only a prelude to the furious battles at Kettle and San Juan hills, the heavily fortified ridges that guarded the approach to Santiago. The Rough Riders had been assigned a support role behind several regiments of regular troops, but as the casualties mounted and as communications between the generals in the rear and frontline troops broke down, Roosevelt moved his Rough Riders into the thick of the action. By the time the fighting had ended, 90 of the 450 Rough Riders who had entered the battle lay killed or wounded. A bullet grazed Roosevelt's wrist, but he was not seriously wounded. In this climactic battle Roosevelt had long wished for, he seemed as immortal as a Greek god, especially to the awestruck journalists who were reporting this fight to the millions of avid newspaper readers back home. "Mounted high on horseback, and charging the rifle-pits at a gallop and quite alone," wrote Richard Harding Davis, the famed *New York Herald* and *Scribner's* reporter, Roosevelt "made you feel that you would like to cheer."[21]

In the Cuban campaign, Roosevelt brought to life the mythic past he had invented for the American people in *The Winning of the West*. In the climactic Kettle Hill–San Juan Hill battle that symbolized the triumph of America over savagery and the confluence of the many streams of humanity into one American people, Roosevelt himself played the starring role. But there was a problem. Just as the arrival of the black man on the North American continent had compromised the great white nation taking shape there, so, too, the presence of black U.S. troops on Kettle Hill and San Juan Hill interfered with the nation's triumph—or at least with Roosevelt's enjoyment of that triumph.

Roosevelt had been able to keep blacks out of the Rough Riders, but he could not keep them out of the United States army in Cuba. Four regular regiments—a substantial percentage of the U.S. Army—were black (although commanded by white officers), and they were among the most experienced and reliable American troops. The Negro Ninth and Tenth cavalry regiments fought well at Las Guásimas and played an even more vital role in the taking of Kettle and San Juan hills. The Tenth Cavalry had been the frontline troops on Kettle Hill, and in that battle lost more of their officers (eleven of twenty-two) than any other regiment. When Roosevelt called for a charge up the hill, they promptly joined in; meanwhile, several platoons of the Ninth Cavalry reached the summit of Kettle Hill from a different direction at the same moment as Roosevelt. Black troops from both regiments and, even more important, from the Twenty-Fourth Infantry Division, fought hard for San Juan Hill as well.[22]

When Roosevelt reached the top of San Juan Hill, he found himself the effective commander of the Rough Riders, the Ninth and Tenth Negro cavalries, and three other cavalry regiments. The chaos of battle had willy-nilly produced a true American melting pot—the heterogeneity of the Rough Riders further diversified by the presence of both white and black regulars—and the pot had served its purpose well, as all these diverse troops had fought as a single, cohesive unit. White regulars, the heavily southwestern Rough Riders, the journalists, and even Roosevelt himself all heaped praise on the black soldiers, who returned to the United States as heroes. The Tenth Cavalry marched in a parade down Washington's Pennsylvania Avenue and received President William McKinley's salute. When Roosevelt bid farewell to the Rough Riders in October, he toasted the black soldiers: "The Spaniards called them 'Smoked Yankees,'" he said, "but we found them to be an excellent breed of Yankees. I am sure that I speak the sentiments of officers and men in the assemblage when I say that between you and the other cavalry regiments there exists a tie which we trust will never be broken." The Rough Riders, reported a black soldier of the Tenth Cavalry, roared their approval.[23]

Roosevelt might have seized on evidence of the intermixing of black and white troops to celebrate the melting pot as a mechanism that could fashion a single nation out of all the different racial, ethnic, and regional groups who resided in the United States. But he had never been entirely comfortable with the presence of blacks fighting alongside whites on Kettle and San Juan hills. In fact, he had been alarmed by the mixing, by "the different regiments being *completely intermingled*—white regulars, colored regulars, and Rough Riders." He believed that complete and unregulated mixing—as had happened in Mexico and other Latin countries—produced mediocre races. The indiscriminate mingling of black and white troops in the heat of battle, moreover, threatened to explode the myth that regulated assimilation produced racially superior Americans and to disrupt the reenactment of assimilation carefully orchestrated by Roosevelt himself. The black troops had to be put in their place—a place separate from and subordinate to that of white Americans.[24]

Roosevelt took on this task when he began publishing his history of the Rough Riders in *Scribner's Magazine* in 1899. In recounting the seizure of San Juan Hill, Roosevelt interrupted his triumphalist narrative to criticize the shortcomings of the Negro troops. While these troops were excellent fighters, they were "peculiarly dependent upon their white officers"; left on their own—as many had been by the time they arrived on the summit of San Juan Hill, given the high casualty rate among the officers of the Ninth and Tenth—they faltered, even ran. Roosevelt recalled having to draw his revolver on black troops who seemed to be leaving their positions without permission. Only after he had threatened to shoot them did they return to the forward lines.[25]

Presley Holliday, a black soldier of the Tenth Cavalry, remembered the incident differently. He described a chaotic situation as night was falling on San Juan Hill amid many calls for soldiers to carry the wounded to the rear and to procure rations and trenching tools for the troops at the summit. Both Rough Riders and black soldiers responded to those calls, which created the impression of many soldiers leaving the battle scene. That is what Roosevelt apparently saw when he drew his revolver and aimed it at the black troops. But, according to Holliday, Lt. Robert F. Fleming of the Tenth (a white officer) quickly reassured Roosevelt that the black soldiers had been following orders; the next day, Roosevelt even visited members of the Tenth Cavalry and apologized to them.[26]

It is, of course, difficult to know exactly what went on at dusk, when all the soldiers, including Roosevelt himself, were exhausted from the fight and may have had difficulty seeing and thinking clearly. It is possible that some black troops may have been too quick to leave the still insecure summit for the safety of the rear when the opportunity arose. Holliday admitted that some of the Tenth Cavalry's newer recruits became nervous at being separated from the bulk of their regiment and at being in such close proximity to white soldiers. But even if nervousness prompted them to look for opportunities to leave the summit, it was not adequate reason for Roosevelt to challenge the worth of the black fighting man. There had been instances in Cuba of white soldierly cowardice and of blacks proving themselves to be the more stalwart troops; indeed, the colored Twenty-Fourth Infantry had been called upon to charge San Juan Hill—and did—only after the white Seventy-First New York had panicked and refused to attack. Roosevelt ignored this and other incidents of white cowardice and black valor, determined as he was to charge that only black troops lacked the self-reliance and hardy individualism to become their own men, to become true Americans. In that chaotic and confusing moment on San Juan Hill, Roosevelt was certain he had uncovered incontrovertible evidence of the black soldiers' "peculiar dependence" on white officers. Whereas the Rough Riders, in Roosevelt's eyes, had shown themselves equal to the Kentucky backwoodsmen in every respect, the black cavalry troops had demonstrated once again what Roosevelt viscerally believed: that blacks were not truly fit for combat, that they lacked the qualities needed to participate as equals in the great nation that Daniel Boone and his fellow frontiersmen had willed into existence in the eighteenth century.[27]

These were devastating charges in 1899, especially when leveled by a person of Roosevelt's stature. Emboldened by the Supreme Court decision in *Plessy v. Ferguson* (1896), the South was disfranchising blacks and excluding them from institutions that had been designated white—schools, restaurants, stores, parks, and many places of employment. In the North, whites were pushing blacks out of the skilled trades and service jobs that had long supported a small but vibrant black middle class. The Spanish-American War took on special significance in this context. African Americans hoped that their impressive record of service would compel the U.S. military to open officer ranks to them, and that the achievement of that status could then bolster their quest for equality, integration, and belonging in other areas of American life as well. How could a nation permit officers of its own army to be denied the right to vote, to sit on juries, or to use public accommodations? Most whites, Roosevelt among them, evidently agreed that the nation could not tolerate this contradiction. They sought to resolve it, however, not by tearing down racial barriers, but by reinforcing and justifying the ones already in place. Just as most blacks could not successfully discharge the responsibilities of citizenship, so, too, Roosevelt and others argued, they could not be entrusted with leading troops into battle. The black demand for officer status was rebuffed. In this climate it did not take long for whites to challenge the fighting abilities of black soldiers, even when they were commanded by white officers. By the First World War, few blacks were given combat roles. The nation had stripped virtually all blacks of the right to fight and die for their country. The sacrifices and heroism of the Ninth and Tenth cavalries had become but a dim memory to whites. White southerners, meanwhile, were reintegrating themselves into the military. As a result of the Spanish-American War, efforts to re-create the United States as a white nation had borne fruit.[28]

The centrality of race to the definition of Roosevelt's America was apparent, too, in the treatment of the Cubans and Filipinos, ostensible allies of the Americans in the fight against the Spaniards. Finding a savage foe in the Spanish-American War proved a more difficult task than Roosevelt and others had anticipated. Despite their alleged savage behavior at Las Guásimas, the Spanish soldiers soon revealed that they were far whiter and more civilized than the Americans had expected. Meanwhile, U.S. troops were unnerved by their encounters with Cuban troops, who were often poorly dressed and inadequately provisioned. American soldiers were particularly upset by the Cuban troops' practice of stripping corpses (of friend and foe alike) of clothing, food, guns, and any other usable items and by their penchant for begging. And they were stunned that Cuban troops were overwhelmingly dark in complexion. The U.S. troops knew little of the Cubans' long struggle for independence, of the hardships they had had to endure, and of why they had chosen guerrilla tactics against the Spanish. The Americans, influenced by Hearst and Pulitzer newspapers, had imagined that Cubans were a people much like themselves—freedom loving, civilized, and white. Hence, they were shocked to discover that the Cubans exhibited traits they could define as primitive and undignified. From this perspective, the black Cubans, not the Spanish, were the island's true savages.[29]

The Cubans themselves, however, never became a savage foe against whom the Americans felt compelled to fight a war of extermination—that honor went to the Filipinos. The Cubans instead became a childlike ally in need of American mentoring, assistance, and protection. On these grounds, the United States justified its refusal to grant the Cubans the political independence they sought. Instead, it made the island into a virtual colony, taking on the "white man's burden" of uplifting a darker race. In such ways the Spanish-American War reinforced Americans' sense of themselves as a white, superior people.[30]

Roosevelt's Civic Nationalism

It is tempting to interpret Roosevelt's nationalism as simply an American expression of what European scholars label ethnic, or romantic, nationalism. Such nationalism locates the essence of the nation in the *Volk*, defined as a people who share the same blood, history, language, and land. The *Volk*, in the eyes of ethnic nationalists, did not change much over time; it was thought of as an entity standing outside history, a force of moral and biological purity that could eradicate the alleged evils of modernity: corruption, materialism, promiscuity, and racial mixing.[31]

Many individuals and groups in the United States subscribed to such ethnoracialist notions, the Ku Klux Klan being the best known. But Roosevelt was not among them. The notion that the European peoples represented pure biological entities made no sense to him, for he understood that war and conquest had made the Europeans far more hybridized

than most cared to admit. Roosevelt celebrated hybridity: the world's greatest peoples, after all—the English, the Americans, the Australians—had
emerged from melting pots. Even prior to the Revolution, Roosevelt had
once written, "we were then already, what we are now, a people of mixed
blood." The smelting, Roosevelt believed, had to be controlled by a skilled
puddler if it was to produce the best and most efficient result; but properly
regulated racial mixing would always produce peoples superior to those
that had remained pure. In his celebration of hybridity, Roosevelt was very
much a modern and at odds with such members of his gentry class as Henry
Cabot Lodge, Madison Grant, and Frederic Remington, who longed for a
pure Anglo-Saxon America.[32]

Roosevelt instead was a civic nationalist who imagined the nation, to
use Michael Ignatieff's words, "as a community of equal, rights-bearing
citizens united in patriotic attachment to a shared set of political practices
and values." Such a national community was open, in theory at least, to all
those who resided in a nation's territory, irrespective of their ethnicity, race,
or religion. It was democratic, for it vested "sovereignty in all of the people."[33] In practice, Roosevelt's national community was open to anyone who
could claim European origins or ancestry. Roosevelt paid little attention
to whether those Europeans had come from eastern or western Europe,
from Catholic, Protestant, or Jewish backgrounds, or from the ranks of the
rich or the poor; to all he extended the invitation to become American. He
assumed a different posture toward blacks, Asians, and other nonwhites. He
did not attempt to exclude them from the political community as thoroughly as he had excluded them from his nationalist mythology. In fact,
on numerous occasions he defended the political rights and aspirations of
selected African Americans and Asians who, to his thinking, had achieved
a requisite level of intellectual and moral competence. But he also believed
that the vast majority of nonwhites would not achieve those levels during
his lifetime or for several lifetimes thereafter.

Although racism compromised his civic nationalism, it would be a mistake to dismiss the sincerity of his civic declarations. He felt his civic nationalism, what he called "true Americanism," deeply, and it allowed him
to welcome into American society "lowly" and "racially inferior" European
immigrants whom most people of his class and cultural background despised. It is easy to belittle the progressive character of Roosevelt's inclu-
sionary attitudes toward European immigrants, now that anti-Catholicism

and anti-Semitism have largely vanished as significant American ideologies and all Euro-Americans are thought to belong to the same white race. But Roosevelt's embrace of Catholic and Jewish Europeans was not popular among many native-born Protestant Americans of his time who were alarmed by the arrival of so many immigrants from supposedly primitive regions in eastern and southern Europe.[34] Many immigrants, in turn, responded to Roosevelt's warmth with appreciation, enthusiasm, and votes. His civic nationalism also gave nonwhite Americans something to work with, for its democratic and egalitarian ethos allowed them to believe they could yet find a way to gain full citizenship rights and thus to include themselves in the great national experiment. The American creed of a Gunnar Myrdal and the integrationist dream of a Martin Luther King Jr. sprang from the same taproot of civic nationalism that Theodore Roosevelt espoused.

Roosevelt's civic nationalism was rooted partly in a political commitment to rewarding merit in ways uncompromised by prejudice or cronyism. From the earliest days of his political career, Roosevelt had wanted to purge government of favoritism and corruption and to ensure that government appointments would be reserved for the best qualified. That meant adopting civil service procedures that relied on impartial merit tests rather than on ties of party, friendship, or nationality.[35] But Roosevelt's civic nationalism also reflected his affection for "huge, polyglot, pleasure-loving" New York, where people from all walks of life had found a way to live together. Roosevelt valued what he saw as New Yorkers' inclination to put aside their prejudices, and he believed that city leaders ought to encourage this broad-mindedness. He was proud to call himself a friend of Otto Raphael, a Jewish policeman, who, like Roosevelt, was "'straight New York.'" As police commissioner in 1895–97, Roosevelt became famous for his midnight strolls with Jacob Riis, the journalist and social reformer (himself an immigrant), ostensibly to catch deadbeat cops who were asleep on the job; but Roosevelt loved just as much the exposure these excursions gave him to the hidden communities and activities of New York City life. "These midnight rambles are great fun," he once wrote. "My whole work brings me in contact with every class of people in New York. . . . I get a glimpse of the real life of the swarming millions."[36]

There was a voyeuristic element to this, just as there had been in Riis's sensationalist exposé, *How the Other Half Lives*.[37] But there was also a desire to break down the barriers that had separated New Yorkers from each other and to prod all citizens of the "great city" to cross neighborhood and ethnic boundaries. Some scholars have argued that Roosevelt's openness to immigrants extended only to the so-called old immigrants from Great Britain, Germany, and Scandinavia who supposedly belonged to superior and easily assimilable races. The "new immigrants" from eastern and southern Europe, in this view, received no welcome from Roosevelt, for they were considered to lack the racial makeup to succeed in America.[38] While some evidence supports this view, other evidence does not. It cannot account, for example, for Roosevelt's endorsement of Israel Zangwill's play *The Melting-Pot* when it opened on Broadway in 1908. The protagonist, the musically talented but penniless David Quixano, belongs to a "new immigrant" Russian Jewish family. David's mother, father, and sisters have been slain in the Kishinev pogrom of 1903. David flees to New York, where he seizes the opportunity America gives him, writes his American symphony, marries the gentile girl of his dreams, and becomes a proud American.[39]

Roosevelt was moved by Zangwill's insistence that even immigrants whose origins lay in the allegedly inferior races of eastern Europe could come to be numbered among the most successful and best of Americans. It mattered, too, that David succeeds in America not by maintaining his Jewish heritage, but by assimilating to American culture. The words Zangwill puts in David's mouth could have come from Roosevelt's own pen: "America is God's Crucible, the great Melting-Pot where all the races of Europe are melting and reforming! . . . Germans and Frenchmen, Irishmen and Englishmen, Jews and Russians—into the Crucible with you all! God is making the American." No wonder Roosevelt wrote Zangwill, "I do not know when I have seen a play that stirred me as much."[40]

An even more impressive demonstration of Roosevelt's comfort with the new immigrants occurred in 1913, in the midst of a strike by women garment workers in New York City. Roosevelt traveled to Henry Street and St. Mark's Place to witness the strike firsthand and to interview the strikers about their grievances and ambitions. On Henry Street he encountered young women whom some observers would have described as the most pathetic examples of the new immigration: They were the "lowest and poorest paid workers that we saw," Roosevelt noted. Their supposed racial background was equally "base," for many were Turkish Jews who could not even speak Yiddish, let alone English. They were thus cut off not only from

American culture but also from the Yiddish-speaking Jewish community and labor movement in New York City.[41]

It would have been easy for Roosevelt to find fault with these women and to deplore an immigration policy that had let them in. But he was moved by their plight, feeling "deep sympathy for them personally." We must take care of them, he argued, for they represent the "mothers of . . . *our* American citizenship for the next generation." One can discern in Roosevelt's reaction a Victorian paternalism that stressed the need to save these poor damsels from their distress (although his preferred remedy, unionization of the women, was not paternalist at all). Such a judgment, however, too readily ignores Roosevelt's unambiguous invitation to these women to become part of the American nation. In going out among these poor Turkish Jewish women, mixing easily with them ("gather around me and tell your stories," he implored at one point), and treating them as the mothers of future Americans, Roosevelt was showing ample solicitude and ease with a group of new immigrants.[42]

Roosevelt's willingness to grant those immigrant women, or any women, the rights and duties of men was another matter. The centrality of the warrior to Roosevelt's narratives of nation building, his admiration for muscular individuals willing to use force, and his abhorrence of effeminacy in men underscore the gendered character of his nationalism. Men, Roosevelt believed, were society's natural leaders; nations rested on the homosocial bonds arising among men who shared the perils of combat. Women's nature did not allow them to succeed at men's work, and the admission of females to the army and other sacred institutions of male comradeship would only compromise nation building.

But women's inferiority did not mean that they, or at least the Euro-Americans among them, were to be excluded from the nation. Their contributions as wives and mothers were essential both to the creation of new male citizens and to those citizens' moral education; women were, as Roosevelt had declared of the women strikers in New York City, the "mothers . . . of our citizenship."

Roosevelt enlarged his conception of women's political role over the first two decades of the twentieth century. His interest in the conditions of workers and the immigrant poor not only led him to advocate unionization for women workers, but also brought him into contact with women Progressives such as Jane Addams and Florence Kelley who advocated woman suffrage and the extension of other rights to women. Roosevelt actually became a supporter of woman suffrage, while suffragists and feminists found in Roosevelt's civic nationalism the language to justify their struggle for equality. But Roosevelt never became a feminist or a believer in the fundamental equality of men and women. He supported suffrage because he believed women voters would help to cleanse politics of corruption and vice and, in so doing, strengthen men, enhancing their ability to pursue national virtue and glory. In such ways did Roosevelt's civic nationalism retain its gendered cast.[43]

Civic Nationalism and the Problem of Race

In the abstract, the task of reconciling civic nationalism with racial nationalism was straightforward. Roosevelt simply argued that certain races—notably Asians and African Americans—could not meet the fundamental requirements of American citizenship. "Only the very highest races have been able" to make a success of self-government, he wrote in a letter in 1908, and it would be foolish, even contemptible, to assume that "utterly undeveloped races" could function on an even footing with whites in a democracy.[44]

The practical work of exclusion was in some cases as easily accomplished as the ideological work. That was certainly true in regard to the Chinese, whom Roosevelt despised. The Chinese Exclusion Act of 1882, which barred Chinese immigrant laborers from entering the country, ensured that the Chinese American population would not become large enough to pose a real problem to American democracy. Congress kept this policy of exclusion in place until the 1940s. Roosevelt did not want to exclude the Japanese, a people whom he admired, but he nevertheless engineered a policy of exclusion once anti-Japanese agitation in California made one, in Roosevelt's eyes, a political necessity.[45]

The work of reconciling civic and racial nationalist principles in regard to black Americans was another matter altogether because the relatively easy remedy of an exclusionary immigration law could not solve the "Negro problem." The corollary to immigration exclusion—the repatriation of blacks to Africa—seemed too impractical by the early 1900s even to propose as public policy.

With regard to blacks, Roosevelt never deviated much from the view he expressed to his friend Owen Wister in 1906: "I entirely agree with you that as a race and in the mass they are altogether inferior to whites."[46] He rarely protested the segregationist regime that, during the years of his presidency, reshaped social relations in the American South. As president, he actually appointed fewer blacks to federal positions than his predecessor William McKinley. During these years, Roosevelt continued to denigrate the fitness and honor of black soldiers. In 1906, he ordered the dishonorable discharge of 167 men of the all-black Twenty-fifth United States Infantry Regiment, alleging that they were covering up for a few soldiers who may have assaulted a white woman and participated in a raid against the white residents of Brownsville, Texas. The facts of the case were hotly debated and were never truly clarified. But this did not stop Roosevelt from expelling from the army scores of black soldiers, including five who had been awarded the Congressional Medal of Honor for their heroism in Cuba and the Philippines. It is unlikely Roosevelt would have meted out equally harsh treatment to white soldiers accused of a coverup.[47]

Yet this same man earned the loyalty of blacks and the enmity of southern whites because on occasion he violated the color line in sensational and highly publicized ways. He enraged southern whites when he appointed a black man, William D. Crum, to the collectorship of the port of Charleston, South Carolina, a prestigious federal post, and he infuriated them again when he shut down the post office in Indianola, Mississippi, to punish local whites who had run their African American postmaster, Minnie M. Cox, out of town. Roosevelt's greatest racial "crime" occurred within months of his inauguration, when he invited Booker T. Washington to the White House for lunch. Not only did Roosevelt thus become, in the words of the *Washington Bee*, "the first President of the United States to entertain a coloured man." He also committed, in the words of one observer, "the one unpardonable violation of the Southern racial code"—"the breaking of bread between the races on equal terms." With the exception of interracial sexual intercourse, there could be no more "ultimate and positive expression" of a commitment to social equality. Many southern whites never forgave Roosevelt for the transgression.[48]

Why did he do it? Recently, historians have treated Roosevelt's high-profile meetings with and appointments of blacks as part of a cynical political game in which Roosevelt was attempting to secure his southern base among black Republicans; once he decided that the political payoff from that base was too small, he stopped appointing blacks and began courting southern whites instead.[49]

Roosevelt no doubt made such calculations, but it would be a mistake to interpret his entire approach to the race question as Machiavellian. If Roosevelt, in general, endorsed the notion that the white race was supreme, he was nonetheless impatient with the idea that the two major American races ought to have no contact with each other. In personal terms, Roosevelt was an adventurer and boundary crosser who bristled at attempts to restrict his freedom of association. If he wanted to meet with a black—or a Jew or a Catholic—under conditions of equality, he would not tolerate anyone telling him he had no right to do so. In political terms, Roosevelt grounded this right in his civic nationalist belief that Americans ought to respect—and open their homes and businesses to—anyone willing to work hard and live honorably, regardless of his or her racial or religious background. That is why Roosevelt, on many occasions and at great length, declared his commitment to treating "each black man and each white man strictly [according to] . . . his merits as a man, giving him no more and no less than he shows himself worthy to have."[50] Roosevelt, in other words, could not entirely contain his behavior within the boundaries called for by the racialized nation he had labored so hard to imagine and create. This was true even of his efforts to redirect American politics through the New Nationalist program he unveiled in 1910, which became the ideological foundation of the Progressive Party he founded in 1912. Roosevelt worked hard in this campaign to do what he had done on San Juan Hill—to bring European immigrants closer to the center of American life while keeping blacks and other racial minorities on the periphery. By many measures he was successful in doing so. But Roosevelt continued to violate the southerners' racial code in other ways.

The New Nationalism

The New Nationalism, a political project developed by the Progressive journalist Herbert Croly in 1908, was intended to offer class-torn America a comprehensive plan of economic and political reconstruction. Croly called for a large central state to regulate the predatory practices of big industry and to reinvigorate American life with a spirit of cooperation and selflessness. Croly's program gave Roosevelt a name for the steps he had already taken as president to enlarge the federal government in order to control corporations and to offer all Americans, no matter how impoverished or disadvantaged, a "square deal." Just back from an African safari in 1910 and looking for a way to reenter American politics after his premature retirement from the presidency in 1909, Roosevelt embraced Croly's New Nationalism as his own.[51]

Croly's New Nationalism also allowed Roosevelt to address a glaring weakness in his earlier formulations of civic nationalism. Roosevelt's nationalism had always contained within it the promise of economic opportunity and advancement to those who worked hard and lived honorably. But the civic nationalist philosophy he had formulated in the 1890s, with its focus on equal civil and political rights for all citizens, could not deliver on that promise. Politically, this philosophy owed a great deal to classical liberalism, especially in its insistence that individual emancipation would follow upon the removal of artificial constraints on political and civic participation. Thus, Roosevelt had believed that the ending of discriminatory treatment in public and private life would give European immigrants and other disadvantaged Americans ample opportunity to partake of the American dream. But he had failed to gauge the negative effects of industrialization on individual opportunity and virtue. Belatedly, and after much prodding from the labor movement in New York City, Roosevelt acknowledged that grinding poverty was preventing workers, even those with full political and civil rights, from achieving economic security and the leisure necessary to cultivate their civic virtue. The poor needed what the English economist T. H. Marshall would later call social rights: rights to limits on the hours of work, to a decent wage, to compensation for work-related injuries, and to social insurance for themselves and their families. Once they possessed such social rights, citizens could gain economic security and reach their fullest moral and intellectual potential. The New Nationalism made the attainment of social rights central to its program. Every man, Roosevelt declared, would then be able "to reach the highest point to which his capacities . . . can carry him." In this way the promise of civic nationalism would be fulfilled.[52]

As a New Yorker, Roosevelt understood how large a proportion of the working class were immigrants and their children. His New Nationalist program was meant to bring them into the nation, not just politically and culturally, but economically as well. As his movement gathered momentum, Roosevelt attracted to it leading social welfare Progressives, including Paul Kellogg, Jane Addams, and Frances Kellor, who had labored intensively with immigrants in their neighborhoods, schools, and workplaces. For these reformers, the plight of the European immigrants—their inadequate wages, the slum conditions in which they lived, the infectious diseases from which they suffered, and the urban vices to which some of them had succumbed (prostitution, gambling, and political corruption)—symbolized much that was wrong with the United States. Progressive reformers called for better working conditions, higher wages, improved housing and sanitation, playgrounds to give children more wholesome recreation, Americanization programs to teach immigrants English, and public museums and libraries to cultivate immigrants' minds. As they gathered with Roosevelt in Chicago in 1912 to found the Progressive Party, these reformers were giddy with the belief that their concerns had moved from obscure charity and academic conferences to the very center of American politics. "A great party," Addams declared in her speech seconding Roosevelt's nomination, "has pledged itself to the protection of children, to the care of the aged, to the relief of overworked girls, to the safeguarding of burdened men." The Progressive Party had become "the American exponent of a world-wide movement toward juster social conditions." In the process, it helped define an agenda that would remain central to American reform for fifty years.[53]

But the issue of race intruded on this program of nationalist renewal. The Progressive Party had raised blacks' hopes, drawing many African American voters to Roosevelt. Even those who remained suspicious of Roosevelt found in the Progressive pledge to help the most disadvantaged Americans a compelling reason to throw their support behind the new movement. In the summer of 1912, black Republicans in several southern states left their party and put together delegate slates to send to the Progressive Party's convention. But Roosevelt and his supporters refused to seat them, choosing to honor the credentials of lily-white delegations from those states instead.[54]

The black delegates were the properly elected ones, but Roosevelt, seeing an opportunity to build a Progressive base among southern whites dissatisfied with the Democratic Party, brushed propriety aside. The southern whites whom Roosevelt wanted to woo would join the Progressive Party only on the condition that the party endorse the principles of white supremacy, and that meant an acceptance of segregation and black disfranchisement in the South. Roosevelt acquiesced in that demand, prevailing upon the Progressive convention committee to deny southern black delegates their seats.[55]

From the perspective of his civic nationalism, this should not have been a difficult move for Roosevelt to make or justify. He could have stressed how few southern blacks had raised themselves to a level where they would be capable of handling the political responsibilities already vested in whites. But Roosevelt felt compelled to mount a far more complex defense, for his decision to subordinate blacks had drawn a firestorm of criticism within and beyond the Progressive Party.[56]

Roosevelt stressed the impotence and corruption of black Republicanism in the South, the base from which the Progressives would have drawn their support. He emphasized his support for black participation in the North and proudly pointed to the black men who had been elected members of delegations from thirteen northern and border states. "The Progressive Party," Roosevelt declared, "is already, at its very birth, endeavoring in these States, in its home, to act with fuller recognition of the rights of the colored man than ever the Republican party did." Finally, he insisted that racial progress in the South would come, not from highhanded northern attempts to force a new racial order on that recalcitrant region, but from the many well-intentioned "white men in the South sincerely desirous of doing justice to the colored man." Only these "men of justice and of vision as well as of strength and leadership," Roosevelt wrote, can do for the colored man "what neither the Northern white man nor the colored men themselves can do": secure the right of free political expression "to the negro who shows he possesses the intelligence, integrity, and self-respect which justify such right of political expression in his white neighbor." The white delegates to the Progressive convention, Roosevelt implied, were precisely the sort of wise southern men who would work on the Negro's behalf.[57]

Roosevelt's rationalizations could not hide how much his actions had violated the spirit of the Fourteenth and Fifteenth amendments, which forbade discrimination against citizens on the basis of color, or how much southern white Progressives wanted to perpetuate white supremacy, not upend it. And to ask southern blacks to trust their fate to well-intentioned white neighbors was not only to insult their capacity for political self-mobilization, but also to demand that they acquiesce in their own subordination.

Roosevelt's fellow Progressives attacked him on all these grounds as well as on others. But Roosevelt stuck to his guns, and a majority of Progressives assented to his policy. Yet, despite his victory, Roosevelt had hurt himself with the white South. His public pronouncements on the decision to exclude the black delegates were apologetic and long-winded; they all included lengthy iterations of his civic nationalist conviction that every American be guaranteed "his right to life, to liberty, to protection from injustice" without regard to creed, birthplace, social station, or color. In his communications and speeches, Roosevelt also listed the many efforts by the Progressive Party in the North to guarantee blacks their political rights. None of this went over very well with white southerners who were contemplating joining Roosevelt's crusade. And then, on the eve of the election, Roosevelt further alienated his potential white southern supporters by committing another "unpardonable violation of the Southern racial code": He dined with two blacks in a Rhode Island hotel, reminding white supremacists everywhere of his original sin—his White House lunch, more than a decade earlier, with Booker T. Washington. The Progressive Party's southern campaign was a fiasco, netting Roosevelt many fewer votes than he had won as a Republican in 1904.[58]

There are at least two ways to interpret the events of 1912. The first is to emphasize the hold that the racial nationalist tradition exercised over the imagination of Roosevelt and others. Throughout his life, Roosevelt believed that most nonwhites belonged to inferior races with limited capacities for self-government. Only the few individuals within those races who had "achieved" the level of Europeans were to be rewarded with a full complement of civil and social rights. This kind of thinking permitted Roosevelt and his supporters at the Progressive Party's convention in 1912 to reinscribe African American subordination into their liberal politics, a precedent that would haunt liberalism for more than fifty years.

But it is equally striking that, in upholding racial nationalism in 1912, Roosevelt created a political and personal mess for himself. Unlike his excision of black soldiers from the Rough Rider narrative, an act he had executed in 1899 without shame or hesitation, Roosevelt was troubled by his exclusion of black delegates from the Progressives' convention. In the uncertain terms in which he rationalized this exclusion and in the inconsistency of his behavior on the race question, one can detect the influence of the civic nationalist ideal. This ideal could—and did—destabilize Roosevelt's racial myths and practices, even as it failed to undercut them altogether.

In Roosevelt's actions in 1912, then, can be discerned the true American dilemma: a national identity divided against itself. On the one hand,

Roosevelt and others conceived of America as a land meant for Europeans, a land in which blacks had either a subordinate place or no place at all. On the other hand, they subscribed to a civic nationalist ideal that welcomed all law-abiding residents into the polity and disavowed distinctions based on race. How were the opposing conceptions of national identity to be reconciled into a single American creed? Sometimes this dilemma came into full view, as it did in 1912; other times it was obscured, as images of the two Americas developed separately from each other, dominating different political and cultural forms. But both sprang with equal force from the same source, American nationalism, and both animated American politics with equal intensity.

Eventually, the contradiction between the civic and racialized forms of American nationalism became too great for large numbers of Americans to tolerate. But that moment took a long time to arrive. Only in the 1960s did a great battle erupt over the desirability of upholding a nation so steeped in racialized notions of belonging. But equally puzzling is the question of how American nationalism flourished for so long in such a divided state. One answer is easy: that, when push came to shove, racial nationalism was the only tradition that mattered to white Americans. As much as these Americans, even the liberals among them, expressed a commitment to equal rights, they always believed that whites were better and more deserving than people of color.

Roosevelt's case, however, suggests a more complex and confusing answer: that the kind of restrictive definition of social order called for by the racial nationalist tradition proved too constraining to human imagination. As committed as Roosevelt was to celebrating the United States as a white nation, he never felt entirely comfortable living within such racially rigid borders. Roosevelt had always been an adventurer, drawn to frontiers, whether they were located in the American West, in Cuba, or in immigrant districts in New York City. In his historical writing he celebrated the mixing of peoples; in his personal life, he enjoyed his encounters with the Turkish Jewish women workers in New York, with Booker T. Washington in the White House, and even, initially, with the black soldiers on San Juan Hill. For such an individual, having two nations—a racial nation and a civic nation—may have been better than having one, for it allowed him to satisfy quite different strivings. He could pursue social order through racial hierarchy even as he found personal satisfaction through his freedom to associate with individuals of widely divergent nationalities, races, and vocations. From this perspective, the divided or double character of American nationalism poses much less of a problem; while it undoubtedly caused moments of embarrassment and political failure, it also may have helped to sustain nationalists like Roosevelt who could not find in only one conception of the nation satisfaction for their ambitions and needs.

One can discern in this need to inhabit "two nations" an implicit critique of the very notion that nationhood was an effective vehicle for social bonding and personal fulfillment. In Roosevelt's mind, this critique could never have become explicit. He was a man of his time, which meant that he associated absolute devotion to one nation with the highest civic virtue. He would have regarded the notion that he himself inhabited two nations as abhorrent, much as he detested those Americans, ranging from nostalgic immigrants to Anglophiliac would-be aristocrats, who dared to suggest that they loved some European nation as much as they loved America. But Roosevelt was also human, and his humanity sometimes overflowed the vessel—the nation—into which he so insistently poured all his strivings and aspirations.

Notes

This essay is a revised version of an essay originally appearing in the *Journal of American History* 86 (December 1999): 1280–1307.

1. For the classic definition of the American civic creed, see Gunnar Myrdal, *An American Dilemma: The Negro Problem and Modern Democracy*, 2 vols. (1944; reprint, New York: Harper and Row, 1972), 1:3–25.

2. John Higham, *Strangers in the Land: Patterns of American Nativism* (1955; reprint, New Brunswick: Rutgers University Press, 1992), 131–57; Cecilia Elizabeth O'Leary, *To Die For: The Paradox of American Patriotism* (Princeton: Princeton University Press, 1999), 129–49; Alexander Saxton, *The Rise and Fall of the White Republic: Class Politics and Mass Culture in Nineteenth-Century America* (New York: Verso, 1990), 293–383; Andrew Gyory, *Closing the Gate: Race, Politics, and the Chinese Exclusion Act* (Chapel Hill: University of North Carolina Press, 1998).

3. Theodore Roosevelt, *The Winning of the West: An Account of the Exploration and Settlement of Our Country from the Alleghanies to the Pacific*, vols. 8 and 9 of *The Works of Theodore Roosevelt*, 20 vols., ed. Hermann Hagedorn (New York: Scribner, 1926). In addition to Roosevelt's writings, the following account draws on Thomas G. Dyer, *Theodore Roosevelt and the Idea of Race* (Baton Rouge: Louisiana State University Press, 1980); George Sinkler, *The Racial Attitudes of American Presidents: From Abraham Lincoln to*

Theodore Roosevelt (Garden City, N.Y.: Doubleday, 1971), 308–73; Richard Slotkin, Gunfighter Nation: The Myth of the Frontier in Twentieth-Century America (New York: Atheneum, 1992), 29–122; Gail Bederman, Manliness and Civilization: A Cultural History of Gender and Race in the United States, 1880–1917 (Chicago: University of Chicago Press, 1995), 170–215; and Saxton, Rise and Fall of the White Republic, 349–83.

4. Roosevelt, Winning of the West, in Works, 8:100–101. See Frederick Jackson Turner, The Significance of the Frontier in American History, ed. Harold P. Simonson (New York: Dover Publications, 1980), 29–58; and Richard White, "Frederick Jackson Turner and Buffalo Bill," in The Frontier in American History, ed. James R. Grossman (Berkeley: University of California Press, 1994), 6–65.

5. Theodore Roosevelt, "Manhood and Statehood," address (1901), Works, 13:455.

6. Roosevelt might have claimed that American culture was essentially English or Anglo-Saxon; at times, he came close to labeling the backwoodsmen's culture Scotch-Irish. But he pulled back from both claims, perhaps because either would have implied that his own heritage—mixed, but primarily Dutch—lay outside the core American culture. Roosevelt, Winning of the West, in Works, 8:89.

7. Ibid., 8; Theodore Roosevelt to Albion Winegar Tourgee, Nov. 8, 1901, in The Letters of Theodore Roosevelt, 8 vols., ed. Elting E. Morison (Cambridge, Mass.: Harvard University Press, 1951), 3:190–91.

8. Theodore Roosevelt, "National Life and Character," 1894, in Works, 13:212–13; Roosevelt to Tourgee, Nov. 8, 1901, in Letters, 3:190–91. Roosevelt's class analysis of the slave trade was shared by many white laboring men and sanctioned a racialized class consciousness. See Saxton, Rise and Fall of the White Republic.

9. Theodore Roosevelt, "The Manly Virtues and Practical Politics," 1894, in Works, 13:32.

10. Theodore Roosevelt, "True Americanism," 1894, ibid., 19. See also Theodore Roosevelt, "The Strenuous Life," 1899, ibid., 319, and passim.

11. Theodore Roosevelt, "American Ideals," 1895, ibid., 3–4; "Grant," 1900 speech, ibid., 430–41.

12. Walter LaFeber, The New Empire: An Interpretation of American Expansion, 1860–1898 (Ithaca: Cornell University Press, 1963), 80–101, William H. Harbaugh, The Life and Times of Theodore Roosevelt (New York: Oxford University Press, 1975), 99.

13. Theodore Roosevelt, The Rough Riders (New York: Bartleby, 1902), 22–23.

14. Ibid., 17–22, 28–32, 50, 52, esp. 17; Roosevelt to Henry Fairfield Osborn, Dec. 21, 1908, in Letters, 6:1434–36; Edmund Morris, The Rise of Theodore Roosevelt (New York: Modern Library, 1979), 618; Slotkin, Gunfighter Nation, 103.

15. Here my interpretation diverges from that of Slotkin, who sees in the Rough Riders a replication of the racial mix that conquered the frontier. Slotkin, Gunfighter Nation, 104.

16. The one black in the regiment was Roosevelt's body servant, Marshall. Roosevelt. Rough Riders, 67.

17. Ibid., 18, 51, 52, 116–17; Morris, Rise of Theodore Roosevelt, 620–21, 639–40, 647; Harbaugh, Life and Times, 106.

18. Morris, *Rise of Theodore Roosevelt*, 623; Roosevelt, *Rough Riders*, 46–78. On the war itself, see David F. Trask, *The War with Spain in 1898* (New York: Bison Books, 1981); and Philip S. Foner, *The Spanish-Cuban-American War and the Birth of American Imperialism, 1895–1902*, 2 vols. (New York: Monthly Review Press, 1972).

19. Gerald Linderman, *The Mirror of War: American Society and the Spanish-American War* (Ann Arbor: University of Michigan Press, 1974), 114–73.

20. Roosevelt, *Rough Riders*, 79–118, esp. 110, 115.

21. Richard Harding Davis, *Notes of a War Correspondent* (New York, 1910), 96; Roosevelt, *Rough Riders*, 119–64; Morris, *Rise of Theodore Roosevelt*, 650–56.

22. William H. Leckie, *The Buffalo Soldiers: A Narrative of the Negro Cavalry in the West* (Norman: University of Oklahoma Press, 1967); Albert L. Scipio II, *Last of the Black Regulars: A History of the Twenty-Fourth Infantry Regiment, 1869–1951* (Silver Spring, Md.: Roman, 1983); Roosevelt, *Rough Riders*, 132–64; Theophilus G. Steward, *The Colored Regulars in the United States Army* (1904; reprint, New York: Humanity Books, 1969).

23. John Hope Franklin and Alfred A. Moss Jr., *From Slavery to Freedom: A History of Negro Americans* (New York: Knopf, 1988), 271; Roosevelt, *Rough Riders*, 145–52; Willard B. Gatewood Jr., *"Smoked Yankees" and the Struggle for Empire: Letters from Negro Soldiers, 1898–1902* (Urbana: University of Illinois Press, 1971), 76–77; Frank Friedel, *The Splendid Little War* (Boston: Little Brown, 1958), 173; Herschel V. Cashin et al., *Under Fire with the Tenth Cavalry* (1899; reprint, New York: Bellwether, 1970); Edward A. Johnson, *History of Negro Soldiers in the Spanish-American War, and Other Items of Interest* (1899; New York, 1970), 39–81; Steward, *Colored Regulars in the United States Army*, 191–220, 236–55.

24. Roosevelt, *Rough Riders*, 145 (emphasis added). Amy Kaplan, "Black and Blue on San Juan Hill," in *The Cultures of United States Imperialism*, ed. Amy Kaplan and Donald E. Pease (Durham: Duke University Press, 1993), 219–36.

25. Roosevelt, *Rough Riders*, 149, 150–52.

26. Presley Holliday to editor, *New York Age*, May 11, 1899, in Gatewood, *"Smoked Yankees,"* 92–97.

27. Ibid., 95–96, 97, 72–73, 76–81; Anthony Lukas, *Big Trouble: A Murder in a Small Western Town Sets off a Struggle for the Soul of America* (New York: Simon and Schuster, 1997), 134–35.

28. *Plessy v. Ferguson*, 163 U.S. 537 (1896); John W. Cell, *The Highest Stage of White Supremacy: The Origins of Segregation in South Africa and the American South* (Cambridge: Cambridge University Press, 1982); Gatewood, *"Smoked Yankees,"* 79–81, 87. See also Willard B. Gatewood Jr., *Black Americans and the White Man's Burden* (Urbana: University of Illinois Press, 1975); Bernard C. Nalty, *Strength for the Fight: A History of Black Americans in the Military* (New York: Free Press, 1986), 78–124; and Ann J. Lane, *The Brownsville Affair: National Crisis and Black Reaction* (Port Washington, N.Y.: Kennikat Press, 1971).

29. Roosevelt, *Rough Riders*, 81; Morris, *Rise of Theodore Roosevelt*, 646; Kaplan, "Black and Blue on San Juan Hill," 223–26; Linderman, *Mirror of War*, 114–47.

30. Stuart Creighton Miller, *"Benevolent Assimilation": The American Conquest of the Philippines, 1899–1903* (New Haven: Yale University Press, 1982); Richard Drinnon, *Fac-*

ing West: The Metaphysics of Indian-Hating and Empire Building (Minneapolis: University of Minnesota Press, 1980), esp. 307–51; Slotkin, *Gunfighter Nation*, 106–22; Foner, *Spanish-Cuban-American War;* Louis A. Perez, *Cuba under the Platt Amendment, 1902–1934* (Pittsburgh: University of Pittsburgh Press, 1986).

31. On the history of ethnic nationalism in Europe, see Rogers Brubaker, *Citizenship and Nationhood in France and Germany* (Cambridge, Mass.: Harvard University Press, 1992); and Michael Ignatieff, *Blood and Belonging: Journeys in the New Nationalism* (New York: Mulberry Books, 1993).

32. Slotkin, *Gunfighter Nation*, 97; Roosevelt, "True Americanism," 24–25; Roosevelt, *Winning of the West*, in *Works*, 8:17; G. Edward White, *The Eastern Establishment and the Western Experience: The West of Frederic Remington, Theodore Roosevelt, and Owen Wister* (New Haven: Yale University Press, 1968); Higham, *Strangers in the Land*, 68–157 and *passim*.

33. Ignatieff, *Blood and Belonging*, 5.

34. Higham, *Strangers in the Land*, 52–105, 158–93.

35. Harbaugh, *Life and Times*, 13–49, 69–92.

36. Theodore Roosevelt, *Theodore Roosevelt: An Autobiography* (1913; reprint, New York: Macmillan, 1927), 175, 179–80; Roosevelt to Anna Roosevelt, June 16, 1895, in *Letters*, 1:463.

37. Jacob A. Riis, *How the Other Half Lives: Studies Among the Tenements of New York* (1890; reprint, New York: Charles Scribner's Sons, 1971).

38. See, for example, Slotkin, *Gunfighter Nation*, 189–92.

39. Israel Zangwill, *The Melting-Pot: Drama in Four Acts* (1909; reprint, New York, 1923), 2 and *passim*.

40. Ibid., 33; Roosevelt to Israel Zangwill, Oct. 15, 1908, in *Letters*, 6:1288.

41. Roosevelt to Michael A. Schaap, Jan. 24, 1913, in *Letters*, 7:696–701.

42. Ibid.; Annelise Orleck, *Common Sense and a Little Fire: Women and Working-Class Politics in the United States, 1900–1965* (Chapel Hill: University of North Carolina Press, 1995), 77–78 (emphasis added).

43. Arnaldo Testi, "The Gender of Reform Politics: Theodore Roosevelt and the Culture of Masculinity," *Journal of American History* 81 (March 1995): 1509–33; Robyn Muncy, "Trustbusting and White Manhood in America, 1898–1914," *American Studies* 38 (Fall 1997): 21–42; Roosevelt, *Theodore Roosevelt: An Autobiography*, 161–67; Theodore Roosevelt, *The Foes of Our Own Household* (New York, 1917), esp. 232–73; Bederman, *Manliness and Civilization*, 170–215; Nancy F. Cott, "Marriage and Women's Citizenship in the United States, 1830–1934," *American Historical Review* 103 (December 1998): 1440–74.

44. Roosevelt to Arthur Hamilton Lee, March 7, 1908, in *Letters*, 6:965.

45. Lucy Salyer, *Laws Harsh as Tigers: Chinese Immigrants and the Shaping of Modern Immigration Law* (Chapel Hill: University of North Carolina Press, 1995), 94–138; Gyory, *Closing the Gate*. On Roosevelt's admiration for the Japanese, see Roosevelt to George Otto Trevelyan, Sept. 12, 1905, in *Letters*, 5:22; and Gary Gerstle, *American Crucible: Race and Nation in the Twentieth Century* (Princeton: Princeton University Press, 2001), 60–61.

46. Roosevelt to Owen Wister, April 27, 1908, in *Letters*, 5:226.

47. Alfred Holt Stone, *Studies in the American Race Problem* (New York: Dunleith, 1908), 313; Lane, *Brownsville Affair*.

48. Stone, *American Race Problem*, 243–49, 315, 319. Those wanting to believe in Roosevelt's commitment to racial equality could find other examples of good deeds. As civil service commissioner, he had eliminated from exams given in southern cities questions regarding applicants' religion, political orientation, and race; the result was that greater numbers of black applicants entered government service. As governor of New York, he outlawed racial discrimination in the state's public schools. Ibid., 312; Harbaugh, *Life and Times*, 127–28.

49. Joel Williamson, *The Crucible of Race: Black-White Relations in the American South since Emancipation* (New York: Oxford University Press, 1984), 354.

50. Roosevelt to Tourgee, Nov. 8, 1901, in *Letters*, 3:190. See also Roosevelt to Owen Wister, ibid., 5:221–30, esp. 228.

51. Herbert Croly, *The Promise of American Life* (1909; reprint, Boston: E. P. Dutton, 1989); George E. Mowry, *Theodore Roosevelt and the Progressive Movement* (Madison: University of Wisconsin Press, 1946); Arthur S. Link, *Woodrow Wilson and the Progressive Era, 1910–1917* (New York: Harper and Brothers, 1954), 1–24.

52. Howard Lawrence Hurwitz, *Theodore Roosevelt and Labor in New York State, 1880–1900* (New York: Columbia University Press, 1943); T. H. Marshall, *Citizenship and Social Class and Other Essays* (Cambridge: Cambridge University Press, 1950), 11; Theodore Roosevelt, *The New Nationalism* (New York: The Outlook Company, 1910), 11, and *passim*.

53. Daniel Levine, *Jane Addams and the Liberal Tradition* (Madison: University of Wisconsin Press, 1971), 190–91; John Allen Gable, *The Bull Moose Years: Theodore Roosevelt and the Progressive Party* (Port Washington, N.Y.: Kennikat Press, 1978), 6, 40; Jane Addams, *Twenty Years at Hull House* (New York, 1910); Rivka Shpak Lissak, *Pluralism and the Progressives: Hull House and the New Immigrants, 1890–1919* (Chicago: University of Chicago Press, 1919). On the Progressive reformers' engagement with the new immigrants and their problems, see also, Paul U. Kellogg, "The Pittsburgh Survey," *Charities and the Commons* 21 (January 1909): 517–26; Margaret Byington, *Homestead: Households of a Mill Town* (New York, 1910); and Paul U. Kellogg, ed., *The Pittsburgh District: Civic Frontage* (New York, 1914).

54. Gable, *Bull Moose Years*, 60–74.

55. Ibid.; George E. Mowry, "The South and the Progressive Lily White Party of 1912," *Journal of Southern History* 6 (May 1940): 237–47; Dewey W. Grantham Jr., "The Progressive Movement and the Negro," *South Atlantic Quarterly* 54 (October 1955): 461–77; Arthur S. Link, "The Negro as a Factor in the Campaign of 1912," *Journal of Negro History* 32 (January 1947): 81–99.

56. Grantham, "Progressive Movement and the Negro"; Link, "Negro as a Factor in the Campaign of 1912."

57. Arthur S. Link, ed., "Correspondence Relating to the Progressive Party's 'Lily White' Policy in 1912," *Journal of Southern History* 10 (November 1944): 483–88; Theodore Roosevelt, "The Progressives and the Colored Man," 1912, in *Works*, 17:304–05.

58. Link, ed., "Correspondence Relating to the Progressive Party's 'Lily White' Policy in 1912," 482; Mowry, "South and the Progressive Lily White Party of 1912," 246; Link, "Negro as a Factor in the Campaign of 1912," 97–98.

Margaret Sanger and the Racial Origins

of the Birth Control Movement

The birth control movement of the early twentieth century is typically seen as a critical step in women's progress toward political and social equality. But despite its association with women's emancipation and personal rights, the birth control movement developed and implemented a racialized conception of the social ends of reproduction. The movement's chief crusader, Margaret Sanger, personified the mixed legacy of family planning as both a means to liberate women from compulsory childbearing and a means to control the reproduction of people considered socially inferior. Sanger devoted her life to championing women's right to practice contraception, in defiance of prevailing law, social convention, and the Catholic Church.[1] She founded the American Birth Control League in 1921, which joined with other groups in 1939 to form the Birth Control Federation of America, eventually becoming America's leading family planning organization, the Planned Parenthood Federation of America. Sanger is still idolized by many reproductive rights activists and organizations as the mother of birth control and one of America's most outspoken feminists.[2] Yet Sanger's early alliances with eugenicists and the promotion of eugenic thinking tied the distribution of birth control to the ideals of racial betterment and population control. The birth control movement's racial origins produced an exclusionary understanding of which citizens are entitled to reproductive freedom that continues to influence reproductive health and welfare policies to this day.

Sanger's original defense of birth control was vehemently feminist. Her advocacy centered on the emancipation of women. She traced her commitment to birth control to the desperate condition of the poor immigrant women she visited as a public health nurse in New York, women saddled with numerous unwanted pregnancies and endangered by self-induced abortions. She saw women's ability to control their own reproduction as essential to their freedom and equal participation in society. Access to birth control would also allow women to freely express their sexuality without fear of pregnancy. She sought to liberate women's sexual pleasure from the confines of maternity, marriage, and Victorian morality. "No woman can call herself free until she can choose consciously whether she will or will not be a mother," Sanger declared in her 1920 book, *Woman and the New Race*.[3] Sanger also stressed the importance of contraceptives that women could control themselves, rather than those that depended on men's cooperation, preferring diaphragms to the more common contraceptive methods of condoms and withdrawal.

Women's right to birth control became a subject of national attention when Sanger was arrested twice for violating federal and state anticontraception laws. Her first arrest, in 1914, occurred when the Post Office banned several issues of her magazine, *The Woman Rebel*, and the U.S. attorney's office charged her with violating the Comstock Law. Passed by Congress in 1873, the Comstock Law classified information about contraceptives as obscene and made its circulation through the mail a crime. Facing a possible forty-five-year sentence, Sanger fled to Europe. She returned a year later to publicize the issue of birth control. Under public pressure, the government dropped the charges in 1916. That same year, Sanger opened the first contraceptive clinic in the United States, located in the Brownsville section of Brooklyn, where she distributed diaphragms—known as "pessaries"—to hundreds of women. Ten days later, police raided the clinic, arresting Sanger and her sister, Ethel Byrne, the clinic's nurse. Sanger was convicted of violating the New York criminal law banning distribution of contraceptives and sentenced to thirty days in the workhouse.

Several scholars who have studied the birth control movement in America remark on how its original feminist vision of voluntary motherhood was soon overshadowed by the gender-neutral goal of family planning and population control.[4] What began at the turn of the century as a crusade to free women from the burdens of compulsory, endless childbearing became by the Second World War a method of sound social policy. The concern for women's right to control their own reproduction was superseded by concern for the nation's fiscal security and ethnic makeup. As the political theorist and activist Angela Davis puts it, "What was demanded as a 'right' for the privileged came to be interpreted as a 'duty' for the poor."[5]

The career of Margaret Sanger demonstrates how the ideals of the birth control movement were interpreted along racial lines and how birth control can be used to achieve coercive reproductive policies as well as women's liberation. Of course, Sanger should not be made to shoulder all of the blame for the repressive aspects of the birth control movement. Although its most prominent figure, she did not single-handedly create the political forces that shaped the meaning of birth control.[6] But Sanger's shifting alliances reveal how the prevailing racial order influenced the meaning of reproductive freedom—whether reproductive technologies were used for women's emancipation or their oppression. As the movement veered from its radical, feminist origins toward a eugenic agenda, birth control became a tool to regulate the poor, immigrants, and black Americans.

Sanger's Alliance with Eugenicists

At the time Sanger launched her crusade for birth control, the eugenics movement in America had embraced the theory that intelligence and other personality traits are genetically determined and therefore inherited.[7] This hereditarian belief, coupled with the reform approach of the Progressive Era, fueled a campaign to remedy America's social problems by stemming biological degeneracy. The eugenicists advocated the rational control of reproduction in order to improve society. Many advocated positive eugenics, which encouraged the breeding of superior citizens and voluntary cooperation in forming the most desirable unions. The movement's most lasting legacy, however, is its coercive enforcement of negative eugenics, which aimed to prevent genetically inferior—and therefore socially "unfit"—people from procreating. By 1913 twenty-four states and the District of Columbia had enacted laws forbidding marriage by people considered genetically defective, including epileptics, imbeciles, paupers, drunkards, criminals, and the feebleminded. Influenced by the testimony of eugenics lobbyists such as Harry Hamilton Laughlin, Congress passed the National Origins Act of 1924 (also known as the Johnson-Reed Act), imposing national quotas that effectively cut off immigration from southern and eastern Europe. As James R. Barrett and David Roediger observe, southern and eastern Europeans who came to the United States between 1895 and 1924 acquired an "inbetween status"—above African Americans and Asian Americans but below the older white immigrants of Nordic ancestry.[8] Eugenicists also advocated compulsory sterilization to improve society by eliminating its "socially inadequate" members. In 1914, Laughlin, superintendent of the Eugenic Record Office, prepared a two-volume report that proposed a schedule for sterilizing fifteen million people over the next two generations as well as a model sterilization law to accomplish this plan.[9]

In *Buck v. Bell* (1927), the U.S. Supreme Court upheld the constitutionality of eugenic sterilization laws.[10] The Court approved the sterilization of a seventeen-year-old girl named Carrie Buck who had been committed to the Virginia Colony for Epileptics and Feebleminded when she became pregnant as a result of rape.[11] Laughlin testified in support of the sterilization order that Buck belonged to the "shiftless, ignorant, and worthless class of anti-social whites of the South," concluding that her sexual depravity was "a typical picture of the low-grade moron."[12] The colony also submitted testimony that Buck's seven-month-old daughter was mentally below average. Justice Oliver Wendell Holmes explained the state's prevailing interest in preemptively sterilizing people with hereditary defects: "It is better for all the world if, instead of waiting to execute degenerate offspring for crime, or to let them starve for their imbecility, society can prevent those who are manifestly unfit from continuing their kind." Holmes, himself an ardent eugenicist, gave eugenic theory the imprimatur of constitutional law in his infamous declaration, "Three generations of imbeciles are enough." In the years following the *Buck v. Bell* decision, the number of states with compulsory sterilization laws grew to thirty.

Eugenic sterilization enforced social judgments cloaked in a scientific rationale. The economic crisis of the Great Depression increased interest in sterilization as a means of preventing the birth of children who would need public assistance. The eugenics movement was also energized by issues of race. In the 1930s, it turned its attention from the influx of undesirable immigrants to the black population in the South. The location of most sterilizations shifted from the West, where California led in the number of involuntary operations, to southern states.[13] Southern segregationists threatened by black political advancement borrowed theories from northern liberals, who were the chief exponents of eugenics philosophy. Eugenicists were also worried that intermingling between blacks and whites would deteriorate the white race. By 1940, thirty states had passed statutes barring interracial marriage. Antimiscegenation laws, which remained constitutional until 1967, were a eugenic measure.[14]

After the First World War, Sanger's rhetoric linked birth control less with feminism and more with eugenics. Her insistence on women's right to sexual gratification cost her support from the women's movement, which emphasized maternal virtue and chastity.[15] Feminists of Sanger's time grounded their public activism in the moral superiority of motherhood. Eugenics gave the birth control movement a national mission and the authority of reputable science.[16] By framing her campaign in eugenic terms, Sanger could demonstrate that birth control served the nation's interests. Birth control not only promoted women's health and freedom, but also constituted an essential element of America's quest for racial betterment. The language of eugenics, moreover, gave scientific credence to the movement's claim that birth control was an aspect of public health and improved the national welfare. It helped to contest religious objections to birth control as interfering with God's will and to counter inferences that it encouraged sexual promiscuity.

Sanger opposed the Galtonian approach to eugenics, which advocated primarily positive measures to improve the human race. She devoted an entire chapter of her 1922 book, *The Pivot of Civilization*, to criticizing the "dangers of cradle competition" and explaining the advantages of birth control to lower the birthrate of the unfit.[17] The study of eugenics, Sanger argued, had demonstrated that "uncontrolled fertility is universally correlated with disease, poverty, overcrowding, and transmission of hereditable traits." Sanger warned that society's failure to curb reckless breeding by the unfit had already launched a devastating degeneration of the population. Sanger painted a stark picture of the resulting social conditions, writing that eugenicists had shown "that society at large is breeding an ever-increasing army of under-sized, stunted and dehumanized slaves; that the vicious circle of mental and physical defect, delinquency and beggary is encouraged, by the unseeing and unthinking sentimentality of our age, to populate asylum, hospital and prison."[18] Sanger argued that a program of positive eugenics would be unable to prevent the dangers posed by reckless breeding because "the most responsible and most intelligent members of society are less fertile ... [and] the feebleminded are the most fertile." This imbalance, she wrote, constituted "the great biological menace to the future of civilization."

Sanger felt it would be difficult to persuade the intelligent classes to discontinue family planning and to participate in a program of "competitive childbearing" for the benefit of society. Rather, it was the negative side of eugenics that attracted Sanger. She believed that negative eugenics had far greater potential for arousing public concern: "On its negative side it shows us that we are paying for and even submitting to the dictates of an ever-increasing, unceasingly spawning class of human beings who never should have been born at all."[19] Sanger advocated access to birth control as the most practical method of reducing the birthrate of the less desirable classes. "Eugenics without birth control seemed to me a house built upon the sands. It could not stand against the furious winds of economic pressure which had buffeted into partial or total helplessness a tremendous proportion of the human race," Sanger remembered in her autobiography. "The eugenists wanted to shift the birth control emphasis into less children for the poor to more children for the rich. We went back of that and sought first to stop the multiplication of the unfit. This appeared the most important and greatest step towards race betterment."[20] Declaring birth control "the very pivot of civilization," Sanger concluded, "As a matter of fact, Birth Control has been accepted by the most clear thinking and far seeing Eugenists themselves as the most constructive and necessary means to racial health."[21]

Sanger ultimately convinced leading eugenicists of the efficacy of increasing access to birth control. The American Birth Control League turned from legislative lobbying to organizing clinics because clinics could immediately work to reduce the birthrates of their socially inadequate patients.[22] The eugenics movement supported Sanger's birth control clinics as a means of reaching groups whose high fertility rates were thought to threaten the nation's racial stock and culture. Sanger, in turn, complied with the eugenicists' recommendation that her clinics record race and national origin on patient history cards, providing a source of data on the fertility rates of different racial groups.

The American Birth Control League championed an explicitly eugenic policy of promoting birth control among the socially unfit. The League's "Principles and Aims" opened with the following statement: "The complex problems now confronting America as the result of the practice of reckless procreation are fast threatening to grow beyond human control. Every-where we see poverty and large families going hand in hand. Those least fit to carry on the race are increasing most rapidly."[23] Its first aim was to "enlighten and educate all sections of the American public in the various aspects of the dangers of uncontrolled procreation and the imperative ne-cessity of a world program of Birth Control," and it endorsed "sterilization of the insane and feebleminded and the encouragement of this operation upon those afflicted with inherited or transmissible diseases." Its board of directors included such avowed racists as Lothrop Stoddard, the author of *The Rising Tide of Color*, and C. C. Little, the president of the Third Race Betterment Conference. The League maintained close ties with the Ameri-can Eugenics Society, the Human Betterment Association, the American Genetics Association, and other eugenic groups by sharing information about birth control. As the nation slumped into economic depression, the League argued that birth control was essential to reducing the number of children on public relief.

The alliance of the eugenics and birth control movements bolstered the contemporaneous struggle for women's emancipation. At a time when white women were largely confined to the domestic realm, eugenics included women as active participants in a crusade of scientific and political impor-tance. Because eugenics concerned the quality of offspring, its prescriptions were often directed at women and women's role in society. The League's "Principles and Aims" declared, for example, "Every mother must realize her basic position in human society. She must be conscious of her respon-sibility to the race in bringing children into the world." Many eugenicists recognized that women could better promote the interest of improving the race if they had greater knowledge of maternal health and greater control over their careers and sexuality.[24] Thus, the eugenics movement promoted an exclusionary conception of women's liberation in the service of racist social ends.

Birth Control Clinics for Blacks

In January 1939 the American Birth Control League and the Birth Control Clinical Research Bureau joined forces to become the Birth Control Fed-eration of America (BCFA), with Sanger as honorary chairman of the board. That same year BCFA established a Division of Negro Service. In her impor-tant social history of the birth control movement, *Woman's Body, Woman's*

Right, Linda Gordon emphasizes the racist motivation behind the movement's interest in educating blacks about controlling their fertility. Sanger defended her proposal for a "Negro Project" in 1938 in seemingly racist terms: "The mass of Negroes, particularly in the South," asserted the proposal for the project, "still breed carelessly and disastrously, with the result that the increase among Negroes, even more than among whites, is from that portion of the population least intelligent and fit, and least able to rear children properly."[25] But analyzing of the project's purpose becomes more complicated when we acknowledge that Sanger was quoting verbatim none other than the great civil rights leader W. E. B. Du Bois from an article he wrote for *Birth Control Review* in June 1932.[26]

Du Bois and other prominent blacks were not immune from the elitist thinking of their time and sometimes advocated birth control for poorer segments of their own race in terms painfully similar to eugenic rhetoric. Yet using birth control as a tool of racial betterment had a different meaning for blacks than for most whites in terms of both strategies and goals. For eugenicists and many white birth control advocates, improving "the race" meant reducing the number of births among people considered genetically inferior, and they considered all blacks to be genetically inferior to whites. Gordon notes that the proposal for the Negro Project followed up the statement about the unfit *among* Negroes with a chart comparing the overall increase of the black population to that of whites, revealing "overt white supremacy."[27]

Blacks like Du Bois employed eugenic thinking in an effort to improve the black race, focusing primarily on class distinctions among African Americans. In addition, they understood that racial progress was ultimately a question of racial justice: it required transformation of the unequal economic and political relations between blacks and whites. Sanger, by contrast, "felt all reform began and ended with birth control," writes Donald Pickens.[28] White eugenicists promoted birth control as a way of preserving an oppressive racial structure. Blacks promoted birth control as a way of toppling it. Still, Du Bois's embrace of a eugenic approach to social betterment reveals the pervasive acceptance of eugenics as a progressive ideology.[29]

It would thus be misleading to paint a picture of the early birth control movement as diametrically opposed to the interests of black citizens. Contrary to the prevalent interpretation, the birth control movement was not simply "thrust upon an unwilling black population."[30] Many black women were already regulating their fertility when the birth control movement got under way. As George S. Schuyler observed in *Birth Control Review* in 1932, "If anyone should doubt the desire on the part of Negro women and men to limit their families, it is only necessary to note the large scale of 'preventive devices' sold in every drug store in the various Black Belts and the great number of abortions performed by medical men and quacks."[31]

Black activists played a critical role both in the national debate about birth control and in the establishment of local family planning clinics. Official segregation meant that all birth control facilities established in the South in the early 1930s were for white women only, and blacks themselves insisted on expanding family planning services to their communities. Prominent blacks such as Du Bois had chastised the birth control movement for failing to address the needs of black people. The BCFA's national advisory council on Negro issues boasted an impressive roster, including Du Bois; Mary McLeod Bethune, founder and head of the National Council of Negro Women; Walter White, executive director of the NAACP; Reverend Adam Clayton Powell Jr., of the Abyssinian Baptist Church in Harlem; and Professor E. Franklin Frazier. The black women's club movement was instrumental in expressing black women's support for birth control and for increasing the numbers of family planning clinics available in black communities. Their guiding concern for racial justice, however, distinguished their understanding of birth control from the dominant conception linked to eugenic thinking and practice.

Black supporters of birth control opposed the eugenic notion that certain races were inherently inferior. The leading blacks in the birth control movement never presented contraception as a means of eliminating hereditary defects; rather, birth control addressed such problems as high maternal and infant mortality rates that resulted from social and economic barriers. Du Bois and other blacks active in the birth control movement adamantly opposed sterilization, the chief tool of eugenicists. The *Pittsburgh Courier*'s editorial policy, for example, favored birth control but urged blacks to oppose sterilization programs. Du Bois warned in 1936 in his *Courier* column that these programs "fall upon colored people and it behooves us to watch the law and the courts and stop the spread of the habit."[32]

The birth control movement's alliance with eugenicists and its paternalistic attitude toward blacks led to a debate among the white leadership about the best method of bringing birth control to black communities.

Sanger succeeded in 1938 in obtaining a twenty-thousand-dollar grant from Albert Lasker, a prominent advertising executive, to finance an educational campaign among southern blacks using primarily black fieldworkers. Clarence J. Gamble, an influential member of the board of directors and heir to the Proctor and Gamble fortune, had a different vision. He proposed that the grant be used to set up a demonstration project run by white doctors and aimed at proving to southern officials that birth control could help reduce the number of blacks on public relief. Sanger and Gamble strategized about using black workers to most effectively disseminate birth control information among the uneducated black population. In a letter to Gamble in 1939, Sanger defended the training of black doctors to promote birth control among their own people: "While the colored Negroes have great respect for white doctors, they can get closer to their own members and more or less lay their cards on the table, which means their ignorance, superstitions and doubts. They do not do this with the white people."[33] Sanger also proposed training black ministers to dispel suspicion among "their more rebellious members." "We do not want word to go out that we want to exterminate the Negro population," Sanger warned.

This correspondence highlights two important aspects of the provision of birth control to blacks: black people were suspicious of white-controlled birth control programs from the very beginning, and white-controlled programs had no intention of allowing black people to take the reins. Gordon points out as well that Sanger, in her paternalistic reliance on black doctors and ministers under supervision of white BCFA officials, did not contemplate "the possibility of popular, grassroots involvement in birth control as a cause."[34] Sanger's view that many blacks were too ignorant and superstitious to use contraceptives on their own reflected a popular racial stereotype held over from slavery. On the other hand, Sanger had far more confidence than most people of her day in black women's ability and willingness to take advantage of birth control services.

In 1939, the BCFA's Division of Negro Service launched two pilot projects. One project, in Nashville, Tennessee, operated clinics at a black settlement house called Bethlehem Center and at Fisk University, staffed by black doctors and nurses. Nine black public health nurses made home visits to domestics who were unable to visit the clinic during the day. The second project operated programs in several rural counties of South Carolina that trained black nurses to provide contraceptive instruction. But, as Sanger's letter to Gamble showed, the BCFA remained firmly in control of the projects' policies. Gamble reiterated in a memo in 1939, "There is great danger that we will fail because the Negroes think it a plan for extermination. Hence let's appear to let the colored run it."[35] Even if the Negro Project did not intend to exterminate the black population, it facilitated the goals of eugenicists. Eugenicists considered southern blacks to be especially unfit to breed on the basis of a theory of "selective migration," which held that the more intelligent blacks tended to migrate to the North, leaving the less intelligent ones behind. Selective migration was thought to explain the embarrassing finding that blacks from northern cities had scored higher on the army intelligence tests than some groups of southern whites. By 1939, both North and South Carolina had made birth control one of their official public health services—at a time when Massachusetts and Connecticut still had laws making the use of contraceptives a crime.[36]

Another clinic was established earlier in Harlem through a joint effort between the National Urban League and Sanger's Birth Control Clinical Research Bureau. In 1924, James Hubert, the executive secretary of the New York chapter of the Urban League, approached Sanger about the possibility of opening a clinic in a black neighborhood in New York City, where Sanger's organization had been operating a clinic for over a year.[37] Over the next several years Sanger met with Urban League representatives to discuss plans to establish a clinic in Harlem. After ten thousand dollars was raised to fund the clinic, its doors opened in February 1930 on the second floor of a storefront on Seventh Avenue, off 138th Street. The Harlem clinic offered the same services as the Clinic Research Bureau's main branch, providing gynecological examinations, contraceptive information, and diaphragms. Nearly two thousand patient visits were recorded in the first year and several thousand each following year. Until 1933, however, about half of these patients were white women referred from downtown.[38] The Harlem clinic had a separate advisory board, the Harlem Advisory Council, to help run the clinic and raise funds. In her letter soliciting members for the council, Sanger expressed her goal for the body: "To determine the best methods to use for educating the public concerning the aims and purposes of Birth Control" as well as to gain the confidence of black public health professionals.[39]

Despite its advisory council and widespread support for its work, the Harlem clinic did not escape the black community's ambivalence about birth control. Many potential patients suspected that the clinic was really intended to promote race suicide rather than racial betterment. Some Harlem residents believed that black people's progress in America depended on numerical proliferation and that birth control would hasten racial extinction. Others feared that white doctors would use them as guinea pigs in medical experiments. The placard identifying the clinic as the Clinical *Research* Bureau and its exclusively white staff only helped to fan suspicions. More black women began to use the clinic after it moved to the Urban League building and hired a black physician and social worker and two black nurses.

Although Sanger hoped that the Harlem clinic would demonstrate blacks' ability to use birth control effectively, she nevertheless resisted giving the Harlem Advisory Council control over the clinic's operation. She felt that her clinic met a need that "the race did not recognize" for itself.[40] She, like other whites in the birth control movement, saw the role of black leaders and health professionals as facilitating white-led organizations' efforts among the black population. They incorporated blacks in their advocacy to help raise funds and to give legitimacy to the movement's projects in black communities. But black members of advisory councils were neither invited to participate in national planning nor allowed to manage the clinics that served black patients.

Despite its limited role, the Harlem council succeeded in influencing the clinic's approach to issues of race. In addition to the change in the staff's racial composition, the clinic's promotional materials began to respond to the Harlem residents' fears of race suicide and experimentation. For example, the Harlem clinic's pamphlets inserted the word "harmless" in its description of contraceptives and distinguished between birth control and sterilization, emphasizing that birth control is "merely a temporary means of preventing undesired pregnancies."[41]

As the Depression made it increasingly difficult to fund the Harlem clinic, Sanger was forced in 1935 to relinquish management of the clinic to the New York City Committee of Mothers' Health Centers, affiliated with the American Birth Control League. The committee slashed the clinic's services and treated the Advisory Council with even greater paternalism than Sanger had, prompting council member Mabel Staupers to write, "If the Birth Control Association wishes the cooperation of Negroes . . . I feel that we should be treated with the proper courtesy that is due us and not with the usual childish procedures that are maintained with any work that is being done for Negroes."[42] The League closed the clinic a year later.

Was Sanger a Racist?

Was Sanger a racist or a savvy political strategist? Did she advocate birth control for the less fit because she believed they were inferior or did she exploit the rhetoric of racial betterment in order to gain support for women's reproductive freedom? These questions help us examine Sanger's campaign as a case study in the role of political language and objectives in forming our understanding of reproductive freedom and citizens' rights more generally. Recent scrutiny of Sanger's collaboration with eugenicists, and especially Gordon's portrayal of her motives as racist, have tarnished Sanger's heroic persona. In contrast, other scholars have defended her strategic alliance with eugenicists as an effective political move.[43] The historian Carole McCann argues that eugenicists were important to Sanger's crusade "because they provided a sexually neutral language with which to speak publicly about reproduction."[44] Similarly, in *Woman of Valor*, Ellen Chesler describes Sanger's association with eugenicists as a tenuous attempt to counter religious opposition to birth control.[45] Sanger also had to overcome the powerful and respected eugenics movement's resistance to birth control out of concern that it would hasten the decline of birthrates among the upper classes.

But the link between eugenics and the birth control movement is far more significant than this political facilitation. The language of eugenics did more than legitimate birth control. It defined the purpose of birth control, shaping the meaning of reproductive freedom and the identification of those entitled to have it. Birth control became a means of controlling a population, not of increasing women's reproductive autonomy. Birth control in America was defined from the movement's inception in terms of race and could never be properly understood apart from race again.

McCann argues further that although Sanger appropriated the terminology of eugenics, her position on racial betterment differed significantly from that of the eugenics movement. Sanger adopted the eugenicists' view of the dangers of racial deterioration, says McCann, but she rejected their biological explanation of its cause. Charles Valenza, the director of public information for Planned Parenthood of New York City, similarly defended Sanger, writing that "charges that Sanger's motives for promoting birth control were eugenic are unfounded."[46] Sanger believed instead that racial degeneration resulted from social factors, especially economic pressures, rather than from inherent genetic defects. She held uncontrolled fertility responsible for bringing children into conditions of poverty and deprivation.

McCann and Valenza both point out that three leading historians of this period, James Reed, Gordon, and David Kennedy, all incorrectly attribute to Sanger a quotation reprinted in *Birth Control Review* for May 1919: "More children from the fit, less from the unfit—that is the chief issue of birth control." "She did not make that statement and, in fact, criticized it," McCann asserts.[47] But this disagreement merely reflects Sanger's objection to the positive eugenics tenet that the rich should have larger families. She wholeheartedly endorsed the negative eugenics portion of the admonition. Besides, why should we consider Sanger's personal motives more important than the eugenic ideas she disseminated in her books, magazine, and propaganda and implemented in her clinics?

Sanger was not a racist either, argue McCann and Valenza. They claim that she had precisely the same interest as black leaders such as Du Bois in educating poor blacks about family planning in order to improve their health and chances for success in America. "I think it is magnificent that we are in on the ground floor," Sanger wrote in a private letter to a benefactor, "helping Negroes to control their birthrate, to reduce their high infant and maternal death rate, to maintain better standards of health and living for those already born, and to create better opportunities to help themselves, and to rise to their own heights through education and principles of democracy."[48] Even in her most eugenical book, *The Pivot of Civilization*, Sanger did not tie fitness for reproduction to any particular ethnic group.

It appears that Sanger was motivated by a genuine concern to improve the health of the poor mothers she served rather than by a desire to eliminate their stock. Sanger believed that all their afflictions arose from their unrestricted fertility, not from their genes or racial heritage. For this reason, I agree that Sanger's views were distinct from those of her eugenicist colleagues. Sanger nevertheless promoted two of the most perverse tenets of eugenic thinking: that social problems are caused by the reproduction of the socially disadvantaged and that their childbearing should therefore be deterred. In a society marked by racial hierarchy, these principles led to policies designed to reduce nonwhite women's fertility. The judgment of who is fit and who is unfit, of who should reproduce and who should not, incorporated the racist ideologies of the time. Sanger, moreover, used her birth control clinics to bolster the prevailing racial hierarchy that placed blacks in a position inferior to whites.

Valenza's contention that "in theory the eugenics movement was not racist; its message was intended to cross race barriers for the overall betterment of humanity" misses this point. Eugenic theory did not transcend the American racial order; it was fed, nurtured, and sustained by racism. And eugenic theory served to legitimate the racist social structure, providing a supposedly scientific explanation for white supremacy.

Conclusion

The racial origins of the birth control movement left an imprint on the meaning of reproductive freedom that continues to influence public policy today. In 1990, for example, the *Philadelphia Inquirer* published an editorial shockingly reminiscent of the rhetoric of the eugenic era. In "Poverty and Norplant: Can Contraception Reduce the Underclass?" the deputy editor of the editorial page, Donald Kimelman, proposed the long-acting contraceptive Norplant as a solution to inner-city poverty, arguing that "the main reason more black children are living in poverty is that the people having the most children are those least capable of supporting them."[49] Kimelman endorsed giving women on welfare financial incentives to encourage them to use the contraceptive. Although public outcry forced the *Inquirer* to print an apology, the editorial's premise was reflected in scores of legislative proposals to address poverty, welfare dependency, and maternal substance abuse by pressuring poor women to use birth control.[50]

Another legacy is ambivalence about family planning in black communities. Black women's experience of abusive birth control practices, including coercive sterilization, created widespread anxiety among African Americans that white-operated family planning programs were a potential means of racial genocide, although black women continued to seek access to contraceptives. In the 1960s, for example, many black nationalist men adopted the position that birth control was a form of racial genocide that should be rejected by black women, who should bear more children "for the revolution." Black women challenged these attempts to enlist their bodies and began to articulate a distinct black feminist view of reproductive freedom.[51]

Although some blacks believe that white-controlled family planning literally threatens black survival, I take the position that racist birth control policies serve primarily an ideological function. The chief danger of these programs is not the physical annihilation of a race or social class. Even during the eugenics movement, family planning policies never reduced the black birthrate enough to accomplish this result. Rather, the chief danger of these policies is to legitimate an oppressive social structure. Proposals to solve social problems by curbing black reproduction make racial inequality appear to be a product of nature rather than power. By identifying procreation as the cause of black people's condition, they divert attention away from the political, social, and economic forces that maintain America's racial order. This harm to the entire group compounds the harm to individual members who are denied the freedom to have children. Donald MacKenzie observed that eugenic social theory is "a way of reading the structure of social classes onto nature."[52] In the same way, the primary threat to the black community posed by coercive birth control schemes is not the actual elimination of the black race; it is the biological justification of white supremacy. Whatever its motivation, Margaret Sanger's alliance with eugenicists inscribed in the origins of the birth control movement this exclusionary understanding of citizenship and reproductive freedom.

Notes

1. David M. Kennedy, *Birth Control in America: The Career of Margaret Sanger* (New Haven: Yale University Press, 1970); Ellen Chesler, *Woman of Valor: Margaret Sanger and the Birth Control Movement in America* (New York: Simon and Schuster, 1992).

2. See, e.g., Ellen Chesler, "Margaret Sanger," *The Nation* (special issue on American Rebels), July 21, 2003.

3. Margaret Sanger, *Woman and the New Race* (New York: Brentano's, 1920), 94.

4. See, e.g., Carole R. McCann, *Birth Control Politics in the United States, 1916–1945* (Ithaca: Cornell University Press, 1994); Linda Gordon, *Woman's Body, Woman's Right: A Social History of Birth Control in America* (New York: Grossman, 1976).

5. Angela Davis, "Racism, Birth Control, and Reproductive Rights," in *From Abortion to Reproductive Freedom: Transforming a Movement*, ed. Marlene Gerber Fried (Boston: South End Press, 1990), 15, 20.

6. McCann criticizes accounts of the birth control movement written by Ellen Chesler, Linda Gordon, David Kennedy, and others for representing the development of the

movement as a consequence of Margaret Sanger's will, independent of historical context. McCann, *Birth Control Politics*, 3–4.

7. David J. Kevles, *In the Name of Eugenics: Genetics and the Uses of Human Heredity* (New York: Knopf, 1985); Mark Haller, *Eugenics: Hereditarian Attitudes in American Thought* (New Brunswick, N.J.: Rutgers University Press, 1963).

8. James R. Barrett and David Roediger, "Inbetween Peoples: Race, Nationality and the 'New Immigrant' Working Class," in *Against Exceptionalism*, ed. Rick Halpern and Jonathan Morris (London: Macmillan, 1997).

9. Harry Hamilton Laughlin, *The Legal and Administrative Aspects of Sterilization: Report of Committee to Study and to Report on the Best Practical Means of Cutting Off the Defective Germ-Plasm in the American Population* (Cold Springs Harbor, N.Y.: Eugenics Record Office, 1914).

10. *Buck v. Bell*, 274 U.S. 200 (1927).

11. Stephen Jay Gould, "Carrie Buck's Daughter," *Constitutional Commentary* 2 (1985): 331.

12. Robert J. Cynkar, "*Buck v. Bell*: 'Felt Necessities' v. Fundamental Values?" *Columbia Law Review* 81 (1981): 1418, 1438.

13. Elaine Tyler May, *Barren in the Promised Land: Childless Americans and the Pursuit of Happiness* (New York: Basic Books, 1995), 110.

14. See *Loving v. Virginia* 388 U.S. 1 (1967).

15. McCann, *Birth Control Politics*, 58.

16. Ibid., 100.

17. Margaret Sanger, "Dangers of Cradle Competition," in *The Pivot of Civilization* (New York: Brentano's, 1922), 170–89.

18. Ibid., 175.

19. Ibid., 187.

20. Margaret Sanger, *An Autobiography* (1938; reprint, New York: Dover, 1971), 374–75.

21. Sanger, *Pivot of Civilization*, 189.

22. McCann, *Birth Control Politics*, 180.

23. "Principles and Aims of the American Birth Control League," appendix to Sanger, *Pivot of Civilization*, 277.

24. Kevles, *In the Name of Eugenics*, 64–66.

25. Gordon, *Woman's Body, Woman's Right*, 332.

26. W. E. B. Du Bois, "Black Folk and Birth Control," *Birth Control Review* 16 (June 1932): 166.

27. Gordon, *Woman's Body, Woman's Right*, 332.

28. Donald K. Pickens, *Eugenics and the Progressives* (Nashville, Tenn.: Vanderbilt University Press, 1968), 84.

29. Daylanne K. English, *Unnatural Selections: Eugenics in American Modernism and the Harlem Renaissance* (Chapel Hill: University of North Carolina Press, 2004).

30. Jessie M. Rodrique, "The Black Community and the Birth-Control Movement," in *Unequal Sisters: A Multicultural Reader in U.S. Women's History*, ed. Ellen Carol DuBois and Vicki L. Ruiz (New York: Routledge, 1990), 333.

31. George S. Schuyler, "Quantity or Quality," *Birth Control Review* 16 (June 1932): 165, 166.

32. Quoted in Rodrique, "The Black Community and the Birth-Control Movement," 338.

33. Margaret Sanger to Clarence J. Gamble, Dec. 10, 1939, 2.

34. Gordon, *Woman's Body, Woman's Right*, 332.

35. Quoted ibid., 333.

36. "Birth Control: South Carolina Uses It for Public Health," *Life*, May 6, 1940, 64–68.

37. McCann, *Birth Control Politics*, 139.

38. Ibid., 141–42.

39. Quoted ibid., 142.

40. Ibid., 151, quoting Margaret Sanger to Julius Rosenwald, Oct. 9, 1929.

41. Ibid., 156.

42. Ibid., 158, quoting Mabel Staupers to Margaret Sanger, April 2, 1935.

43. James Reed, *The Birth Control Movement and American Society: From Private Vice to Public Virtue* (Princeton: Princeton University Press, 1978); Charles Valenza, "Was Margaret Sanger a Racist?" *Family Planning Perspectives* 17 (January–February 1985): 44.

44. McCann, *Birth Control Politics*, 58, 99–134.

45. Chesler, *Woman of Valor*, 214–15.

46. Valenza, "Was Margaret Sanger a Racist?" 44.

47. McCann, *Birth Control Politics*, 112; Valenza, "Was Margaret Sanger a Racist?" 44–46.

48. Margaret Sanger to Albert Lasker, July 9, 1942, quoted in Valenza, "Was Margaret Sanger a Racist?" 46.

49. Donald Kimelman, "Poverty and Norplant: Can Contraception Reduce the Underclass?" *Philadelphia Inquirer*, December 12, 1990, A18.

50. Dorothy Roberts, *Killing the Black Body: Race, Reproduction, and the Meaning of Liberty* (New York: Vintage, 1999), 104–245.

51. Jennifer Nelson, *Women of Color and the Reproductive Rights Movement* (New York: New York University Press, 2003).

52. Donald A. MacKenzie, *Statistics in Britain, 1865–1930: The Social Construction of Scientific Knowledge* (Edinburgh: Edinburgh University Press, 1981), 18.

W. E. B. Du Bois and the Race Concept

W. E. B. Du Bois (1868–1963) was a propagandist and a scientist, in that order. As a young pioneer of empirical research in sociology, he initially believed that scientific proof of the oppression of black people in the United States would move sensible, educated whites to see the wrongs of racism. Their eyes finally opened, they would join with the "talented tenth" of educated black elites to eliminate discrimination. His faith in science as the solver of social problems was shattered, however, by the mad rationality of lynching and segregation. This moved Du Bois to place science in the service of propaganda in order to solve the problem of the color line, which in his classic *The Souls of Black Folk* (1903) he had famously declared to be the problem of the twentieth century. As a cofounder of the National Association for the Advancement of Colored People (NAACP) in 1909 and the editor of its journal, *The Crisis*, for twenty-four years, Du Bois continued to use the best in scientific research to explain the world, but as a propagandist he now used such knowledge (to paraphrase Michel Foucault) for cutting. Du Bois sought to understand the world in order to change it. Alternating between working at Atlanta University (1897–1910, 1934–44) and with the NAACP (1910–34, 1944–48), Du Bois synthesized scholar and activist, sociologist and muckraker, scientist and propagandist.

This combination of scientific rigor and propagandistic value is particularly evident in Du Bois's evolving understanding of what he called the "race concept." In refuting nineteenth-century theories of Negroid inferiority and Caucasoid superiority, his work comported with the best science of the day while delivering stinging hammer blows against the system of white world supremacy. Objective research served a normative function. By disproving the natural existence of races, Du Bois showed that the racial order is neither natural nor just the result of the determination of one group to maintain its power over others. The result of this merging of science and propaganda was an original theory of race that is finally being recognized today, particularly in the field of critical whiteness studies.[1] Du Bois's mature theory of "the race concept" prefigures contemporary notions of race as a social construction. Du Bois theorizes race as a product of power and resistance rather than of biological inheritance, connecting race to class relations in American capitalism. Further, his political theory explains how race creates collectivities of people—which he refers to as worlds—and forges hierarchical relations between them. Finally, it reflects scientific advances while serving two of his overarching goals: to explain racial hierarchy as a form of undemocratic power and to create a constituency to fight it.

Unfortunately, an understanding of the political nature of Du Bois's conception of race has been obscured by charges of essentialism. Inaugurated by K. Anthony Appiah's article "The Uncompleted Argument: Du Bois and the Illusion of Race," a cottage industry has grown around the question of whether Du Bois's notion of race is thoroughly social constructivist or whether, as Appiah argues, it maintains an essentialist trace that Du Bois was unable to shed: "For the purpose that concerned him most—understanding the status of the Negro—Du Bois was thrown back on the scientific definition of race, which he officially rejected."[2] The debate over Appiah's thesis has produced much interesting work but, strictly speaking, it is anachronistic. Du Bois struggled to understand the racial order given the categories of his day; the criterion of social construction was not available to him. Yet he continually challenged and surpassed the racial truths of his day. In the process, he was not afraid to surpass his own beliefs on race, eventually arriving at a conception that would now be recognized as social constructivist.[3] Yet the purpose of Du Bois's theory of race is not to refute essentialism. It is to undermine the undemocratic power of "the white world." A definition of race was useful to Du Bois only insofar as it served this goal.

An examination of Du Bois's critique of the white world is therefore central to understanding his evolving conception of race. His mature concept, developed in the 1930s and 1940s, locates the relations of the classes at the root of this power. In such works as *Black Reconstruction* (1935) and *Dusk of Dawn* (1940) he argues that slavery, colonialism, segregation, privilege, and exploitation not only perpetuate racial hierarchy but also create the "worlds of race" themselves. The white world is a product of a peculiar cross-class alliance between capitalists and a section of the working class, which receives certain privileges in exchange for its complicity with the system of capitalism. The black or dark world, meanwhile, consists of those excluded from and subordinated by this alliance. Membership in either world, Du Bois emphasizes, is less the result of biology or ancestry than of a social-political system that collects humans into races or worlds for the purpose of class rule.

Du Bois comes to argue that the solution to the problem of the color line lies in ending the white world's power. This can be accomplished only through the collective political effort of the dark world. This struggle holds the potential for radical social transformation as well as the end of racial hierarchy. Du Bois's dialectical conception of racial conflict explains why he embraces black "self-segregation" at the same time as he converts to Marxism and develops a social constructivist conception of race. Du Bois encourages the creation of a "Negro nation within the nation," an idea that derives from his belief that the dark world is the democratic antithesis of the white world. The white world is a form of political and social power that threatens democracy in the United States and across the globe, while the dark world holds the future of democracy.

By connecting race to class relations, critiquing the antidemocratic tendencies of the white world, and asserting the democratic possibilities of the dark one, Du Bois's political theory of race not only confirms that race is a social construction but also reveals the fundamentally political nature of that construction. It indicates that racial discrimination will be abolished not by the elimination of race altogether, as today's advocates of color blindness urge, or by equality among races, as multiculturalists call for, but by the abolition of the power of the dominant world. One intriguing implication of Du Bois's theory of race, then, is that democracy may require not so much the end of white racism as the very dissolution of the white world itself.

Du Bois's Evolving Conception of Race

All conceptions of race are politically motivated; Du Bois's is no different. What is different, as Tommy Lott points out, is that, unlike his contemporaries, Du Bois seeks to craft a basis for group loyalty without relying on biological essentialism.[4] This was an evolutionary process for Du Bois. In early work such as "The Conservation of Races" (1897), he expresses his belief that races exist by nature. Science has been able to distinguish at least two and possibly three races, while History (in the Hegelian sense of the term) discerns eight. A race is "a vast family of human beings, generally of common blood and language, always of common history, traditions, and impulses, who are both voluntarily and involuntarily striving together for the accomplishment of certain more or less vividly conceived ideals of life."[5] Each race possesses a unique set of physical characteristics, a common history, a temperament, and a "spiritual message" for the world. The Negro race, however, has yet to deliver its full message. The only way it can do so, he maintains, is to develop as a race. The message cannot be delivered if Negroes assimilate or "self-obliterate" into white America. The desire to "conserve" the Negro race, however, leads to a dilemma: are American Negroes Americans or Negroes? "What, after all, am I? Am I an American or am I a Negro? Can I be both?"[6] The answer for the early Du Bois is, American in citizenship, political ideals, language, and religion and Negro in all other respects. In order to deliver to the world their gift of song, humor, spirit, and pathos, Negroes must build "race organizations" such as Negro colleges, business organizations, and newspapers. This understanding of race permeates Du Bois's most famous work, *The Souls of Black Folk*. The Negro, after "the Egyptian and Indian, the Greek and Roman, the Teuton and Mongolian," is a seventh race (reduced from eight for literary purposes), born oppressed yet possessing an innate gift of culture, toil, spirit, and a "second-sight" into American life caused by a sense of "double consciousness" (am I black or am I American?).[7]

In "The Conservation of Races" and *The Souls of Black Folk*, race is a scientific category referring to common ancestry and physical characteristics and a world-historic category referring to common history, temperament, and destiny. Consistent with much thinking at the beginning of the twentieth century (thinking influenced by the Chevalier de Lamarck's biological theories rather than by Charles Darwin's), Du Bois utilizes the notion of blood in his definition of race. Blood defines races according to physical as well as cultural attributes and assumes that both are hereditary.[8] Given that the concept of blood mixes genetic and cultural elements, the early Du Bois sees little need to distinguish between the biological and sociohistorical aspects of his race concept. By today's standards this notion of race is essentialist because it assumes that races can be distinguished scientifically according to physical and behavioral characteristics and that each race has a destiny and a gift to contribute to civilization. If this were Du Bois's final word on race, Appiah's critique would require little comment.[9] Yet Du Bois continued to write for sixty-five years after "The Conservation of Races" and *The Souls of Black Folk*, and his understanding of race changed dramatically in that time. Unfortunately, most analyses of Du Bois's conception of race, including Appiah's, have overlooked the development of his thought, focusing almost exclusively on "Conservation."[10]

Du Bois's evolving conception of race can be divided into three periods.[11] The first dates from "The Conservation of Races" until about 1906, when Du Bois became familiar with the work of the anthropologist Franz Boas, who argued that racial differences are rooted in culture rather than in biology.[12] Even more significant than Boas's influence, however, was the Atlanta race riot of 1906, which, together with the climate of lynching that permeated the South, taught Du Bois that science was of limited use in explaining race friction. Racial prejudice is not a product just of ignorance, as he had once assumed, but of deep-rooted rational and irrational beliefs among whites. Reason alone cannot solve this problem. Propaganda is necessary. After witnessing the knuckles of a lynched man on display in the window of an Atlanta grocery store, Du Bois grimly concluded, "One could not be a calm, cool, and detached scientist while Negroes were lynched, murdered, and starved."[13]

These experiences led Du Bois to reject biological and world-historic notions of race. In this middle period, which lasts until approximately 1930, culture and geography replace biology and destiny as explanations for race. *The Negro* (1915), for example, begins by asking, "What is a Negro?" Du Bois immediately dismisses attempts to answer the question scientifically: "In fact it is generally recognized today that no scientific definition of race is possible. Differences, and striking differences, there are between men and groups of men, but they fade into each other so insensibly that we can only indicate the main divisions of men in broad outlines."[14] He acknowledges three types of humans, Negro, Mongolian, and Caucasian, but these are merely variations of a single human type whose differences are the result of climate and environment, not essence. Furthermore, the three supposed races contain such variation within them and overlap so much with each other that all are essentially mixed or mulatto; African mulattoes have merely been "darkened" over the course of history while European mulattoes have been "bleached."[15] Thus, while Du Bois recognizes differences that group people into broad races, he denies any biological basis for such differences, and he does not recognize any distinctive character or world-historic essence of a race. He does write of the "disposition" of the Negro, asserting, for example, that the Negro in Africa is "among the most lovable of men," one whose life is marked by "ceremony and courtesy." Yet the African's character is a product of his social condition, his "primitive life," not of his racial essence. The primitive African's endearments and foibles are little different from those of primitive Germans or Chinese, "and the more we study the Negro the more we realize that we are dealing with a normal human stock which under reasonable conditions has developed and will develop in the same lines as other men."[16]

Du Bois's final, mature conception of race was brought on by his conversion to Marxism in the early 1930s as well as by his growing disillusionment with the philosophy and strategy of the NAACP (he resigned from the organization in 1934, though not permanently). Du Bois explains the evolution of his thinking in his autobiography, *Dusk of Dawn* (1940). Du Bois admits that he once believed in the scientific existence of races, citing "The Conservation of Races" as emblematic of this early view. But he soon became skeptical of scientific definitions of race because they kept changing: one rested on evolutionary developmental differences, another on brain weight, another on culture, still another on psychology. These multiple and conflicting definitions were increasingly implausible. Du Bois then provides a family genealogy to show how absurd the notion of fixed, distinct races is. His Dutch, French, and African ancestry proves that his early conception of race was wrong, for the walls of race are not clear and straight, and there are no "mutually exclusive races."[17] Further, he acknowledges that his upbringing, tastes, and mores are more European than African and that he has had to retroactively construct his "African racial feeling," having almost no connection to Africa save by a song sung by his great-grandmother and passed down through his mother's side. Nevertheless, Du Bois feels a much stronger bond to Africa than to Europe, which leads him to ask, "What is it between us [himself and Africa] that constitutes a tie which I can feel better than I can explain?" The connection, he concludes, is historical and political, forged through the "social heritage of slavery":

> But one thing is sure and that is the fact that since the fifteenth century these ancestors of mine and their other descendants have had

a common history; have suffered a common disaster and have one long memory. The actual ties of heritage between the individuals of this group vary with the ancestors that they have in common and many others: Europeans and Semites, perhaps Mongolians, certainly American Indians. But the physical bond is less and the badge of color relatively unimportant save as a badge; the real essence of this kinship is its social heritage of slavery; the discrimination and insult; and this heritage binds together not simply the children of Africa, but extends through yellow Asia and into the South Seas. It is this unity that draws me to Africa.[18]

By this mature period Du Bois understands racial identity as socially constructed. Furthermore, he augments his critique of biological definitions of race with a materialist explanation of the existence of race. Central to this explanation is his analysis of white labor and its collusion with capital. Long a critic of white working-class racism, in the 1930s he uses this criticism to link the reproduction of the racial order to class struggle.

The Two Worlds and the Cross-Class Alliance

In an argument that recalls the *Communist Manifesto*, Du Bois in *Dusk of Dawn* describes the United States as a nation divided into two worlds, one white and the other black or dark. (His frequent use of the term *world* instead of *race* underscores his political rather than essentialist understanding of race.) The white world claims to uphold democracy but practices racial tyranny. It conceives of its liberties not as universal rights but as privileges reserved for its members. The dark world, meanwhile, struggles mightily under the limitations of movement, education, liberty, and opportunity imposed by the white world. The result is a struggle between two hostile camps. In its quest for domination, however, the white world has unwittingly called into existence the people who will wield weapons against it. Just as the proletariat will dig the grave of the bourgeoisie and build communism, Du Bois asserts that "we black folk are the salvation of mankind."[19]

The essence of the racial order is domination, Du Bois stresses, and the basis of such domination is power, not congenital differences between peoples:

Thus, it is easy to see that scientific definition of race is impossible; it is easy to prove that physical characteristics are not so inherited as to make it possible to divide the world into races; that ability is the monopoly of no known aristocracy; that the possibilities of human development cannot be circumscribed by color, nationality, or any conceivable definition of race; all this has nothing to do with the plain fact that throughout the world today organized groups of men by monopoly of economic and physical power, legal enactment and intellectual training are limiting with determination and unflagging zeal the development of other groups; and that the concentration particularly of economic power today puts the majority of mankind into a slavery to the rest.[20]

Racial groups, then, are constituted by the class structure of American society and of the planet. Yet Du Bois does not simply reduce race to class and equate white with bourgeoisie and black with proletariat. The secret of the white world's power cannot lie in its ownership of capital alone, for the majority of whites do not own any. Rather, the white world's power rests on an *alliance* between capital and a section of the working class.

Du Bois explains this cross-class alliance in the United States in a key but often ignored text, *Black Reconstruction*.[21] In the North and the South, from the antebellum era to the Great Depression (the book was published in 1935), poor whites have colluded with elites to subordinate African Americans. Poor whites manned slave patrols, mob black neighborhoods, lynch black people, and defend segregation. The function of these practices is to divide the working class, facilitating continued capitalist domination. As a reward for ensuring elite rule, working-class whites receive sundry "public and psychological wages": suffrage, access to public accommodations, leniency from the legal system, better schools and neighborhoods, greater economic opportunities, and an elevated social status in which the poorest white is in some ways equal in standing to the wealthiest—and always superior to any black person.[22] The emerging labor movement placed the protection of these privileges ahead of its interests in challenging capital. "The white serfs, as they were transplanted in America," Du Bois wrote, "began a slow, but in the end, effective agitation for recognition in American democracy. And through them has risen the modern American labor movement. But this movement almost from the first looked for its triumph along the ancient paths of aristocracy and sought to raise the white servant and laborer on the backs of the black servant and slave."[23]

The acquiescence of white labor to capital through the cross-class alliance has three consequences. First, it provides the class foundation for Jim Crow, enabling white unity at the expense of black people. Second, it deflects class conflict. Rather than uniting with other workers on the basis of class interests, the white proletariat unites with elites on the basis of racial interests. This corrupts class consciousness among white workers, frustrating the struggle for "industrial democracy" (Du Bois's term for socialism): "The possibility of [industrial democracy] has long been foreseen and emphasized by the socialists, culminating in the magnificent and apostolic fervor of Karl Marx and the communists; but it is hindered and it may be fatally hindered today . . . by the persistent determination . . . to keep the majority of people in slavish subjection to the white race."[24] Third, the alliance is the material foundation of race itself. The racial order is a system that divides humanity into two worlds. Members of the cross-class alliance form the white world, while those excluded from it are thrown into the dark one. This alliance is not the only force that constructs race, for, as I argue below, the culture and will of the dark world are also important, but it is its class base.

Du Bois's mature critique of the cross-class alliance and the white world culminates his stinging critique of racial subordination begun in his youth. This political conception of race drives his later scholarship even where he appears to fall into essentialist language. In *The World and Africa* (1947), for example, Du Bois uses the terms *Negroid*, *Caucasoid*, and *Mongoloid* in his discussion of who inhabited ancient North African civilization. The use of such terms would seem to indicate a residual essentialism, particularly his argument about the primary contribution of Negroids in building ancient Egypt. However, he explicitly rejects any scientific definition of race in the book, employing the *-oid* terms provisionally, he explains, to generally refer to those peoples descended from Africa, Europe, and Asia, respectively. Ultimately, he argues, the effect of the slave trade is that there are really only two races in the modern world: "Human Beings and Negroes."[25]

DuBois's critique of the cross-class alliance also underlies the association between race and culture that he makes in his mature works. In the introduction to the first issue of his journal *Phylon*, in 1940, for example, Du Bois explains that the journal will use the terms *race* and *culture* more or less interchangeably in order to "emphasize that view of race which regards it as cultural and historical in essence, rather than primarily biological and psychological." He goes on to define races as

> the greater groups of human kind which by outer pressure and inner cohesiveness, still form and have long formed a stronger or weaker unity of thought and action. Among these groups appear both biological and psychological likenesses, although we believe that these aspects have in the past been overemphasized in the face of many contradictory facts. While, therefore, we continue to study and measure all human differences, we seem to see the basis of real and practical racial unity in culture. We use then the old word in new containers.[26]

Du Bois here notes two ways in which race-cultures are formed, "outer pressure" and "inner cohesiveness." "Inner cohesiveness" refers to the shared habits, values, and customs of a group, while "outer pressure" refers to racial subordination.[27] Given that the experience of slavery brought the black world together initially, culture or inner cohesiveness is an effect of outer pressure. Individuals find themselves thrown together by social structures; self-activity within these structures allows individuals to cohere as a people. The means by which populations are distilled into particular races is political even if race tends to express itself culturally.[28] Thus, even when he defines race as culture, the lines demarcating races are drawn by power.

As Arnold Rampersad points out, mature texts like *The World and Africa* and *Black Folk: Then and Now* may use essentialist terminology such as Negroid in asserting the African contribution to world civilization, but such use is intended "to generate out of a combination of fact, intuition, faith, and hope a mythos of Africa that would guide the modern black in directing himself."[29] In other words, these histories of the culture of Negroid peoples have a propagandistic function: to inspire black pride and collective action. This can be demonstrated through a deliberately idiosyncratic use of Marxian categories: on the one hand, the purpose of Du Bois's theory of race is to refute all attempts to validate a biological *race-in-itself*, those scientific theories that assert the objective existence of races. Such theories inevitably encourage comparison between races and estimations as to which one is more or less advanced. As such, they typically justify white domination. To the extent that a race-in-itself exists, it is a social product of history, geography, culture, and power, not of nature. On the other hand, his theory facilitates the construction of a *race-for-itself*, a collective united by a common experience of racial subordination and resistance to it. Like Marx's class-for-itself, the black or dark world becomes a race-for-itself when it is conscious of its oppression and determined to abolish it. Du Bois's definition of race as culture and his use of terms like *Negroid* are used propagandistically to forge a race-in-itself. His political task is to forge a strong dark world that can challenge white world tyranny.[30]

The Dark World and Internationalist Nationalism

Like many people during the Depression, Du Bois was certain that capitalism had failed. Soviet Russia was the harbinger; the future was socialist. But the path to industrial democracy is obstructed, Du Bois argues, by the racial prejudice of the white working class. White labor, indifferent to the suffering of the black masses, refuses to acknowledge any relationship between its well-being and the condition of African Americans: "Today it is white labor that keeps Negroes out of decent low-cost housing, that confines the protections of the best unions to 'white' men, that often will not sit in the same hall with black folk who already have joined the labor movement. . . . It mobs white scabs to force them into labor fellowship. It mobs black scabs to starve and kill them."[31] White labor is too concerned with maintaining its racial privileges to grasp its historic task of building the new society. The burden falls to black folk. Du Bois argues that black unity is the only logical path to socialism in the face of white chauvinism. African Americans must continue to resist segregation, but they must also take advantage of the segregation already imposed on them, using it to pool black resources into a parallel economy. The object of this "deliberate and purposeful segregation" is not to build black capitalism, as some have argued, but to accumulate black capital collectively through consumers' unions and cooperatives in order to provide an economic base of strength from which to eventually negotiate the dismantling of Jim Crow.[32] Such a project would show Americans that capital could be accumulated cooperatively, revealing the future in the present and putting black folk in the vanguard of the coming economic revolution. Given the cross-class alliance, the creation of a "separate nation within a nation" is the American path to industrial democracy.[33]

Du Bois argues that by preferring racial privilege to expanded democracy white labor has lost any claim to universality. The dark world has replaced the proletariat in general as Marx's "universal class." Just as the capitalists' factories educate the proletariat in how to create communism, so the white world's Jim Crow will teach the dark world to free itself and thereby build a new world within the shell of the old. As the antithesis of the white world, dark peoples "are the supermen who sit idly by and laugh and look at civilization. . . . We who exalt the Lynched above the Lyncher, and the Worker above the Owner, and the Crucified above Imperial Rome."[34] Moreover, in freeing itself the dark world frees all humanity because there is no one beneath it to subordinate. Du Bois's Marxian theory of racial struggle provides a new context for his most famous declaration regarding the problem of the twentieth century: "The proletariat of the world consists not simply of white European and American workers but overwhelmingly of the dark workers of Asia, Africa, the islands of the sea, and South and Central America. These are the ones who are supporting a superstructure of wealth, luxury, and extravagance. It is the rise of these people that is the rise of the world. The problem of the twentieth century is the problem of the color line."[35]

Appiah argues that Du Bois's nationalism is incompatible with a sociohistorical conception of race. Du Bois's biographer David Levering Lewis similarly claims it "reintroduce[s] . . . racial essentialism through the back door."[36] If the basis of dark world unity rests on purported common genetic or psychological characteristics, this would be the case. But Du Bois's nationalism reflects an attempt to build a race-for-itself out of a people whose common inheritance is slavery and segregation, not blood. Du Bois substitutes the dark world for the proletariat as the universal class not out of essentialism but out of his Marxian-inflected analysis of the possibility of socialism given the cross-class alliance.

Black nationalism for Du Bois, then, serves internationalist and humanist objectives.[37] "American Negroes have got to plan for their economic salvation," he insists. "And this social survival of colored folk in America means in a real sense the survival of colored folk in the world and the building of a full humanity instead of a petty white tyranny."[38] By challenging white world domination, the dark world creates opportunities to expand democracy for all: "So today, if we move back to increased segregation it is for the sake of added strength to abolish race discrimination; if we move back to racial pride and loyalty, it is that eventually we may move forward to a great ideal of humanity and a patriotism that spans the world."[39] Black unity challenges the cross-class alliance and thereby creates opportunities to build industrial democracy. Ironically, the more committed Du Bois is to Marxism, the more firmly he embraces black nationalism as necessary to transcend the dichotomy between "Human Beings and Negroes." As he declares, "A belief in humanity means a belief in colored men."

Throughout all three periods of his evolving conception of race, Du Bois seeks to "conserve" blackness. That impulse is initially due to his essentialist desire to preserve a race-in-itself, but by his mature period it reflects a desire to forge a race-for-itself, a political force seeking self-determination in the ultimate interest of democracy for all. The mature Du Bois emphasizes the particular beauty and humanity of African Americans not to divine essential characteristics of a race but to assert the humanity of the dark world and to impress upon it its world-historic task: to save democracy from the tyranny of whiteness.

The End of the White World

The future, Du Bois is certain, belongs to the dark world. What, then, of the white world? Du Bois never explicitly contemplated the fate of the white world in a post–Jim Crow era. A Germanophile, he sometimes associated whiteness with European culture, so perhaps he envisioned a cultural pluralism in which whites and their culture coexist with the world's peoples of color on a plane of equality rather than supremacy. Yet if the heart of the white world is empire, exploitation, and privilege, as he asserts, perhaps the end of white domination is not pluralism but the dissolution of the white world itself. "The democracy which the white world seeks to defend does not exist," Du Bois argues, for whites' racial interests too often override their democratic aspirations.[40] The task of defending and expanding democracy, then, falls to the dark world. Of course, whites are welcome to join in this task and are ultimately necessary to its success, but this requires that whites abandon the privileged standing that defines them as white in the first place. The destruction of the cross-class alliance, it seems, would leave whiteness with little meaning other than as an overly vague and hence largely useless description of skin color and European culture. One startling implication of Du Bois's mature theory of race, then, is its implication that a free society implies not just the end of racial discrimination but also the abolition of the white world. Perhaps this is what Du Bois means when he writes, "In the activities of such a [free] world, men are not compelled to be white in order to be free."[41]

Du Bois never drew these conclusions himself. Others have, however, including James Baldwin, the historian David Roediger, and the journal *Race Traitor*, the last two explicitly claiming the legacy of Du Bois.[42] These white world abolitionists, I suggest, are the heirs of a Du Boisian conception of race, one which calls for the unity of the dark world rather than color blindness, which contemplates the dissolution of the white world rather than multiculturalism, and which augurs not the fulfillment of liberal democracy but a challenge to it.

Notes

Thanks to Lawrie Balfour, Bruce Baum, Lisa Disch, John Medearis, and David Roediger for critiquing early versions of this chapter.

1. For examples of this influence, see David R. Roediger, *The Wages of Whiteness: Race and the Making of the American Working Class* (New York: Verso, 1991); Noel Ignatiev, *How the Irish Became White* (New York: Routledge, 1995); Joel Olson, *The Abolition of White Democracy* (Minneapolis: University of Minnesota Press, 2004).

2. Anthony Appiah, "The Uncompleted Argument: Du Bois and the Illusion of Race," *Critical Inquiry* 12, no. 1 (1985): 29. A sample of articles engaging Appiah's thesis includes Houston Baker, "Caliban's Triple Play," in *"Race," Writing, and Difference*, ed. Henry Louis Gates Jr. (Chicago: University of Chicago Press, 1986); William J. Moses, "W. E. B. Du Bois's 'The Conservation of Races' and Its Context: Idealism, Conservatism, and Hero Worship," *Massachusetts Review* 34, no. 2 (1993): 275–94; Lucius Outlaw, "'Conserve' Races? In Defense of W. E. B. Du Bois," in *W. E. B. Du Bois on Race and Culture: Philosophy, Politics, and Poetics*, ed. Bernard W. Bell, Emily Grosholz, and James B. Stewart (New York: Routledge, 1996); John Shuford, "Four Du Boisian Contributions to Critical Race Theory," *Transactions of the Charles S. Peirce Society* 37, no. 3 (2001): 301–37; Paul C. Taylor, *Race: A Philosophical Introduction* (Cambridge: Polity, 2003).

3. Nahum Dimitri Chandler, "The Economy of Desedimentation: W. E. B. Du Bois and the Discourses of the Negro," *Callaloo* 19, no. 1 (1996): 78–93.

4. Tommy L. Lott, *The Invention of Race: Black Culture and the Politics of Representation* (Malden, Mass.: Blackwell, 1999), 60.

5. W. E. B. Du Bois, "The Conservation of Races," *The American Negro Academy Occasional Papers, No. 2* (Washington: American Negro Academy, 1897), 7. Although how races differ precisely, he is unsure. "That there are differences between the white and black races is certain, but just what those differences are is known to none with an approach to accuracy." W. E. B. Du Bois, "The Study of the Negro Problems," *Annals of the American Academy of Political and Social Sciences* 9 (January 1898): 19.

6. Du Bois, "Conservation of Races," 11.

7. W. E. B. Du Bois, *The Souls of Black Folk* (New York: Signet Classic, 1969), 45.

8. George W. Stocking Jr., "The Turn-of-the-Century Concept of Race," *Modernism/Modernity* 1, no. 1 (1994): 4–16; Adolph L. Reed Jr., *W. E. B. Du Bois and American Political Thought: Fabianism and the Color Line* (New York: Oxford, 1997), 120–24.

9. Yet as Thomas Holt argues, even the conception of race articulated in "The Conservation of Races" already hints at the socially and historically constructed conception of race Du Bois articulates in his later works: "W. E. B. Du Bois's Archaeology of Race: Re-Reading 'The Conservation of Races,'" in *W. E. B. Du Bois, Race, and the City: The Philadelphia Negro and Its Legacy*, ed. Michael B. Katz and Thomas J. Sugrue (Philadelphia: University of Pennsylvania Press, 1998).

10. Appiah, for example, devotes seven pages to a discussion of "The Conservation of Races" and scarcely two on Du Bois's crucial *Dusk of Dawn*. For other analyses that over-emphasize "Conservation" and slight Du Bois's mature texts, see Bernard R. Boxill, "Du Bois on Cultural Pluralism," in Bell et al., *Du Bois on Race and Culture*; Tommy L. Lott, "Du Bois on the Invention of Race," *Philosophical Forum* 24, no. 1–3 (1992–93): 166–87; Reed, *Du Bois and American Political Thought*, chap. 7.

11. The following argument sharpens the distinctions between these periods for analytical purposes. The mature Du Bois, for example, while embarrassed by his earlier writings on race, thought them more inadequate than wrong, and one can still detect Lamarckian traces (e.g., use of the word *blood*) in mature writings such as "Miscegenation," in *Against Racism: Unpublished Essays, Papers, Addresses, 1887–1961*, ed. Herbert Aptheker (Amherst: University of Massachusetts Press, 1985). For arguments that emphasize continuity in Du Bois's thought, see William E. Cain, "From Liberalism to Communism: The Political Thought of W. E. B. Du Bois," in *Cultures of United States Imperialism*, ed. Amy Kaplan and Donald E. Pease (Durham: Duke University Press, 1993); and Anthony Monteiro, "Being an African in the World: The Du Boisian Epistemology," *Annals of the American Academy of Political and Social Science* 568 (March 2000): 220–34.

12. David Levering Lewis, *W. E. B. Du Bois: Biography of a Race, 1868–1919* (New York: Henry Holt, 1993), 351–52.

13. W. E. B. Du Bois, *Dusk of Dawn: An Essay Toward an Autobiography of a Race Concept* (New Brunswick, N.J.: Transaction, 1995), 67.

14. W. E. B. Du Bois, *The Negro* (Mineola, N.Y.: Dover, 2001), 7.

15. Du Bois, *The Negro*, 13. His use of the term *mulatto* bears resemblance to contemporary concepts such as hybridity and mestiza. However, Du Bois does not embrace mixed-race identity as preferable to black identity; he does not argue either that race is "beyond Black and white" because we are all mixed. For Du Bois, a bipolar racial order operates despite the mulatto or hybrid character of humanity. This is evident in his autobiography, for Du Bois was of mixed African and European descent, yet he never seeks to identify as mixed or multiracial, given that American society defines him unequivocally as a Negro. See *Dusk of Dawn*, chap. 5.

16. Du Bois, *The Negro*, 82.

17. Du Bois, *Dusk of Dawn*, 116; Lewis, *Biography of a Race*, 174.

18. Du Bois, *Dusk of Dawn*, 117.

19. Ibid., 141.

20. Ibid., 137–38.

21. For one of the few normative analyses of *Black Reconstruction*, see Lawrie Balfour, "Unreconstructed Democracy: W. E. B. Du Bois and the Case for Reparations," *American Political Science Review* 97, no. 1 (2003): 33–44. For an extended discussion of the two worlds and the cross-class alliance in Du Bois's work, see Olson, *Abolition of White Democracy*, chapter 1.

22. W. E. B. Du Bois, *Black Reconstruction in America 1860–1880* (New York: Atheneum, 1992), 700–701.

23. W. E. B. Du Bois, *The Gift of Black Folk: Negroes in the Making of America* (Boston: Stratford, 1924), 137.

24. W. E. B. Du Bois, *Black Folk: Then and Now* (1939; reprint, Millwood, N.Y.: Kraus-Thompson, 1975), 382.

25. W. E. B. Du Bois, *The World and Africa: An Inquiry Into the Part which Africa Has Played in World History* (New York: Viking Press, 1947), 116.

26. W. E. B. Du Bois, "Apology," reprinted in *W. E. B. Du Bois: A Reader*, ed. David Levering Lewis (New York: Henry Holt, 1995), 215.

27. Du Bois, "Apology," 215.

28. Du Bois, *Dusk of Dawn*, 152–53.

29. Arnold Rampersad, *The Art and Imagination of W. E. B. Du Bois* (Cambridge, Mass.: Harvard University Press, 1976), 230.

30. One difference between Du Bois and Marx is that, as I suggest below, the purpose of constructing a race-for-itself is not to abolish all races, as a class-for-itself would abolish all classes, but to abolish specifically the power of the white world. Du Bois never calls for the withering away of the dark world.

31. W. E. B. Du Bois, "A Negro Nation Within the Nation" (1935), in Andrew G. Paschal, ed., *A W. E. B. Du Bois Reader* (New York: Collier, 1971), 73.

32. Matthew Pratt Guterl makes this error in *The Color of Race in America 1900–1940* (Cambridge, Mass.: Harvard University Press, 2001).

33. W. E. B. Du Bois, "The Negro and Social Reconstruction" (1936), in Du Bois, *Against Racism*, 144; "Negro Nation Within the Nation"; *Dusk of Dawn*, chap. 7; *The Autobiography of W. E. B. Du Bois* (New York: International, 1968), chap. 17. See also Thomas C. Holt, "The Political Uses of Alienation: W. E. B. Du Bois on Politics, Race, and Culture, 1903–1940," *American Quarterly* 42, no. 2 (1990): 301–23.

34. Du Bois, *Dusk of Dawn*, 149.

35. Du Bois, *Black Folk*, 383.

36. David Levering Lewis, *W. E. B. Du Bois: The Fight for Equality and the American Century 1919–1963* (New York: Henry Holt, 2000), 456.

37. Sterling Stuckey, *Slave Culture: Nationalist Theory and the Foundations of Black America* (New York: Oxford University Press, 1987); Kenneth Mostern, "Postcolonialism after W. E. B. Du Bois," *Rethinking Marxism* 12, no. 2 (Summer 2000): 61–80.

38. Du Bois, "Negro and Social Reconstruction," 150.

39. Ibid., 156; Du Bois, *Dusk of Dawn*, 311.

40. Du Bois, *Dusk of Dawn*, 169.

41. W. E. B. Du Bois, "The Problem of Humanity" (1944), in Paschal, *W. E. B. Du Bois Reader*, 370.

42. James Baldwin, "On Being 'White' . . . And Other Lies," *Essence*, April 1984, 90–92; David Roediger, *Toward the Abolition of Whiteness* (London: Verso, 1994); Noel Ignatiev and John Garvey, eds., *Race Traitor* (New York: Routledge, 1996).

Displacing Filipinos, Dislocating America

Carlos Bulosan's *America Is in the Heart*

"He is an educated servant," said the lady of the house. "He was a schoolteacher in the Philippines. And he went to college here."

"You can hire these natives for almost nothing," said her husband. "They're only too glad to work for white folks."

"You said it," one of the men said. "But I would rather have niggers and Chinamen. They don't have a college education, but they know their places."

"And I won't have a Filipino in my house, when my daughter is around," said one of the women.

"Is it true that they are sex-crazy?" The man next to her asked. "I understand that they go crazy when they see a white woman."

—CARLOS BULOSAN, *AMERICA IS IN THE HEART*

White American anxieties over race, empire, class, sexuality, and masculinity converge in this scene from Carlos Bulosan's autobiographic novel *America Is in the Heart* (1946). The conversation is overheard by the novel's young protagonist, Allos, in the library of his brother Macario's employer, a movie director. The dubious praise heaped upon the servant as colonial subject and cheap labor is later qualified by the discomfort caused by his suspect place in the American racial hierarchy. The anonymous white man observes that "niggers" and "Chinamen" "know their places" in the class and racial hierarchy, but Filipinos do not. The Filipino offers a twist to the hierarchy in that he is an American colonial subject educated in a U.S. territory, the Philippines, an American insular appurtenance from 1898 to 1946. Unlike his racialized counterparts in the racial hierarchy, the Filipino's unplaced-ness is perhaps not so much due to his ignorance of his station but to the peculiar place allotted to him in U.S. imperial history.

The United States claimed the Philippine archipelago as property in the aftermath of the Spanish-American War (1898) and the bloody Philippine-American War (1899–1902) in which one out of every seven Filipinos was killed.[1] Thwarting the national aspirations of the short-lived Philippine republic (1896–98), the United States incorporated the peoples of the Philippine archipelago as a U.S. territory in 1898. Throughout the first decades of the twentieth century, debates around the Philippine question and the status of the U.S. colonies in relation to the Constitution were crucial to the definition of American citizenship and Americanness. The possibility of a citizen existing outside the U.S. terrestrial and cultural compass prompted the Supreme Court to define the political relationship between the United States proper and U.S. property. The nature of these territories, including Puerto Rico, Hawaii, and Guam, and their relationship to the U.S. polity came under debate in the Supreme Court and Congress from 1898 through the 1930s, in a series of court cases collectively known as the Insular Cases.[2] The Court arguments and congressional debates held that the "Constitution did not follow the flag" in the territories. That is, constitutional rights and citizenship did not automatically extend to the territories upon their acquisition. Much like the ruling in *Plessy v. Ferguson* (1896), the problem before Congress and the Supreme Court was how to legalize and constitute separate (but not equal) national entities in relation to the American polity. Debates about tariff and territory shaped this doctrine to shore up American boundaries. Subsequently, the controversy over commerce and citizenship constituted two types of Americans subjects for the new century: the imperial citizen and its uncanny unincorporated double, the colonial national.

Between 1898 and 1946, American manifest destiny, extending itself into the Pacific, expanded the colonial educational system and the governmental bureaucracy in the archipelago. Through the doctrine of benevolent assimilation the people of the newly acquired islands were to be taught how to be self-governing. The occupying American administration placed a high premium on public education modeled after the American system, inculcating in Filipinos American ideals of freedom and equality through the colonial education system.[3] Under the *pensionado* program, beginning in 1903, hundreds of young men and women, many from the Philippine elite, went to the United States for their university education. However, the major influx of Filipinos into the United States was a response not to education but to labor demands. As a result of the ban on Japanese and Chinese immigration into the United States and its territories as laborers, by the 1920s over one hundred thousand Filipinos went to work on the plantations of Hawaii and along the West Coast, from the Alaskan canneries to the California harvest fields.[4] Most of the laborers were men who lived in Filipino bachelor communities in which the proportion of men to women was twenty-two to one, a circumstance that stifled the possibility of heterosexual formation and reproduction of Filipino families. Unlike other Asian migrants, Filipinos were known to consort with Mexicans and native-born white women. Furthermore, the gender imbalance in the Filipino community increased fears of miscegenation among whites despite the national prohibition against interracial relationships. The Filipino's entry into the metropole as labor during the mid-1920s came at the height of activity by the Ku Klux Klan and nativist sentiment, which subjected Filipinos to intense violence and enforced segregation. The onset of the Great Depression further increased hostility against Filipino workers on the West Coast, who were perceived to be taking jobs away from white men.

The nationalist demand for independence in the archipelago and the nativist demand for Filipino expatriation at home led the U.S. government to shut its borders to Filipinos through the passage of the Tydings-McDuffie Act in 1934. The act promised independence to the Philippines within ten years and cut immigration from the Philippines to the United States to a mere fifty persons per year, finalizing a history of legalized Asian exclusion beginning with the Chinese Exclusion Act of 1882. The Tydings-McDuffie Act also left Filipinos who resided in the United States without any kind of citizenship. By refusing repatriation such residents lost their Philippine citizenship, and by remaining on the continent they were, as Asiatics, under the terms of the act, "aliens ineligible for U.S. citizenship," casting them further into political and social limbo.

Carlos Bulosan was born on November 2, 1911, at the height of American colonization of the Philippines, to a small landholding family in a small provincial agricultural village called Binalonan in the northern Philippines.[5] The time between his arrival in the United States in 1930 as part of the wave of Filipino labor immigration and the publication of *America Is in the Heart* in 1946 saw the shift of the Filipino's status from American national to inassimilable alien. By 1932, Bulosan was publishing poetry and essays in local Filipino papers and in American journals like *Poetry* and *Lyric*, and he was included in an anthology of American poets edited by Helen Hoyt. Bulosan was a principal contributor to *New Tide*, a radical literary magazine, the rise of which he dramatizes in *America Is in the Heart*. Bulosan, suffering from tuberculosis, was confined from 1935 to 1938 in Los Angeles General Hospital, where, with the help of Dorothy and Sanora Babb, writers who brought him books and encouraged his writing, he dedicated years of self-study to American literature. (The Babb sisters appear as the Odell sisters in the novel.) During the 1930s and 1940s Bulosan became a radical labor organizer, editor, and publisher. Amid the antifascist campaign of the Second World. War, Bulosan established himself as a prominent Filipino writer when the public's focus turned to the Philippines as an American territory in the war's Pacific theater. After the publication of his poetry collection *Letter from America*, which marked his emergence as a Filipino American writer, Bulosan appeared in *Who's Who in America* in 1941. His fiction and essays were widely read, particularly his bestselling wartime short story collection *Laughter of My Father*. He also published in *Harper's*, *The New Yorker*, and *Saturday Evening Post*. He died in Seattle, Washington, on September 11, 1956. His published works include short stories, essays, poetry, memoirs, and a posthumously published novel, *Cry and Dedication* (1995).

His best-known work is his composite autobiography *America Is in the Heart*, written in 1943 and published in 1946.[6] Set in the Philippines and the United States between the end of the First World War and the beginning of the Second, the novel narrates an American national's voyage from the poverty of the rural Philippines to the brutality and violence of the harvest trail in the rural American West Coast. Bulosan's novel recounts the "personal history" of a Filipino American composite, Allos, who overcomes the violence of racism and labor struggles and whose experience exposes the difficulties and contradictions of the colonial relationship between the Philippines and the United States and the exploitative conditions of the laborer in the American West.

The first part of the novel recounts Bulosan's boyhood in Binalonan. Through Allos (nickname for Carlos), Bulosan narrates how the emergence of industry and modernization gradually pushed out small farmers and destroyed the peasant economy. The small plots of land his family cultivated were sold one by one to pay for his brother Macario's education in Manila, the administrative capital of American-controlled Philippines. The family's resources depleted, the fifteen-year-old Allos goes to the United States to find work. The second part of the novel traces Allos's burdened movement as a migrant worker from Alaska down the Pacific coast. He soon discovers that "it was a crime to be a Filipino in California" (121). He is reunited with his brother Amado, who has become a bootlegger. To survive, Allos learns to steal, hustle, and gamble. His life takes a turn when he visits a friend who convinces him to write for a union organizing publication, *The New Tide*.

The third section relates Allos's involvement in the American labor movement. He narrowly escapes an attempted lynching but is left, along with two other labor organizers, badly hurt and beaten. Later, he finds out he has tuberculosis. Unable to work physically, he commits himself to writing for and about the Filipino proletariat in the United States and the Philippines. In the final section, Allos allies himself with leftist and progressive writers working for minority rights and unity. He is involved in the trade union movement and the Committee for the Protection of Filipino Rights, which lobbied for Filipinos' right to become naturalized American citizens. After many setbacks, he joins the communists and, making use of the vast literary knowledge he has acquired during his hospital stay, initiates political education programs among Filipino agricultural workers. The book ends with the bombing of Pear Harbor, which proves to be a setback for the labor and Filipino movements. He bids farewell to his friends who have chosen to join the U.S. armed forces in the segregated Filipino regiments in the United States and territorial Hawaii.

In the 1960s, the formation of the United Farm Workers union by César Chávez and Dolores Huerta and the Delano grape strike of 1965, in which Filipinos and Mexicans acted in concert to demand better working conditions for farmworkers, renewed interest in Bulosan's life and works. In 1973, the University of Washington Press reissued *America Is in the Heart*, which was received as a voice of anticolonialism in support of the cause of the working class. The critics Epifanio San Juan, Elaine Kim, and Rachel Lee have explored different facets of Bulosan's work. Bulosan criticism led by San Juan and Petronilo Daroy has explored the class-consciousness shaping the novel and reflecting Bulosan's own political commitment as a labor organizer and radical writer seeking to unite the causes of peasants and workers on both sides of the Pacific.[7] *America Is in the Heart* reflects the collective struggles of thousands of Filipino immigrants who were recruited to the United States for employment by the promise of prosperity only to face racism, severe unemployment, and legal prohibitions. In the novel, Bulosan articulates a Filipino/American internationalist consciousness that serves as a counterpoint to prevailing notions of postwar ethnic assimilationism as well as a critique of U.S. colonialism, class exploitation, and racist violence. Throughout the 1970s, the autobiography offered a voice to a progressive politics that connects class and antiracist struggle with the struggles for national liberation in the colonized world.

Through his personal history, very much contiguous with and contingent upon American history, Bulosan insists upon exposing the open sores of the American narrative: "I would like to tell the story of our life in America. It's a great wrong that a man should be hungry and illiterate and miserable in America" (261). His personal history reveals a different sort of American history, one that interrogates the dominant one and interrupts the fixity of the nationalist and racist imaginary. In this fictionalized autobiography, Bulosan recounts a series of horrors and tragedies about his life in the United States, yet he concludes by reaffirming quite melodramatically his commitment to America as an emancipatory project: "It came to me that no man—no one at all—could destroy my faith in America again. It was something that had grown out of my defeats and successes, something shaped by my struggles for a place in this vast land . . . it was something that grew out of the sacrifices and loneliness of my friends, of my brothers in America and my family in the Philippines—something that grew out of our desire to know America, and to become part of her great tradition, and to contribute something toward her final fulfillment" (326). The protagonist, once the object of the American colonial project, resignifies and expands the "American project" so that he could play an active part in its fulfillment as a historical process. When the protagonist discovers that he is able to "understand this vast land through our own [Filipino] experiences, I was sure now that we were at last beginning to play our own role in the turbulent drama of history" (312–13).

The "struggles for a place" in the narrator's profession of faith in America are the pretext of Bulosan's narrative, its unwritten driving force. This faith that grows out of the desire "to know" and "to become part" of an America that has continually refused to give Filipinos proper U.S. citizenship in the first half of the twentieth century governs the novel's writing as an event.

The incorporation of the protagonist's collective tragedy and loss both here and in the Philippines and making them visible as part of the American literary tradition serves to challenge the authority of this very tradition and its pretensions to dictate the network of meaning and signs assigned to America. To know America is to produce a relationship with the sign of America—a relationship prompted by an impossible desire given the disenfranchisement of the Filipino as colonial and racialized labor. Yet the kind of knowing Bulosan privileges in this effort to become part of America depends upon the relentless recounting of violent acts committed upon the protagonist's body and psyche, displaying for the reader the process of dis-integration of the Filipino masculine body and offering in its place a disembodied voice which makes claims upon a fantastical "America."

This display of the body produced for others begins when Allos is a child in the Philippines. His first encounter with a white American is motivated by his economic need and the American's voyeuristic desires. To earn money for his impoverished family, Allos leaves Binalonan and goes to Baguio, a small, modernized city that had become the American settlers' resort town, favored for its cool temperatures and high elevation. The pubescent Allos finds work in the public market performing odd jobs for the traders and surviving on the food his temporary employers offer or discard:

> My clothes began to wear out. I was sick from eating what the traders discarded. One day an American lady tourist asked me to undress before her camera, and gave me ten centavos. I had found a simple way to make a living. Whenever I saw a white person in the market with a camera, I made myself conspicuously ugly, hoping to earn ten centavos. But what interested the tourists most were the naked Igorot women and their children. . . . They seemed to take particular delight in photographing young Igorot girls with large breasts and robust mountain men whose genitals were nearly exposed, their G-strings bulging large and alive. (67)

Allos offers his young body to the white female voyeur, overriding the gender hierarchy in favor of the racial hierarchy that imperialism imposes. After the first request to disrobe before the camera, Allos decides to put his body on display for commercial exchange. Knowing the part he has to play, he covers his body with dirt to make himself look more like the Igorot "natives," a neighboring northern hill-tribe people. Thus misrecognized, he performs as the native for the colonizer's racial and erotic gaze. Campo-manes and Gernes read this passage as "a visual metaphor for the defini-tion of Pinoys as racial and historical others, exploitable and stripped of the habiliments of dignity."[8] At the time of the novel's writing this steady gaze characterized the colonial relationship wherein the islands were displayed to the world as the American democratic experiment in Asia.

Allos's subsequent migration to the United States and entry into the white American home to help his brother Macario as a servant creates the opportunity to replay this scene with a difference. After the sixteen-year-old Allos overhears the discussion by the movie director and his friends about the untrustworthiness of Filipino servants, Allos accidentally sees the lady of the house unclothed while serving her breakfast in the bedroom:

> She came back to the room without clothes, the red hair on her body gleaming with the tiny drops of water. It was the first time I had seen the onionlike whiteness of a white woman's body. I stared at her, natu-rally, but looked away as fast as I could when she turned in my direc-tion. She had caught a glimpse of my ecstasy in the tall mirror, where she was nakedly admiring herself.
> "What are you staring at?" she said.
> "Your body, madam, " I said, and immediately regretted it.
> "Get out!" She pushed me into the hall and slammed the door.
> (141)

The momentary expression of prohibited desire by the native servant across class and race lines is perceived by the mistress as being impertinent and is immediately rejected. For this scene to follow the one that discusses preda-tory Filipino male sexuality is almost comical. The impudent stare of the young brown man intrudes upon the white woman "admiring herself" in the mirror. "Naturally," the narrator offers in weak defense, he stares, and the reader too gets a glimpse of the "tiny drops of water" gleaming on the lady's red hair, not the hair on her head, one notes, but that on her body. This natural stare focused on the painstaking and erotic details of the wom-an's "onionlike whiteness" is an uninvited one, to be sure, and Allos follows this intrusion by brazenly admitting to watching her body. This gaze is as erotic and sensual as the imperial gaze upon the Igorots' near-naked bod-ies. Unlike Allos's self-exposing performance for the lady tourist, the white woman here is completely disrobed and not by request. In fact, Allos must steal a glimpse precisely because he knows it to be illicit. Indeed he takes pleasure in the stolen glance—an ecstatic one, as the mirror has revealed to the reader and the mistress.

Allos's voyeurism is contained by the social interdiction established by racial and class hierarchies. In the tropical resort the aforementioned American lady tourist desires to capture the erotic savagery of Filipinos, a desire sanctioned by imperial power. For the colonized body to look back, as Allos does at the movie director's wife, is unseemly and disruptive. The American lady tourist feels she can gaze without impunity at the native's genitals and can request that the native disrobe for her. Like the mistress and her mirror, what the lady tourist captures in her camera is a narcissistic expression of her superiority, desire, and, most important, the privilege of having such a desire. Both white women's means of looking—mirror and camera—share this trait of imperial narcissism, a privilege to have desire not available to the colonized object, whose subjectivity, desire, and body are evacuated in the same process of imperial self-reflection.

Allos's desirous but perhaps accidental glance foreshadows the discipline he would later face as an adult for committing such transgressions. The native under pain of violence or even death cannot share in the imperial subject's desiring gaze. In order to take part in it, he must be concealed. He can only steal those glances and watch the looker watching herself. In the scene I quoted to begin the essay, Allos catches other people's conversation; in this boudoir scene, he surreptitiously catches a glance. In both spaces of the house, one more public than the other, he is concealed by virtue of his servant status, but this special status as part of the household yet wholly apart enables him to appropriate and collect narratives and images in which he is not meant to be a participant. The liminal space allotted to the Filipino in the household and in America at large prescribes a disembodied narrative voice emanating from a concealed body—a necessity dictated by laws, social hierarchy, and survival within this network of proscriptions. The consequence of evincing the physical signs of having desire, whether in the form of an impudent stare or a brazen response, ranges from ejection to harsh discipline to even the violent destruction of that body.

The outlet for Filipino male sexuality is limited by the prohibition of interracial liaisons with white women, the paucity of Filipina women, and the abject state of the racially segregated Filipino homosocial spaces. The novel reveals the limited movement of the Filipino as it traces Allos's movement as a migrant worker from the Alaska canneries to Seattle and down along the West Coast. Allos, in search of a home, travels in boxcars and finds himself in the harsh, lawless conditions of Chinatown ghettoes and in the underworld of gambling houses, dance halls, prostitutes, and gangsters. This is the place America has set aside for Filipinos, he discovers: a lonely bachelor society contained vigilantly in marginalized and criminalized spaces. He is made invisible, as visibility comes at the dangerous price of brutal erasure. Outside these homosocial spaces, encounters with white men would result in violence.

As an adult, Allos encounters his first ambush by a white racist mob on a Filipino harvester campsite as a labor organizer:

> Then I saw them pouring the tar on Jose's body. One of them lit a match and burned the delicate hair between his legs.
> "Jesus, he's a well-hung son of a bitch!"
> "Yeah!"
> "No wonder those whores stick to them!"
> Why were these men so brutal and sadistic? A tooth fell out of my mouth, and blood trickled down my shirt. The man called Lester grabbed my testicles with his left hand and smashed them with his right fist. (208)

This castration scene unflinchingly portrays the violent consequences of crossing racial, class, sexual, and political borders proscribed by the white, propertied social order. The castration implicit in the burning of Jose's pubic hair and explicit in the crushing of Allos's genitals asserts white male control over the brown bodies' sexual and political agency but also evinces the projection of white sexual and political anxieties. For the white racist, the disciplining of the brown body through violence keeps the Filipino in his racial and political place in the West, much as the devastating terror of lynching of the black body in the South kept blacks in their place. The spectacular excess of a ravaged Filipino body, with its genitals disfigured, serves as a cautionary tale for other Filipinos and dissenting class voices to remain silent and unseen. The disturbing negation of the Filipino male body in the discursive realm, as in the library scene, takes on brutal materiality in this scene. This socially sanctioned white lawlessness is a manifestation of the systemic dispensability of the Filipino and racialized others in American society. The Filipino's discursive and material annihilation are of a piece.

When Allos publishes his first book of poetry, he reconciles with his estranged brother, Amado, who leaves Allos a letter before going away to become a transporter in the U.S. Navy at the onset of the Second World War:

> I'm not as well read as you are, but I know that a little volume of poetry can give something to the world. I could have striven to raise myself as you have done, but I came upon a crowd of men that destroyed all those possibilities. However, I'm glad that I remained what I am, because it will give you a chance to see your own brother in darkness; in fact it will give you another chance to look at yourself when you were like me. My lostness in America will give you reason to work harder for your ideals, because they are my ideals too.
>   "I did not have a rich and easy life, but it was my own. I would like to live it over again. . . . You are my brother. (322–23)

Amado, the "brother in darkness," offers himself as the foil for the protagonist's own coming into public light with his newly published book of poetry. Amado does not apologize for his choices; on the contrary, his life becomes an offering to Allos to be integrated into his brother's literary corpus. Unlike the lady's mirror, the mirror Amado offers to Allos as his reflection is the abject origins of himself: "It will give you another chance to look at yourself when you were like me." The letter affirms not only their family ties, but also their ties to each other, strengthened through their common frustrated desires and shared abjection. As Allos promised in the beginning, "Yes, I will be a writer and make all of you live again in my words" (57). Allos's literary body made public becomes the repository for their shared abjection, to make possible the reintegration of masculinity, family, and community, beyond a bodily integration.

Bulosan erases his personal story to make room for others stories; his person disappears, and in its place appears a composite collection of stories once rendered invisible and inaudible by the disavowal of American politics and letters. Importuned, even authorized, by those around him, Bulosan recollects others' narratives of violation for the reader. Bulosan explains his autobiographical project: "I would like to tell the story of our life in America . . . for all the world to see" (261). The retelling of multiple anecdotal experiences and unofficial stories shapes the work into a composite sum greater than its parts. As Campomanes and Gernes point out, Bulosan distills the tragic story of the collective Pinoy, an affectionate term used by

Filipinos to refer to other Filipinos, to make sense and connect the individual isolation each feels in colonial dislocation and class displacement. This composite autobiography as a group event displaces the individual narrator, the purported object of the "autobiography," to redirect individual events toward the political narration of America.

Campomanes's and Gernes's generative study has highlighted the epistolary form as a central metaphor of *America Is in the Heart* and Bulosan's other writings as the author's creation of his literary self. The epistolary form assumes at once an intimacy and a distance. A personal network of belonging mitigates the alienating distance between sender and receiver, bringing with it a network of shared signs. As a letter writer, according to Campomanes and Gernes, "the narrator himself, and by implication, Bulosan, becomes figuratively translated so that he, in turn, can function as a translator, a cultural mediator and a spokesman for those rendered speechless by history."[9] In this light, Bulosan's autobiographical missive reaches beyond the intended reader to be overheard by others. To extend the epistolary motif, Bulosan the writer and reteller of Filipino American experience acts as the cultural and locutionary copula among the variously dislocated Filipinos in the Philippines and the United States and between Filipinos and the greater American society. The travails of peasants in the Philippines and of migrant Filipino workers in the United States articulate direct links between colonial and class dispossession to reconfigure the very location of "America" itself across the Pacific. If the epistolary articulation connotes intimacy in all its forms, then the heart as interiority invokes the love letter and the visible production of his voice and his America.

In the end, the reader encounters America again in Allos's recollection of a memory disguised as a dream. When he is implicated as a communist agitator and is forced to leave Los Angeles, he dreams that his family is starving in his village. In the dream his mother is "starving herself so that her children would have something to eat." He runs away from home and from the poverty it symbolizes. He is later arrested for vagabondage. A kind police officer takes pity on him while he is in jail and feeds him and drives him home. When Allos tells the officer he is from Binalonan, the policeman says, "I used to have a friend from your town. He became a maker of songs in America." (282). "He who was so kind, gentle and good. Would I see him again somewhere? Would I? Were all people from America like him? . . . Suddenly it came to me: it was not a dream. It had actually happened to me when I was a little boy in Binalonan. It had come back to me in a dream, because I had forgotten it. How could I forget one of the most significant events in my childhood? How could I have forgotten a tragedy that was to condition so much of my future life?" (280–83). It is the first time that Allos hears of America. America began as a dream. His fantastic relation to America originates here. The forgotten incident is remembered in a dream when he is again alone and running, much as in his boyhood attempt to run away from a hostile environment. The childhood incident introduced him to America as a place of fantastic promise, a place untouched by poverty and destruction. "He who was so kind, gentle and good" symbolized the America he would continue to pursue. Yet the dream itself is a memory of another. Allos's American fantasy haunts and disrupts his narrative of migration and political action.

The spatial dislocation and temporal asynchrony posed by the narrator's ambivalent relationship to American culture constitute Bulosan's narrative strategies. The intrusion of this dream-memory, the recall of the Philippines, and the insertion of his past into the present mark the anxiety of original dislocation. With the onset of industrialization he was forced to leave the poverty of his home in the Philippines. The memory of the breakdown of his family in the Philippines through death and immigration is relived and relieved by acts of kindness by those he later encounters in America. In one instance, he encounters a woman named Eileen: "Eileen was undeniably the America I had wanted to find in those frantic days of fear and flight, in those acute hours of hunger and loneliness. This America was human, good and real" (235). America as fantasy figures itself in those who offer him material, physical, and intellectual support.

The play of identification and disidentification with America rests on the repeated intrusion of this fantasy at moments of crisis. The anxiety as dream reveals itself exactly at moments of "fear and flight" and "hunger and loneliness." Campomanes draws parallels between the structures of *America Is in the Heart* and of Richard Wright's *Native Son* (1940), published three years before Bulosan's novel was written. He suggests that the two novels share the tripartite structure of Fear, Flight, and Fate. Chapter 4 of *America Is in the Heart* announces not only the protagonist's survival but also the part Fantasy plays in constituting the other three elements. The (un)timely intrusion of fantasy displaces the subject, and the recognition of disjuncture leads Allos to wonder throughout the novel "why . . . America

[was] so kind and cruel" (147) and "why Filipinos were brutal yet tender, nor was it easy for me to believe that they had been made this way by the reality of America." (152). The incongruity between his fantasy and reality fuels his search for his fantastical America. In this sense, America is never completely signified or signifiable as a cultural or political program in the novel. For Allos, America is a series of gestures: the random act of kindness, an emotion, and a once-forgotten memory. The reality of the United States cannot live up to Allos's memory and fantasies.

Allos characterizes his colonial anxiety as a literal time lag. "I was pursued by my own life," he confesses (222). In the course of his work with the American labor movement, Allos learns that he has tuberculosis, which would incapacitate him for years and require an operation to remove the ribs on one side of his body. His prolonged stay at the hospital affords him time to read, write, and later publish his poetry. He takes refuge in his books. As the world contracts to apartments, hospital beds, and camp-grounds precisely because of racial segregation, the body recedes, and the immateriality of books and ideas moves to the fore: "These then were the writers who acted as my intellectual guides through the swamp of culture based on property" (266). Unable to work physically, he "catches up" on his reading. He reads and begins to identify with the Euro-American literary tradition. Bulosan's political project in writing the novel depended upon finding a coherent paradigm in which the Filipino experience in the United States can find expression. He insists upon inserting the Filipino presence into the American story. If part of Allos's story is his search for America, then the terrestrial United States would resist easy narration precisely because of its fantastical American double.

If impoverishment, racism, and violence had destroyed his fantasy of America, a radical literary culture would render it meaningful: "There was something definitely American, something positively vital, in all of them—but more visible in Hart Crane, Malcolm Cowley, William Faulkner, and also their older contemporaries, Carl Sandburg, John Gould Fletcher, Vachel Lindsay. I could follow the path of these poets, continue their tradition." The tradition of radical American literature allowed him to "catch up" and offered the philosophical and cultural lineage to which he could link his experiences and begin to give meaning to "all that was starved and thwarted in my life" (62). His feverish reading habits and his compulsion to list repeatedly the authors he has to read seek to ease even as they underscore his anxiety. His intellectual pursuits and invocations would authorize and legitimate his own writing: "I wrote every day and the past began to come back to me in one sweeping flood of memories. The time had come, I felt, for me to utilize my experiences in written form. I had something to live for now and to fight the world with; and I was no longer afraid of the past. I felt that I would not run away from myself again" (305).

By the end of his autobiography, Allos exorcises this haunting past through his ability to assign meaning to events in his life. By locating himself in a radical history and a literary tradition, he reconciles his subjectivity, gaining access to a narrative of cultural and historical agency to counter the ahistorical stasis imposed by imperialism. Referring to the democratic aspirations of the American writers Mark Twain and William Saroyan, Allos says, "It came to me that the place did not matter: these sensitive writers reacted to the social dynamics of their time. I too reacted to my time. I promised myself that I would read ten thousand books when I got well. I plunged into books boring through the earth's core, leveling all seas and oceans, swimming in the constellations" (312). America ceases to be a locatable place and becomes a site of universalism, "swimming in the constellations." America as trope is manifest through the narration of migration, daily survival, and, most important, fantasy, "the desire to know America."

Here, Bulosan's America ceases to be a fixed place and is transformed into a trope of unfulfilled and unsignifiable desire. The American colonizer had a vision of bringing his Filipino colonial wards into his civilizing narrative. At somewhat cross-purposes, the Filipino Carlos Bulosan argues that the proletarian Filipino has a role in the formulation of the American project as promise: "America is not bound by geographical latitudes. America is not merely a land or an institution. America is in the hearts of men" (189). Therefore, if the Filipino is to be a place-holder at all in or as the American project, as a cultural and historical agent, he would seem to mark the indeterminacy and incoherence of the project's teleology and the secure identification of America.

Notes

I want to express gratitude to the students in my American tropics seminar for rereading this novel with me. Many thanks to Oscar Campomanes and Donette Francis for conversations spanning two decades, and to John Vincent, whose generosity with his time and ideas has made writing this essay a pleasure.

Epigraph: Carlos Bulosan, *America Is in the Heart* (1946; reprint, Seattle: University of Washington Press, 1973), 141. Page references for this text hereafter will be given in parentheses.

1. Estimates of Filipinos killed directly or indirectly (through military strategies of starvation and internment) range from a conservative one hundred thousand to as high as one million.

2. The Insular Cases pertain to a set of cases litigated from 1901 to 1922 and involving the U.S. territories: nine cases in 1901, of which seven involved Puerto Rico, one the Philippines, and one Hawaii; and thirteen cases from 1904 to 1914 and 1922, five involving Puerto Rico, six the Philippines, one Hawaii, and one Alaska. Cf. Juan R. Torruela, *The Supreme Court and Puerto Rico: The Doctrine of Separate and Unequal* (San Juan: Editorial de la Universidad de Puerto Rico, 1985), 240.

3. See Constantino, *The Miseducation of the Filipino* (s.n., 1966); Glen May, *Social Engineering in the Philippines* (Westport, Conn.: Greenwood Press, 1980); Onofre D. Corpuz. *An Economic History of the Philippines* (Manila: University of the Philippines Press, 1997).

4. Susan Evangelista. *Carlos Bulosan and His Poetry: A Biography and Anthology* (Seattle: University of Washington Press, 1985).

5. Bulosan's birthdate is unclear. Because of his fictionalizing of his biography and the casual organization of his writing, several dates for his birth have been cited in different works.

6. Published by Harcourt, Brace, the publisher of his first collection of short stories, *Laughter of My Father* (1944).

7. Cf. Elaine Kim, *Asian American Literature* (Philadelphia: Temple University Press, 1982), 43–57; Marilyn Alquizola, "Subversion or Affirmation: The Text and the Subtext of *America Is in the Heart*," in *Asian Americans: Comparative and Global Perspectives*, ed. Shirley Hune et al. (Pullman: Washington State University Press, 1991); Rachel Lee, *The Americas of Asian American Literature: Gendered Fictions of Nation and Transnation* (Princeton: Princeton University Press, 1999); Sau-ling Cynthia Wong, *Reading Asian American Literature: From Necessity to Extravagance* (Princeton: Princeton University Press, 1993); Petronilo Daroy, "Carlos Bulosan: The Politics of Literature," *St. Louis Quarterly* 6, no. 2 (June 1968); Epifanio San Juan, *Carlos Bulosan and the Imagination of the Class Struggle* (New York: Oriole Editions, 1972). San Juan has also compiled Bulosan's work and written many critical pieces on him.

8. Oscar Campomanes and Todd S. Gernes, "Two Letters from America: Carlos Bulosan and the Act of Writing," *MELUS* (fall 1988): 21.

9. Ibid., 22.

Looking through *Sidney Brustein's Window*

Lorraine Hansberry's New Frontier, 1959–1965

A Raisin in the Sun . . . is about an American family's conflict with certain of the
monetary values of this society. And its characters were Negroes. As indeed are
the characters of several other of my plays. But many of the characters in my
other plays are also white. I write plays about various matters which have both
Negro and white characters in them, and there is really nothing else that I can
think of to say about the matter.

—LORRAINE HANSBERRY, *NEW YORK TIMES*, OCTOBER 31, 1964

This essay explores the career of the playwright Lorraine Hansberry in
the aftermath of the commercial success of her first play, *A Raisin in
the Sun* (1959). As the title suggests, I pay particular attention to Hansberry's second Broadway play, *The Sign in Sidney Brustein's Window*, which
opened on Broadway in the fall of 1964 and closed the following January.
Hansberry has yet to be fully understood as a key public intellectual of the
cold war years. The overwhelming success of *A Raisin in the Sun*, coupled
with the emphatic critical and commercial failure of *The Sign in Sidney
Brustein's Window*, has left people with an incomplete and truncated sense
of Hansberry's thinking. Whatever its flaws as theater, *The Sign in Sidney Brustein's Window* is a bold attempt to break out of the intellectual
straightjacket of the cold war and create an American polity in which there
are no unspoken words, no forbidden subjects. According to Hansberry,
Americans did indeed need a New Frontier, but one very different from
the one heralded by President John F. Kennedy. Hansberry's New Frontier
would require Americans to work hard to understand the social and political forces behind the communism of Fidel Castro, not overthrow it. On

Hansberry's New Frontier, Americans would debate for the first time since the Civil War the relationship between race and class. On her New Frontier artists and scholars who explored relationships between revolutions in the postcolonial world and domestic crises over civil rights in the United States would be given a hearing and a real opportunity to find an audience.

To a degree, the social revolution of the 1960s would bring some of Hansberry's hopes to fruition. By the late 1960s, the university-based student movement would create, for a time, the kind of dialogue she had in mind and tried to start. Defeat in Vietnam would shine a light into dark corners of the American republic—such as the abuses of power by the president and other agencies of the executive branch. Within five years of the fall of South Vietnam, however, American politics "righted itself" again with the election of Ronald Reagan and the reaffirmation of the old cold war faith.

To the extent that these events, which took place in the fifteen years after Hansberry's death in 1965, influenced her reputation, they kept it frozen on *A Raisin in the Sun*. Because the reception for *The Sign in Sidney Brustein's Window* had been so roundly negative and the surrounding circumstances so tragic (Hansberry and her play were dying simultaneously painful public deaths), the keepers of the Hansberry legacy kept Hansberry in the public eye primarily by keeping new, expanded versions of *A Raisin in the Sun* before the public—each version giving an allegedly clearer sense of the playwright's prescient radicalism. Thus, even a discussion of her much less well-known second play must begin with the consequences to her of the first. Hansberry was not, as she was sometimes portrayed in the mass circulation periodicals of the day, just a very brainy housewife from Greenwich Village who sat down to write and, two years later, had an award-winning play on Broadway. *A Raisin in the Sun* was not Hansberry's first statement as a public intellectual, only her most widely known. She began her public life in New York City under the tutelage of the legendary singer Paul Robeson, whose screen career was ended by the red scare. Robeson was, in the words of Ossie Davis and Ruby Dee, two political colleagues of Hansberry's whose professional careers would also be lifted by *A Raisin in the Sun*, the "headmaster of our little circle."[1]

Hansberry published some of her first words as a writer for Robeson's newspaper, *Freedom*, protesting against government harassment of the Left. Hansberry, like her mentors W. E. B. Du Bois and Robeson, believed that "we must look toward and work for a socialist organization of society as the next great and dearly won universal condition of mankind."[2] Whether she was a card-carrying communist or not, Hansberry was very interested in the experiments with socialist theory underway at that time in Cuba and elsewhere in the developing world.[3]

Hansberry, Robeson, and Du Bois were among the thousands of putative communists, socialists, and fellow travelers who had no interest in operating as agents of a foreign power against their fellow citizens (much less in creating an American Soviet). They believed most deeply in an ideal that was yet to be realized—a system in which privation and alienation *could not* exist. Hansberry's focus was less on defending other communist governments than it was on correcting injustices within her own land. In public remarks made at the height of the Cuban missile crisis, Hansberry opposed the Kennedy administration's quarantine of Cuba, defended the right of the "Cuban people [to choose] their destiny," and attacked a Chinese incursion into India.[4] Nearly 90 percent of her statement, however, called for the intellectual leaders of the United States to speak more directly to the politics of their time and help "empty the Southern jails of . . . those students whose imprisonment for trying to insure what is already on the book [*sic*] is our national disgrace."[5]

I highlight Hansberry's ideological dissent from orthodoxy to restore complexity to our historical sense of the cold war past. Seeing importance and value in Hansberry's body of work does not require that we accept her word on all important matters, such as the necessity of a socialist future, or that we embrace her rhetorical excesses, such as her scathing broadbrush attack on American intellectuals who opposed Castro as slaves to an official American party line.[6] Hansberry was a gifted, flawed, and perceptive human being who was working to a very high standard as she wrestled with the most important and most complicated issues of her time.

Hansberry, *A Raisin in the Sun*, and the Public

In order to understand the author of *A Sign in Sidney Brustein's Window*, one must first understand what happened to Hansberry as the author of *A Raisin in the Sun*. That play is about the divisions created within the Younger family when they receive a check for ten thousand dollars, the payoff on the life insurance policy on the recently deceased Walter Lee Younger.[7] In the mind of his wife, Lena, thirty-five hundred dollars will provide the down payment on a house with a yard in which her grandson, Travis, can play. The money holds out the promise of escape from the cramped Southside Chicago walk-up that has been the family home since Walter and Lena came north a little more than forty years earlier during the first phase of the Great Migration. The balance of the funds will be used to finance the medical education of her daughter Beneatha. Lena Younger's thirty-five-year-old son, Walter Lee Jr., a chauffer, has other plans—secret plans—for the money. He hopes to use it to buy a liquor store in the neighborhood with his business partners, Willy Harris and a man named Bobo.

Lena makes certain that the thirty-five hundred dollars designated for a nicer home in the suburbs is set aside. She then dramatically acknowledges her unwitting role in Walter Lee Jr.'s feelings of defeat by giving him responsibility for the remaining sixty-five hundred dollars. Hansberry then has Walter Lee Jr. promptly lose the nest egg to the unreliable Willy Harris. Humiliated by his incompetence as a deal maker, he must face his family. Walter Lee, in a misguided effort to correct his mistake, comes close to making an even greater one: he decides to accept an offer of an even greater amount of money from a homeowners' association determined to keep its suburban neighborhood lily-white. Ultimately, however, fortified by his family's unity on principle, Walter Lee Jr. preserves the family honor by turning back this bribe and insisting that the Youngers must move ahead—even though they recognize that they will face organized and possibly even violent opposition from their new neighbors. There is no promise in *A Raisin in the Sun* of happiness achieved in an effortless integration into an all-white neighborhood. The Younger family sets off knowing they will face determined opposition in their new neighborhood.

While the reviewers of the play did not entirely overlook its social themes, the authenticity of the characterizations was seen as an overriding strength. In his review for the *New York Times*, Brooks Atkinson expressed a judgment that would become the consensus of the critics. While noting "occasional crudities in the craftsmanship," Atkinson argued that these "are redeemed by . . . Hansberry's . . . simple honesty."[8] Critics for *Newsweek*, *Time*, and *Life*, each of which reached nationwide readerships numbering in the millions, treated the challenges faced by the Youngers as the problems of one family, rather than of one class or race. *Life* magazine honored Hansberry's artistic achievement by claiming that the members of the

Younger family were portrayed as human beings rather than "social problem cases";[9] *Time* honored the play's "bread and butter virtues—conflict, a valid moral struggle, character development and people one can care about and respect";[10] *Newsweek*, which hailed *A Raisin in the Sun* as "one of the most stirring and revealing productions of the year," treated the play as a domestic drama fused together by a series of powerful "emotional crises that repeatedly smash through the barriers between players and playgoers."[11] For these reviewers, the play "belongs to the long and simple annals of the poor" written in the "language of the heart."[12]

Among the leading journals of liberal opinion Hansberry also fared well, but these reviewers, many of whom were perhaps somewhat closer to Hansberry ideologically, saw an overreliance on traditional plot devices getting in the way of a compelling drama. Gerald Weales of *Commentary* and Richard E. Hayes of *Commonweal* admired Hansberry's skill with characterization but also found that, according to Hayes, the play did not "break the mold of received experience" and relied a bit too heavily on well-worn conventions of the "domestic drama."[13] Tom F. Driver of the *New Republic* went even further, suggesting that the play succeeded commercially because of "our sentimentality over the 'Negro question.'" Hansberry had created a "moving . . . theatrical experience, but the emotions it generates are not relevant to the social and political realities."[14] The *New Yorker's* Kenneth Tynan, an admirer of *A Raisin in the Sun*, did "wish that the dramatist had refrained from idealizing such a stolid old conservative" as the family's matriarch, Lena Younger.[15] Only Harold Clurman of *The Nation*, himself a veteran of the radical theater movement of the 1930s, thanked Hansberry for writing from a "definite point of view, . . . with no eye toward meritorious possibilities in home ownership and public relations." Not only this, but Clurman saluted the play for "throw[ing] light on aspects of American life quite outside of . . . race."[16]

A Raisin in the Sun succeeded with the broad American audience because, as Davis wrote in 1965, they were reassured that "the play didn't have to be about Negroes at all" and that it was "a living demonstration of our mythic conviction that underneath, all of us Americans . . . are pretty much alike."[17] When Hansberry argued that her play was about "honest-to-God, believable, many-sided people who happened to be Negroes," she meant something very different from what some of the play's admirers meant when they used the same universalistic language.[18] Many of those who embraced

A Raisin in the Sun did so, at least in part, because they saw the Youngers as embarked on the same journey of seemingly inevitable upward mobility that other Americans had experienced. They assumed that the Youngers would move to Clybourne Park and win over the neighbors. As we shall see, Hansberry's own life experience taught her otherwise.[19] Thus, it is equally possible that the Youngers would meet a similar fate and confront obstacles that even Mama's faith could not overcome.

That such a misunderstanding should take place between this author and her public is not surprising. In the intellectually claustrophobic atmosphere of the 1950s, the pull of a certain kind of ideological and aesthetic traditionalism was exceptional among the authors as well as the consumers of popular culture. Is it not possible that such circumstances might have caused Hansberry to clothe her intended themes more thickly in traditional dramatic garb than she might otherwise have in order to reach a mass audience? Hansberry, for instance, framed her story as a family drama, so much so that, as she acknowledged, "the family so overwhelms the play that Walter Lee necessarily fails as the true symbol he should be, even though *his* ambitions, *his* frustrations, and *his* decisions are those which decisively drive the play on."[20] Not only this, but there was widespread confusion about the extent to which *A Raisin in the Sun* was autobiographical. Only in the *New Yorker* did a detailed profile of the author appear, told principally in Hansberry's own words. Only here would a significant number of readers find the full story of how *A Raisin in the Sun* grew from a defeat in the Hansberry family. The Hansberrys, however, unlike the Youngers, were a wealthy Chicago family, but even that economic advantage and a Supreme Court decision had not been enough to enable Carl Hansberry, Lorraine's father, to achieve his version of the American dream. He died an exile in Mexico.[21]

Despite the biographical detail contained in the *New Yorker* article, however, nowhere in that profile does Hansberry indicate how far she deviated from the reigning norms of American public opinion. To the extent that she dissents from such norms, it is couched in the very traditional public language of the 1950s: "I don't want anyone else to do my housework. I've always done it myself. I believe you should do it yourself. I feel very strongly about that."[22] This omission should not cause one to question either Hansberry's integrity or her courage. She had been through the ideological wars of the early cold war years, and she understood the narrow foundations of American political discourse. Hansberry's Federal Bureau of Investigation (FBI) file confirms that she lived her political life in the open, in full view of the organization. The bureau sent an agent to see *A Raisin in the Sun*, and he reported that it contained nothing explicitly reflecting the Communist Party program. The agent claimed that most of the audience overlooked the "propaganda messages" without identifying what they might be.[23] The wonder is that she was not red-baited when she first became famous in 1959. On the other hand, the theater was far less subject to blacklisting than motion pictures and television, which had mass audiences. By the time *A Raisin in the Sun* became a motion picture in 1961, it had been certified safe for mass consumption by the enthusiastic embrace of the critics.

Hansberry's forcefully eloquent dissents on everything from the interpretation of *A Raisin in the Sun* to the content of American foreign policy reached not millions but mere thousands of people, the vast majority of whom lived in one or two neighborhoods of New York City. In addition, although Hansberry was quite busy between the debut of *A Raisin in the Sun* and the premiere of *The Sign in Sidney Brustein's Window*, the fact that she had no other work before the general public in the intervening five years meant that the writers for mass circulation magazines who had praised *A Raisin in the Sun* and its author had no reason to revisit the playwright in greater depth.

Hansberry Dissents

Hansberry's fullest statement of what she had intended to portray in her work appeared in the *Village Voice* for August 12, 1959, a few months after the debut of *A Raisin in the Sun*. It is part of Americans' folklore to believe they are a people surrounded by possibilities and limited only by the individual's ability to imagine them. Hansberry deftly counters this expression of American exceptionalism by suggesting that Walter Lee Jr. must act within the confines of his time and place—the racist and economically stratified America of the 1950s:

> In Walter Lee Younger's life somebody *has* to die for ten thousand bucks to pile up—if then. Elsewhere in the world, in the face of catastrophe, he might be tempted to don the saffron robes of acceptance. . . .

Or, history being what it is turning out to be, he might wander down to his first Communist Party meeting. But here in the dynamic and confusing postwar years on the South Side of Chicago, his choices of action are equal to those gestures only in symbolic terms. . . . Revolution seems alien to him in his circumstances (America), and it is easier to dream of personal wealth than a communal state wherein universal dignity is supposed to be a corollary. Yet his position in time and space does allow for one other alternative: he may take his place on any of a number of frontiers of challenge (such as helping to break down restricted neighborhoods) which are admittedly limited because they do not threaten the basic social order.[24]

As American politics moved onto the brilliantly lit stage of the Kennedy New Frontier, Hansberry was both observing that moment and exploring a new frontier of her own. By January of 1961 Hansberry had seen her first play embraced in terms that differed from her own intellectual ambitions and her own perceptions about what she had put forward. She had also completed *The Drinking Gourd*, a crackling dramatization of the economic and cultural forces behind American slavery. The script had been commissioned by the National Broadcasting Company but was shelved along with the network's plans to dramatize the many dimensions of the Civil War.[25] Even though Hansberry, after *A Raisin in the Sun*, was presumably the very definition of bankable, her script was never produced.[26]

As conflict over desegregation sharpened during the early 1960s, Hansberry was concerned less about how to counter the overt racism of a Bull Connor or a George Wallace than with how to educate the well-intentioned members of the American liberal establishment. In the late spring of 1963, as police violence against civil rights protesters in Birmingham, Alabama, dominated the national news, Hansberry joined the singer Harry Belafonte, the social scientist Kenneth Clark, the writer James Baldwin, and others in a confrontational meeting with Attorney General Robert F. Kennedy. Belafonte had called the meeting out of his conviction that the Kennedy administration did not understand the breadth and depth of African American anger and determination to achieve a significant change in their status in American society. As Hansberry reflected back on that historic encounter with a leader of the New Frontier, she argued that John and Robert Kennedy were like many other well-intentioned white Americans of their time: "I think that when they are confronted with their [own] prejudice, it tends to melt away." Nonetheless, these leaders shared with other Americans "a great naiveté about what it is like to be a Negro."[27]

This was not Hansberry's only encounter with cold war liberals who were having difficulty understanding the true scope of the civil rights crisis. In June of 1964—during the nation's first of four "long, hot summers" of civil unrest—Hansberry and her colleagues Davis, Dee, and John Killens, among others, addressed a community meeting at Town Hall in New York City: it was entitled "Black Revolution and White Backlash." The audience was drawn from some of the city's most politically liberal precincts. Yet even in these surroundings the fears for the future expressed by Hansberry and her colleagues drew the wrath and alarm of the moderator, David Susskind, a leading television personality of the period and a self-identified liberal. Susskind interpreted the participants' words as "carefully couched calls for violence . . . dangerous, irresponsible and ineffective talk."[28] Their transgression seems to have been to suggest that African American public opinion, especially among the young, had reached a potentially dangerous level. Dee feared that the time might come "when the black worker winds up in the street fighting the whiter worker over the fewer and fewer jobs left by automation."[29] Hansberry also spoke to the dangerous mood in the country, symbolized by "Negroes my own age and younger [who] say that we must lie down in the streets and . . . do whatever we can, take to the hills if necessary with some guns and fight back."[30]

That the general public might find such language threatening in 1964 (or today for that matter) is not remarkable. That such words would provoke such unrest among self-described advanced liberals, radicals, and socialists is more noteworthy. Although the atrophy of political discourse during the red scare of the 1950s may have played a part in these sharp exchanges, it is also evidence of a more enduring chasm: the historical distance between blacks and whites. As LeRoi Jones (better known today as Amiri Baraka), another discussant at that meeting, said in his opening statement, "If there is going to be [an honest dialogue], it would have to be new because I don't think there has ever been an honest dialogue between white Americans and black Americans."[31] The words spoken by Hansberry, Dee, and others on that night did not cause riots in Harlem, Watts, or Detroit over the next four years. These citizens were analyzing the present and predicting the immediate future. They spoke directly and presciently to the crisis that lay ahead for their country. The opposition that Dee, Hansberry, and others faced that night also reflected the fact that, beginning in 1964, the race crisis was finally being recognized as a national one.

Between 1959 and 1965, in addition to *The Drinking Gourd* and Hansberry's political work, she was composing the libretto for an opera on the life of the Haitian revolutionary Toussaint L'Ouverture and *Les Blancs*, a play conceived in the summer of 1960, when the Congo was flaring as the latest point of collision point between the politics of the cold war and the movement for decolonization. In that drama, as in *A Raisin in the Sun*, the action centered on a man who must gradually acknowledge the inevitability of having to make a choice—in this case, between being an upholder of the colonial order and being a leader who uses the advantages of his class to lead his people on a path toward genuine nationhood.[32] According to her former husband, Robert Nemiroff, Hansberry was working on this script steadily from the spring of 1960 until her death.[33]

Perhaps Hansberry interrupted her work on these and other projects to write *The Sign in Sidney Brustein's Window* in order to address the short-sightedness and ignorance that she perceived to exist among left-of-center Americans. The lack of understanding Hansberry observed in Robert Kennedy extended well beyond him to her avowedly bohemian neighbors in Greenwich Village. In an essay in the *Village Voice* criticizing Jean Genet's *The Blacks: A Clown Show*, Hansberry is reminded that the misreading of *A Raisin in the Sun* occurred not only in mainstream publications but in the "little magazines" of Greenwich Village, "in which Nelson Algren agrees in print with Jonas Mekas that *A Raisin in the Sun* is, of all things, a play about 'insurance money' and/or 'real estate.'" The glibness and ease with which some bohemians and radicals interpreted the desire of African Americans to leave unsafe neighborhoods in the "ghetto" as proof that they have sold out and become "hell-bent for suburbia" greatly offended Hansberry. Was the price of solidarity between African Americans and these supposed allies an implicit agreement between the two groups that blacks should simply become "a massive set of fraternals" to these alienated whites?[34]

As a document of and about American society in the middle years of the cold war, *The Sign in Sidney Brustein's Window* is an ambitious reflection on the role of the intellectual in society. And although McCarthyism is nowhere mentioned, it is there nonetheless. As Hansberry's friend James Baldwin observed after seeing the play, *The Sign in Sidney Brustein's Win-*

dow was about "the degree we have, all of us, permitted ourselves to retreat from what we once were." Baldwin was shocked "at the distance one decade, the era of McCarthy, has driven between us and our own ability to commit ourselves."[35] In this her second play, Hansberry is, in part, working through her experiences as an intellectual activist since *A Raisin in the Sun*—from the misinterpretation of her play in so many quarters to the confrontations over the direction of social reform with Robert Kennedy and with the audience at Town Hall.

Although one of its major characters, Alton Scales, is "dark" in skin color, the son of a Pullman porter and a domestic worker, his experience as an "American Negro" and his unwillingness to take the "white man's leavings" are not what *The Sign in Sidney Brusten's Window* is about.[36] The characters in Sidney's world *have overcome* racism, but they are not yet free, because they are unable to act on their beliefs about American society (including its continuing racism).

At the center of the action of the play is Sidney Brustein, a former radical who has come halfheartedly to the conclusion that it is best to "keep your conscience to yourself—Readers don't want it and feel pretty damn sure that they can't afford it. . . . Above all else, avoid the impulse to correct. . . . It's the only form of compassion left."[37] Sidney is, most recently, the owner of a failed coffeehouse. In a gesture that casts doubt on the real depth of his alienation he has purchased a small local newspaper that "is going to stay clear of politics. *Any* kind of politics."[38] He is also in a marriage that seems to be nearing its end. Sidney's wife, Iris, formerly his acolyte, has lived through Sidney's fall from political commitment firsthand and can no longer stand either his moods or his demands; she is tired of Sidney's pretense of moral superiority and is on the verge of leaving the "starving artist" life for an acting career in television commercials.

Sidney's personal drama is played out against the backdrop of a local election campaign in which a reform candidate is challenging the local party machine for a city council seat. Over the course of the play we meet the rest of Sidney's inner circle: Alton Scales, a former communist ("No more since Hungary . . . type Red") who works part time at a local bookstore; Sidney's sister-in-law Mavis, "the Mother Middle-Class itself"; Gloria Parodus, also Sidney's sister-in-law and "a big-time high-fashion whore"; David Ragin, an earnest young gay playwright, and one of the many writing in the fashionable absurdist mode of Jean Genet, Samuel Beckett, and others; and Wally O'Hara, the pragmatic reformer who is running to challenge not only the party machine but also the criminal syndicate that, while Burstein stayed home nursing his grudges, has turned Sidney's neighborhood into the "second largest narcotics drop in the city."[39]

The most important quality of *The Sign in Sidney Brustein's Window* is the vividness and complexity of Hansberry's characterizations. As in *A Raisin in the Sun*, these are memorable people with whom one, to varying degrees, can identify. At the same time, Hansberry has an all-too-mechanistic way of moving the action along to a predictable conclusion. Those looking for some development of how Sidney evolves from a quarrelsome intellectual isolationist back into one of the "committed" again will find little more than Gloria's suicide and Wally O'Hara's sellout to the machine. These developments appear so abruptly as to seem to be little more than clumsy authorial interventions to make a key point while getting to the final curtain on time. It is also puzzling that a play about politics contains so few direct comments on the fundamental issues and divisions in American politics.

As in *A Raisin in the Sun*, the personal comes through more strongly than the political: Sidney isn't sure who he is or what he is doing; he seems to be a mess in need of sorting out because that is who he is. Mavis, the sometimes unthinking catalogue of stereotypes and uninformed conventional wisdom, is also the only one with the moral acuity to argue against the notion that Gloria's vocation is merely "her choice"—a choice implicitly equal in consequence to every other. When Gloria commits suicide after Alton Scales refuses to marry her once he discovers how she earns a living, Hansberry saves some of her most eloquent and moving prose for Alton's misguided declaration of independence from having "the white man's leavings in my house."[40] In the final scene of *The Sign in Sidney Brustein's Window*, Sidney, faced with the loss of his sister-in-law and with Wally O'Hara's sellout to the party bosses and the drug syndicate, decides to go outside and "make something strong of this sorrow."[41]

Although *The Sign in Sidney Brustein's Window* was not without its admirers, the critical reception was generally negative. Richard P. Cooke, writing for the *Wall Street Journal*, welcomed the play but found it to be "packed too full with ideas and situations."[42] Offering a similar verdict, Walter Kerr, of the *New York Herald Tribune*, lauded the ambition and complexity of Hansberry's characterizations and her uncommon understanding that each of us "has in some way worked out his own . . . accommodation to his weaknesses." Hansberry's sure grasp of her theme ultimately overrode a certain awkwardness in construction, which was also a product of her ambition.[43]

The general circulation magazines that had broadcast the triumph of *A Raisin in the Sun* to a national audience now broadcast the failure of *The Sign in Sidney Brustein's Window*. The *New Yorker* and *Newsweek* were roundly dismissive. The *New Yorker's* John McCarten found Hansberry's portrait of political life in Greenwich Village to bear little resemblance to reality.[44] *Newsweek* castigated the playwright for "plundering from every playwright around" and drowning herself and her audience in "borrowed bitchery."[45] *Time* found the work to be "overloaded, over written and overwrought" and advised Hansberry "to recover the dramatic directness of her prize-winning first-play *A Raisin in the Sun*."[46]

Ultimately, the simultaneous death of Hansberry and the commercial failure of *The Sign in Sidney Brustein's Window* placed all the more weight on *A Raisin in the Sun* to represent Hansberry to the world. This sad conjunction of events was also perhaps a powerful force behind Nemiroff's "informal autobiography" of Hansberry, *To Be Young, Gifted, and Black*. This, rather than the highly flawed *The Sign in Sidney Brustein's Window*, could be Hansberry's last public word to the world. *To Be Young, Gifted, and Black* was Nemiroff's effort to project Hansberry's relevance into the future by providing evidence of her personal struggles and political radicalism to a generation of activists convinced that *A Raisin in the Sun* was irrelevant to their struggles.[47]

The Hansberry Legacy

On Saturday, January 16, 1965, Lorraine Hansberry was laid to rest. William E. Farrell, writing in the *New York Times*, recorded that a crowd of more than six hundred, including Malcolm X, "overflowed . . . the pews and aisles of Harlem's Presbyterian Church of the Master" to say a final public farewell. Robeson, "looking heavier and healthier than when he arrived here from London last winter to end his self-exile," delivered the eulogy. " 'It was a privilege,' " Robeson told the audience, "in a voice still compelling in its richness and resonance," " 'to know Lorraine. Her roots were deep in her people's history.' " Dee remembered her friend as "an artist of real promise [who was] beginning to shed light on the fear, pain and hope of our time."[48]

As we try to make sense of Hansberry's legacy, it is very easy to look back at Hansberry and her audience and see only the innocence of each. But present-day readers would do well to look at their own times also and admit the continuing pertinence of Hansberry's "homely, working-class *Raisin*" to our own large and continuing social problems.[49] Since 1954, the American legal and political systems have sought to desegregate American society through the social institution of the public school. When Americans look at the present and recognize frankly the widespread failure to find ways to overcome underlying patterns of segregation by race and by income, candor requires that they acknowledge that *A Raisin in the Sun* remains a document very clearly addressed to them.

The Sign in Sidney Brustein's Window is a critique of the cold war intellectual from an entirely original perspective. If she had wanted, Hansberry could have made her play, for example, about a New Frontier, think tank academic with ethically compromising ties to the defense establishment. Instead, she looked at the world she knew best—the world of the leftist bohemian, a self-constructed outsider. She found much to admire and much that called for sharp examination. Those who bound "in and out of the Communist Party" or become exclusively absorbed in the "abstractions flowing out of London or Paris" or "Zen, action painting or even just Jack Kerouac" are no more free from the necessity of moral compromise and no less capable of causing human suffering than anyone else.[50]

Hansberry chose to meet a relentlessly rough, unruly, and discordant world head on. That was, in the broadest sense, her lifework. In her short public life, one can discover a largely unknown new frontier, a piece of intellectual territory that will help one to understand more completely the political era known by that phrase and to make one's way through a troubled present.

Notes

Epigraph: Lorraine Hansberry, "Village Intellect Revealed," *New York Times*, October 31, 1964, 2:3.
1. Ossie Davis and Ruby Dee, *With Ossie and Ruby: In Life Together* (New York: William Morrow, 1998), 276.
2. Lorraine Hansberry, "The Legacy of W. E. B. Du Bois," *Freedomways* 5, no. 1 (1965): 20.
3. My understanding of Lorraine Hansberry's politics has been strengthened by Judith Smith's intricate treatment of it in *Visions of Belonging: Family Stories, Popular Culture, and Postwar Democracy, 1940–1960* (New York: Columbia University Press, 2004).

4. Lorraine Hansberry, "Challenge to Artists," *Freedomways* 3, no. 1 (1963): 34–35.

5. Ibid.

6. "Few . . . American intellectuals had it within them to be ashamed that their 'discovery' of the 'betrayal' of the Cuban Revolution by Castro just happened to coincide with the change of heart of official American government policy" (Hansberry, "Village Intellect Revealed," 3).

7. For a fuller treatment of this play, see my *The Work of Democracy: Ralph Bunche, Kenneth B. Clark, Lorraine Hansberry, and the Cultural Politics of Race* (Cambridge, Mass.: Harvard University Press, 1995), 180–87.

8. Brooks Atkinson, "The Theater: 'A Raisin in the Sun,'" *New York Times*, March 12, 1959, 27.

9. "Negro Talent in a Prize-winning Play," *Life*, April 27, 1959, 137.

10. "New Plays on Broadway," *Time*, March 23, 1959, 60.

11. "With a Wallop," *Newsweek*, March 23, 1959, 76.

12. "New Plays on Broadway," 58.

13. Richard E. Hays, "Weathers of the Human Heart," *Commonweal*, April 17, 1959, 81–82. See also Gerald Weales's "Thoughts on 'Raisin in the Sun,'" *Commentary*, June 1959, 527–30.

14. Tom F. Driver, "A Raisin in the Sun" [review], *New Republic*, April 13, 1959, 21.

15. Kenneth Tynan, "Ireland and Points West," *New Yorker*, March 21, 1959, 101.

16. Harold Clurman, "A Raisin in the Sun" [review], *The Nation*, April 4, 1959, 301–02.

17. Ossie Davis, "The Significance of Lorraine Hansberry," *Freedomways* 5, no. 3 (1965): 399.

18. Quoted in Nan Robertson, "Dramatist Against the Odds," *New York Times*, March 8, 1959, II:2.

19. "Playwright," *New Yorker*, May 9, 1959, 33–35.

20. Lorraine Hansberry, "An Author's Reflections: Willy Loman, Walter Younger and He Who Must Live" (1959), in *The Village Voice Reader: A Mixed Bag from the Greenwich Village Newspaper*, ed. Daniel Wolf and Edwin Fancher (New York: Doubleday, 1962), 195.

21. "Playwright," 34.

22. Ibid., 33.

23. Keppel, *Work of Democracy*, 177.

24. Hansberry, "Author's Reflections," 198.

25. Keppel, *Work of Democracy*, 218–27.

26. Robert Nemiroff, "A Critical Background" [to *The Drinking Gourd*], in *Lorraine Hansberry: The Collected Last Plays*, ed. Robert Nemiroff (New York: Random House, 1972), 151. Whether the series was canceled in part because of ideological concerns about Hansberry will never be known. What can be quite well established is that the political environment made the subject of racial conflict too sensitive for broadcast over a medium with such a large national audience. Hansberry's experience with NBC conformed to a well-established pattern in prime-time television with regard to race. The failure of "The Nat King Cole Show" to get a commercial sponsor despite strong ratings is well known. According to Daisy Fullilove Balsley, Rod Serling, one of the most important screenwriters of television's golden age," met with sponsor censorship and network interference when he tried to produce a script he wrote dramatizing the Emmett Till case (Till was a black teenager who was kidnapped and lynched in Mississippi for whistling at a white woman); in the end, the revisions were so extensive that any connection to the real event was lost ("A Descriptive Study of References Made to Negroes and Occupational Roles Represented by Negroes in Selected Mass Media" [Ph.D. diss., University of Denver, 1959], 11–12).

27. Diane Fisher, "Birth Weight Low, Jobs Few, Death Comes Early," *Village Voice*, June 6, 1963, 9.

28. "Black Revolution and White Backlash," [transcript of Town Hall meeting], *National Guardian*, July 4, 1964, 4.

29. Ibid.

30. Ibid., 6.

31. Ibid., 4.

32. Keppel, *Work of Democracy*, 217.

33. Hansberry, *The Collected Last Plays*, 31–33.

34. Hansberry, "Genet, Mailer, and the New Paternalism," *Village Voice*, June 1, 1961, 10.

35. Quoted in Robert Nemiroff, "The 101 'Final' Performances of *Sidney Brustein*," introduction to Lorraine Hansberry, *The Sign in Sidney Brustein's Window* (Random House, 1965), xlii–xliii.

36. These details are found in Hansberry, *The Sign in Sidney Brustein's Window*, 6, 101.

37. Ibid., 7.

38. Ibid., 21.

39. Ibid., 53, 63, 50, 24.

40. Ibid., 101–02.

41. Ibid., 143.

42. Richard P. Cooke, "Hansberry's Success," *Wall Street Journal*, October 19, 1964, 20.

43. Walter Kerr, "The Tidy Play and the Untidy," *New York Magazine* [Sunday Supplement of the *New York Herald Tribune*], November 2, 1964, 10.

44. John McCarten, "Hansberry's Potpourri," *New Yorker*, October 24, 1964, 93.

45. "Borrowed Bitchery," *Newsweek*, October 26, 1964, 101–02.

46. "Theater," *Time*, October 23, 1964, 67.

47. Lorraine Hansberry, *To Be Young, Gifted, and Black: An Informal Biography*, adapted by Robert Nemiroff (New York: New American Library, 1969).

48. William E. Farrell, "Six Hundred Attend Hansberry Rites: Robeson Delivers Eulogy," *New York Times*, January 17, 1965, 88.

49. Hansberry, "Genet, Mailer, and the New Paternalism," 10.

50. Farrel, "Six Hundred Attend Hansberry Rites," 88.

James Baldwin's "Discovery of

What It Means to Be an American"

It is to history that we owe our frames of reference, our identities, and our aspirations. And it is with great pain and terror that one begins to realize this.
—JAMES BALDWIN, "WHITE MAN'S GUILT" (1965)

This world is white no longer, and it will never be white again.
—JAMES BALDWIN, *NOTES OF A NATIVE SON* (1955)

In 2004 the African American writer James Baldwin (1924–87) joined the ranks of those Americans whose lives have been memorialized on a U.S. postage stamp (fig. 1). A partial tally of the other American persons, institutions, and artifacts so honored by the Postal Service in 2004 offers a glimpse into the variety of American hopes and dreams: Wilma Rudolph, the African American sprinter who won three gold medals in the Olympic Games of 1960; the white actor John Wayne; the white children's writer Theodor Seuss Geisel (Dr. Seuss); the African American actor, singer, and political activist Paul Robeson; the white composer Henry Mancini; R. Buckminster Fuller, the white futurist and inventor of the geodesic dome; the Lewis and Clark Bicentennial; the white dramatist Moss Hart; the U.S. Air Force Academy; "The Art of Disney: Friendship."[1]

Yet Baldwin—along with his fellow radical Robeson—arguably fits paradoxically on this list. One of the most influential U.S. writers and critics of the second half of the twentieth century, he unquestionably deserves the honor. Furthermore, Baldwin's inclusion in this array of American originals is surely meant to signal the arrival of a postracist America that celebrates its great minority critics. That said, Baldwin vigorously challenged the existing American reality, which in his view was too often a racist nightmare.

FIGURE 1 James Baldwin (1924–87) stamp, USA. James Baldwin Stamp Design © 2004 United States Postal Service. All Rights Reserved. Used with Permission of USPS and James Baldwin Estate.

And while Ida B. Wells-Barnett claimed Exiled as a narrative voice, Baldwin actually spent much of his adult life in self-imposed exile in France. "I left America," he wrote in 1959, "because I doubted my ability to survive the fury of the color problem here."[2] Baldwin also went to Europe to confront his Americanness. As a gay man, he was assailed within hypermasculinist strains of black nationalism in the United States, such as that articulated by the Black Panther Eldridge Cleaver.[3]

Baldwin's great achievement was to lay bare the harsh conflict between American dreams and illusions of innocence, on the one hand, and American duplicities and racialized realities, on the other. He contributed richly to a critical tradition—which included, among others, W. E. B. Du Bois and the Swedish economist Gunnar Myrdal—that conceived the contradiction between the history of American racism and the "American Creed" of freedom and justice for all as a "white problem" rather than as "the Negro problem."[4] For white Americans, the limitations of the American dream, the barriers to realizing it fully and inclusively, have been obscured historically through their complicity with white racism, institutionalized in immigration policy, labor and housing markets, and access to good schools. Owing to their advantaged status within the American racial order, white

Americans have generally been too quick to regard the United States as a free and equal meritocracy.

At the same time, Baldwin, no less than Thomas Jefferson and Abraham Lincoln, held on to a positive vision of America. For him, America symbolized, among other things, an as-yet-unrealized, radically democratic possibility. The mythic "land of the free and the home of the brave" has been bound up with white racism, feigned white innocence, and guiding assumptions about the normative American as racially white, attitudes that have obscured pronounced class divisions. But America also signified both a distinctive, hybrid, vernacular national culture and a set of political ideals—freedom, equality, democracy, and pluralism—that gesture toward a new social order "beyond the Old World concepts of race and caste and class."[5]

I focus here on Baldwin's analysis during the 1950s and early 1960s of the black-white divide of Jim Crow America. His chief contribution to rethinking what it means (or might mean) to be an American lies in how he framed the central challenge that arises out of two warring visions of America: that for the United States to achieve the egalitarian democratic promise of America, its people, especially its white citizens, must squarely confront the myth of American innocence with respect to the history of racism in the United States. He made clear how difficult it would be to "achieve our country."[6]

Baldwin and American Nationality

In his essay "The Discovery of What It Means to Be an American," Baldwin said that "the principal discovery an American writer makes in Europe is just how complex" is the "fate" of being an American. The American writer confronts a thick web of historical associations that swirl around the word *American*, which "remains a new, almost completely undefined and extremely controversial proper noun."[7] He went on to recall his surprise to learn that he, the "son of a slave," was undeniably American. Considering his fellow white Americans in Europe, he said, "It turned out to make very little difference that the origins of white Americans were European and mine were African—they were no more at home in Europe than I was. The fact that I was the son of a slave and they were the sons of free men meant less, by the time we confronted each other on European soil, than the fact

that we were both searching for our separate identities" (DWM, 17–18).[8]
Baldwin later recounted that his initial discovery of his Americanness "was
not . . . a matter for rejoicing. It was a great shock. . . . The fact that I had to
leave my country in order to realize that I was a part of it, or that it was a
part of me."[9]

He underscored this duality of American nationality when he recalled
his experience of listening to the recordings of Bessie Smith, the great African American blues singer of the 1920s, in Switzerland in the 1950s, after
suffering what he calls "a species of a breakdown":

> It was Bessie Smith, through her tone and her cadence, who helped
> me dig back to the way I myself must have spoken when I was a picka-
> ninny, and to remember the things I had heard and seen and felt. I
> had buried them very deep. I had never listened to Bessie Smith in
> America (in the same way that, for years, I would not touch water-
> melon), but in Europe she helped to reconcile me to being a "nigger."
>
> I do not think that I could have made this reconciliation here.
> Once I was able to accept my role—as distinguished, I must say, from
> my "place"—in the extraordinary drama which is America, I was re-
> leased from the illusion that I hated America.[10]

The "tone and cadence" of Bessie Smith were not only that of a so-called
Negro in the United States of the mid-twentieth century; they were also
distinctly American.[11] They expressed a sensibility that spoke particularly
to African Americans' struggles within and against their particular place
in the racialized hierarchy of the United States at the time. Simultaneously,
her music also spoke more broadly of and to a larger American national
vernacular culture.[12] Listening to Smith sing, then, brought Baldwin back
not just to "the way I myself must have spoken when I was a pickaninny,"
but also to his inescapable American identity.

In part, Baldwin was reiterating Du Bois's notion of the "double consciousness" of Negro Americans. "One ever feels his two-ness," Du Bois said
in 1903, "an American, a Negro; two souls, two thoughts, two unreconciled
strivings; two warring ideals in one dark body."[13] Thus, Baldwin explained
in "The American Dream and the American Negro" (1965),

> it comes as a great shock to discover that the country which is your
> birthplace and to which you owe your life and your identity has not,

in its whole system of reality, evolved any place for you. The disaffection and the gap between people, only on the basis of their skins, begins there and accelerates throughout your whole lifetime. You realize that you are 30 and you . . . have been through a certain kind of mill and the most serious effect is again not the category of disaster—the policeman, the taxi driver, the waiters, the landlady, the banks, the insurance companies, the millions of details . . . which spell out to you that you are a worthless human being. . . . But what is worse is that nothing you have done, and as far as you can tell nothing you *can* do, will save your son or your daughter from having the same disaster.[14]

He put a slightly different spin on this point in *The Fire Next Time* (1963): "The American Negro is a unique creation; he has no counterpart anywhere, and no predecessors. . . . The world is white and [he is] black."[15] That is, although the term *Negro* has been used to refer to people of African origins in contexts other than the United States, being an American Negro constituted a unique racialized identity and social status—a status produced by the specific social, political, economic, and cultural history of the United States but not accepted fully as American.[16]

For all his concern with the plight of black Americans, however, one of Baldwin's central insights into American nationality was that the racialized aspects of U.S. history shaped the identities of white Americans and the pursuit of the America dream as deeply as they shaped the identities of black Americans. Speaking to white Americans about racial falsehoods, he said, "If I'm not what I've been told I am, then it means that *you're* not what you thought *you* were *either!* And that is the crisis."[17] He developed this point further while pondering his experience as a black man and an American living in a small Swiss village in the early 1950s:

> In this long battle, . . . the white man's motive was the protection of his identity; the black man was motivated by the need to establish an identity. And despite the terrorization which the Negro in America endured and endures sporadically until today, despite the cruel and inescapable ambivalence of his status in his country, the battle for his identity has long ago been won. He is not a visitor to the West, but a citizen there, an American; as American as the Americans who despise him, the Americans who fear him, the Americans who love him. . . .

The time has come to recognize that the interracial drama acted out on the American continent has not only created a new black man, it has created a new white man, too. No road whatever will lead Americans back to the simplicity of this European village where white men still have the luxury of looking on me as a stranger.[18]

In Baldwin's assessment, this struggle over intertwined identities has profound significance for the idea of America as a nation dedicated to ideals of equality, liberty, and democracy. It means that these ideals are bound together in America ideology with the white supremacy that white Americans adopted from their European heritage:

One must . . . recognize that morality is based on ideas and that all ideas are dangerous . . . because ideas can only lead to action and where action leads no man can say. And dangerous in this respect: that confronted with the impossibility of remaining faithful to one's beliefs, and the equal impossibility of becoming free of them, one can be driven to the most inhuman excesses. The ideas on which American beliefs are based are not, though Americans often seem to think so, ideas which originated in America. They came out of Europe. And the establishment of democracy on the American continent was scarcely as radical a break with the past as was the necessity, which Americans faced, of broadening this concept to include black men.[19]

In short, the American dream of a democratic society requires a radical reconfiguring of old European notions of the people. Rather than making the radical break from Europe necessary to achieve a truly democratic nation, however, white Americans declared their commitment to the idea of democracy but retained white supremacy. In contrast, Baldwin saw a fateful difference between European racism and that of white Americans: Europe's "colored" subjects remained—at least until relatively recently—in "Europe's colonies, at which remove they represented no threat whatever to European identity." Meanwhile, the black presence in the United States had fundamentally shaped American ideology and identity: "Even as a slave, [the black man] was an inescapable part of the social fabric and no [white] American could escape having an attitude toward him."[20] Elsewhere he remarked, "The Negro problem in America can[not] even be discussed coherently without bearing in mind . . . the history, traditions, customs, the moral assumptions and preoccupations of the country. . . . No one in America escapes its effects and everyone in America bears some responsibility for it." Regarding the impact of this history on American beliefs, he says, "It was impossible, for one thing, for Americans to abandon their beliefs, not only because these beliefs alone seemed to justify the sacrifices they had endured and the blood that they had spilled, but also because these beliefs afforded them their only bulwark against a moral chaos as absolute as the physical chaos of the continent it was their destiny to conquer. But in the situation in which Americans found themselves, these beliefs threatened an idea which, whether or not one likes to think so, is the warp and woof of the heritage of the West, the idea of white supremacy."[21]

Baldwin also explored how the legacy of white supremacy and racial status has shaped American national identity in relation to the pursuit of socioeconomic status and material success. He maintained that the question of "minority rights" in the United States must be considered in terms of an examination of what constitutes "the majority" since "the society in which we live is an expression—in some way—of majority will."[22] By "the majority" he meant the group with the dominant influence on the national culture.[23] With regard to early American history the majority could be identified with the aristocracies of Virginia and New England, which were largely of "Anglo-Saxon stock and . . . created . . . our Anglo-American heritage." In the long run these aristocracies had a declining influence because they "referred to a past condition; . . . to the achievements . . . of a stratified society; and what was evolving in America had nothing to do with the past."[24]

Moreover, the waves of European immigrants in the late nineteenth century and early twentieth significantly reconfigured the question of American identity with respect to the relationship between the majority and minorities: "The old forms . . . gave way before the rush of Italians, Greeks, Spaniards, Irishmen, Poles, Persians, Norwegians, Swedes, Danes, wandering Jews from every nation under the heaven, Turks, Armenians, Lithuanians, Japanese, Chinese, and Indians. Everybody was suddenly in the melting pot, as we like to say, but without any intention of being melted." They came "to make their lives, achieve their futures, and to establish a new identity." What's more, their diversity "presented a problem for the [old] Puritan God, who had never heard of them," and most of them soon "took their places as a minority, a minority because their influence was so slight and because it was their necessity to make themselves over in the image of their new and unformed country."[25] Concerning the impact of these groups on American identity, Baldwin explains, "There were no longer any universally accepted forms or standards, and since all the roads to the achievement of an identity had vanished, the problem of status in American life became and it remains today acute. In a way, status became a kind of substitute for identity, and because money and the things money can buy is the universally accepted symbol here of status, we are often condemned as materialists. In fact, we are much closer to being metaphysical because nobody has ever expected from things the miracles that we do."[26]

Baldwin explained this displacement of the question of American identity by the pursuit of socioeconomic status—in effect, the creation of an American identity *defined by* the pursuit of socioeconomic status and material success—in light of the country's racial status hierarchy. He noted that such immigrant groups as the Irish, Swedes, and Danes "can no longer be considered in any serious way as minorities," and that "American minorities can be placed on a kind of color wheel." Therefore, "when we think of the American boy, we don't usually think of a Spanish, Turkish, a Greek, or a Mexican type, still less of an Oriental type. We usually think of someone who is kind of a cross between the Teuton and the Celt." This "national self-image" symbolized "hard work and good clean fun and chastity and piety and success. It leaves out of account, of course, most of the people in the country, and most of the facts of life." Moreover, this image "has almost nothing to do with what or who an American really is. . . . Beneath this bland, this conqueror image, a great many unadmitted despairs and confusions, and anguish and unadmitted crimes and failures hide."[27]

His phrasing here was imprecise for his own purposes. Insofar as this "conqueror image" of the Teutonic-Celtic white American set the status ordering of "the color wheel," it actually had a great deal "to do with what or who an American really is." Yet his more immediate point was that so many actual Americans do not fit the normative Teutonic-Celtic American image. Speaking "as a member of the nation's most oppressed minority," he insisted that "before we can do very much in the way of clear thinking or clear doing as relates to the minorities in this country, we must first crack the American image and find out and deal with what it hides."[28] The iconography of the supposedly typical American has shifted notably since the 1960s.[29] Nonetheless, what this image symbolized has changed much less. For instance, the experience of white Americans still sets the standard for generalized American notions of equal opportunity, hard work, and merit.[30]

The "White Problem"

One way Baldwin "crack[ed] the American image" open was to apprehend the country's race problem as fundamentally a white problem. White racial identity dominated the "wheel of color" and framed the "rung-by-rung ascension" to social status in the "prevailing notion of American life." The fact that the American way of life confronted even the white majority with the ever-present possibility of slipping down the socioeconomic status rungs indicated "one of the real reasons for the status of the Negro in this country. In a way, the Negro tells us where the bottom is: because he is there, . . . beneath us, we know where the limits are and how far we must not fall."[31] (The comedian Richard Pryor, reflecting on the identity crisis he had in 1967, has given a succinct account of this racialized status: "I was a Negro for twenty-three years. I gave that shit up. No room for advancement.")[32]

Regarding the white problem, Baldwin said that "before one can really talk about the Negro problem in this country, one has got to talk about the white people's problem."[33] The "race problem" was fundamentally the white people's problem because it was rooted in persistent delusions among self-described white people of white supremacy, the whiteness of their country, and white innocence with respect to the racism and privilege enacted by white Americans.[34] White people have great difficulty acknowledging that from the beginning of U.S. history black Americans were "a source of cheap labor and everything white people did thereafter in relation to the Negroes was a way of justifying this."[35] Moreover, because of their investments in their whiteness, white people have too readily accepted the dubious proposition that "America is still the land of opportunity . . . [where] inequalities vanish before a determined will."[36] In short, white Americans too typically have a naive, self-serving view of this history. They are generally "far more hopeful, far more innocent, far more irresponsible, far less aware of the terrible, black, ugly facts of life than black people can afford to be."[37]

Baldwin spelled out the contemporary significance of the white problem in 1964 in a round-table discussion entitled "Liberalism and the Negro" sponsored by *Commentary* magazine. He criticized the philosopher Sidney

Hook's idea of "rising expectations [in the United States] as to what decent conduct should be," which Hook attributed to improvements in education. Baldwin considered rising expectations in terms of increasing material well-being and social status. More to the point, he maintained that this notion applied uniquely to European immigrants, "that is, people who came to this country voluntarily and who managed, once they got here, to achieve a way of life and a whole attitude toward reality and toward themselves which they could not have achieved if they had remained wherever they came from in Europe." The problem with the European immigrants' narrative—and the core of the white problem—was its failure to comprehend that this experience of rising expectations was contrary to the experience of black Americans: "The black experience is entirely different. You find yourself in a slum and you realize at a certain point that no amount of labor, no amount of hard work, no amount of soap is going to get you out of that slum."[38]

Baldwin explored the problem of white innocence most directly in "The White Problem" (1963). Speaking in the year marking "one hundred years of Negro freedom" and in the shadow "of the crisis in Birmingham," he asked people to reconsider two lines from the U.S. national anthem: "Oh, say, does that star-spangled banner still wave / O'er the land of the free and the home of the brave."[39] This mythic America made it seem both easy and exceptional to be an American, at least for white Americans. Given this mindset, "if one tries to define the proper noun, *American*, one will discover that the noun equates with a catalogue of virtues, and with something called, plaintively enough, 'I-Am-American Day.'"[40] Yet insofar as Americans faced squarely the gap between the myth of America ("land of the free and the home of the brave") and the harsh, sometimes brutal, reality of white racial domination in the United States, then they would be forced to learn that being an American is something of a dilemma, a "complex fate." "The beginnings of this country have nothing whatever to do with the myth we have created about it."[41] "There is an illusion about America," Baldwin wrote in another essay, "a myth about America to which we are clinging which has nothing to do with the lives we lead and I don't believe that anybody in this country who has really thought about it or really almost anybody who has been brought up against it—and almost all of us have in one way or another—this collision between one's image of oneself and what one actually is is always very painful."[42]

It is not quite right, then, to say that the country was established by Europeans dedicated to the foundation of a free society: "They came here because they thought it would be better here than wherever they were." Now, "part of the dilemma of this country is that it has managed to believe the myth it has created about its past, which is another way of saying that it has entirely denied its past." White Americans in particular have been inclined to ignore or evade the fact that "a great many crimes were committed . . . to create the country called America."[43]

Regarding contemporary problems, the issue is not so much the historical crimes, such as the decimation of Native Americans and the enslavement of Africans, which cannot be erased, but the American mythology that minimizes these crimes and elides responsibility for them. One of the "hidden reasons for the tremendous popularity of the cowboy-Indian legend in American life," Baldwin said, is that these "stories are designed to reassure us that no crime was committed." Since the people who settled the country "were Christian, and since they had already decided that they came here to establish a free country," the only way they could justify the enslavement of Africans was to deny their humanity, even though "they could recognize a man when they saw one." This lie "is the basis of our present trouble." The real problem is presumed white innocence: "What is most terrible is that American white men are not prepared to believe my version of the story, to believe that it happened. In order to avoid believing that, they have set up in themselves a fantastic system of evasions, denials, and justifications, which system is about to destroy their grasp of reality, which is another way of saying their moral sense."[44] White Americans have "a very curious sense of reality—or, rather, perhaps, I should say, a striking addiction to irreality."[45]

According to Baldwin, when we understand the American race problem as the white problem rather than as the Negro problem we gain a much clearer sense of the means necessary to change it. Thinking in terms of "the Negro problem" tends to suggest policies that would help black Americans to be "fitted into American civilization, or American society, . . . as it's now constituted."[46] "White Americans," he said in *The Fire Next Time*, "find it impossible to divest themselves of the notion that they are in possession of some intrinsic value that black people need, or want. And this assumption—which, for example, makes the solution to the Negro problem depend on the speed with which Negroes accept and adopt white standards—is revealed in all sorts of ways. . . . It is the Negro, of course, who is presumed to have to become equal—an achievement that not only proves the comforting fact that perseverance has no color but also that overwhelmingly corroborates the white man's sense of his own value."[47] In just this spirit Hook proposed "a temporary crash program to improve the position of the Negro community" in the United States.[48] Baldwin, for his part, called for a different approach: "White people will have to ask themselves precisely why they found it necessary to invent the nigger; for the nigger is a white invention, and white people invented him out of terrible necessities of their own."[49]

Subsequent events have born out the deeper wisdom of Baldwin's view. In certain respects, President Lyndon Johnson's short-lived War on Poverty agenda answered Hook's call for "a temporary crash program" for black Americans.[50] This program was certainly justified by racism, both historical and ongoing, against African Americans and by its wider legacy.[51] Yet in light of Baldwin's analysis the most striking thing about Johnson's War on Poverty was not that it failed to end poverty and racism in the United States but that it quickly generated a white backlash against redistributive social welfare policies, especially those policies most clearly aimed at overcoming the inequalities faced by black Americans.[52]

Toward a New America

Baldwin also looked beyond the white problem to reenvision American nationality. The racial tensions that plagued the United States, he concluded, "have little to do with real antipathy" and are not really even about color or race.[53] The "fact of color" was a politically constructed fact that could, if confronted, illuminate submerged realities of American life.[54] Most notably, it indicated some problems inherent in the American dream of a "rung by rung" ascension to ever higher socioeconomic status. This conception of the promise of American life encouraged Americans to draw sharp distinctions between winners and losers and to naturalize (and often racialize) this divide. Baldwin insisted that Americans have failed to make the more life-affirming possibilities of the American dream "into a reality" because of "the nature of that dream and with the fact that we Americans, of whatever color, do not dare to [critically] examine it."[55] He later observed that the prevailing American dream harmed not only a disproportionate number of people of color, but also poor and working-class white people who "take refuge in their whiteness" and fail to question how the economic structure of the United States relegates them to being "the instrument[s] of someone else's profit."[56]

As Lawrie Balfour notes, Baldwin himself remained wedded to "a kind of American exceptionalism. He contends that the United States is uniquely positioned to overcome racial injustice and to create a new, more democratic way of life."[57] Nonetheless, it is important to grasp the radical promise of his American exceptionalism. His claim was not that the United States was likely to achieve a fully nonracial, democratic way of life but that it was uniquely situated to do so: "We are the strongest nation in the world, but this is not for the reasons that we think. It is because we have an opportunity which no other nation has of moving beyond the Old World concepts of race and class and caste, and create, finally, what we must have had in mind when we first began speaking of the New World. But the price for this is a long look backward whence we came and an unflinching assessment of the record."[58] That is, precisely because of the profound gap between American myth and the American (racialized) reality, the United States was uniquely positioned to achieve—and to become a model of—a truly free, egalitarian, democratic society. But this would require Americans, especially white Americans, to confront the conflicted record of U.S. history and leave behind the myth that America is a white nation. It would also require white Americans to come to grips with the chimera of their whiteness—the false comfort of taking refuge in this racial fiction as a source of social status and a defense against insecurities and disappointments of the American way of life.

Baldwin's democratic dream was an American dream and thus a kind of American nationalism insofar as it stemmed from his connection to this particular national history and culture. As Balfour says, this raises questions "at a time of such enormous economic and political interpenetration of national borders." Additionally, Baldwin's emphasis on the black-white divide, a product of his historical moment, has some limitations in light of the growth of Latino and Asian American populations since the 1960s.[59] And some of Baldwin's claims about the dire prospects that all black Americans face are now somewhat (although not completely) dated. That said, Baldwin's vision should be refined and complicated rather than dismissed.[60] While the black-white divide does not exhaust the complexities of racial politics in the United States, Baldwin shed much light on the ways in which race and racism have distorted America nationalism and American dreams. For example, while many African Americans have in fact worked their way "out of that slum" Baldwin's analysis helps his readers to grasp why too many have not.

Finally, his emphasis on the white problem illuminates what remains a central feature of politics in the United States. Notably, despite widespread talk of how President George W. Bush won the presidential election of 2004 because of Republican appeals to moral values, a more striking feature of the voting patterns was the persistence of a form of white identity politics.[61] Furthermore, while nation-states in general and the United States in particular continue politically to order the world, Baldwin's critical rethinking of American nationality and the American ethos remains highly relevant. It offers invaluable resources for crafting a more just and democratic American domestic polity with a more just and less self-aggrandizing role in the wider world. As Baldwin suggested in the mid-1960s, the struggle for racial justice in the United States was "analogous to, indissoluble from, the struggle of the dispossessed all over the world."[62]

Notes

Thanks to Duchess Harris, Ben Keppel, and Dean Robinson for comments on earlier drafts of this essay.

Epigraphs: James Baldwin, "White Man's Guilt," in Baldwin, *The Price of the Ticket: Collected Nonfiction, 1948–1985* (New York: St. Martin's Press, 1985), 410; James Baldwin, *Notes of a Native Son* (1955; reprint, New York: Bantam, 1968), 149.

1. See http://shop.usps.com.

2. James Baldwin, *Nobody Knows My Name: More Notes of a Native Son* (New York: Dell, 1961), 17.

3. Henry Louis Gates Jr., *Thirteen Ways of Looking at a Black Man* (New York: Vintage, 1997), 11–13.

4. See W. E. B. Du Bois, "The Souls of White Folk," in *Black on White: Black Writers on What It Means to Be White*, ed. David R. Roediger (New York: Schocken Books, 1998), 184–99; Gunnar Myrdal, *An American Dilemma: The Negro Problem and Modern Democracy* (1944; reprint, New York: Harper and Row, 1962), lxxv–lxxvi.

5. Baldwin, "The Creative Process," in *James Baldwin: Collected Essays*, ed. Toni Morrison (New York: Library of America, 1998), 672.

6. James Baldwin, *The Fire Next Time* (1963; reprint, New York: Vintage Books, 1993), 105. Baldwin's overall analysis of American mythology and nationality was wide ranging. In his early novels *Giovanni's Room* and *Another Country*, as well as in a later essay, he examined how the "American ideal of sexuality appears to be rooted in the American idea of masculinity." See Baldwin, "Freaks and the American Ideal of Manhood,"

in *James Baldwin*, 815; *Giovanni's Room* (New York: Dial Press, 1956); *Another Country* (New York: Dial Press, 1962). He also challenged dominant cultural patterns that "universalized heterosexual culture" as part of American nationhood. See Roderick A. Ferguson, "The Parvenu Baldwin and the Other Side of Redemption: Modernity, Sexuality, and the Cold War," in *James Baldwin Now*, ed. Dwight McBride (New York: New York University Press, 1999), 234; Marlon B. Ross, "White Fantasies of Desire: Baldwin and the Racial Identities of Sexuality," in *James Baldwin Now*, 13–55; Magdalena J. Zaborowska, "Mapping American Masculinities: James Baldwin's Innocents Abroad, or *Giovanni's Room* Revisited," in *Other Americans, Other Americas: The Politics and Poetics of Multiculturalism*, ed. Magdalena J. Zaborowska (Aarhus, Denmark: Aarhus University Press, 1998), 119–31.

7. Baldwin, *Nobody Knows My Name*, 17.

8. Ibid., 17–18.

9. James Baldwin and Margaret Mead, *A Rap on Race* (Philadelphia: J. B. Lippincott, 1971), 85–86.

10. Baldwin, *Nobody Knows My Name*, 18–19.

11. For a related discussion of Baldwin's response to Bessie Smith, see Josh Kun, "Life According to the Beat: James Baldwin, Bessie Smith, and the Perilous Sounds of Love," in *James Baldwin Now*, 307–28.

12. See Ralph Ellison, "Blues People," in *Shadow and Act* (New York: Vintage Books, 1972), 247–58; James Baldwin, "If Black English Isn't a Language, Then Tell Me, What Is?" in *James Baldwin*.

13. W. E. B. Du Bois, *The Souls of Black Folk* (1903; reprint, Mineola, N.Y.: Dover Publications, 1994), 2.

14. Baldwin, "The American Dream and the American Negro," in *James Baldwin*, 715.

15. Baldwin, *Fire Next Time*, 84, 25.

16. Baldwin, *Nobody Knows My Name*, 24–54.

17. Baldwin, "A Talk to Teachers" (1963), in *James Baldwin*, 682.

18. James Baldwin, *Notes of a Native Son*, 147, 148–49.

19. Ibid., 145.

20. Ibid., 144–45.

21. Ibid., 146.

22. Baldwin, *Nobody Knows My Name*, 107.

23. Here he rejected the idea that the majority can be defined in terms of power rather than influence (*Nobody Knows My Name*, 109). Elsewhere he emphasized relative power and powerlessness. See *Fire Next Time*, 96; James Baldwin, "A Letter to Americans," *Freedomways* 8 (spring 1968): 112–16.

24. Baldwin, *Nobody Knows My Name*, 108–09.

25. Ibid., 109–10.

26. Ibid., 110.

27. Ibid.

28. Ibid., 110–11.

29. One example of changing imagery is *Time* magazine's computer-generated "Eve," its multiracial "New Face of America" (1993). See David Roediger, *Colored White: Transcending the Racial Past* (Berkeley: University of California Press, 2002), 10–15.

30. George Lipsitz, *The Possessive Investment in Whiteness: How White People Profit from Identity Politics* (Philadelphia: Temple University Press, 1998), chap. 1.

31. Baldwin, *Nobody Knows My Name*, 111, 110.

32. Richard Pryor, quoted in Hilton Als, "A Pryor Love," *New Yorker* 75, September 13, 1999, 75.

33. Baldwin, in James Baldwin, Nathan Glazer, Sidney Hook, and Gunnar Myrdal, "Liberalism and the Negro: A Round-Table Discussion," *Commentary* 37, March 1964, 27. See also Martin Luther King Jr., "Racism and the White Backlash," in *Where Do We Go From Here: Chaos or Community?* (Boston: Beacon Press, 1968).

34. Ibid., 38.

35. Ibid., 27.

36. Baldwin, *Nobody Knows My Name*, 58.

37. Ibid., 37. Baldwin later explained that white people not only wrongly think of America as a white country, but "they delude themselves into thinking that they are [white]." See Baldwin, "The Price of the Ticket" (1985), in *James Baldwin*, 835–36, 842.

38. Baldwin, "Liberalism," 32.

39. James Baldwin, "The White Problem," in *100 Years of Emancipation*, ed. Robert A. Goldwin (Chicago: Rand McNally, 1964), 80.

40. Ibid., 82.

41. Ibid.

42. Baldwin, *Nobody Knows My Name*, 126; Baldwin, "Talk to Teachers," 683–86.

43. Baldwin, "White Problem," 83.

44. Ibid., 84–86.

45. Baldwin, "Nothing Personal" (1964), in *James Baldwin*, 702.

46. Baldwin, "Liberalism," 27.

47. Baldwin, *Fire Next Time*, 94–95. On this point, see Lawrie Balfour, "Finding the Words: Baldwin, Race Consciousness, and Democratic Theory," in *James Baldwin Now*, 83–93.

48. Sidney Hook, in "Liberalism," 26.

49. Baldwin, "White Problem," 88.

50. The Kerner Commission Report (1968) on urban unrest later made an ambitious clarion call for such a program, but it was not answered. See *Report of the National Advisory Commission on Civil Disorders*, with a special introduction by Tom Wicker (New York: Bantam Books, 1968).

51. Johnson himself laid out part of the justification for such "race conscious" compensatory policies in 1965: "You do not take a person, who for years has been hobbled by chains and liberate him, bring him up to the starting line of a race and then say 'you are free to compete with all the others,' and still justly believe that you have been completely fair" (quoted in Isaac Kramnick, "Equal Opportunity and the 'Race of Life,'" *Dissent* 28 [Spring 1981]: 178).

52. Clayborne Carson notes that the presidential election of 1964 was the last one in which "a majority of white voters supported a Democratic candidate. It would also be the last one in which a majority of white voters and black voters supported the same presidential candidate." Subsequently, the majority of white voters have tended to see the Democratic Party as the party of minority interests. See Carson, "Parting the Country," *Dissent* 45 (Summer 1998): 111.

53. Baldwin, *Fire Next Time*, 95.

54. Baldwin said in *The Fire Next Time*, "America, of all Western nations, has been best placed to prove the uselessness and the obsolescence of the concept of color. But it has not dared to accept this opportunity" (93).

55. Ibid., 88.

56. James Baldwin, "An Open Letter to My Sister, Angela Y. Davis" (1971), in Angela Y. Davis et al., *If They Come in the Morning: Voices of Resistance*, with a foreword by Julian Bond (New York: Signet Books, 1971), 22–23.

57. Lawrie Balfour, *The Evidence of Things Not Said: James Baldwin and the Promise of American Democracy* (Ithaca: Cornell University Press, 2000), 137.

58. Baldwin, "Creative Process," 672.

59. Balfour, *Evidence of Things Not Said*, 137.

60. For other efforts to refine and extend Baldwin's vision, see Balfour, *Evidence of Things Not Said*; Rebecca Aanerud, "Now More Than Ever: James Baldwin and the Critique of White Liberalism," in *James Baldwin Now*, 56–74; George Shulman, "Race and the Romance of American Nationalism in Martin Luther King, Norman Mailer, and James Baldwin," in *Cultural Studies and Political Theory*, ed. Jodi Dean (Ithaca: Cornell University Press, 2000); and the essays by Ferguson, Ross, and Zaborowska cited in n. 6.

61. According to the *New York Times*, 22 percent of voters said that moral values mattered most to them, and 80 percent of these voters voted for Bush. (The 20 percent of voters who named economy or jobs went overwhelmingly for Kerry, while the 19 percent who named terrorism overwhelmingly favored Bush.) Seventy-eight percent of white evangelical or born-again Christians (23 percent of all voters) went for Bush, while Protestants in general (54 percent of voters) favored Bush 59 to 40 percent; Catholics went 52/47; Jews, 25/74. The results broken down by racial identification were as follows: white people (77 percent of all voters) favored Bush over Kerry 58 to 41 percent; blacks (11 percent of voters) overwhelmingly favored Kerry over Bush, 88 to 11 percent; Hispanic/ Latino voters (8 percent of voters) favored Kerry over Bush, 53 to 44 percent; and Asians (2 percent of voters) favored Kerry over Bush, 56 to 44 percent. In short, Bush's reelection was largely a triumph of white identity politics. See Katherine Q. Seelye, "Moral Values Cited as a Defining Issue of the Election," *New York Times*, November 4, 2004, P4; Colin Kidd, " 'My God Was Bigger than His,' " *London Review of Books*, November 4, 2004, 15–18; Tim Wise, "What's the Matter with White Folks?: Racial Privilege, Electoral Politics and the Limits of Class Populism," *LiP Magazine* (Spring 2005).

The election of Barack Obama as U.S. president in 2008 did not radically alter this pattern of white identity politics. Among white voters nationally Obama lost to John McCain, although there were notable regional and class differences in voting among whites. Obama beat McCain handily among the other major racialized groups in the United States. See Michael Tomasky, "How Historic a Victory?," *New York Review of Books* 55 (December 18, 2008), 44–47; www.cnn.com/ELECTION/2008/results/polls.

62. Baldwin, in James Baldwin and Budd Schulberg, "Dialogue in Black and White" (1964–65), in *James Baldwin: The Legacy*, ed. Quincy Troupe (New York: Simon and Schuster, 1989), 159. Baldwin also said that the achievement of a truly democratic society was partly dependent on how those people who have learned to think of themselves as white responded to "the revolution now occurring in the world." See Baldwin, *Nobody Knows My Name*, 63.

Afterword

Racially Writing the Republic and Racially Righting the Republic

FIGURE 1 "The Flag Is Bleeding" (1967), by Faith Ringgold, The American People Series #18, oil on canvas, 72 in. x 96 in. © Faith Ringgold 1967.

It can be depressing to confront the degree to which race still matters in American society. Despite decades of suffering, sacrifice, and struggle, people who are not white confront starkly unequal access to housing, health care, education, and employment in the Unite States. Hate crimes and housing discrimination oppress communities of color while newspapers, television programs, and talk radio shows recruit readers, viewers, and listeners to partake in the sadistic pleasure of recreational hate.

The authors of *Racially Writing the Republic* teach that America's problems did not begin yesterday and that they will not be solved tomorrow. Racial considerations have long been at the center of the nation's political culture, social relations, spatial organization, and interpersonal imaginations. White supremacy has not been a spasmodic, aberrant, and irrational departure from the norm as Americans have often been led to believe by their educators, journalists, and political leaders. Rather, it has been a persistent presence in the construction of individual and collective identities from the colonial era to the present.

Yet the chronicles of racial domination and resistance in *Racially Writing the Republic* also provide the tools needed to "right" the racial republic, to reckon with the long fetch of racism in American lives and replace it with social justice. The hour is late and the odds are long, but, as Dr. Martin Luther King used to say, it is never the wrong time to do right.

All of the essays in *Racially Writing the Republic* help explain why American is still wrestling with the realities of racism some 40 years after the assassination of Martin Luther King Jr., nearly 55 years after the Supreme Court's *Brown v. Board* decision, and more than 140 years after the Emancipation Proclamation. The long history of race in the past haunts the present. As Laura Janara notes in her essay on Tocqueville, nothing from the past ever goes away completely. Expectations about the privileges of whiteness pervade contemporary debates about affirmative action, immigration, environmental pollution, and educational inequality. Inside aggrieved communities of color, frustrated aspirations for justice not only fail to disappear, but, in the words of one of Langston Hughes's most famous poems, they stink like rotten meat, sag like a heavy load, and sometimes they explode.[1]

Part of the problem stems from the fact that racism has never been only about race. Racism serves as a crucible in which other cruelties are created, learned, and legitimated. It recruits adherents to the idea that injustice is natural, necessary, and inevitable. The essays in this book demonstrate how destructive racist actions and ideas have also served historically productive purposes for those who embraced them. John Kuo Wei Tchen reveals how slave owners in the midst of waging a revolutionary war for their own freedom turned racial otherness into commodities, collecting porcelain plates and dishes from China to prove themselves refined, dignified, and worthy of ruling a new nation and a new empire. Duchess Harris, Bruce Baum, Catherine A. Holland, and Gary Gerstle show that Thomas Jefferson, Abraham Lincoln, and Theodore Roosevelt, respectively, constructed their understandings of white freedom by insisting on denying blacks the full fruits of liberty, despite the importance of African Americans to their own personal and public successes.

Laura Janara explores the writings of Tocqueville to disclose how whites in the early national period used white supremacy to build an imaginary fraternity among white men, one designed to temper the passions unleashed by aggressive economic competition and its resulting status anxieties. Gwendolyn Mink explains how "race feeling" provided the basis for labor solidarity during the early years of the American Federation of Labor. Allegiances to white supremacy provoked militant actions by white workers, yet they also divided the working class dreadfully while arming employers with ways to make concessions to the privileges of whiteness without yielding to labor on fundamental class questions about wages, hours, and working conditions. Dorothy Roberts examines the vexed relationship between birth control and eugenics in the thought and politics of Margaret Sanger. Roberts reveals how birth control advocates turned to the language of eugenics to legitimate their cause with the broader public, only to discover that this language transformed their crusade to win reproductive autonomy for women into a vehicle for controlling and oppressing communities of color.

Yet while the depth, dimensions, and duration of white supremacy give every reason for pessimism, the racial record of the United States also includes a long history of antiracism. *Racially Writing the Republic* reveals how activists, artists, intellectuals, and ordinary citizens from all walks of life have left us legacies of affiliations, alliances, identities, and identifications replete with the tools one needs to unwrite the hurts of history and to put the republic and its citizens on the path to making things right. Just as it is depressing to consider the reach and scope of white supremacy in our past and present, it is invigorating, encouraging, and inspiring to contemplate the long history of antiracism that Americans inherit from the past and that persists today.

In many cases, it has been the very horrors of racial oppression that have pointed the way toward antiracist emancipatory ideas and actions. Patricia

Schechter discloses in this book that it was the Memphis lynchings of 1893 that set Ida B. Wells-Barnett on her path as an antiracist public intellectual. Schechter shows how Wells-Barnett turned hegemony on its head, moving her listeners by "talking through tears" and transforming her sense of isolation and exile into a political and moral stance that replaced allegiance to a temporal homeland with a commitment to world-transcending citizenship. Joel Olson explains a similar moment in the life of W. E. B. Du Bois—when the lurid sight of the knuckles of a lynched black man in a store display window after the Atlanta Riot of 1906 convinced Du Bois that education needed to be accompanied by agitation, legislation, and litigation. Du Bois saw reason for hope, however, inside the very dynamics of white supremacy because he recognized that the quest for domination by the white world had produced a reactive solidarity among the darker races, unwittingly creating people determined to wield weapons against a system that both demeaned and demonized them. Similarly, Jerry Thompson details how brutal repression and systematic disenfranchisement impelled Juan Nepomuceno Cortina to launch military actions in defense of people of Mexican ancestry in Texas in the mid-nineteenth century. Cortina defended the interests of his people on both sides of the U.S.–Mexico border, fashioning a cause that could not be contained within the borders of a single nation-state. Cari M. Carpenter's explication of the politics of translation in the life of Sarah Winnemucca shows how univocal national narratives can provoke covert and indirect forms of discursive resistance from members of aggrieved communities.

The antiracist acts and ideas examined in *Racially Writing the Republic* often move beyond reactive self-defense to propose the radical reconstruction of society itself. Allan Punzalan Isaac shows how Carlos Bulosan responded to the imperial project of the United States to remake Filipinos in the image of North Americans with literary work that envisioned Filipino immigrants like himself playing a role in remaking the United States a more democratic and inclusive nation. Ben Keppel calls attention to Lorraine Hansberry's lesser-known play *The Sign in Sidney Brustein's Window* to demonstrate that Hansberry's critique of white supremacy required her to argue that political quiescence and cowardice grow organically from the defensive privatism of bourgeois social relations. Similarly, Bruce Baum delineates James Baldwin's arguments that democracy itself could never survive unless the nation divested itself of its posture of innocence about the racial crimes of its history.

Some readers of *Racially Writing the Republic* might be willing to concede the centrality of white supremacy in the past, but not in the present. For them, the fourteen essays in this book have archaeological value in uncovering dimensions of the past no longer visible in the present. In their view, the Supreme Court's *Brown v. Board* decision of 1954 and the Civil Rights Act of 1964 and the Voting Rights Act of 1965 relegate the histories in this book to the prehistory of the genuine democracy that became fully consolidated by 1965.

Such a perspective cannot explain why the civil rights laws were written to be so weak—why fair housing and fair hiring laws contain no provision for cease-and-desist orders, why the penalties for violating them remain so low that they comprise merely a cost of doing business for discriminators. This stance does not explain why fair housing enforcement is left largely to citizen initiative rather than to the actions (and subpoena powers) of the attorney general or the Department of Housing and Urban Development. It does not account for the enormous backlog of cases at the Equal Employment Opportunity Commission or for the reluctance of judges to require malefactors convicted of deliberate employment discrimination to pay even court costs and attorney fees, much less punitive damages likely to discourage others from discriminatory practices.[2]

In his chapter on Hansberry, Keppel asks readers to look at school desegregation to measure the degree to which our society has addressed or redressed the republic's racial inscription. The history of *Brown v. Board* presents a sobering assessment and a significant challenge to anyone attempting to right the republic at the present time.

"Getting around *Brown*" is the name of a fine book by Gregory Jacobs about school desegregation in Columbus, Ohio. It is also the best phrase to describe the most powerful force within the political culture of the United States during the past half century.[3] Contrary to the celebratory stories occasioned by the fiftieth anniversary of *Brown v. Board*, deliberate, collective, organized white resistance to the desegregation of opportunities and life chances in American society remains pervasive, powerful, and predominant in every region of the country. Getting around *Brown* has been the main mechanism for mobilizing a sense of group position among whites, for protecting and augmenting the value of past and present discrimination, and for enabling elite individuals and interests to build a conservative consensus within national political life.

Evading the desegregation mandate of the *Brown* decision has been the single most important dynamic within the U.S. political system, a practice encouraged and legitimated by both political parties, protected by the judiciary, subsidized by the tax code, and sustained by a complex combination of public and private policies. In their efforts to get around *Brown*, elite white leaders and their followers enact powerful identity politics based on assertions of group rights, while condemning communities of color for "playing the race card" and shunning individualism. Getting around *Brown* entails evasions of moral and legal responsibility in order to protect the unfair gains and unjust enrichments that accrue to whites as a consequence of systematic and illegal housing discrimination and widespread intentional educational inequality.

Less than two years after the Supreme Court issued the *Brown* decision, the sociologist Herbert Blumer offered an analysis of race prejudice that would prove extraordinarily prescient. Speaking at the dedication of the Robert E. Park building on the campus of Fisk University in Nashville, Blumer explained that race prejudice was not primarily a matter of private, personal, and individual attitudes, but a matter of group position—a fusing of public, political, and institutional actions designed to protect privileges and advantages. He granted that members of dominant groups often express personal disdain for those they view as inferior, alien, and intrinsically different. Yet they do so, Blumer argued, largely out of fear that the subordinated group threatens their entitlement to important privileges and prerogatives.

Blumer made no prediction about the implementation of *Brown v. Board*, but he did note that individuals with standing, prestige, authority, and influence within the dominant group had the power to "manufacture events to attract public attention and to set lines of issue in such a way as to predetermine interpretations favorable to their interests."[4] Resistance to school desegregation, to busing, to equalizing expenditures on education across school districts—and later, resistance to affirmative action—became precisely those kinds of events. Elite whites with standing, prestige, authority, and power chose to portray judicial efforts to implement desegregation mandates as cataclysmic occurrences, as events more threatening to the nation than the segregation and discrimination that caused the courts to act in the first place.

The ferocious opposition to desegregation led by southern demagogues has been well chronicled.[5] Ninety southern members of the U.S. House of Representatives and all but three of the region's twenty-two U.S. senators signed the Southern Manifesto in March 1956 declaring the *Brown* ruling illegitimate. They urged "massive resistance" by citizens.[6] In order to resist desegregation, Senator Harry Byrd of Virginia and the chief executive of the state, Governor Lindsay Almond, worked together to make operation of public schools a local option for the state's counties and cities. Their efforts enabled the Prince Edward County board of supervisors to evade a federal court order to desegregate by abolishing the county's entire public school system in 1959, creating instead a foundation to run all-white private schools paid for by tax credits from the county and tuition grants by the state. Seventeen hundred black students in the county went without any education at all for five years, until the Supreme Court ruled Prince Edward County's scheme unconstitutional.[7]

Governor Orville Faubus of Arkansas called out the National Guard to prevent nine black students from enrolling in Little Rock's Central High School in 1957. When President Dwight Eisenhower placed the guard under federal control to carry out the orders of the Supreme Court, the governor closed all four high schools in Little Rock for the 1958–59 academic year to prevent them from becoming integrated.[8] Political leaders in Alabama championed a successful effort to amend the state constitution in 1956, authorizing the legislature to abolish public education and to allocate state funds and allow the use of state facilities for segregated private schools for whites in order to frustrate the implementation of *Brown v. Board*.[9] In Georgia, the legislature made it a crime for state or local officials to disburse public funds for desegregated schools. South Carolina repealed its laws making school attendance mandatory, while Louisiana and Mississippi passed laws forbidding children from attending integrated schools.[10]

Less well chronicled, however, have been the actions of white elites from other regions of the country aimed at frustrating the most effective measures likely to implement the mandate of *Brown*. President Eisenhower refused to endorse *Brown v. Board* openly, contenting himself with a condemnation of "the extremists on both sides." As Vincent Harding, Robin D. G. Kelley, and Earl Lewis point out, with that comment the president equated "courageous children and their communities who were working for democratic change with men and women who defied the Supreme Court, dynamited buildings, and assassinated leaders."[11] In the Justice Departments of the Eisenhower and John F. Kennedy administrations, timid approaches to enforcing *Brown v. Board* raised the percentage of black students attending schools with whites in the states of the Old Confederacy from zero in 1955 to 2 percent in 1964. Peter Irons notes that this pace would have postponed full integration for an additional five centuries.[12] Despite this incremental pace, 52 percent of northern whites told pollsters in 1966 that they felt the government was pushing integration "too fast."[13]

Richard Nixon secured the endorsement of the segregationist ex-Democrat and ex-Dixiecrat senator Strom Thurmond of South Carolina in the presidential campaign of 1968 in return for a pledge to reduce federal action on behalf of school desegregation.[14] He campaigned against "extremists" whom he described as those in favor of "instant integration."[15] After his election, Nixon disregarded the school desegregation guidelines issued in the Civil Rights Act, nominated resolute opponents of busing to the Supreme Court, and in his reelection campaign in 1972 urged Congress to pass legislation overturning court-ordered busing for purposes of desegregation.[16]

Most community and political leaders in the North proved to be as resolute as their southern counterparts in their defense of school segregation. In a desegregation case in Columbus, Ohio, *Penick v. Columbus Board of Education*, the federal district court judge Robert M. Duncan outlined the many methods used by the local school board over the years to create and maintain segregated schools. Duncan delineated a clear and consistent pattern of gerrymandering pupil assignment areas, building new schools only in sites where their neighborhood populations would be all white or all black, creating noncontiguous and optional attendance zones, and making racially based hiring and appointment decisions. A Republican appointed to the bench by Nixon, Duncan concluded that "the real reason the courts are in the school desegregation business is the failure of other government entities to confront and produce answers to the many problems in this area pursuant to the law of the United States."[17]

In Los Angeles, segregated schools were mandatory by law in the nineteenth century. De facto segregation persisted in the twentieth century to such a degree that the California Supreme Court in 1976 declared the local school district "among the most segregated in the entire country."[18] In 1963 black students filed a class action lawsuit, *Crawford v. Board of Education of the City of Los Angeles*, to end policies that established South Gate High School as mostly all white and Jordan High School as mostly all black, even though the two schools were located less than two miles apart. White parents and political leaders in South Gate claimed they opposed the merger for nonracial reasons. They contended that they did not want their children to have to walk across dangerous Alameda Street, even while the segregated arrangement required black children to cross the equally busy and equally dangerous Firestone Boulevard.[19] When the California state judge Alfred Gitelson ruled on the case in 1970 he concluded that the Los Angeles school board "knowingly, affirmatively, and in bad faith . . . segregated, *de jure*, its students to create and perpetuate segregated schools." He ordered the school board to adopt a plan to desegregate as the remedy for the injury done to minority students for decades of mistreatment.

Governor Ronald Reagan immediately said the order was "utterly ridiculous," a decision that "goes beyond sound reasoning and common sense." President Nixon condemned Judge Gitelson's order as "probably the most extreme judicial decree so far."[20] In the Supreme Court's decision upholding desegregation and the legality of the judge's decision, Justice William Rehnquist coached antibusing opponents about how they could amend the state constitution in order to invalidate busing mandated by state, but not federal, judges. Armed with that suggestion, white political leaders in California placed a proposition on the ballot to prevent state judges from ordering busing. The proposition passed with nearly 70 percent of the vote.[21]

School desegregation efforts faced massive resistance in the North and the South. Yet even in the face of clear evidence of the wholesale refusal to comply with the *Brown* decision, the courts did not begin to evaluate proposed remedies for segregation critically until 1968 in the case *Green v. County School Board of New Kent County, Virginia*.[22] Federal courts did not direct school districts to adopt specific remedies such as busing until 1971, with the *Swann v. Charlotte-Mecklenberg Board of Education* case, and the Supreme Court did not announce that the time for "all deliberate speed" had run out until the *Milliken v. Bradley* cases I and II, were decided, respectively, in 1974 and 1977.

By inviting and condoning more than two decades of delay, the Supreme Court enabled the systematic denial of black children's constitutional rights. The Court elevated the comfort of white parents and their representatives into a constitutionally protected right, simply because they argued that re-mediation inconvenienced them and interfered with their expected privi-leges.[23] Yet when the courts finally ran out of patience with two decades of getting around *Brown*, elite white leaders responded by characterizing the resort to busing to achieve desegregation as an epochal event. They repre-sented busing as an injury to whites to be treated more seriously than the original injury done by segregation's systematic denial of the constitutional rights of black and Latino children.

Busing had been a standard practice during the era of segregation, but it was viewed differently when used for purposes of school desegregation. No white leaders had opposed busing when it served as the primary mechanism for segregating schools. None argued that the concept of the neighborhood school should override the imperatives of segregation. In the *Swann* deci-sion, Supreme Court Chief Justice Warren Burger noted that eighteen mil-lion children—39 percent of the total population of K–12 students—already rode buses to school during the 1969–70 academic year.[24]

Yet when the Supreme Court endorsed busing for purposes of racial de-segregation, white elites from all sections of the country joined to condemn the practice. In 1971 the liberal Democrats Edith Green of Oregon and James O'Hara of Michigan joined the Michigan Republican William Broomfield in encouraging the House of Representatives to vote overwhelmingly for a resolution delaying the implementation of any court order mandating bus-ing until all appeals had been exhausted: the resolution passed by a vote of 235 to 126.[25]

In the *Milliken v. Bradley* (1974) desegregation case, federal district judge Stephen A. Roth ruled that the city schools in Detroit had been deliberately segregated by the school board's decisions to build new schools in either all-white or all-black neighborhoods and to allow white students to escape from largely black schools while forbidding black students to transfer to predominately white schools. Moreover, because the Michigan Supreme Court had ruled repeatedly that education in the state "is not a matter of local concern, but belongs to the state at large," Roth ordered an interdis-trict busing program between the city of Detroit and its suburbs. Although nearly three hundred thousand children in the three-county area covered by Judge Roth's ruling already rode buses to school, politicians from both major political parties condemned Roth's resort to busing for the purposes of desegregation.[26] None of the many vocal and visible opponents of Judge Roth's decision addressed the extensive evidence cited by the judge that private sector actions in real estate and home lending followed school segregation patterns or that whites had come to expect the schools their children attended would be better funded and better equipped than schools with a majority of black students in them.[27]

The Supreme Court overruled Judge Roth in *Milliken v. Bradley*, citing the sanctity of the principle of "local autonomy of school districts" and the value that citizens "rightly" place on neighborhood schools. Yet as Justice Thurgood Marshall pointed out in his dissenting opinion, school district lines in Michigan were not based on neighborhoods or even municipalities. The state drew district lines in such a way that the Detroit metropolitan area included eighty-five districts. Some suburbs contained as many as six school districts, while one school district served five cities. Two districts spread over three counties, and seventeen districts stretched across two counties.

The Court majority also evaded the violations of federal and state fair housing laws that produced black cities surrounded by white suburbs. Speaking for the majority in a 5–4 decision, Justice Potter Stewart ignored the voluminous evidence Judge Roth cited connecting residential racial segregation in Detroit and its suburbs to a plethora of actions by city, county, and state agencies. Stewart offered a stupefyingly disingenuous suggestion: that segregation in Detroit and its suburbs stemmed from "unknown or unknowable causes."[28]

Jamin Raskin notes that the Supreme Court's ruling in *Milliken v. Bradley* gave "judicial impetus and imprimatur to white flight."[29] It rewarded suburban areas for segregation, granting those that had successfully excluded blacks from residence an exemption from desegregation remedies. It advised white parents—including those who became party to the *Milliken* case because they objected to the state of Michigan denying their children a desegregated education—that the only way to secure optimal educational resources for their children was to move away from areas where blacks lived.

The Court's decision in *Milliken v. Bradley* drew widespread support and emboldened the opponents of desegregation. During the administration of President Jimmy Carter, Congress voted to prohibit the executive branch from cutting off federal funds to school districts resisting desegregation (as mandated by the Civil Rights Act of 1964) if those cases entailed mandatory busing as a remedy.[30] In *Milliken v. Bradley II*, the court permitted educational enrichment in segregated inner city schools as an allowable remedy for past discrimination but overturned those so-called sweeteners in 1995 in *Missouri v. Jenkins*. The Court argued in *Missouri v. Jenkins* that such remedies made central city schools *too* attractive to voluntary transfers by suburban whites, therefore violating the ban against interdistrict remedies enunciated in *Milliken v. Bradley*. The federal Emergency School Aid Act of 1975 allocated funds for schools under desegregation decrees to retrain staff, hire race relations counselors, and develop curricular materials sensitive to the needs of minority students. The Reagan administration, however, eliminated the program in 1981, effectively terminating federal investment in integrated schools.[31]

Perhaps the most egregious demonstration of the Court's epistemology of ignorance appears in its refusal to acknowledge the link between housing discrimination and school segregation. Although the Burger Court recognized in 1971 in the *Swann* case that segregated and unequal schools shape housing choices, subsequent rulings have denied that link.[32] While holding the Denver school system responsible for policies that intentionally segregated black and Latino students in the *Keyes* decision (1973), for example, Justice Lewis Powell absolved the district of responsibility to remedy "geographical separation of the races" that "resulted from purely natural and neutral non-state causes." In a decision on segregation in Austin, Texas, in 1976 Justice Rehnquist likewise asserted (without proof) that "economic pressures and voluntary preferences are the primary determinants of residential patterns." He waxed poetic on that theme in reviewing the case in Columbus, Ohio, in 1977, claiming that residential segregation in the region resulted from a "mélange of past happenings prompted by economic considerations, private discrimination, discriminatory school assignments or a desire to reside near people of one's own race or ethnic background."[33]

In attributing residential segregation to "natural," "neutral," "voluntary" desires, the Court has accepted the fictions of guilty defendants in desegregation cases. The attorney James P. Gorton, who represented school districts in suburban St. Louis and Atlanta against desegregation orders, boasted to a reporter that he and his colleagues had established that "people live in specific school districts and urban areas based on job needs, personal preferences, and other factors—not because of race."[34] Yet an enormous body of unchallenged and uncontradicted evidence demonstrates the contrary. Researchers have found consistently that the racial composition of a neighborhood is more important to whites than housing quality, level of crime, environmental amenities, and location.[35] Even putatively nonracial considerations such as the reputation of local schools often contain perceptions about the racial identities of the student body.[36] In the early years of school desegregation cases, judges drew on overwhelming evidence that residential segregation stemmed from a combination of private discriminatory acts including mortgage redlining, real estate steering, and blockbusting, and public policies such as urban renewal, allocating Section 235 funds to certain areas of cities only, and placement decisions about public housing projects, subsidized developments, and schools.[37] As late as 1987, a circuit court established a mutually constitutive relationship between housing and school segregation in Yonkers, New York, fashioning a remedy that required integrated housing as well as integrated schools.[38] Yet the Rehnquist Court consistently distorted the facts in order to excuse this systematic discrimination. According to its reasoning, the existence of segregation in housing is attributed to nonracial causes, arguing that no whites move away from municipalities to secure the benefits they gain from neighborhoods and schools that are prohibited to blacks. Existing segregation is instead attributed to race-neutral causes that are beyond the concern of the courts. When it comes to school desegregation plans, however, the Court rejects them because they might cause white flight while still maintaining that blacks live in ghettos because they choose to live near other members of their race. Whites are thus judged not currently race conscious in their selection of neighborhoods and schools, but they might become so, the Court complains, if faced with desegregation.[39]

Black and Latino students disproportionately find themselves segregated by race and by class in schools with fewer resources than "majority white" schools, less experienced teachers, and more undiagnosed and untreated disabilities. After declining to around 62 percent in the early 1980s because of court-ordered desegregation, the proportion of black students in segregated schools has reverted back to the levels of the 1960s. Seventy percent of black students attended segregated schools in 1999, compared with 77 percent in 1968.[40] None of the twenty-five largest cities in the United States has a majority of white students in its school system.[41] The proportion of black students in "majority white" schools declined by 13 percent during the 1990s.[42]

The schools that serve minority and high-poverty populations lack key science and math courses, offer few advanced placement courses, and have inferior equipment and supplies. Capital investments in schools located in high-poverty areas are 31 percent less than similar investments in middle-class areas. The wealthiest school districts spend 56 percent more per student than the poorest ones.[43]

Residential racial segregation compounds the problems of poverty even more. Over 80 percent of hypersegregated black and Latino schools are located in areas of concentrated poverty, compared to only 5 percent of schools with an overwhelmingly white population.[44] Hypersegregated schools with black or Latino enrollments of 90 percent or greater are fourteen times more likely to have a majority of impoverished students than schools with white majorities. Poor neighborhoods have high incidences of lead poisoning and asthma among residents, and schools serving these neighborhoods encounter high percentages of students who are hungry, have undiagnosed and untreated developmental disabilities, and whose families move so often because of scarce housing opportunities that they never develop a relationship with school personnel.[45] Pervasive housing segregation means that middle-class black students are much more likely to have high percentages of poor classmates than white students.

Education is even more important to blacks and Latinos than to whites because members of those groups are much less likely to receive inheritances from parents or to have access to family business networks. Blacks and Latinos are more likely to live far away from employment centers. Yet school inequality and segregation leave them with inferior educational opportunities. Unfair impediments to education and asset accumulation for some people, however, translate into unfair gains and unjust enrichments for others. Opposition to school desegregation has enabled whites to preserve and augment advantages initially secured as a result of overt de jure segregation in an earlier era. As Gary Orfield argues, the superiority of suburban schools is taken for granted as a right attendant to homeownership, while desegregation is viewed as a threat to a system that passes racial advantages from one generation to the next. In Orfield's words, "Whites tell pollsters that they believe that blacks are offered equal opportunities, but fiercely resist any efforts to make them send their children to the schools they insist are good enough for blacks." At the same time, "the people who oppose busing minority students to the suburbs also tend to oppose sending suburban dollars to city schools."[46]

Yet getting around *Brown* does not work only to the disadvantage of aggrieved communities of color. By rendering racial inequality in the United States natural, necessary, and inevitable, getting around *Brown* forms the basis for a broader social warrant rooted in inequality, hostile privatism, defensive localism, and a notion of citizenship as the consumption of government services and the hoarding of scarce resources. By transforming the meaning of the Fourteenth Amendment from the prohibition of subjugation into a measure that prevents government agencies from recognizing and remedying racial inequality, getting around *Brown* severs all citizens from the traditions most responsible for fairness, equity, and justice in the national life. It replaces the dreams of freedom of aggrieved people with a social warrant for selfishness.

The legacy of getting around *Brown* has helped produce a framework of besieged whiteness that grievously distorts the role of the nation in the world and the presence of the world inside the nation. The evisceration of the social wage at home and the export of industrial production to low-wage countries overseas have produced an influx of immigrant low-wage workers into the American economy. Rather than recognizing the influx of immigrants as a consequence of efforts by the United States to control markets, raw materials, labor, and sites for investment overseas, many whites perceive immigration in racial terms, as a threat to the expected privileges of whiteness. Immigrants from Asia, Latin America, and Africa enter a country with a racialized history, a country that condemns hard-working exploited laborers as parasites, while portraying the pampered consumers who profit from the exploitation of immigrant labor as heroic producers beset by an immigrant invasion. At the same time, however, immigrants are enticed to become "honorary whites" by making gains at the expense of other communities of color. Blacks are recruited to anti-immigrant mobilizations. The historical legacy of getting around *Brown* stands in the way of the just aspirations of African Americans, American Indians, Asian Americans, and Latino Americans for equal access to employment, education, housing, and health care.[47]

Addressing the consequences of centuries of discrimination will be difficult and costly. Yet the costs of not acting are even greater. If we do not address our problems today, they will only become worse and more expensive to correct in the future. Moreover, everyone suffers from discrimination, not just its direct victims. Discrimination misallocates resources and rewards unwise economic actors. The national and global economic crisis created by the meltdown of the subprime mortgage market in 2008 is merely the most recent and one of the more visible manifestations of how racial injuries harm all of society.

Getting around getting around *Brown* will be a difficult task. It requires not only gaining victories in individual cases and arenas, but also the development of a social movement capable of generating a new social warrant. It necessitates restoring the antisubjugation dimensions of the Fourteenth Amendment and distinguishing them from their antidiscrimination applications. It entails establishing disparate and unfavorable racial impact as the basis for judging civil rights violations, even if the discriminators have been cunning enough to avoid articulating their racist intent openly. It compels Americans to confront the evasions of getting around *Brown* directly by demanding full enforcement of fair housing laws, by filing suit against the perpetrators of home loan discrimination, real estate steering, insurance redlining, predatory lending, and the myriad other means used to keep the nation's neighborhoods separate and unequal. Most important, it forces Americans to relearn the lessons of the past by producing the kinds of collective learning that come from collective action, to engage in struggles for rights, resources, and recognition that can generate new ways of knowing and new ways of being.

Four decades ago, Martin Luther King Jr. talked increasingly about "the fierce urgency of now." In words that seem even more poignant and relevant today than they did in 1967, King defined clearly the task facing those committed to righting the republic. In an appeal to his followers to act now, before it is too late, King explained that what they do can be more important than what they think, that the books they read and the books they write sometimes compel them to put their books down and to fashion instead a different future. King observed,

We are now faced with the fact that tomorrow is today. We are confronted with the fierce urgency of now. In this unfolding conundrum of life and history, there is such a thing as being too late. Procrastination is still the thief of time. Life often leaves us standing bare, naked, and dejected with a lost opportunity. The tide in affairs of men does not remain at flood—it ebbs. We may cry out desperately for time to pause in her passage, but time is adamant to every plea and rushes on. Over the bleached bones and jumbled residues of numerous civilizations are written the pathetic words "too late." There is an invisible book of life that faithfully records our vigilance or our neglect.[48]

Notes

1. Langston Hughes, "A Dream Deferred," in *The Collected Poems of Langston Hughes*, ed. Arnold Ramparsad (New York: Vintage, 1995), 426.

2. George Lipsitz, *The Possessive Investment in Whiteness: How White People Profit from Identity Politics* (Philadelphia: Temple University Press, 2006), 24–47.

3. Gregory S. Jacobs, *Getting Around Brown: Desegregation, Development, and the Columbus Public Schools* (Columbus: Ohio State University Press, 1998).

4. Herbert Blumer, "Race Prejudice as a Sense of Group Position," *Pacific Sociological Review* 1, no.1 (spring 1958): 6.

5. Curtis M. Vaughan, *Faubus's Folly: The Story of Segregation* (New York: Vantage, 1959); Roy Reed, *Faubus: The Life and Times of an Arkansas Prodigal* (Fayetteville: University of Arkansas Press, 1997); Numan Bartley, *The Rise of Massive Resistance: Race and Politics in the South During the 1950s* (Baton Rouge: Louisiana State University Press, 1969); Robbins Gates, *The Making of Massive Resistance: Virginia's Politics of Public School Desegregation, 1954–1956* (Chapel Hill: University of North Carolina Press, 1964); Dan T. Carter, *The Politics of Rage* (New York: Simon and Schuster, 1995).

6. Vincent Harding, Robin D. G. Kelley, and Earl Lewis, "We Changed the World, 1945–1970," in *To Make Our World Anew: A History of African Americans*, ed. Robin D. G. Kelley and Earl Lewis (New York: Oxford University Press, 2000), 473.

7. Peter Irons, *Jim Crow's Children: The Broken Promise of the Brown Decision* (New York: Penguin Books, 2002), 80–94.

8. James T. Patterson, *Brown v. Board of Education: A Civil Rights Milestone and Its Troubled Legacy* (New York: Oxford University Press, 2001), 109–13.

9. Richard A. Pride, *The Political Use of Racial Narratives: School Desegregation in Mobile, Alabama, 1954–1992* (Urbana: University of Illinois Press, 2002), 26.

10. Patterson, *Brown v. Board of Education*, 99.

11. Harding, Kelley, and Lewis, "We Changed the World," 473.

12. Irons, *Jim Crow's Children*, 190.

13. Jill Quadagno, *The Color of Welfare: How Racism Undermined the War on Poverty* (New York: Oxford University Press 1994), 30.

14. Ibid., 127.

15. Irons, *Jim Crow's Children*, 241.

16. Gary Orfield, "School Desegregation after Two Generations: Race, Schools, and Opportunity in Urban Society," in *Race in America: The Struggle for Equality*, ed. Herbert Hill and James E. Jones Jr. (Madison: University of Wisconsin Press, 1993), 240.

17. Jacobs, *Getting Around Brown*, 57, 62.

18. *Crawford v. Board of Education of the City of Los Angeles* 17 CAL 3d 280 287 n2 (1976).

19. Becky M. Nicolaides, *My Blue Heaven: Life and Politics in the Working-Class Suburbs of Los Angeles, 1920–1965* (Chicago: University of Chicago Press, 2002), 301–02.

20. Joseph S. Ettinger, "The Quest to Desegregate Los Angeles Schools," *Los Angeles Lawyer* (March 2003): 57.

21. Clayborne Carson, "Two Cheers for *Brown v. Board of Education*," *Journal of American History* 91, no. 1 (June 2004): 27; Ettinger, "Quest to Desegregate," 62.

22. Nathaniel R. Jones, "Civil Rights After *Brown*: 'Stormy the Road We Trod,'" in *Race in America*, 100.

23. Wiley A. Branton, "Race, the Courts, and Constitutional Change in Twentieth-Century School Desegregation Cases after *Brown*," in *African Americans and the Living Constitution*, ed. John Hope Franklin and Genna Rae McNeil (Washington: Smithsonian Institution Press, 1995), 86; Cheryl I. Harris, "Whiteness as Property," *Harvard Law Review* 106, no. 8 (June 1993): 1756.

24. Irons, *Jim Crow's Children*, 221.

25. Ibid., 227.

26. Ibid., 238.

27. Jones, "Civil Rights After *Brown*," 103; Harris, "Whiteness as Property," 1756.

28. Patterson, *Brown v. Board of Education*, 178–81; Gary Orfield, Susan Eaton, and the Harvard Project on School Desegregation, *Dismantling Desegregation: The Quiet Reversal of Brown v. Board of Education* (New York: New Press, 1996), 296.

29. Jamin B. Raskin, *Overruling Democracy: The Supreme Court vs. the American People* (London: Routledge, 2003), 160.

30. Gary Orfield, "Turning Back to Segregation," in *Dismantling Desegregation*, 16.

31. J. B. Wellish et al., *An In-Depth Study of Emergency School Aid Act (ESAA) Schools: 1975–1976* (Santa Monica, Calif.: Systems Development Corporation, 1977); R. P. Nathan et al., *The Consequence of Cuts: The Effects of the Reagan Domestic Program on State and Local Governments* (Princeton: Princeton University Press, 1983).

32. Drew S. Days III, "The Current State of School Desegregation Law: Why Isn't Anybody Laughing?" in *In Pursuit of a Dream Deferred*, ed. John A. Powell, Gavin Kearney, and Vina Kay (New York: Peter Lang, 2001), 163.

33. Days, "Current State of School Desegregation Law," 175.

34. C. Verspereny, "Desegregation Case Defense Outlined," *St. Louis Post-Dispatch*, July 18, 1982, quoted in Amy Stuart Wells and Robert L. Crain, *Stepping Over the Color Line:*

African American Students in White Suburban Schools (New Haven: Yale University Press, 1997), 259.

35. R. D. Taub, D. G. Taylor, and J. A Dunham, *Paths of Neighborhood Change: Race and Crime in Urban America* (Chicago: University of Chicago Press, 1984); Craig St. John and Nancy A. Bates, "Racial Composition and Neighborhood Evaluation," *Social Science Research* 19 (March 1990): 47–61.

36. Thomas M. Shapiro, *The Hidden Cost of Being African American: How Wealth Perpetuates Inequality* (New York: Oxford University Press, 2004), 271.

37. Meredith Lee Bryant, "Combating School Resegregation through Housing: A Need for a Reconceptualization of American Democracy and the Rights It Protects," in *In Pursuit of a Dream Deferred*, 56–58.

38. Bryant, "Combating School Resegregation," 58.

39. Gary Orfield, "Unexpected Costs and Uncertain Gains of Dismantling Desegregation," in *Dismantling Desegregation*, 96.

40. Shapiro, *Hidden Cost of Being African American*, 143.

41. Irons, *Jim Crow's Children*, 289.

42. Chungmei Lee, "Is Resegregation Real?" (Cambridge, Mass.: Harvard Civil Rights Project Report, 2004), 6.

43. Shapiro, *Hidden Cost of Being African American*, 145.

44. Jack M. Balkin, "Brown as Icon," in *What "Brown v Board of Education" Should Have Said*, ed. Jack M. Balkin (New York: New York University Press, 2002), 6.

45. Orfield, "Unexpected Costs and Uncertain Gains," 83.

46. Gary Orfield, "School Desegregation After Two Generations: Race, Schools, and Opportunity in Urban Society," in *Race in America*, 245, 240.

47. While all antiracists need to address the specificity of antiblack racism in the United States, as the authors in this volume demonstrate so clearly, racial projects in the United States cannot be understood exclusively through a black–white binary. See Lipsitz, *Possessive Investment in Whiteness*; and George Lipsitz, "Abolition Democracy and Global Justice," *Comparative American Studies* 2, no. 3 (2004): 271–87.

48. Martin Luther King Jr., "Why I Oppose the Vietnam War" (April 4, 1967), in *A Testament of Hope: The Essential Writings and Speeches of Martin Luther King, Jr.* (San Francisco: Harper, 1990), 243.

Bibliography

Adams, John. 1961–66. *Diary and Autobiography of John Adams*, ed. L. H. Butterfield. Cambridge, Mass.: Belknap Press of Harvard University Press.

Aldridge, A. Owen. 1993. *The Dragon and the Eagle: The Presence of China in the American Enlightenment*. Detroit: Wayne State University Press.

Anderson, Benedict. [1983] 1999. *Imagined Communities: Reflections on the Origin and Spread of Nationalism*. New York: Verso.

Anderson, Dwight G. 1982. *Abraham Lincoln: The Quest for Immortality*. New York: Alfred A. Knopf.

Andrews, Charles M. 1916–17. "Boston Merchants and the Non-Importation Movement." *Transactions of the Colonial Society Massachusetts* 19:159–259.

Appiah, Anthony. 1985. "The Uncompleted Argument: Du Bois and the Illusion of Race." *Critical Inquiry* 12 (1): 21–37.

Appleby, Joyce. 2003. *Thomas Jefferson*. New York: Henry Holt.

Aptheker, Herbert, ed. 1985. *Against Racism: Unpublished Essays, Papers, Addresses, 1887–1961*. Amherst: University of Massachusetts Press.

Bailyn, Bernard. 1996. "Sally and Her Master." *Times Literary Supplement* (November 15): 4.

Bailyn, Bernard, Robert Dallek, David Brion Davis, Donald Herbert Donald, John K. Thomas, and Gordon S. Wood, eds. 1992. *The Great Republic: A History of the American People*. Vol. 1. Lexington, Mass.: D. C. Heath.

Baldwin, James. 1955. *Notes of a Native Son*. New York: Bantam.

———. 1961. *Nobody Knows My Name: More Notes of a Native Son*. New York: Dell Publishing.

———. [1963] 1993. *The Fire Next Time*. New York: Vintage Books.

———. 1968. "A Letter to Americans." *Freedomways* 8 (Spring).

———. 1985. *The Price of the Ticket: Collected Nonfiction, 1948–1985*. New York: St. Martin's Press.

Baldwin, James, Nathan Glazer, Sidney Hook, and Gunnar Myrdal. 1964. "Liberalism and the Negro: A Round-Table Discussion." *Commentary* 37 (March): 25–42.

Baldwin, James, and Margaret Mead. 1971. *A Rap on Race*. Philadelphia: J. B. Lippincott.

Balfour, Lawrie. 2000. *The Evidence of Things Not Said: James Baldwin and the Promise of American Democracy*. Ithaca: Cornell University Press.

Balkin, Jack M., ed. 2002. *What "Brown v Board of Education" Should Have Said*. New York: New York University Press.

Ball, Terence. 1995. *Reappraising Political Theory: Revisionist Studies in the History of Political Thought*. Oxford: Oxford University Press.

Barkeley Brown, Elsa. 1994. "Negotiating and Transforming the Public Sphere: African American Political Life in the Transition from Slavery to Freedom." *Public Culture* 7 (Fall): 106–46.

Barrett, James R., and David R. Roediger. 1997. "Inbetween Peoples: Race, Nationality and the 'New Immigrant' Working Class." In *American Exceptionalism? U.S. Working-Class Formation in an International Context*, ed. Rick Halpern and Jonathan Morris. New York: St. Martin's Press.

Bartley, Numan. 1969. *The Rise of Massive Resistance: Race and Politics in the South During the 1950s*. Baton Rouge: Louisiana State University Press.

Basler, Roy P., ed. 1959. *The Collected Works of Abraham Lincoln*. Vol. 1. New Brunswick, N.J.: Rutgers University Press.

Bederman, Gail. 1995. *Manliness and Civilization: A Cultural History of Gender and Race in the United States, 1880–1917*. Chicago: University of Chicago Press.

Bell, Bernard W., Emily Grosholz, and James B. Stewart, eds. 1996. *W. E. B. Du Bois on Race and Culture: Philosophy, Politics, and Poetics*. New York: Routledge.

Bennet, Lerone, Jr. 2000. *Forced Into Glory: Abraham Lincoln's White Dream*. Chicago: Johnson.

Benson, Lee. 1961. *The Concept of Jacksonian Democracy*. Princeton: Princeton University Press.

Bhabha, Homi K., ed. 1999. *Nation and Narration*. London: Routledge.

Blackmar, Elizabeth. 1989. *Manhattan for Rent, 1785–1850*. Ithaca: Cornell University Press.

Blumer, Herbert. 1958. "Race Prejudice as a Sense of Group Position." *Pacific Sociological Review* 1 (spring): 3–7.

Boesche, Roger, ed. 1985. *Alexis de Tocqueville: Selected Letters on Politics and Society*. Berkeley: University of California Press.

Bourdieu, Pierre. 1984. *Distinction: A Social Critique of the Judgement of Taste*. Cambridge, Mass.: Harvard University Press.

Braxton, Joanne M. 1989. *Black Women Writing Autobiography: A Tradition within a Tradition*. Philadelphia: Temple University Press.

Breen, T. H. 1986. "An Empire of Goods: The Anglicization of Colonial America, 1690–1776." *Journal of British Studies* 25: 467–99.

———. 1988. "'Baubles of Britain': The American and Consumer Revolutions of the Eighteenth Century." *Past and Present* 119 (May): 73–104.

Brewer, Rose. 1993. "Theorizing Race, Class, Gender: The New Scholarship of Black Feminist Intellectuals and Black Women's Labor." In *Theorizing Black Feminisms: The Visionary Pragmatism of Black Women*, ed. Stanlie M. James and Abena P. A. Busia. New York: Routledge.

Bridges, Amy. 1984. *A City in the Republic*. Cambridge: Cambridge University Press.

Brodie, Fawn M. 1974. *Thomas Jefferson: An Intimate History.* New York: W. W. Norton.

Brown, Gillian. 1990. *Domestic Individualism: Imagining Self in Nineteenth-Century America.* Berkeley: University of California Press.

Brown Ruoff, LaVonne A. 2001. "Reversing the Gaze: Early Native American Images of Europeans and Euro-Americans." In *Native American Representations: First Encounters, Distorted Images, and Literary Appropriations,* ed. Gretchen M. Bataille. Lincoln: University of Nebraska Press.

Brubaker, Rogers. 1992. *Citizenship and Nationhood in France and Germany.* Cambridge, Mass.: Harvard University Press.

Bryce, James. 1910. *The American Commonwealth.* New York: Macmillan.

Bulosan, Carlos. 1946. *America Is in the Heart.* Seattle: University of Washington Press.

Burstein, Andrew. 2005. *Jefferson's Secrets: Death and Desire at Monticello.* New York: Basic Books.

Bushman, Richard L. 1992. *The Refinement of America: Persons, Houses, Cities.* New York: Alfred A. Knopf.

Camp, Stephanie M. H. 2000. "Sally Hemings and Thomas Jefferson." *Mississippi Quarterly* 53 (spring): 275–83.

Carby, Hazel V. 1987. *Reconstructing Womanhood: The Emergence of the Afro-American Woman Novelist.* Cambridge, Mass.: Harvard University Press.

Carpenter, F. B. 1866. *Six Months at the White House with Abraham Lincoln: The Story of a Picture.* New York: Hurd and Houghton.

Carroll, Peter N., and David W. Noble. 1973. *The Restless Centuries: A History of the American People.* Minneapolis: Burgess.

———. 1977. *The Free and the Unfree: A New History of the United States.* New York: Penguin.

Carson, Clayborne. 1998. "Parting the Country." *Dissent* 45 (Summer): 108–11.

———. 2004. "Two Cheers for Brown v. Board of Education." *Journal of American History* 91 (1) (June): 26–31.

Carter, Dan T. 1995. *The Politics of Rage.* New York: Simon and Schuster.

Cashin, Herschel V. 1970. *Under Fire with the Tenth Cavalry.* Reprint of 1899 edition. New York: F. Tennyson Neely.

Cell, John W. 1982. *The Highest Stage of White Supremacy: The Origins of Segregation in South Africa and the American South.* Cambridge: Cambridge University Press.

Chandler, Nahum Dimitri. 1996. "The Economy of Desedimentation: W. E. B. Du Bois and the Discourses of the Negro." *Callaloo* 19 (1): 78–93.

Chaplin, Joyce C. 1997. "Natural Philosophy and an Early Racial Idiom in North America: Comparing English and Indian Bodies." *William and Mary Quarterly* 54 (1): 229–52.

Chesler, Ellen. 1992. *Woman of Valor: Margaret Sanger and the Birth Control Movement in America.* New York: Simon and Schuster.

Cochran, David Carroll. 1999. *The Color of Freedom: Race and Contemporary American Liberalism.* Albany: State University of New York Press.

Commager, Henry Steele. 1950. *The American Mind.* New Haven: Yale University Press.

Commager, Henry Steele, ed. 1988. *Documents of American History*. Englewood Cliffs, N.J.: Prentice Hall.

Connolly, William E. 1994. "Tocqueville, Territory and Violence." *Theory, Culture, and Society* 11 (February): 19–41.

Cook, Jacob Ernest. 1982. *Alexander Hamilton*. New York: Charles Scribner & Sons.

Coolidge, Mary Roberts. 1969. *Chinese Immigration*. New York: Arno Press.

Cooper, Anna Julia. 1988. *A Voice from the South: By a Black Woman from the South*. Edited by M. H. Washington. New York: Oxford University Press.

Corpuz, Onofre D. 1997. *An Economic History of the Philippines*. Manila: University of the Philippines Press.

Cott, Nancy. 1973. "Notes Toward an Interpretation of Antebellum Childrearing." *Psychohistory Review* 7 (4): 4–20.

———. 1998. "Marriage and Women's Citizenship in the United States, 1830–1934." *American Historical Review* 103 (December): 1440–74.

Crenshaw, Kimberlé, Neil Gotanda, Gary Peller, and Kendall Thomas, eds. 1995. *Critical Race Theory: The Key Writings that Formed the Movement*. New York: New York Press.

Croly, Herbert. 1909. *The Promise of American Life*. Boston: E. P. Dutton.

Cross, Ira. 1935. *History of the Labor Movement in California*. Berkeley: University of California Press.

Cynkar, Robert J. 1981. "*Buck v. Bell*: 'Felt Necessities' v. Fundamental Values?" *Columbia Law Review* 81 (November): 1418–61.

Dao, James. 2003. "A Family Get-Together of Historic Proportions." *New York Times*, July 14, 2003.

Daroy, Petronilo. 1968. "Carlos Bulosan: The Politics of Literature." *St. Louis Quarterly* 6 (June): 193–206.

Davis, Angela Y., ed. 1971. *If They Come in the Morning: Voices of Resistance*. New York: Signet Books.

Davis, David Brion. 1999. "The Culmination of Racial Polarities and Prejudice." *Journal of the Early Republic* 19 (Fall): 757–76.

Davis, Ossie. 1965. "The Significance of Lorraine Hansberry." *Freedomways* 5 (3): 397–402.

Davis, Ossie, and Ruby Dee. 1998. *With Ossie and Ruby: In Life Together*. New York: William Morrow.

Davis, Richard Harding. 1910. *Notes of a War Correspondent*. New York: Charles Scribner's Sons.

Dawson, Raymond. 1967. *Chinese Chameleon*. Oxford: Oxford University Press.

de Beaumont, Gustave. [1958] 1999. *Marie, or, Slavery in the United States*. Translated by Barbara Chapman. Baltimore: Johns Hopkins University Press.

de León, Arnoldo. 1983. *They Called Them Greasers: Anglo Attitudes toward Mexicans in Texas, 1821–1900*. Austin: University of Texas Press.

———. 1993. *Mexican Americans in Texas: A Brief History*. Arlington Heights, Ill.: Harlan Davidson.

de Tocqueville, Alexis. 1909. *Voyage en Amérique*. Edited by R. C. Ford. Boston: D. C. Heath.

———. 1969. *Democracy in America*. Translated by George Lawrence. New York: Doubleday.

de Tracy, Count Antoine Louis Claude Destutt. 1970. *A Treatise on Political Economy*. Translated by T. Jefferson. New York: A. M. Kelley.

Dean, Jodi, ed. 2000. *Cultural Studies and Political Theory*. Ithaca: Cornell University Press.

Degler, Carl N. 1984. *Out of Our Past: The Forces that Shaped Modern America*. 3d ed. New York: Harper Colophon Books.

Dell, Robert M., and Charles A Huguenin. 1970. "Vermont's Royall Tyler in New York's John Street Theatre: A Theatrical Hoax Exploded." *Vermont History* 38 (2).

Deloria, Philip J. 1998. *Playing Indian*. New Haven: Yale University Press.

Deloria, Vine, Jr., and Clifford Lytle. 1984. *The Nations Within: The Past and Future of American Indian Sovereignty*. New York: Pantheon.

Denker, Ellen Paul. 1985. *After the Chinese Taste: China's Influence in America, 1730–1930*. Salem, Mass.: Peabody Museum of Salem.

Detweiler, Susan Gray. 1982. *George Washington's Chinaware*. New York: Harry N. Abrams.

Dobie, J. Frank. 1985. *A Vaquero of the Brush Country*. Austin: University of Texas Press.

Dolbeare, Kenneth M., ed. 1996. *American Political Thought*. 3d ed. Chatham, N.J.: Chatham House.

Donald, David Herbert. 2001. *Lincoln Reconsidered: Essays on the Civil War Era*. New York: Vintage.

Drescher, Seymour, and Stanley L. Engerman, eds. 1998. *A Historical Guide to World Slavery*. Oxford: Oxford University Press.

Drinnon, Richard. 1980. *Facing West: The Metaphysics of Indian-Hating and Empire Building*. Minneapolis: University of Minnesota Press.

DuBois, Ellen Carol, and Vicki L. Ruiz, eds. 1990. *Unequal Sisters: A Multicultural Reader in U.S. Women's History*. New York: Routledge.

Du Bois, W. E. B. 1897. "The Conservation of Races." In *The American Negro Academy Occasional Papers, No. 2*. Washington: American Negro Academy.

———. 1898. "The Study of the Negro Problems." *Annals of the American Academy of Political and Social Sciences* 9 (January).

———. 1924. *The Gift of Black Folk: Negroes in the Making of America*. Boston: Stratford.

———. 1932. "Black Folk and Birth Control." *Birth Control Review* 16 (June).

———. 1939. *Black Folk: Then and Now*. Millwood, N.Y.: Kraus-Thompson.

———. 1947. *The World and Africa: An Inquiry Into the Part which Africa Has Played in World History*. New York: Viking Press.

———. 1968. *The Autobiography of W. E. B. Du Bois*. New York: International.

———. 1969. *The Souls of Black Folk*. New York: Signet Classic.

———. 1992. *Black Reconstruction in America 1860–1880*. New York: Atheneum.

———. 1995. *Dusk of Dawn: An Essay Toward an Autobiography of a Race Concept.* New Brunswick, N.J.: Transaction.

———. 2001. *The Negro.* Mineola, N.Y.: Dover.

Du Halde, Jean Baptiste. 1736. *The General History of China, containing a Geographical, Historical, Chronological, Political and Physical Description of the Empire of China.* London: John Watts.

Dyer, Thomas G. 1980. *Theodore Roosevelt and the Idea of Race.* Baton Rouge: Louisiana State University Press.

Dyson, Michael Eric. 1997. "The Labor of Whiteness, the Whiteness of Labor, and the Perils of Whitewashing." In *Audacious Democracy: Labor, Intellectuals, and the Social Reconstruction of America,* ed. Steven Fraser and Joshua B. Freeman. Boston: Houghton Mifflin.

Eaves, Lucille. 1910. *History of California Labor Legislation.* Berkeley: University of California Press.

Ellis, Joseph J. 1997. *American Sphinx: The Character of Thomas Jefferson.* New York: Alfred A. Knopf.

———. 2000. "Jefferson: Post-DNA." *William and Mary Quarterly,* 3d series (57): 125–38.

English, Daylanne K. 2004. *Unnatural Selections: Eugenics in American Modernism and the Harlem Renaissance.* Chapel Hill: University of North Carolina Press.

Fitzpatrick, John C., ed. 1940. *The Writings of George Washington.* Vol. 16. Washington: United States Government Printing Office.

Foner, Eric. 1970. *Free Soil, Free Labor, Free Men: The Ideology of the Republican Party before the Civil War.* New York: Oxford University Press.

———. 1980. *Politics and Ideology in the Age of the Civil War.* New York: Oxford University Press.

Foner, Philip S. 1972. *The Spanish-Cuban-American War and the Birth of American Imperialism, 1895–1902.* 2 vols. New York: Monthly Review Press.

Foote, Shelby. 1998. *The Civil War: A Narrative.* Alexandria, Va.: Time-Life Books.

Foster, Frances Smith. 1993. *Written by Herself: Literary Production by African American Women, 1746–1892.* Bloomington: Indiana University Press.

Fowler, Don D., and Catherine S. Fowler, eds. 1971. *Anthropology of the Numa: John Wesley Powell's Manuscripts on the Numic Peoples of Western North America, 1868–1880.* Washington: Smithsonian Institution Press.

Frankenberg, Ruth. 1994. *White Women, Race Matters: The Social Construction of Whiteness.* Minneapolis: University of Minnesota Press.

Franklin, Benjamin. 1959–78. *The Papers of Benjamin Franklin.* Edited by Leonard W. Labaree. New Haven: Yale University Press.

Franklin, John Hope, and Genna Rae McNeil, eds. 1995. *African Americans and the Living Constitution.* Washington: Smithsonian Institution Press.

Franklin, John Hope, and Alfred A. Moss Jr. 1988. *From Slavery to Freedom: A History of Negro Americans.* New York: Knopf.

Franklin, V. P. 1996. *Living Our Stories, Telling Our Truths: Autobiography and the Making of the African-American Intellectual Tradition*. Oxford: Oxford University Press.

Frazier, Charles. 1997. *Cold Mountain*. New York: Atlantic Monthly Press.

Frederickson, George M. 2002. *Racism: A Short History*. Princeton: Princeton University Press.

———. 1981. *White Supremacy: A Comparative Study in American and South African History*. Oxford: Oxford University Press.

Friedel, Frank. 1958. *The Splendid Little War*. Boston: Little, Brown.

Furber, Holden. 1976. *Rival Empires of Trade in the Orient, 1600–1800*. Minneapolis: University of Minnesota Press.

Gable, John Allen. 1978. *The Bull Moose Years: Theodore Roosevelt and the Progressive Party*. Port Washington, N.Y.: Kennikat Press.

Gabriel, Ralph Henry. 1940. *The Course of American Democratic Thought*. New York: Ronald Press.

Gates, Henry Louis, Jr. 1997. *Thirteen Ways of Looking at a Black Man*. New York: Vintage.

Gates, Henry Louis, Jr., ed. 1985. *"Race," Writing, and Difference. Critical Inquiry* 12 (Autumn). Special issue.

Gates, Robbins. 1964. *The Making of Massive Resistance: Virginia's Politics of Public School Desegregation, 1954–1956*. Chapel Hill: University of North Carolina Press.

Gatewood, Willard B., Jr. 1971. *"Smoked Yankees" and the Struggle for Empire: Letters from Negro Soldiers, 1898–1902*. Urbana: University of Illinois Press.

———. 1975. *Black Americans and the White Man's Burden*. Urbana: University of Illinois Press.

Gerber Fried, Marlene, ed. 1990. *From Abortion to Reproductive Freedom: Transforming a Movement*. Boston: South End Press.

Gerstle, Gary. 2001. *American Crucible: Race and Nation in the Twentieth Century*. Princeton: Princeton University Press.

Giddings, Paula. 1984. *When and Where I Enter: The Impact of Black Women on Race and Sex in America*. New York: William Morrow.

Goldman, Emma. 1977. *Living My Life*. New York: New American Library.

Goldwin, Robert A., ed. 1964. *100 Years of Emancipation*. Chicago: Rand McNally.

Gompers, Samuel. 1931. *Seventy Years of Life and Labor*. Vol. 1. New York: E. P. Dutton.

Gordon, Linda. 1976. *Woman's Body, Woman's Right: A Social History of Birth Control in America*. New York: Grossman.

Gordon-Reed, Annette. 1997. *Thomas Jefferson and Sally Hemings: An American Controversy*. Charlottesville: University of Virginia Press.

Gould, Stephen Jay. 1985. "Carrie Buck's Daughter." *Constitutional Commentary* 2:331–39.

Grantham, Dewey W., Jr. 1955. "The Progressive Movement and the Negro." *South Atlantic Quarterly* 54 (October): 461–77.

Green, Jack P., and J. R. Pole, eds. 2000. *A Companion to the American Revolution.* Malden, Mass.: Blackwell.

Greenhouse, Linda. 2007. "Justices, 5-4, Limit the Use of Race for School Integration." *New York Times,* June 29, 2007, A1, A20.

Guterl, Matthew Pratt. 2001. *The Color of Race in America 1900–1940.* Cambridge, Mass.: Harvard University Press.

Gyory, Andrew. 1998. *Closing the Gate: Race, Politics, and the Chinese Exclusion Act.* Chapel Hill: University of North Carolina Press.

Hagedorn, Hermann, ed. 1923–26. *The Works of Theodore Roosevelt.* 20 vols. New York: Scribner.

Haller, Mark. 1963. *Eugenics: Hereditarian Attitudes in American Thought.* New Brunswick: Rutgers University Press.

Hamilton, Alexander. 1948. *Gentleman's Progress: Itinerarium of Dr. Alexander Hamilton.* Edited by Carl Bridenbaugh. Chapel Hill: University of North Carolina Press.

———. 1961. *Alexander Hamilton's Pay Book.* Edited by E. P. Panagopoulos. Detroit: Wayne State University Press.

Haney-López, Ian F. 1996. *White by Law: The Legal Construction of Race.* New York: New York University Press.

Hannaford, Ivan. 1996. *Race: The History of an Idea in the West.* Washington: Woodrow Wilson Center Press.

Hansberry, Lorraine. 1961. "Genet, Mailer, and the New Paternalism." *Village Voice* (June 1): 10–15.

———. 1962. *The Village Voice Reader: A Mixed Bag from the Greenwich Village Newspaper.* Edited by Daniel Wolf and Edwin Fancher. New York: Doubleday.

———. 1963. "Challenge to Artists." *Freedomways* 3 (1): 34–35.

———. 1965a. "The Legacy of W. E. B. Du Bois." *Freedomways* 5 (1).

———. 1965b. *The Sign in Sidney Brustein's Window.* New York: Random House.

———. 1969. *To Be Young, Gifted, and Black: An Informal Biography.* Adapted by Robert Nemiroff. New York: New American Library.

Harbaugh, William H. 1975. *The Life and Times of Theodore Roosevelt.* New York: Oxford University Press.

Harnar, Nellie Shaw. 1974. *The History of the Pyramid Lake Indians 1843–1959 and Early Tribal History 1825–1834.* Sparks, Nev.: Dave's Printing and Publishing.

Harris, Cheryl I. 1993. "Whiteness as Property." *Harvard Law Review* 106 (June): 1709–95.

Harris, Trudier, ed. 1991. *Selected Writings of Ida B. Wells- Barnett.* New York: Oxford University Press.

Higham, John. 1992. *Strangers in the Land: Patterns of American Nativism.* New Brunswick: Rutgers University Press.

Hill, Herbert, and James E. Jones Jr., eds. 1993. *Race in America: The Struggle for Equality.* Madison: University of Wisconsin Press.

Hofstadter, Richard. 1974. *The American Political Tradition.* New York: Vintage Books.

Holland, Catherine A. 2001a. "Notes on the State of America: Jeffersonian Democracy and the Production of a National Past." *Political Theory* 29 (April).

———. 2001b. *The Body Politic: Foundings, Citizenship, and Difference in the American Political Imagination*. New York: Routledge.

Hollinger, David. 2000. "The Ethno-Racial Pentagon." In *Race and Ethnicity in the United States: Issues and Debates*, ed. S. Steinberg. Malden, Mass.: Blackwell.

Holt, Thomas C. 1990. "The Political Uses of Alienation: W. E. B. Du Bois on Politics, Race, and Culture, 1903–1940." *American Quarterly* 42 (2): 301–23.

Honour, Hugh. 1961. *Chinoiserie: The Vision of Cathay*. New York: Harper and Row.

Hopkins, Sarah Winnemucca. 1994. *Life Among the Piutes: Their Wrongs and Claims*. Reno: University of Nevada Press.

Horsman, Reginald. 1981. *Race and Manifest Destiny: The Origins of American Racial Anglo-Saxonism*. Cambridge, Mass.: Harvard University Press.

———. 2000. *The New Republic: The United States of America 1789–1815*. Essex: Longman/Pearson Education.

Hughes, Langston. 1995. *The Collected Poems of Langston Hughes*. Edited by Arnold Rampersad. New York: Vintage.

Hulsether, Mark. 1993. "Evolving Approaches to U.S. Culture in the American Studies Movement: Consensus, Pluralism, and Contestation for Cultural Hegemony." *Canadian Review of American Studies* 23 (2): 1–55.

Hume, David. 1752. "On Luxury." In *Political Discourses*. Edinburgh: A. Kincaid and A. Donaldson.

———. 1997. "Negroes . . . naturally inferior to the whites." In *Race and the Enlightenment*. Edited by Emmanuel Chukwudi Eze. Oxford: Blackwell.

Hune, Shirley, ed. 1991. *Asian Americans: Comparative and Global Perspectives*. Pullman: Washington State University Press.

Hurwitz, Howard Lawrence. 1943. *Theodore Roosevelt and Labor in New York State, 1880–1900*. New York: Columbia University Press.

Ignatieff, Michael. 1993. *Blood and Belonging: Journeys in the New Nationalism*. New York: Mulberry Books.

Ignatiev, Noel. 1995. *How the Irish Became White*. New York: Routledge.

Ignatiev, Noel, and John Garvey, eds. 1996. *Race Traitor*. New York: Routledge.

Irons, Peter. 2002. *Jim Crow's Children: The Broken Promise of the Brown Decision*. New York: Penguin Books.

Irvin Painter, Nell. 1992. "Hill, Thomas, and the Use of Racial Stereotype." In *Race-ing Justice, En-Gendering Power: Essays on Anita Hill, Clarence Thomas, and the Construction of Social Reality*, ed. Toni Morrison. New York: Pantheon.

———. 1996. *Sojourner Truth: A Life, A Symbol*. New York: W. W. Norton.

Jacobs, Gregory S. 1998. *Getting Around Brown: Desegregation, Development, and the Columbus Public School*. Columbus: Ohio State University Press.

Jacobson, Matthew Frye. 1999. *Whiteness of a Different Color: European Immigration and the Alchemy of Race*. Cambridge, Mass.: Harvard University Press.

James, Joy. 1997. *Transcending the Talented Tenth: Black Leaders and American Intellectuals*. New York: Routledge.

James, William. 1890. *The Principles of Psychology*. New York: Henry Holt.

Janara, Laura. 2002. *Democracy Growing Up: Authority, Autonomy and Passion in Tocqueville's Democracy in America*. Albany: State University of New York Press.

Johnson, Donald B., and Kirk H. Porter. 1961. *National Party Platforms, 1840–1960*. Urbana: University of Illinois Press.

Johnson, Edward A. 1899. *History of Negro Soldiers in the Spanish-American War, and Other Items of Interest*. New York: Kessinger.

Jordan, Winthrop D. 1969. *White Over Black: Attitudes Toward the Negro, 1550–1812*. Baltimore: Penguin Books.

Joshi, S. T., ed. 1999. *Documents of American Prejudice: An Anthology on Race from Thomas Jefferson to David Duke*. New York: Basic Books.

Kaeppler, Susanne. 1986. *The Pornography of Representation*. Minneapolis: University of Minnesota Press.

Kaplan, Amy, and Donald E. Pease, eds. 1993. *The Cultures of United States Imperialism*. Durham, N.C.: Duke University Press.

Katz, Michael B., and Thomas J. Sugrue, eds. 1998. *W. E. B. Du Bois, Race, and the City: The Philadelphia Negro and Its Legacy*. Philadelphia: University of Pennsylvania Press.

Kauer, Ralph. 1944. "The Workingmen's Party of California." *Pacific Historical Review* 13 (September): 278–91.

Kelley, Robin D. G. 1996. *Race Rebels: Culture, Politics, and the Black Working Class*. New York: Free Press.

Kelley, Robin D. G., and Earl Lewis, eds. 2000. *To Make Our World Anew: A History of African Americans*. New York: Oxford University Press.

Kelly, Isabel T. 1938. "Northern Paiute Tales." *Journal of American Folklore* 51, no. 202 (October–December): 363–437.

Kelsey, Penelope. 2003. "Natives, Nation, Narration: Reading Roanoke in the Renaissance." *ESQ* 49 (1–3): 149–60.

Kennedy, David M. 1970. *Birth Control in America: The Career of Margaret Sanger*. New Haven: Yale University Press.

Keppel, Ben. 1995. *The Work of Democracy: Ralph Bunche, Kenneth B. Clark, Lorraine Hansberry, and the Cultural Politics of Race*. Cambridge, Mass.: Harvard University Press.

Kevles, David J. 1985. *In the Name of Eugenics: Genetics and the Uses of Human Heredity*. New York: Knopf.

Kim, Elaine. 1982. *Asian American Literature*. Philadelphia: Temple University Press.

Kincaid, Jamaica. 1998. "The Little Revenge of the Periphery." *Transition*, no. 73: 68–73.

King, Martin Luther, Jr. 1968. "Racism and the White Backlash." In *Where Do We Go From Here: Chaos or Community?* Boston: Beacon Press.

———. 1990. *A Testament of Hope: The Essential Writings and Speeches of Martin Luther King, Jr*. San Francisco: Harper.

Kleppner, Paul. 1970. *The Cross of Culture: A Social Analysis of Midwestern Politics, 1850–1900*. New York: Free Press.

Knack, Martha, and Omer C. Stewart. 1984. *As Long as the River Shall Run: An Ethnohistory of Pyramid Lake Indian Reservation*. Berkeley: University of California Press.

Knight, Franklin. 1844. *Monuments of Washington's Patriotism Containing a Facsimile of His Public Accounts Kept During the Revolutionary War, June 1775–June 1783*. Washington: Trustees of Washington's Manual Labour School and Male Orphan Asylum.

Koch, Adrienne, and William Peden, eds. 1944. *The Life and Selected Writings of Thomas Jefferson*. New York: Random House.

Kowaleski-Wallace, Elizabeth. 1997. *Consuming Subjects: Women, Shopping, and Business in the Eighteenth Century*. New York: Columbia University Press.

Kramnick, Isaac. 1981. "Equal Opportunity and the 'Race of Life.'" *Dissent* 28 (spring).

Kupperman, Karen Ordahl. 1997. "Presentment of Civility: English Reading of American Self-Presentation in the Early Years of Colonization." *William and Mary Quarterly* 54 (1): 193–228.

LaFeber, Walter. 1963. *The New Empire: An Interpretation of American Expansion, 1860–1898*. Ithaca: Cornell University Press.

Lane, A. T. 1984. "American Trade Unions, Mass Immigration, and the Literacy Test 1900–1917." *Labor History* 25 (winter): 5–25.

Lane, Ann J. 1971. *The Brownsville Affair: National Crisis and Black Reaction*. Port Washington, N.Y.: Kennikat Press.

Lanier, Shannon, and Jane Feldman. 2000. *Jefferson's Children: The Story of One American Family*. Introduction by Lucian K. Truscott IV. New York: Random House.

Lape, Noreen Groover. 1998. "'I would rather be with my people, but not to live with them as they live': Cultural Liminality and Double Consciousness in Sarah Winnemucca Hopkins's *Life Among the Piutes: Their Wrongs and Claims.*" *American Indian Quarterly* 22 (Summer): 259–79.

Laughlin, Harry Hamilton. 1914. *The Legal and Administrative Aspects of Sterilization: Report of Committee to Study and to Report on the Best Practical Means of Cutting Off the Defective Germ-Plasm in the American Population*. Cold Springs Harbor, N.Y.: Eugenics Record Office.

Leckie, William H. 1967. *The Buffalo Soldiers: A Narrative of the Negro Cavalry in the West*. Norman: University of Oklahoma Press.

Lee, Chungmei. 2004. *Is Resegregation Real?* Cambridge, Mass.: Harvard Civil Rights Project Report.

Lee, Rachel. 1999. *The Americas of Asian American Literature: Gendered Fictions of Nation and Transnation*. Princeton: Princeton University Press.

Levine, Daniel. 1971. *Jane Addams and the Liberal Tradition*. Madison: Greenwood.

Levy, Michael B., ed. 1988. *Political Thought in America: An Anthology*. 2d ed. Chicago: Dorsey Press.

Lewis, David Levering. 1993. *W. E. B. Du Bois: Biography of a Race, 1868–1919*. New York: Henry Holt.

———. 2000. *W. E. B. Du Bois: The Fight for Equality and the American Century 1919–1963*. New York: Henry Holt.

Lewis, Jan Ellen, and Peter S. Onuf, eds. 1999. *Sally Hemings and Thomas Jefferson: History, Memory, and Civic Culture.* Charlottesville: University of Virginia Press.

Linderman, Gerald. 1974. *The Mirror of War: American Society and the Spanish-American War.* Ann Arbor: University of Michigan Press.

Link, Arthur S. 1944. "Correspondence Relating to the Progressive Party's 'Lily White' Policy in 1912." *Journal of Southern History* 10 (November): 483–88.

———. 1947. "The Negro as a Factor in the Campaign of 1912." *Journal of Negro History* 32 (January): 81–99.

———. 1954. *Woodrow Wilson and the Progressive Era, 1910–1917.* New York: Harper and Brothers.

Lipsitz, George. 1998. *The Possessive Investment in Whiteness.* Philadelphia: Temple University Press.

———. 2004. "Abolition Democracy and Global Justice." *Comparative American Studies* 2 (3): 271–87.

Lorimer, Douglas. 1984. *Colour, Class and the Victorians: English Attitudes to the Negro in the Mid-Nineteenth Century.* Leicester: Leicester University Press.

Lott, Tommy L. 1992–93. "Du Bois on the Invention of Race." *Philosophical Forum* 24 (1–3): 166–87.

———. 1999. *The Invention of Race: Black Culture and the Politics of Representation.* Malden, Mass.: Blackwell.

Lowe, Lisa. 1996. *Immigrant Acts: On Asian American Cultural Politics.* Durham, N.C.: Duke University Press.

Luce, T. James, ed. 1982. *Ancient Writers.* Vol. I. New York: Charles Scribner and Sons.

Lukas, Anthony. 1997. *Big Trouble: A Murder in a Small Western Town Sets Off a Struggle for the Soul of America.* New York: Simon and Schuster.

Macaulay, Catharine. 1775. *An Address to the People of England, Scotland, and Ireland, on the Present Important Crisis of Affairs.* London: E. and C. Dilly.

MacKenzie, Donald A. 1981. *Statistics in Britain, 1865–1930: The Social Construction of Scientific Knowledge.* Edinburgh: Edinburgh University Press.

Magnusson, Lars. 1994. *Mercantilism: The Shaping of an Economic Language.* London: Routledge.

Malone, Dumas. 1970. *Jefferson the President: First Term, 1801–1805.* Boston: Little, Brown.

Mandel, Bernard. 1955. "Samuel Gompers and Negro Workers, 1866–1914." *Journal of Negro History* 40:34–60.

Marable, Manning. 2002. *The Great Wells of Democracy: The Meaning of Race in America.* New York: Basic Books.

Marcus, Greil. 1996. *Invisible Republic: Bob Dylan's Basement Tapes.* New York: Henry Holt.

Marshall, Gail. 1998. *Actresses on the Victorian Stage: Feminine Performance and the Galatea Myth.* Cambridge: Cambridge University Press.

Marshall, T. H. 1950. *Citizenship and Social Class and Other Essays.* Cambridge: Cambridge University Press.

Mason, Alpheus Thomas, ed. 1965. *Free Government in the Making: Readings in American Political Thought*. Oxford: Oxford University Press.

Matovina, Timothy M. 1995. *The Alamo Remembered: Tejano Accounts and Perspectives*. Austin: University of Texas Press.

Matthiessen, Peter. 1983. *In the Spirit of Crazy Horse*. New York: Penguin Books.

Maverick, Lewis A. 1946. *China a Model for Europe*. San Antonio: Paul Anderson.

May, Elaine Tyler. 1995. *Barren in the Promised Land: Childless Americans and the Pursuit of Happiness*. New York: Basic Books.

May, Glen. 1980. *Social Engineering in the Philippines*. Westport, Conn.: Greenwood Press.

McBridge, Dwight, ed. 1999. *James Baldwin Now*. New York: New York University Press.

McCann, Carole R. 1994. *Birth Control Politics in the United States, 1916–1945*. Ithaca: Cornell University Press.

McFeely, William S. 1991. *Frederick Douglass*. New York: W. W. Norton.

McPherson, James M. 1988. *Battle Cry of Freedom: The Civil War Era*. New York: Ballantine Books.

McWilliams, Carey. 1944. *Factories in the Field*. Boston: Little, Brown.

Miller, Stuart Creighton. 1982. *"Benevolent Assimilation": The American Conquest of the Philippines, 1899–1903*. New Haven: Yale University Press.

Miller, William Lee. 2002. *Lincoln's Virtues: An Ethical Biography*. New York: Alfred A. Knopf.

Mills, Charles W. 1997. *The Racial Contract*. Ithaca: Cornell University Press.

Mink, Gwendolyn. 1986. *Old Labor and New Immigrants in American Political Development: Union, Party, and State, 1875–1920*. Ithaca: Cornell University Press.

Mitgang, Herbert. 1970. "The Art of Lincoln." *American Art Journal* 2 (1): 5–8.

Monteiro, Anthony. 2000. "Being an African in the World: The Du Boisian Epistemology." *Annals of the American Academy of Political and Social Sciences* 568 (March): 220–34.

Morgan, Edmund S. 1975. *American Slavery—American Freedom: The Ordeal of Colonial Virginia*. New York: W. W. Norton.

Morgan, Edmund S., and Helen M. Morgan. 1953. *The Stamp Act Crisis: Prologue to Revolution*. Chapel Hill: University of North Carolina Press.

Morgan, Edmund S., and Marie Morgan. 2007. "Our Shaky Beginnings." *New York Review of Books* 54 (April 26): 21–25.

Morison, Elting E., ed. 1951. *The Letters of Theodore Roosevelt*. 8 vols. Cambridge, Mass.: Harvard University Press.

Morris, Edmund. 1979. *The Rise of Theodore Roosevelt*. New York: Modern Library.

Morrison, Toni, ed. 1998. *James Baldwin: Collected Essays*. New York: Library of America.

Moses, William J. 1993. "W. E. B. Du Bois's 'The Conservation of Races' and Its Context: Idealism, Conservatism, and Hero Worship." *Massachusetts Review* 34 (summer): 275–94.

Mostern, Kenneth. 2000. "Postcolonialism after W. E. B. Du Bois." *Rethinking Marxism* 23 (2): 61–80.

Mowry, George E. 1940. "The South and the Progressive Lily White Party of 1912." *Journal of Southern History* 6 (May): 237–47.

———. 1946. *Theodore Roosevelt and the Progressive Movement*. Madison: University of Wisconsin Press.

Muncy, Robyn. 1997. "Trustbusting and White Manhood in America, 1898–1914." *American Studies* 38 (fall): 21–42.

Murphy, Arthur. 1797. *The Orphan of China: A Tragedy*. London: George Cawthorn.

Myrdal, Gunnar. 1972. *An American Dilemma: The Negro Problem and Modern Democracy*. 2 vols. New York: Harper and Row.

Nalty, Bernard C. 1986. *Strength for the Fight: A History of Black Americans in the Military*. New York: Free Press.

Nathan, Richard P., Fred C. Doolittle, et al. 1983. *The Consequences of Cuts: The Effects of the Reagan Domestic Program on State and Local Governments*. Princeton: Princeton University Press.

Nelson, Jennifer. 2003. *Women of Color and the Reproductive Rights Movement*. New York: New York University Press.

Nemiroff, Robert, ed. 1972. *Lorraine Hansberry: The Collected Last Plays*. New York: Random House.

Ngai, Mae M. 1999. "The Architecture of Race in American Immigration Law: A Reexamination of the Immigration Act of 1924." *Journal of American History* 86 (June): 67–92.

Nichols, Frederick Doveton, and Ralph E. Griswold. 1977. *Thomas Jefferson, Landscape Architect*. Charlottesville: University Press of Virginia.

Nicolaides, Becky M. 2002. *My Blue Heaven: Life and Politics in the Working-Class Suburbs of Los Angeles, 1920–1965*. Chicago: University of Chicago Press.

Nicoll, Allardyce. 1927. *A History of Late Eighteenth-Century Drama, 1750–1800*. Cambridge: Cambridge University Press.

Oakes, James. 2007. *The Radical and the Republican: Frederick Douglass, Abraham Lincoln, and the Triumph of Antislavery Politics*. New York: W. W. Norton.

O'Brien, Conor Cruise. 1996. *The Long Affair: Thomas Jefferson and the French Revolution, 1785–1800*. Chicago: University of Chicago Press.

Odell, George C. D. 1970. *Annals of the New York Stage*. New York: AMS Press.

O'Leary, Cecilia Elizabeth. 1999. *To Die For: The Paradox of American Patriotism*. Princeton: Princeton University Press.

Olson, Joel. 2004. *The Abolition of White Democracy*. Minneapolis: University of Minnesota Press.

Onuf, Peter S., ed. 1993. *Jefferson's Legacies*. Charlottesville: University Press of Virginia.

Orfield, Gary, Susan Eaton, and Harvard Project on School Desegregation. 1996. *Dismantling Desegregation: The Quiet Reversal of Brown v. Board of Education*. New York: New Press.

Orleck, Annelise. 1995. *Common Sense and a Little Fire: Women and Working-Class Politics in the United States, 1900–1965*. Chapel Hill: University of North Carolina Press.

Padover, Saul K. 1958. *The Mind of Alexander Hamilton*. New York: Harper and Brothers.

Parks, Suzan-Lori. 1995. *The America Play and Other Works*. New York: Theatre Communications Group.

———. 2002. *Topdog/Underdog*. New York: Theatre Communications Group.

Paschal, Andrew G., ed. 1971. *A W. E. B. Du Bois Reader*. New York: Collier.

Patterson, James T. 2001. *Brown v, Board of Education: A Civil Rights Milestone and Its Troubled Legacy*. New York: Oxford.

Patterson, Orlando. 1997. *The Ordeal of Integration*. New York: Civitas/Counterpoint.

———. 1998. "Jefferson the Contradiction." *New York Times*, November 2, 1998, A27.

Patton, Venetria K., and Ronald Jemal Stevens. 1999. "Narrating Competing Truths in the Thomas Jefferson–Sally Hemings Paternity Debate." *Black Scholar* 29 (4): 8–15.

Perez, Louis A. 1986. *Cuba under the Platt Amendment*. Pittsburgh: University of Pittsburgh Press.

Peterson, Merrill D. 1970. *Thomas Jefferson and the New Nation: A Biography*. New York: Oxford University Press.

Peterson, Merrill D., ed. 1984. *Thomas Jefferson: Writings*. New York: Library of America.

Pickens, Donald K. 1968. *Eugenics and the Progressives*. Nashville, Tenn.: Vanderbilt University Press.

Pierson, George Wilson. 1996. *Tocqueville in America*. Baltimore: Johns Hopkins University Press.

Powell, John A., Gavin Kearney, and Vina Kay, eds. 2001. *In Pursuit of a Dream Deferred*. New York: Peter Lang.

Prashad, Vijay. 2005. "How the Hindus Became Jews: American Racism After 9/11." *South Atlantic Quarterly* 104 (Summer): 583–606.

Pride, Richard A. 2002. *The Political Use of Racial Narratives: School Desegregation in Mobile, Alabama, 1954–1992*. Urbana: University of Illinois Press.

Prucha, Frances Paul. 1984. *The Great Father: The United States Government and the American Indians*. Vol. 2. Lincoln: University of Nebraska Press.

Quandagno, Jill. 1994. *The Color of Welfare: How Racism Undermined the War on Poverty*. New York: Oxford University Press.

Quinn Brown, Hallie. 1988. *Homespun Heroines and Other Women of Distinction*. New York: Oxford University Press.

Raboteau, Albert J. 1994. "African Americans, Exodus, and the American Israel." In *African-American Christianity: Essays in History*, ed. Paul E. Johnson. Berkeley: University of California Press.

Rampersad, Arnold. 1976. *The Art and Imagination of W. E. B. Du Bois*. Cambridge, Mass.: Harvard University Press.

Ramsey, Jarold, ed. 1977. *Coyote Was Going There: Indian Literature of the Oregon County*. Seattle: University of Washington Press.

Raskin, Jamin B. 2003. *Overruling Democracy: The Supreme Court vs. the American People*. New York and London: Routledge.

Reddy, William M. 1987. *Money and Liberty in Modern Europe: A Critique of Historical Understanding*. Cambridge: Cambridge University Press.

Reed, Adolph L., Jr. 1997a. *W. E. B. Du Bois and American Political Thought: Fabianism and the Color Line*. New York: Oxford University Press.

Reed, James. 1978. *The Birth Control Movement and American Society: From Private Vice to Public Virtue*. Princeton: Princeton University Press.

Reed, Roy. 1997. *Faubus: The Life and Times of an Arkansas Prodigal*. Fayetteville: University of Arkansas Press.

Reinhardt, Mark. 1997. *The Art of Being Free: Taking Liberties with Tocqueville, Marx, and Arendt*. Ithaca: Cornell University Press.

Richardson, James F. 1970. *The New York Police: Colonial Times to 1901*. New York: Oxford University Press.

Riis, Jacob A. 1890. *How the Other Half Lives: Studies Among the Tenements of New York*. New York: Charles Scribner's Sons.

Roberts, Dorothy. 1999. *Killing the Black Body: Race, Reproduction, and the Meaning of Liberty*. New York: Vintage.

Roediger, David R. 1994. *Toward the Abolition of Whiteness: Essays in Race, Politics, and Working-Class History*. London: Verso.

———. [1991] 1999. *The Wages of Whiteness: Race and the Making of the American Working Class,*. London: Verso.

———. 2002. *Colored White: Transcending the Racial Past*. Berkeley: University of California Press.

Roediger, David R., ed. 1998. *Black on White: Black Writers on What It Means to Be White*. New York: Schocken Books.

Rogin, Michael Paul. 1975. *Fathers and Children: Andrew Jackson and the Subjection of the American Indian*. Cambridge, Mass.: Harvard University Press.

Roney, Frank. 1931. *Frank Roney, Irish Rebel and California Labor Leader: An Autobiography*. New York: AMS Press.

Roosevelt, Theodore. 1902. *The Rough Riders*. New York: Bartleby.

———. 1910. *The New Nationalism*. New York: The Outlook Company.

———. 1917. *The Foes of Our Own Household*. New York: George H. Doran.

———. 1927. *Theodore Roosevelt: An Autobiography*. New York: MacMillan. Reprint of 1913 edition.

Roth, Rodris. 1988. "Tea-Drinking in Eighteenth-Century America: Its Etiquette and Equipage." In *Material Life in America*, ed. Robert Blair St. George. Boston: Northeastern University Press.

St. John, Craig, and Nancy A. Bates. 1990. "Racial Composition and Neighborhood Evaluation." *Social Science Research* 19 (March): 47–61.

Salyer, Lucy. 1995. *Laws Harsh as Tigers: Chinese Immigrants and the Shaping of Modern Immigration Law*. Chapel Hill: University of North Carolina Press.

Sandmeyer, Elmer. 1939. *The Anti-Chinese Movement in California*. Urbana: University of Illinois Press.

Sanger, Margaret. 1920. *Woman and the New Race*. New York: Brentano's.

——. 1922. *The Pivot of Civilization*. New York: Brentano's.

——. 1938. *An Autobiography*. New York: Dover.

San Juan, Epifanio. 1972. *Carlos Bulosan and the Imagination of the Class Struggle*. New York: Oriole Editions.

Saxton, Alexander. 1970. "Race and the House of Labor." In *The Great Fear: Race to the Mind of America*, ed. Gary B. Nash and Richard Weiss. New York: Holt, Rinehart, and Winston.

——. 1971. *The Indispensable Enemy: Labor and the Anti-Chinese Movement in California*. Berkeley: University of California Press.

——. 1990. *The Rise and Fall of the White Republic: Class Politics and Mass Culture in Nineteenth-Century America*. New York: Verso.

Schechter, Patricia A. 2001. *Ida B. Wells-Barnett and American Reform, 1880–1930*. Chapel Hill: University of North Carolina Press.

Schuyler, George S. 1932. "Quantity or Quality." *Birth Control Review* 16 (June): 165–66.

Scipio, Albert L., II. 1983. *Last of the Black Regulars: A History of the Twenty-Fourth Infantry Regiment, 1869–1951*. Silver Spring, Md.: Roman.

Sekora, John. 1977. *Luxury: The Concept in Western Thought, Eden to Smollet*. Baltimore: Johns Hopkins University Press.

Shapiro, Thomas M. 2004. *The Hidden Cost of Being African American: How Wealth Perpetuates Inequality*. New York: Oxford University Press.

Shipler, David K. 1997. *A Country of Strangers: Blacks and Whites in America*. New York: Knopf.

Shou-yi, Chen. 1936. "The Chinese Orphan: A Yuan Play." *Tien Hsia Monthly* 3 (2).

Shuford, John. 2001. "Four Du Boisian Contributions to Critical Race Theory." *Transactions of the Charles S. Pierce Society* 37 (3): 301–37.

Silbey, Joel. 1977. *A Respectable Minority: The Democratic Party in the Civil War Era, 1860–1868*. New York: W. W. Norton.

Silbey, Joel, Allan G. Bogue, and William H. Flanigan, eds. 1978. *The History of American Electoral Behavior*. Princeton: Princeton University Press.

Singh, Nikhil Pal. 2004. *Black Is a Country: Race and the Unfinished Struggle for Democracy*. Cambridge, Mass.: Harvard University Press.

Sinkler, George. 1971. *The Racial Attitudes of American Presidents: From Abraham Lincoln to Theodore Roosevelt*. Garden City: Doubleday.

Slotkin, Richard. 1992. *Gunfighter Nation: The Myth of the Frontier in Twentieth-Century America*. New York: Atheneum.

Smith, Adam. [1776] 1970. *The Wealth of Nations*. London: Penguin Books.

Smith, John. 1966. "A Little Teatable Chitchat, à la mode; or an ancient discovery reduced to modern practice." In *Dramas from the American Theatre, 1762–1909*, ed. Richard Moody. Cleveland: World Publishing.

Smith, Judith. 2004. *Visions of Belonging: Family Stories, Popular Culture, and Postwar Democracy, 1940–1960*. New York: Columbia University Press.

Smith, Rogers M. 1993. "Beyond Tocqueville, Myrdal, and Hartz: The Multiple Traditions in America." *American Political Science Review* 87 (September): 549–66.

Sowerby, E. Millicent. 1952–59. *Catalogue of the Library of Thomas Jefferson*. Washington: Library of Congress.

Spelman, Elizabeth. 1988. *Inessential Woman: Problems of Exclusion in Feminist Thought*. Boston: Beacon Press.

Spillers, Hortense V. 1989. "'The Permanent Obliquity of an In(pha)llibly Straight': In the Time of the Daughters and the Fathers." In *Changing Our Own Words: Essays on Criticism, Theory, and Writing by Black Women*, ed. Cheryl A. Wall. New Brunswick: Rutgers University Press.

Stadiem, William, and Essie Mae Washington-Williams. 2005. *Dear Senator: A Memoir by the Daughter of Strom Thurmond*. New York: HarperCollins.

Stanton, Lucia. 2000. "The Other End of the Telescope: Jefferson through the Eyes of His Slaves." *William and Mary Quarterly*, 3rd series (57): 140–44.

Stanton, William. 1960. *The Leopard's Spots: Scientific Attitudes toward Race in America, 1815–59*. Chicago: University of Chicago Press.

Steward, Theophilus G. 1969. *The Colored Regulars in the United States Army*. New York: Humanity Books.

Stocking, George W., Jr. 1994. "The Turn-of-the-Century Concept of Race." *Modernism/Modernity* 1 (1): 4–16.

Stone, Alfred Holt. 1908. *Studies in the American Race Problem*. New York: Dunleith.

Stuckey, Sterling. 1987. *Slave Culture: Nationalist Theory and the Foundations of Black America*. New York: Oxford University Press.

Takaki, Ronald. 1994. "Reflections of Racial Patterns in America." In *From Different Shores: Perspectives on Race and Ethnicity in America*, ed. R. Takaki. New York: Oxford University Press.

———. 2001. "Race and the End of History." In *The Good Citizen*, ed. David B. Batstone and Eduardo Mendieta. New York: Routledge.

Taub, Richard D., D. Garth Taylor, and Jan D. Dunham. 1984. *Paths of Neighborhood Change: Race and Crime in Urban America*. Chicago: University of Chicago Press.

Taylor, Alan. 2001. "Blood and Soil." *New Republic* 225 (October 8, 2001): 46–50.

Taylor, Paul C. 2003. *Race: A Philosophical Introduction*. Cambridge: Polity.

Testi, Arnaldo. 1995. "The Gender of Reform Politics: Theodore Roosevelt and the Culture of Masculinity." *Journal of American History* 81 (March): 1509–33.

The Combahee River Collective. 1982. "A Black Feminist Statement." In *But Some of Us Are Brave*, ed. Gloria T. Hull, Patricia Bell Scott, and Barbara Smith. Old Westbury, N.Y.: Feminist Press.

Thompson, Jerry. 1986. *Mexican Texans in the Union Army*. El Paso: Texas Western Press.

———. 1994. *Juan Cortina and the Texas–Mexico Frontier, 1859–1877*. El Paso: Texas Western Press.

———, ed. 1998. *Fifty Miles and a Fight: Major Samuel Peter Heintzelman's Journal of Texas and the Cortina War*. Austin: Texas State Historical Association.

Thompson, Jerry, and Lawrence T. Jones III. 2004. *Civil War and Revolution on the Rio Grande Frontier: A Narrative and Photographic History*. Austin: Texas State Historical Association.

Torruela, Juan R. 1985. *The Supreme Court and Puerto Rico: The Doctrine of Separate and Unequal*. San Juan: Editorial de la Universidad de Puerto Rico.

Trask, David F. 1981. *The War with Spain in 1898*. New York: Bison Books.

Troupe, Quincy, ed. 1989. *James Baldwin: The Legacy*. New York: Simon and Schuster.

Turner, Frederick Jackson. 1994. *The Significance of the Frontier in American History*. Edited by Harold P. Simonson. New York: Dover Publications.

Ukers, William H. 1935. *All About Tea*. New York: Tea and Coffee Trade Journal.

Valenza, Charles. 1985. "Was Margaret Sanger a Racist?" *Family Planning Perspectives* 17 (January–February): 44–46.

Vaughan, Curtis M. 1959. *Faubus's Folly: The Story of Segregation*. New York: Vantage.

Venuti, Lawrence. 2001. *The Translator's Invisibility: A History of Translation*. London: Routledge.

Vose, Clement E. 1967. *Caucasians Only: The Supreme Court, the NAACP, and the Restrictive Covenant Cases*. Berkeley: University of California Press.

Wall, Diana di Zerega. 1987. "At Home in New York: Changing Family Life Among the Propertied in the Late Eighteenth and Early Nineteenth Centuries." Ph.D. diss., New York University.

Wallerstein, Immanuel. 1974. *The Modern World System*. New York: Academic Press.

Washington, George. 1997. *Writings*. Edited by John H. Rhodehamel. New York: Library of America.

———. *George Washington Papers at the Library of Congress 1741–1799*. Manuscripts Division, Library of Congress (available from http://memory.loc.gov).

Weiner, Annette B. 1992. *Inalienable Possessions. The Paradox of Keeping-While-Giving*. Berkeley: University of California Press.

Wellish, J. B. 1977. *An In-Depth Study of Emergency School Aid Act (ESAA) Schools: 1975–1976*. Santa Monica, Calif.: Systems Development Corporation.

Wells, Amy Stuart, and Robert L. Crain. 1997. *Stepping Over the Color Line: African American Students in White Suburban Schools*. New Haven: Yale University Press.

Wells-Barnett, Ida B. 1970. *Crusade for Justice: The Autobiography of Ida B. Wells*. Chicago: University of Chicago Press.

West, Cornel. 2004. *Democracy Matters: Winning the Fight Against Imperialism*. New York: Penguin Press.

Westin, Rubin. 1972. *Racism in U.S. Imperialism: The Influence of Racial Assumptions on American Foreign Policy, 1893–1946.* Columbia: University of South Carolina Press.

White, Deborah Gray. 1993. "The Cost of Club Work, The Price of Black Feminism." In *Visible Women: New Essays on American Activism,* ed. Nancy A. Hewitt and Suzanne Lebsock. Urbana: University of Illinois Press.

White, G. Edward. 1968. *The Eastern Establishment and the Western Experience: The West of Frederic Remington, Theodore Roosevelt, and Owen Wister.* New Haven: Yale University Press.

White, Richard. 1994. "Frederick Jackson Turner and Buffalo Bill." In *The Frontier in American Culture,* ed. James R. Grossman. Berkeley: University of California Press.

Wilentz, Sean. 1997. "Life, Liberty, and the Pursuit of Thomas Jefferson." *New Republic,* March 10, 1997, 32–42.

Williams, Patricia. 1991. *The Alchemy of Race and Rights.* Cambridge, Mass.: Harvard University Press.

———. 2000. "America, Seen Through the Filter of Race: A Conversation on Race." *New York Times,* July 2, 11.

Williamson, Joel. 1984. *The Crucible of Race: Black-White Relations in the American South since Emancipation.* New York: Oxford University Press.

Wills, Gary. 2003. "The Negro President." *New York Review of Books* 50 (November 6): 48–51.

Winant, Howard. 2001. *The World Is a Ghetto: Race and Democracy since World War II.* New York: Basic Books.

———. 2004. *The New Politics of Race: Globalism, Difference, Justice.* Minneapolis: University of Minnesota Press.

Wishy, Bernard. 1967. *The Child and the Republic: The Dawn of American Child Nurture.* Philadelphia: University of Pennsylvania Press.

Wong, Sau-ling Cynthia. 1993. *Reading Asian American Literature: From Necessity to Extravagance.* Princeton: Princeton University Press.

Wood, Gordon S. 1969. *The Creation of the American Republic, 1776–1787.* New York: W. W. Norton.

———. 1982. *The Radicalism of the American Republic.* New York: Alfred A. Knopf.

———. 1998. "The Bloodiest War." *New York Review of Books* 46 (April 9): 41–44.

Woodson, Bryon W., Sr. 2001. *A President in the Family: Thomas Jefferson, Sally Hemings, and Thomas Woodson.* Foreword by Michele Cooley-Quille. Westport, Conn.: Praeger.

Yearley, Clifton. 1972. *The Money Machines: The Breakdown of Reform of Governmental and Party Finance in the North, 1860–1920.* Albany: State University of New York Press.

Zaborowska, Magdalena J., ed. 1998. *Other Americans, Other Americas: The Politics and Poetics of Multiculturalism.* Aarhus, Denmark: Aarhus University Press.

Zinn, Howard. 1995. *A People's History of the United States, 1492–Present.* Revised ed. New York: Harper Perennial.

Contributors

BRUCE BAUM is Assistant Professor of Political Science at the University of British Columbia. He is the author of *Rereading Power and Freedom in J. S. Mill* (University of Toronto Press, 2000) and *The Rise and Fall of the Caucasian Race: A Political History of Racial Identity* (New York University Press, 2006).

CARI M. CARPENTER is Assistant Professor of English at West Virginia University, where she is a member of the Native American Studies Committee. She has published essays on Gertrude Bonnin, Sarah Winnemucca, and feminist technologies in the classroom. She is the author of *Seeing Red: Anger, Sentimentality, and American Indians* (Ohio State University Press, 2008).

GARY GERSTLE is James Stahlman Professor of History at Vanderbilt. He is the author and editor of several books, including *Working-Class Americanism: The Politics of Labor in a Textile City, 1914–60* (1989), *America Transformed: A History of the American People Since 1900* (1999), and *American Crucible: Race and Nation in the Twentieth Century* (Princeton, 2001).

DUCHESS HARRIS is Associate Professor of American Studies at Macalester College. She is the author of *Black Feminist Thought from Kennedy to Clinton* (Palgrave Macmillan, 2009), along with several articles, including "From Kennedy to Combahee: Black Feminist Activism from 1960 to 1980," in *African-American Women in the Civil Rights–Black Power Movement*, ed. V. P. Franklin and Bettye Collier-Thornas (New York University Press, 2001).

CATHERINE A. HOLLAND is Associate Professor of Women's and Gender Studies at the University of Missouri-Columbia. She is the author of *The Body Politic: Foundings, Citizenship, and Difference in the American Political Imagination* (Routledge, 2001).

ALLAN PUNZALAN ISAAC is Assistant Professor of English at Wesleyan University. He is the author of *American Tropics: Articulating Filipino America* (Minnesota, 2006).

LAURA JANARA is Associate Professor of Political Science at the University of British Columbia. She is the author of *Democracy Growing Up: Authority, Autonomy, and Passion in Tocqueville's Democracy in America* (SUNY Press, 2002), which won the American Political Science Association's Foundations of Political Thought 2002 Best First Book Award.

BEN KEPPEL is Associate Professor in History at the University of Oklahoma. He is the author of *The Work of Democracy: Ralph Bunche, Lorraine Hansberry and the Cultural Politics of Race* (Harvard University Press, 1995) and the coeditor (with Jonathan Holloway) of *Black Scholars on the Line: Race, Social Science and American Thought in the Twentieth Century*. He is currently writing a study of the symbolic use of children to embody social injustice in postwar American political culture.

GEORGE LIPSITZ is Professor of Black Studies and Sociology at the University of California, Santa Barbara. His books include *The Possessive Investment in Whiteness: How White People Profit from Identity Politics* (Temple University Press, 2006), *A Life in the Struggle: Ivory Perry and the Culture of Opposition* (Temple University Press, 1995), and *Footsteps in the Dark: The Hidden Histories of Popular Music* (Minnesota, 2007).

GWENDOLYN MINK is Professor of Women's Studies at Smith College. She is the author of several books, including *Old Labor and New Immigrants in American Political Development: Union, Party, and State, 1875–1920* (Cornell University Press, 1986), *Welfare's End* (Cornell, 2002), and *Hostile Environment: The Political Betrayal of Sexually Harassed Women* (Cornell, 2000).

JOEL OLSON is Associate Professor of Political Science at Arizona State University West. He is the author of *The Abolition of White Democracy* (University of Minnesota Press, 2004).

DOROTHY ROBERTS is Professor of Law at Northwestern University Law School. She is the author of *Killing the Black Body: Race, Reproduction, and the Meaning of Liberty* (Pantheon, 1997), for which she won a 1998 Meyers Center Award for the Study of Human Rights in North America.

PATRICIA A. SCHECHTER is Associate Professor of History at Portland State University. She is the author of *Ida B. Wells-Barnett and American Reform, 1880–1930* (University of North Carolina Press, 2001).

JOHN KUO WEI TCHEN is Professor of History and Asian/Pacific Studies at New York University and a cultural activist. He is the author of *New York Before Chinatown: Orientalism and the Shaping of American Culture, 1776–1882* (Johns Hopkins University Press, 1999).

JERRY THOMPSON is Regents Professor of History at Texas A&M International University. His most recent book is *Civil War and Revolution on the Rio Grande Frontier: An Illustrated History* (Texas State Historical Association, 2004).

Index

Brown, William Wells, 62 n. 39

Browne, James, 88

Brownsville, Texas, 83–93, 183

Brownsville section of Brooklyn, 197

Brown v. Board of Education, 13, 18–19, 24 n. 60, 57, 282, 285–90, 295–96

Buchanan, James, 87

Buck v. Bell, 199

Bulosan, Carlos, 4, 6–8, 18, 231–45, 246 n. 5, 284

Burger, Warren (Chief Justice), 290, 292

Burlingame Treaty, 148–49, 151

Bush, George W., 53, 104, 276, 279 n. 61

Bushman, Richard, 29

busing (for desegregation), 289–90

Byrd, Harry, 287

Byrne, Ethel, 197

Cabrera, Tomás, 88, 90

California Immigrant Union, 150–51

Callender, James, 49

Campomanes, Oscar, 238, 242–43

Canales, José Tomás, 81

Canales, Servando, 93

Carpenter, Cari M., 16, 284

Carpenter, Francis Bicknell, 102–3

Cart War, 83, 89

Caucasian Codes, 13, 24 n. 52

Ceremony (Silko), 117

Charlotte-Mecklenberg Board of Education, Swann v. (1971), 289–90, 292

Chávez, César, 235

Chicano Movement, 8

Chi Chun-hsiang, 36

China, U.S. attitudes toward, 15, 27–40, 145–59, 160 n. 10, 160 n. 14, 161 n 34, 161 n. 40, 165, 182, 231–33, 269

Chinese Exclusion Act (1882), 12–13, 17, 155–56, 158–59, 182, 233

chinoiserie, 28–33

Chun-hsiang, Chi, 36

cigar industry, 145–59, 160 n. 15

Cigar Makers' International Union, 149–50, 156

Civil Rights Act (1964), 6, 285, 288, 292

civil rights movement, 1–2, 6–7, 13, 18–19, 45, 56, 139, 185, 248, 254–55

Clark, Kenneth, 254

Cleaver, Eldridge, 264

Clinton, De Witt, 32

Clinton, Mary, 32

Clurman, Harold, 251

Cole, Nat King, 261 n. 26

Columbia Magazine, 29

Columbus, Christopher, 10

Columbus, Ohio, school desegregation in, 285, 288, 292

Columbus Board of Education, Penick v., 288

Committee for the Protection of Filipino Rights, 235

Committee of Mothers' Health Centers (New York City), 207–8

communism, 222, 235, 242, 249, 257

Communist Manifesto, The (Marx), 220

Communist Party, 253–54, 260

Comstock Law, 197

Confucianism, 33–34, 36–37

Congress of Industrial Organizations (CIO), 145–46

Cooper, Anna Julia, 14, 141

Cortina, Juan Nepomuceno, 5, 7–8, 16, 81–93, 284

Cortina War, 16, 82, 84, 89, 91

County School Board of New Kent County, Virginia, Green v. (1968), 289

Cox, Minnie M., 183

Crane, Hart, 244

Crania Americana (Morton), 12

Crawford v. Board of Education of the City of Los Angeles, 289

Crisis, The (journal), 214

Croly, Herbert, 184–85

Crum, William D., 183

Crummel, Alexander, 14

Knack, Martha C., 126 n. 5
Knights of Labor, 13, 158
Knights of St. Crispin, 149–50
Ku Klux Klan (KKK), 11, 163, 177, 233

labor unions, 145–59, 162 n. 49, 181–82, 235–36
La Gran Liga Mexicanista, 81
Lamarck, Chevalier de, 217
Lanier, Shannon, 58–59
Lape, Noreen, 125
Lasker, Albert, 205
Latino discrimination, 5, 12, 16, 21 n. 21, 81–93, 233, 235, 270, 284
Laughlin, Harry Hamilton, 198–99
Lerdo deTejada, Sebastián, 121
Lewis, David Levering, 225
Lewis, Earl, 287–88
Lewis, Jan Ellis, 49
Liberator, The (newspaper), 14
Lincoln, Abraham: election of, 11; Emancipation Proclamation and, 11, 96–110; legacy of, 169; political theory of, 4–5, 7, 16, 96–110, 265, 283
Lipsitz, George, 18–19
Little, C. C., 202
Locke, John, 30, 34, 71
Long Affair, The (O'Brien), 50
Louisiana Purchase, 46
lynching: anti-lynching crusade and, 6, 14, 56, 81, 128–42, 284; during Draft riots, 11; Du Bois's race theories and, 214, 218, 221, 225; Filipino experience of, 235, 240; Lincoln's references to, 110 n. 5; television accounts of, 262 n. 26
Lyons, Maritcha, 132

Macaulay, Catherine, 29
MacKenzie, Donald, 211
Madison, James, 3–4, 19 n. 5
Mahan, Alfred Thayer, 169
Mancini, Henry, 263

Manifest Destiny, 10, 12, 23 n. 47, 78, 81, 232
Marcus, Greil, 24 n. 56
Marsden, W. L., 127 n. 13
Marshall, T. H., 185
Marshall, Thurgood, 291
Marx, Karl, 166, 222, 224–25, 229 n. 30
Marxism, 216, 219, 223, 225–26
Mathews, Victoria Earle, 132
McCain, John, 104, 279 n. 61
McCann, Carole, 208–9, 211 n. 6
McCarthy, Joseph, 18, 256–57
McDougall, Alexander, 38
McKinley, William, 174, 183
McWilliams, Carey, 14
Meeropol, Abel, 14
melting pot, America as, 164, 167, 171, 173–74, 178, 180, 269
Melting-Pot, The (Zangwill), 180
Melville, Herman, 70
Mexican-American War, 5, 12, 16, 81–93, 98, 122–23, 284
Mexican Border Committee, 86
Milliken v. Bradley (1974 and 1977), 289–92
Missouri Compromise, 97
Missouri v. Jenkins (1995), 292
Monroe Doctrine, 78
Monticello Association, 53
Morgan, Edmund, 2 3, 19 n. 5, 80 n. 39
Morris, Gouverneur, 28–29, 31, 38–39
Morris, Robert, 38
Morton, Samuel George, 12
Murphy, Arthur, 35–37
Myrdal, Gunnar, 179, 264

National Association for the Advancement of Colored People (NAACP), 204; founding of, 12–13, 214; nationalism and, 163
National Machinists' Association, 162 n. 49

BRUCE BAUM is an assistant professor in the Department of Political Science at the University of British Columbia. He is the author of *The Rise and Fall of the Caucasian Race: A Political History of Racial Identity* (2006) and *Rereading Power and Freedom in J. S. Mill* (2000).

DUCHESS HARRIS is an associate professor in the Department of American Studies at Macalester College. She is the author of *Black Feminist Thought from Kennedy to Clinton* (2009).

Library of Congress Cataloging-in-Publication Data
Racially writing the republic : racists, race rebels, and transformations of American identity / edited by Bruce Baum and Duchess Harris.
p. cm.
Includes bibliographical references and index.
ISBN 978-0-8223-4435-3 (cloth : alk. paper)
ISBN 978-0-8223-4447-6 (pbk. : alk. paper)
1. Racism—United States—History. 2. Ethnicity—United States—History.
3. United States—Race relations—History. 4. Civil rights—United States.
I. Baum, Bruce David, 1960– II. Harris, Duchess.
E184.A1R32452 2009
305.800973—dc22   2009010101